Perspectives on World Politics

The study of world politics is of crucial importance in understanding and improving contemporary international relations. The growing complexity of the modern world, however, has generated deep divisions among academics. By identifying three broad perspectives, the editors of *Perspectives on World Politics* have imposed a structure on the diverse and conflicting literature found in the discipline and have provided students with coherent sets of conceptual tools for analysing international affairs.

The first perspective on the politics of power and security focuses on the way states contend with the insecurities and dilemmas generated in the anarchic international system. This approach is challenged by the second perspective on the politics of interdependence and transnational relations, which disaggregates both the state and foreign policy to reveal interests and coalitions within and across state boundaries which undermine the idea of a national interest. The third perspective on the politics of dominance and dependence stresses global inequality because the structure of the international system is seen to systematically favour the rich 'centre' countries at the expense of the poor on the 'periphery'.

The second edition, while maintaining the original structure, is substantially revised and updated to encompass developments during the 1980s in the theory and practice of world politics. Attention is paid, for example, to modifications in all three perspectives to the conception of the state. The final section which explores the implications of a perspectival approach to the discipline has also been expanded. The text should appeal to all those interested in world politics both as a field of academic inquiry and as a practical activity.

Richard Little is Senior Lecturer in the Department of Politics and International Relations at the University of Lancaster. **Michael Smith** is Professor in International Studies at Coventry University. Both are established authorities on international relations theory.

Perspectives on World Politics

Second Edition

A Reader edited by
Richard Little and Michael Smith

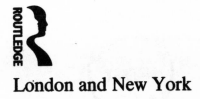

London and New York

First published 1991
by Routledge
11 New Fetter Lane, London EC4P 4EE

Simultaneously published in the USA and Canada
by Routledge
29 West 35th Street, New York, NY 10001

Reprinted 1992, 1994 and 1996

© 1991 Richard Little and Michael Smith

Typeset by Leaper and Gard Ltd, Bristol
Printed in England by Clays Ltd, St Ives plc

British Library Cataloguing in Publication Data
A catalogue record for this book is
available from the British Library.

Library of Congress Cataloguing in Publication Data
A catalogue record for this book is
available from the Library of Congress

ISBN 0–415–05624–1

Contents

Introduction

THE STUDY OF WORLD POLITICS

World politics as an area of academic inquiry and practical activity holds at one and the same time immense promise and immense potential difficulty. Its promise – and a major reason for its attractiveness to students at all levels as well as to politicians and other 'practitioners' – lies in its focus on phenomena which are heavy with implications for the continued existence and flourishing of humankind. Questions of security and prosperity, order and justice, war and peace, and ultimately life and death, have always formed a major preoccupation of those engaged in the field: indeed, the emergence of an identifiable field of study, known widely as International Relations, was one of the less apocalyptic consequences of the First World War, and the growing awareness throughout the twentieth century that international events have important implications for political life at all levels has been accompanied by the expansion and diversification of international studies.

The difficulties and problems which have attended studies of world politics are in many ways the mirror image of its appeal. A focus on global problems, at a time when the ramifications of political activity have extended almost daily, carries with it the problem of complexity and change. Scholars in the field, no less than diplomats and other officials with more direct involvement, become hardened to the fact that many areas of inquiry grow, disappear or are transformed as they are studied. Likewise, the assertions that a comprehensive description of the world political scene ought logically to include the whole of human knowledge, or that the really important elements in global developments are precisely those which are likely to be least accessible, should act as a warning to those who enter the field. A warning, maybe, but not by any means a discouragement: it can be argued that the problems inherent in a study of world politics make of it one of the most challenging fields of inquiry or action available to scholars or practitioners.

There are several major dimensions to the challenge of world politics, which can briefly be noted here. First, there is a challenge of *organization* and *ordering*: how are the phenomena of such a complex field to be moulded into some kind of coherent, ordered description? One expression of this problem can be found in the so-called 'level-of-analysis' problem which has beset international studies and aroused periodic debate. At its simplest, this dilemma reduces itself to a choice of the unit to be studied in any inquiry: is it to be the whole system of world politics, or a particular geographical area, or a set of specific problems, or a particular social or political grouping, or the individual? Such difficulties of choice and discrimination relate closely to the second challenge which can be noted here: the challenge of *theory*. How is it possible to formulate viable and testable theories about an area of complexity and diversity such as world politics? This question especially preoccupies those who conceive of world politics as the concern of social science and who envisage a gradual accumulation of theory and evidence rather akin to that experienced by the natural sciences. The social sciences as a whole have encountered difficulty in attempts to formulate laws of human behaviour, and world politics confronts them with a singularly intractable field. As a result, a third challenge, that of *explanation*, has proved extremely resistant to the assaults of scholarship and analysis: in an area where there is little tried and tested theory, and in which it is a considerable achievement to produce an ordered and coherent description of events, the relationship of cause and effect, of motivation and action, presents a daunting obstacle. These predominantly academic problems spill over into a final area of difficulty: the gap between scholarly investigation and practical politics. It is all too easy to conclude that the challenges of the field are likely to render useless all but the most basic exercises of description, and that attempts at theory are likely to have no practical relevance in the day-to-day conduct of affairs.

Not surprisingly, in the light of such challenges to a growing field of study, the development of world politics as an area of inquiry has been marked by some heated debates. Partly these have been debates over method – the most notable example being furnished by the disputes between so-called 'classical' and 'scientific' schools in the 1960s. Partly also they have been debates over questions of value – over what ought to be the case in world politics, as opposed to what seems to be the case – and here the debates between 'realists' and 'idealists' in the early post-war years provide a major illustration. These debates have been notable for their overwhelming concentration within one academic community – that of the United States – and for their reflections of some at least of the dominant concerns of American policy makers. In the 1970s, however, it became clear that there was more than one version of the 'world' within which world politics occurred: almost simultaneously, American views became less certain and more questioning, and new or existing approaches from other traditions emerged.

The readings in this book are intended directly to attack the questions which arise as soon as it is allowed that there may be more than one version of world politics. In one way, the approach taken has a good deal in common with that implied by a study of the 'level-of-analysis' problem, which alerts the student to the fact that his initial orientation or preconceptions can colour the questions he asks, the methods he employs and the answers he arrives at. Here, however, the focus is not simply on different facets of an agreed 'world' but rather on different versions of the 'world' as a whole, which colour and at the same time reflect issues of method, values and action. The approach is based on the conviction that there exist in the study of world politics certain definable perspectives, which shape the forms of academic activity and practical politics where they are implicitly or explicitly adopted. Three such perspectives form the core of the material assembled here: there may be others which could be identified, and it is not always clear where the boundaries of each perspective lie, but this does not affect the basic premise outlined above. To illustrate the approach in more detail, the next section of this Introduction assesses each in turn, in relation to some central concerns of world politics.

THREE PERSPECTIVES ON WORLD POLITICS

The three perspectives on world politics which provide the framework for the selections of material in this Reader stem from widely differing temporal and political contexts. After what E.H. Carr has described as the initial 'utopian' phase of the study of world politics, there developed during the late 1930s and 1940s a definable focus on *the politics of power and security*. In this first perspective, the stress is laid on the quasi-anarchical nature of the world political system and the consequent concern of states with national security. During the 1960s and 1970s, it became evident that a second perspective had emerged – not to supplant the first in its entirety, but to offer a radically different view based on *the politics of interdependence and transnational relations.* Here, the stress was upon the coexistence and interaction of a mass of politically active groups in the world system and on the consequent problems of bargaining and regulation. At the same time, and from fundamentally different historical and philosophical roots, there had emerged a third perspective based on *the politics of dominance and dependence.* In many ways, this perspective predated the others, since it drew on the work of Marx, Lenin and others in the nineteenth and early twentieth centuries; but it experienced a resurgence with the process of decolonization in the 1950s and 1960s and with the associated problem of economic and social development in new states. How could the poor and weak of the world orientate themselves towards and operate within a global system which seemed to place them at a perpetual disadvantage?

From this discussion, it should be apparent that the problems raised by these perspectives have concrete historical roots, and that they concern not only academic theory but also political action. Some of the implications of these relationships are brought out by the selections in the final section of the Reader, which have been chosen to provide a 'perspective on perspectives'. A good way of exploring these problems further here, and of highlighting the distinctive concerns of each perspective, is by comparing their approach to three central questions of substance in world politics. First, what appear as the significant *actors* in world politics in each case? Second, what view of the global political *process* is implied by each perspective? Finally, what kinds of *outcomes* are emphasized by each approach, and what kind of world do they see as emerging from the actors and processes dealt with?

The politics of power and security

Since this perspective could also be described in terms of 'state-centric politics', there can be no confusion over its assumption of state dominance. This is not to deny that other groups can operate in world politics; rather, it is to assert that the state is dominant to such an extent that other groups gain influence only in so far as they can affect the policies of states. International organizations, economic groupings and other bodies are part of the context within which states operate, but they play an essentially subordinate or contingent role. Perhaps the central attribute which marks the state off from other bodies is its assumed monopoly of the legitimate use of force: as a result of this, states are enabled to pursue their other claims in the international system. Among these claims are those to control of a defined territory, to external sovereignty, and to recognition through exchange of diplomatic missions and admission to international organizations such as the United Nations. The problem is that, although states to this extent form an exclusive 'club', there is also intense competition between the members of the 'club' for scarce resources. In this context, the idea of 'resources' denotes not simply raw materials for the generation of wealth, nor simply the territory which may furnish raw materials, but also things which are much less tangible, such as security. Security – based on territory or other assets – is seen as a limited resource which is central to the concerns of all states but which none can enjoy completely. Nor can all enjoy it in equal measure: at the core of a 'power and security' approach is the assumption that there is an international hierarchy in which military might and economic capacity define the rank of any given state.

The actors in a 'power and security' approach are thus defined as states, commonly seeking to assure their own security and prosperity within the limits of scarce resources. Such a definition is important to a view of the significant processes in world politics, since their importance is clearly derived from the involvement of states. At the level of the state itself, foreign policy can be seen clearly as the process by which national (state) interests are pursued within an insecure world. The assumption is made that states act: in other words, the state moves as a single unit in pursuit of unified objectives. These objectives – and the exertion of power in pursuit of them – constitute the product of a process of rational choice in which the interests and resources of the state in question and of other states are assessed, the implications of particular choices are weighed and action is taken. Foreign policy is a matter of high secrecy and involves only a very restricted elite working on behalf of the state. This follows logically from the assumption that foreign policy is overwhelmingly concerned with matters of national security (both military and economic); in an insecure world, could it be otherwise? Such being the case, it is clear that success or failure in foreign policy is a matter of the appropriate application of power. In any given relationship, the state which most effectively and appropriately wields its power will prevail, with almost mathematical certainty.

A view of foreign policy as being concerned with national security and defence of national interests virtually dictates that the inter-national political system (that is to say, the interstate system) will be characterized by competition and conflict. This is especially likely given the inevitable absence of any institutions accepted by and binding on all members of the system. The interstate system is an 'insecurity community' in which war is an ever-present 'contingent liability', and in which the axiom 'might is right' applies. That it does not apply universally is due to the existence of a core of practices which produce a minimum of international order: international law, the balance of power, the fear of war itself. On the whole, however, the outcome of the 'politics of power and security' is an international system which operates according to a power hierarchy, and in which there is a continuing tension between the concerns and activities of individual states and the demands of the system as a whole. States cannot escape the demands of the system, although it is possible to deflect or balance them in advantageous ways.

The politics of interdependence and transnational relations

Although the state remains a significant – if not the most significant – actor in the second perspective, its role undergoes a transformation. There is a central paradox here – between the growing concern of most states, especially those in industrialized countries, with what goes on in other societies, and the limited ability of many states to achieve their objectives in their ever-broadening area of concerns. The state itself – partly as a consequence – becomes penetrated, by other states or by a variety of other actors, and can no longer lay claim in many cases to the control of territory and the external sovereignty which are the building blocks of the 'politics of power and security'. Notions of power and of a power hierarchy are undermined, since it becomes clear that a state which is 'powerful' or well endowed in one area can be extraordinarily weak in others and vulnerable to its apparent inferiors. Alongside the state emerges a whole range of new, non-state actors which have distinctive areas of concern and arenas of activity. 'Subnational' actors with a base in one state can develop activities which significantly affect the policies of that state in other states or which bypass the state machinery completely. 'Supranational' actors – of which the European Economic Community is the most highly developed example – can in limited areas achieve the ability to override the authority of the state and produce policies which entail a diminution of state sovereignty. 'Transnational' actors, headed by the multinational corporations (MNCs) can establish operations with a multinational base, giving them in theory at least the ability to transfer activities and resources across state boundaries on a large scale. Within this perspective, there are variations in the extent to which the 'death of the state' is predicted or diagnosed:

what is clear, however, is that it is no longer taken for granted as the dominant actor in the international sphere, nor is it seen as the uniform building block of a privileged 'club'. How could it be, when the financial resources of the largest MNCs exceed those of all but a handful of states?

Although the state is no longer, in the 'politics of interdependence and transnational relations', seen as the sole gatekeeper for international political processes, foreign policy does still matter. In this perspective, however, foreign policy is difficult to separate from wider political processes at home and abroad, since its subject matter is of much more immediate impact. The foreign policy system itself thus becomes penetrated, with action emerging not as the result of rational calculation by a unitary decision-making body, but rather as the outcome of complex political and organizational processes. We become aware not only that public and special-interest groups are involved in foreign policy questions, but also that the foreign policy machinery itself is an arena for political competition and dissent. The state becomes disaggregated, and so does the foreign policy process. Externally, the proliferation of channels for action and interaction accompanies the proliferation of issues and their increasing politicization to make foreign policy a matter of delicate management and coalition building rather than the comparatively simple safeguarding of national positions. New actors can intervene to complicate processes, and it is no longer the case that the hierarchy conditions outcomes. Indeed, there is no clear and uncontested hierarchy in newly politicized issue areas, and much activity has to be devoted to the building of rules and institutions to regulate the new agenda.

The international system in these conditions 'explodes'. A system of 'mixed actors' creates the potential for a multitude of coalitions and balances, corresponding to the intersection of novel and existing issues and the absence of a clear or unified global hierarchy. Although it could be said that a global military hierarchy, based especially on nuclear weapons, still exists, such an assertion becomes debatable in conditions where, first, nuclear weapons do not constitute a rational policy instrument and, second, the proliferation of nuclear capacity threatens to complicate the picture and create new instabilities. World politics become simultaneously more diffuse, penetrating new regions and activities, and more interconnected, with linkages between a variety of actors. The resulting conditions of interdependence – between actors and states – increase both the mutual sensitivity of those engaged in world politics and, in many cases, their mutual vulnerability to new forces. The response of those who espouse the second perspective is to call for enhanced mechanisms of management: in a way, they are calling for the *construction* of a system of behaviour of rules and standards (often termed a *regime*) to constrain the actors, whereas in the 'politics of power and security' the hierarchy and the imperatives of national security form a perpetual constraint. For the rather primitive imperatives of the first perspective are substituted a set of beliefs in managerial procedures and the fruits of multilateral negotiation which have to prove themselves in conditions of polyarchy where the sources of power are widely dispersed.

The politics of dominance and dependence

An analysis of world politics based on the examination of dominance and dependence structures implies yet a third view of the role of the actors and of processes which take place in the global system. Although the state still acts as a focus of activity and coercive power, it stands in a particular structural relationship to dominant economic and political interests, which use it as a channel or a support for the pursuit of their aims. The state achieves less autonomy as an actor in world politics, since in many ways it is merely the recruit or the representative of other, more fundamental interests. Where the state is adequate to the task of supporting dominant interests – chiefly those of big capital – then it will be used, but where it fails to match up to the increasingly global needs and activities characteristic of large corporations, then it will be discarded or ignored.

Such a view implies that the real actors in world politics are dominant class or economic interests. It also implies that those in dependent positions within the global structure are systematically prevented from achieving any kind of capacity for autonomous action. A critical stage in the analysis of any actor within this perspective is therefore an assessment of its location within the global structure. In terms of classical imperialist theories, such a location is largely determined by relations between metropolitan powers and colonial areas, which are formalized by territorial occupation and administrative dominance. Where formal territorial imperialism does not exist, as it has not to any marked degree in the 1970s and 1980s outside the Soviet bloc, new concepts become important in the study of relations between dominant and dependent groups. One of the most fruitful of these concepts has been that of centre–periphery relationships, in which the major determinant of international action has been seen as the confrontation between the dominant 'centre' of developed capitalism and the dependent 'periphery' of the less developed areas. The ideas of 'centre' and 'periphery' are not identical with particular groups of *states*, since it is part of this perspective's argument that relations between centre and periphery exist within, as well as between, nations. From this situation emerge a host of cross-cutting relationships, in which the common interests of those at the 'centre of the centre' and the 'centre of the periphery' form a major source of exploitation for peripheral groups.

It is apparent from this discussion that the systematic and structural patterns of dominance and dependence within the international system define the 'actorness' of groups within the system. The processes by which the structure is sustained and developed are equally a reflection of the fundamental imbalance between elements of the system. In the days of the great colonial empires, the mechanisms were formal and institutional as well as social and political in nature: the very rules of international life sanctioned armed intervention and division of territory between the metropolitan European powers. The decline of the nineteenth-century empires during the first two-thirds of the twentieth century was dramatic, but it did not imply that the processes of dominance and dependence had disappeared. In fact, it was possible to discern a distinctive process of 'underdevelopment' which consolidated the continuing dominance of the centre at the expense of the periphery. Such a process in specific cases is sustained by a number of mechanisms: by exploitation, in which the balance of benefits from international processes of exchange is biased towards the centre; by penetration, in which the forms and standards of the centre are pursued by 'recruits' among the elite of peripheral nations at the expense of the mass; and by fragmentation, through which a policy of 'divide and rule' dilutes the potential influence of dependent areas in their struggle against dominant forces. Although there may seem to be changes, and a process of 'development' may seem to take place in dependent areas, this does not alter the brutal basic fact of systematic disadvantage which gives 'structural power' to certain groups at the expense of others.

The outcome of these processes can only be described as a vicious circle. The rich get richer and the poor, in relative terms, can only get poorer as the structures of dominance and dependence are consolidated. In contrast to the view implied by the 'politics of interdependence and transnational relations', attempts at management and reform within the existing structure are ultimately futile; indeed, they are themselves the weapons of those whose central interest is in the continuation of the existing system and of the benefits it confers upon the privileged. In the final analysis, the contradictions and conflicts of interest produced by the prevailing structure can only be resolved by its collapse and its replacement by a more equitable global system. Given that the privileged cannot be expected to connive at their own destruction, such an outcome can only be the result of a traumatic upheaval, possibly induced by the growing internal contradictions of the advanced societies or by the upsurge of revolutionary discontent in the periphery.

An overall view

The preceding discussion has uncovered at least some of the central features of the three perspectives examined. More particularly, it appears that it is possible to distinguish between them according to their approaches to the three questions posed earlier: who are the *actors* in world politics, what are the characteristics of the global political *process*, and what kinds of *outcomes* express the nature of the world system? Although it is wise to be cautious, and to be aware of the dangers inherent in the drawing of boundaries between approaches, the kinds of contrasts which have emerged can be crudely summarized as in Table 1.

It should be clear that the three perspectives examined express broad differences of philosophy and of emphasis in the study of world politics. They may intersect or overlap at particular points, but it would be difficult to argue that they are simply special cases of one broader 'reality'. Three major areas of divergence can be mentioned here in support of such a judgement. First, it is apparent that each perspective embodies a distinctive view of the relationship between the whole and the parts in the world political arena. A view based on the 'politics of power and security' postulates a constant tension between the interests of states and the dynamics of the state system, which creates an atmosphere of insecurity and the possibility of violence. An approach in terms of 'interdependence and transnational relations', on the other hand, enshrines a view of the world as a pluralistic political system within which there is a constant process of mutual and multilateral adaption to events. The 'politics of dominance and dependence', finally, centre upon a world in which the existing structure conditions all political action, and in which the actions and interests of the parts are reflections of the relationships built into the system as a whole.

A second area of divergence, linked to the first, concerns the

Introduction 11

Table 1 The three perspectives on world politics

	Power and security	Interdependence and transnational relations	Dominance and dependence
Actors	States	State and non-state organizations	Economic classes and their representatives
Processes	Competitive pursuit of national interest	Management of global problems	Exploitation and dependency
Outcomes	Limited order within an anarchical society	Rule-governed behaviour in a polyarchical society	Struggle within a centre–periphery structure

possibilities for change or reform in the world system. Whereas the 'politics of power and security' is in many ways a conservative approach to world politics, basing its analysis on the existing distribution of global power, it does admit the possibility of macro-political change as the potential of particular states grows or declines. It does not, however, contemplate a change in the dominant role of the state in general, of the type which is almost a precondition for the 'politics of interdependence and transnational relations'; in this second perspective, the state becomes a variable capable of reform or transformation, and the global system itself is seen as demanding effective management. Such a reformist view, implying that political actions can enable the existing system more effectively to meet the demands of its members, is denied by the 'politics of dominance and dependence'. Since the system embodies structural dominance and dependence, reform is out of the question and the only way of achieving fundamental change is through fundamental transformation.

As a consequence of divergences over the relationship between the whole and parts, and over the possibility of reform or change, the three perspectives finally diverge in terms of their relationship to values and political action. The watchword of those who espouse the 'politics of power and security' is 'political realism', in which the sober and rational calculation of interests and capabilities is a central activity and the means of action should be carefully matched to the demands of particular circumstances. Whilst the need for appropriateness and calculation is by no means denied by the 'politics of interdependence and transnational relations', a major place is accorded to other values based on the possibility of progress and the development of new norms and conventions of behaviour. The 'politics of dominance and dependence' focus far less on the capacity for progress by adaptation and far more on the need for radical political action to exacerbate the contradictions of a system which systematically oppresses some of its members.

With these contrasts, the argument comes almost full circle. At the beginning of this Introduction it was remarked that the study of world politics poses particular challenges for scholar, student and practitioner alike, in terms of description, theory and explanation and in terms of the links between academic endeavour and political actions. None of the three perspectives presented here and in the remainder of this Reader can be seen in isolation from each other or the world in which they have emerged. They offer, to at least a modest degree, an illustration of the ways in which perspectives can shape the form of academic activity and practical politics in a complex world.

A NOTE ON THE SELECTION AND ARRANGEMENT OF MATERIAL

A number of criteria have influenced the selection of material for this Reader. First, in line with the framework outlined in this Introduction, each section is intended to represent as fairly as possible the assumptions shared by authors writing within the perspective; in the case of the final section, the aim was to include material which explicitly assessed the implications of perspectives for the study and practice of world politics. Second, and as a consequence of these initial aims, it has been the concern of the editors to ensure that each individual selection reflects as fully as possible, within the inevitable constraints of space, the chief arguments of its author. Third, wherever possible, the editors have made selections which illustrate the application of ideas within a perspective to particular examples, although no case studies as such have been included. Finally, although it has not been possible, for obvious reasons, to adhere rigidly to an approach based on 'actors, processes and outcomes' within each perspective, such an orientation was implicit in the collection of material.

Each section is preceded by a general introduction to the selections it contains, and each selection by a short introductory summary of content. Since in some cases the original material was accompanied by extensive footnotes and references, the editors decided to edit these in accordance with a uniform set of criteria. Thus notes are included where either there is a quotation in the text, or an author is referred to by name, or direct reference is made to a particular body of literature. It is hoped that this approach combines the maximum of economy in notes with as accurate a reflection as possible of the original author's intentions.

POSTSCRIPT 1990

This Reader was originally produced as part of the package of materials accompanying an Open University Course, *World Politics*, in 1981. As well as forming part of the set reading for the course, and reflecting its general organization and approach, it was also designed to represent trends in the study of world politics which would be of interest and use to students in higher education and the informed reader more generally. Although the course is no longer on offer by the Open University, the Reader is still being used as a university text in North America and Australasia as well as in Europe. It was decided, therefore, that a case could still be made for producing a second edition. The original Introduction has been reproduced because the structure and orientation of the text has not been altered. The purpose of this postscript is to identify the reasons for introducing new material.

During the decade between the planning of the first and second editions of this text, there were some dramatic and extraordinary developments in world politics. Indeed, it is tempting to suggest that a transformation had occurred in the international system. Events in Eastern Europe during 1989, in particular, turned much conventional thinking on its head and caught many academics and policy makers by surprise. At the start of 1990, when this new edition was sent to the publishers, the Soviet empire, which had been such a central feature in the structure of the international system established after the Second World War, was also undergoing unprecedented change. Despite extensive speculation, it was far from clear at the time what the outcome of these momentous developments would be.

The contrast with the condition of world politics in 1980, when the editors were working on the first edition, could not have been more stark. At the end of the 1970s, the Western strategy of containment was looking very fragile. Far from being contained, the Soviet Union seemed to be intent on extending its sphere of influence in Africa, Asia and Latin America, while the West was often seen to be curtailing its overseas interests. At the end of the 1980s, however, it was being argued that the cold war had been 'won' and that liberalism represented the permanent wave of the future. History, however, has a habit of overturning the most confident predictions and the only safe prognostication is that we will always continue to be surprised at least by some future developments in the international system. Indeed, *Perspectives on World Politics* was designed as an antidote to the idea that our knowledge of the world about us can ever be completely secure.

It was not the changes in Eastern Europe and the Soviet Union, however, nor any of the other developments which occurred during the 1980s – such as the Third World debt crisis, the Single European Act or the mounting concern with the environment – which justified the need for a new edition of *Perspectives on World Politics*. The Reader was initially designed to provide students with a guide to the diverse and contradictory literature to be found in the discipline of international relations. Although the primary aim was to reveal that world politics have been subjected to very different interpretations, it was never intended to give students a snapshot of what the world looked like at a particular point in time. Like yesterday's newspaper, such an approach becomes instantly dated. The Reader set out, instead, to present students with some of the competing conceptual tools used to analyse world politics. In the process of exploring these tools, it was hoped to show students how and why divergent perspectives produce radically different pictures of reality. If the strategy worked, moreover, then it meant that the text could not be outdated by subsequent events because a student, having worked through the readings, should be able to identify how contemporary developments in world politics would be interpreted in terms of the three perspectives.

It was relatively unusual at the beginning of the 1980s to organize an entire course about world politics on the basis of competing perspectives. By the end of the decade, however, the strategy was much more widely employed. There was also a widespread tendency to label the perspectives. They were frequently identified as realism, liberalism and socialism or Marxism.[1] These labels, of course, highlight the ideological dimension of the perspectives. The importance of ideology was certainly acknowledged in the first edition of the Reader. In the Introduction, the politics of power and security are related to a conservative or realist posture, the politics of interdependence and transnational relations to a reformist posture and the politics of dominance and dependence to a radical posture. But it is also argued that the three perspectives cannot simply be distinguished on ideological grounds. As the table on p. 11 makes clear, the analytical focus of each perspective is also seen to be different and it can be suggested that the perspectives operate at different levels of analysis. Because of the complex, multifaceted character of the perspectives, therefore, the formulation of restrictive labels to identify the three perspectives was avoided in the first edition. There was also no attempt to give a definitive statement about the epistemological status of the perspectives. Instead, in a fourth section a number of competing views about the nature of the perspectives were identified.

Perhaps inevitably, the idea of competing perspectives has drawn criticism. Susan Strange, a former Professor of International Relations at the London School of Economics, has complained, for example, that by distinguishing competing ideological perspectives students are encouraged to think that there are incompatible views of the world. She likens the perspectives to 'three toy trains on separate tracks, travelling from different starting-points and ending at different (predetermined) destinations, and never crossing each other's path'.[2] On the basis of this criticism, Strange has gone on to insist that it is necessary to break down the ideological barriers which separate the advocates of the three perspectives. Once this is done, she argues, then it becomes possible to develop a much more pragmatic approach to both analysis and policy making, drawing on the insights provided by each perspective.

Strange's position, however, fails to acknowledge that there is no agreement about the direction we should be heading in. The ideological differences cannot be ignored or circumvented. Her position also incorrectly assumes that there is no communication between the different perspectives. While the tracks may never cross – to continue the metaphor – the drivers, if not necessarily all the passengers, are constantly monitoring the progress of the other trains. As a consequence, it can be suggested that because of this interaction all three perspectives altered course to some extent during the 1980s. For example, the first perspective, often identified as realism, became increasingly intrigued by the existence of cooperation in the international arena. The realists denied that interdependence and transnationalism could account for this development. So they began to puzzle about how cooperation rather than conflict can sometimes be generated within the anarchic structure of states. Although signs of this development were present in the first edition of this volume, it became much more pronounced during the 1980s. A change in nomenclature took place, as a consequence, with reference being made to structural realism and neo-realism.

Proponents of the second perspective also modified their position. In the 1970s, it was not unusual to see the argument made that because of transnationalism and interdependence, the state was becoming an obsolete institution. It was even suggested that the multinational corporation could take over from the state as the major instrument of international organization. Such extreme arguments were no longer heard in the 1980s and, under the influence of realism, there was a growing interest in the state. The second perspective accepted that the state plays a crucial and complex role within world politics – competing and cooperating with other actors in the international arena. Although it appeared in the 1970s as if the second perspective was going to dominate the study of world politics, during the course of the 1980s, interest in this perspective began to wane and increasing attention began to be paid to the work of the neo-realists.

The third perspective also shifted ground. In the 1970s, it was not only argued that Third World countries were being exploited by capitalism but also that their economies were being systematically undermined. During the course of the 1980s, however, it became more widely acknowledged within the third perspective that the erosion of Third World economies was not structurally determined by capitalism. On the contrary, it was accepted by some that capitalism was likely to promote economic development in these countries. It also came to be acknowledged that factors like interdependence, transnationalism and information technology are drawing states into an ever tighter network of relations. Theorists linked to the third perspective continued to insist, however, that rather than generating greater equality, these forces are consolidating relations of dominance and dependence within the world economy.

The changes in the orientation of the three perspectives are more complex and contradictory than this summary suggests. Nevertheless, at the risk of over-simplification, the principal reason for preparing a new edition of the Reader was to take some account of these developments. Despite the changes and new orientations in the study of international relations, the three perspectives still seem to provide a useful device for organizing the proliferating literature in this area. It is accepted, though, that the approach does generate problems. From what has already been said, for example, it is apparent that the status of the perspectives raises complex and controversial epistemo-logical questions. As in the first edition, however, it is intended to leave the issue open. To accommodate the growing importance of the issue, however, the fourth section of this edition has been extended.

The problem posed by the existence of competing perspectives is not, in any event, unique to the study of international relations. It is worth noting that a sophisticated debate about the epistemological significance of perspectives took place in the philosophy of the social sciences throughout the 1980s and it is likely to persist through the 1990s.

Producing this new edition of *Perspectives on World Politics* has involved a series of difficult decisions about what to excise and what to include. Overall, about a third of the items have been changed. In the first three sections new items have been added which draw attention to the evolving character of the perspectives. Items which highlight essential features of each perspective have been retained. Inevitably, however, a few items have been excluded which, but for the problem of length, it would have been very desirable to retain. By the same token, the editors are very conscious that there are developments in all three perspectives which have not been taken into account.

Dr Michael Shackleton who helped to produce the first edition of *Perspectives on World Politics* felt unable to collaborate on this new edition because of other commitments. He left British academia some years ago and now works for the European Parliament. The remaining two editors who played an equal role in producing this second edition would like to acknowledge their appreciation of his assistance in the production of the previous edition.

NOTES

1 See, for example, R.D. McKinlay and R. Little, *Global Problems and World Order* (Pinter Publishers, London, 1986).
2 S. Strange, *States and Markets: An Introduction to Political Economy* (Pinter Publishers, London, 1988), p. 16.

Part I

The politics of power and security

INTRODUCTION

The ten extracts in this section have all been written since 1970. This reflects a bias in selection, because the 'power and security', or realist, perspective has traditionally dominated the ways in which political thinkers have conceived of world politics. It would not have been impossible to convey many of the ideas found in this section by concentrating on extracts from Thucydides' *The Peloponnesian War*, Machiavelli's *The Prince* and Hobbes's *Leviathan*. The advantage of doing this would have been to emphasize the great continuities which are discerned by adherents of this perspective; the disadvantages would have been the sacrificing of a focus on the contemporary world arena and the neglect of some recent developments in realist thinking which restored its vigour during the 1980s. Thucydides was considering the Greek city-states, Machiavelli the city-states of Renaissance Italy and Hobbes the 'pre-modern' states of the later Middle Ages. We have chosen, therefore, to restrict the selection to contemporary writers who remain convinced of the central importance of states in world politics and of the issues of power and security to which the coexistence of states gives rise.

All of the extracts rest upon the critical assumption which dominates the perspective: that transactions between states form the essential substance of world politics. Many of the writers use the term 'nation-state' to describe the fundamental building block of the international system. Thus, Stoessinger (1.1) identifies the features common to all nation-states; he goes on to show, however, that although states can be seen as the basic units of world politics, they must be viewed in terms of their power resources, both tangible and intangible. Buzan (1.2) takes up the theme of distinctions between states, but stresses the variations in underlying values which give states their specific characteristics, and relates these to the different forms of state which can be found in the contemporary world. Both Stoessinger and Buzan provide important insights into the diversity which is central to the 'society of states'.

The next two selections, by Clinton (1.3) and Legg and Morrison (1.4), focus not so much on the nature and origins of states as on the objectives they pursue. A key concept for the 'politics of power and security' is that of the 'national interest', and Clinton makes an important distinction between the notions of 'interest in general' and 'interests in particular', the latter referring to specific aims pursued by states in a competitive international arena. For Clinton the task of national policy makers is to balance not only different interests but also different conceptions of national interest in the more general sense. Legg and Morrison take this theme further, by arguing that it is possible to arrive at a rational definition of foreign policy goals, but they also note that the task is complicated by the range and variety of pressures to which policy makers are subjected.

Another key element for realists is that of power. Traditionally, military power and the use of force have been seen as the ultimate expressions of state power, but during the post-1945 period it has often been argued that nuclear weapons in particular have reduced the utility of military strength. Garnett (1.5) strenuously resists this line of argument, arguing that military power remains a pervasive feature of world politics even where it is not translated into the overt use of force. This is not to say that states do not have other means of achieving their goals, and Knorr (1.6) demonstrates the ways in which economic power can be used by them to affect the behaviour of their targets.

What happens, though, when states come into interaction? Traditional realist thinking emphasizes the competitive nature of world politics, of which one classic example is provided by arms races. Jervis (1.7) examines the implications of the attempts by states to maximize their security: according to him, the consequence can be a diminution of security since the competitive quest for advantage can undermine overall international stability. On the other hand, some 'neo-realist' thinkers have stressed the fact that states frequently cooperate. Keohane (1.8) argues that discord and competition produce the need for states to cooperate, and that one major manifestation of this tendency is that of 'international regimes' in a variety of issue areas.

The idea of 'international regimes' to govern state interactions relates closely to notions of international order, which are a perennial concern in the 'politics of power and security'. Bull (1.9) demonstrates that the balance of power can provide a mechanism whereby states attempt both to preserve their independence and to maintain the international system in general – a balance which is often difficult to strike, and which takes a variety of forms. Another form of realist thinking about international order, represented by Krasner (1.10), focuses on the ways in which economic power can be related to other forms of state strength, and economic structures can reflect the broader balance of forces in the international hierarchy.

1.1 The anatomy of the nation-state and the nature of power

John Stoessinger

Source: *The Might of Nations*, 4th edn (Random House, New York, 1973), pp. 7–27.

Stoessinger first identifies a set of components (primarily sovereignty and nationalism but also territorial and economic ties, common language, culture and religion) which combine to establish the structure of the nation-state and help to maintain its cohesion. He then examines a set of tangible (geography, natural resources, population and government) and intangible (national character, morale, ideology and leadership) sources of power available to the nation-state.

THE ANATOMY OF THE NATION-STATE

Our world is made up of over one hundred political units called nation-states. There is hardly a place on this planet that is not claimed by a nation-state. Only a century ago the world still abounded with frontiers and lands that remained unpre-empted. But in our time, man can no longer escape from the nation-state system – unless he migrates to the frozen polar zones or to the stars. The nation-state has become ubiquitous. And everywhere it is the highest secular authority. It may decree that a man die; and, with no less effort, it may offer him the protection that enables him to live. When no state wants him – when man is naked in his humanity and nothing but a man – he thereby loses the very first precondition for his fellows even to be able to acknowledge his existence. Whether it be to be born, to live, or to die, he cannot do without official recognition – the recognition of a nation-state.

This modern-day fact of life is astounding when one considers that the nations that possess this inescapable power of life and death are in many ways only abstractions, figments of the human imagination. For though the power that is brought to bear to implement a nation's will is ultimately physical, the will itself is chiefly the result of human images, images about what a nation is and about why and how its will should be expressed and obeyed.

There are two principal aspects of this universal political image. In the first place, man has endowed the nation-state with a quality that it shares with no other human association – the attribute of *sovereignty*. It is indeed no coincidence that the theory of sovereignty was first formulated in the sixteenth century, at a time when the nation-state system was in process of emerging from the universalism of the medieval world. Its first systematic presentation was contained in the writings of the French political thinker Jean Bodin. Bodin's definition of sovereignty as 'the state's supreme authority over citizens and subjects', set forth in his *De La République* in 1576, is still largely valid today. The nation remains the final arbiter over the lives of its citizens, leaving them recourse to no higher law. And while this is true in peacetime, it is even more totally and dramatically the case in times of war. For in the latter eventuality, the sovereign state has the right to send its citizens to their death and, through its sanction, to transform even the most brutal forms of killing into acts of patriotic heroism. [...] It is sovereignty, more than any other single factor, that is responsible for the anarchic condition of international relations. Bodin conceived of sovereignty as essentially an *internal* phenomenon, 'the state's supreme authority over citizens and subjects'. While the advent of democratic government has rendered this power far less than absolute, no government, democratic or totalitarian, has been willing to yield major portions of its sovereignty in its relations with *other* nation-states. Hence, it would seem that sovereignty in our time is fundamentally a phenomenon of *international* relations, a fact of life in political intercourse among nations. Over three hundred years ago man created the image of Leviathan. In some parts of the world Leviathan is man's servant; in others, he remains the master. But no Leviathan yields to another except by its own consent. Sovereignty, originally no more than a political construct defining man's relationship to the state, has taken on a life of its own on the international scene. In the internal affairs of states, sovereignty has often created political order and stability. In international relations it has led to anarchy.

The second key component that has come into the making of nations has been the phenomenon of *nationalism*. In the broadest terms nationalism may be defined as a people's sense of collective destiny through a common past and the vision of a common future. In a very real sense, a nation's 'personality' is its common past, or history. Empirically, a nation is merely a group of people occupying geographic space. But nations exist much more in time than in space. The history of common triumphs and suffering evokes powerful bonds of solidarity for nations large and small. Common suffering seems to be more important in this respect than are victories. [...]

The vision of a common future constitutes the second ingredient of nationalism. Here, too, man's aspirations as an individual are often projected onto the larger stage of politics and international relations. The unconscious realization that one's personal future may be bleak and devoid of larger meaning is often unbearable. Hence, as Erich Fromm has brilliantly demonstrated in his *Escape from Freedom*, man may seek compensation for his lack of personal future in the reflected glory of the nation's collective future. This form of identification may manifest itself in socially constructive ways; it may also lend itself to nationalism of a more destructive kind, as it did, for example, in Nazi Germany. The process whereby the identification is generated takes place largely in the 'illogical, irrational, and fantastic world of the unconscious'.[1] [...]

It would, of course, be a mistake to claim that the psychological phenomenon of nationalism and the legal institution of sovereignty are the sole foundations of a nation. There are also a number of more 'objective' ingredients that play an essential part. Most prominent among these are territorial and economic ties and the presence of common language, culture, and religion.

Clearly the very first requirement of a nation is that it possess a *geographical base*, a territory of its own. Yet it does not necessarily follow from this that attachment to the soil of the homeland primarily explains the fact of national unity. The insights of social psychology would seem to indicate that an individual may remain attached to a much more specific and limited location, such as his place of birth or the countryside where he was raised. In fact, a person may feel more 'at home' in a spot in a foreign land that reminds him of his youth than in an unfamiliar locale in his own country. Moreover, powerful emotional ties to specific locales may even divide a nation. When this is the case, the nation in question tends to be vulnerable to serious disunity and, frequently, internecine strife. Yet even when strong local attachments are not present, a really active attachment to the national territory as a whole usually results only from powerful nationalistic propaganda.

Another major contributing factor to the existence and unity of a nation lies in its common and interdependent *economic patterns*. Especially has this come to be the case since the advent of modern technology and mass production, with their need for vast national markets. Yet this same economic logic has also tended to undermine the nation-state system. For why limit production and distribution to nationally protected markets? And significantly, the only genuinely 'supranational' organizations in existence in our time are of a primarily economic character. It is therefore incorrect to assert that economic ties reinforce the nation exclusively. Modern technology and the enlargement of markets work equally for the development of economic patterns that reach far beyond national boundaries.

It is similarly difficult to generalize about the part that is played in the making of a nation by the presence of a *common language*. In many countries, as for example the United States, a common tongue is an important integrative factor. In other nations, the fact that the same common language may be spoken in many different versions definitely constitutes a divisive influence. This is very notably the case with the Chinese language, for instance, which consists of hundreds of dialects. Thus, if a native of Shanghai wants to communicate with a Cantonese, he can do so only by falling back on written Chinese or by resorting to some foreign language that both may know. Switzerland, on the other hand, with its three major languages, has achieved a very high degree of national unity. Still other nations have hoped to increase national cohesion by resurrecting a dead language. The revitalization of the Hebrew language in Israel is a case in point. But it is safe to assume that language is a relatively minor factor in Israeli unity. At times the quest for a national language has caused endless internal friction. The attempt to make Urdu the national language of Pakistan met with bitter resistance from that part of the Pakistani population which spoke Bengali. And India, after independence, had to accept English, a 'foreign' language, as its temporary *lingua franca*. Hence the role of language in the life of nations is clearly a rather ambiguous one.

Surely one of the most perplexing concepts is that of '*national character*'. Few social scientists would deny that certain cultural patterns occur more frequently and are more highly valued in one nation than in another. But it is almost impossible to find agreement among scholars on precisely what these common patterns are. In other words, we are faced with the paradox that 'national character' seems to be an indisputable factor but that no one knows exactly what it is. This confusion probably stems from the fact that cultural patterns continue to live as stereotypes. For example, the stereotypes of the 'volatile Frenchman' and of the 'materialistic American' are strictly time-bound. Only a century ago almost opposite images were current. Moreover, patterns may differ from region to region in the same country. And it is never difficult to find exceptions to the prevailing images. On the whole, it would therefore appear that though national character patterns are a fact, their uniqueness and their significance in supporting national unity vary from nation to nation.

The role of *religion*, finally, is equally two-edged. In the United States, religion has neither substantially contributed to nor detracted from national unity. In other countries, Israel for example, religion has proved a very significant factor in making for unity in national terms. Yet in certain other cases religion has played a key part in preventing national unity. Thus it was chiefly the religious friction between Moslems and Hindus that in 1947 made necessary the partition of the Indian subcontinent into two separate nations – India and Pakistan. Religions have probably tended as much to keep nations divided as to aid their unity.

In summary, then, what constitutes a nation in our time may be characterized as follows. First and foremost, it is a sovereign political unit. Second, it is a population that in being committed to a particular collective identity through a common image of past and future shares a greater or lesser degree of nationalism. And finally, it is a population inhabiting a definite territory, acknowledging a common government, and usually – though not always – exhibiting common linguistic and cultural patterns.

Having examined the structure of the nation-state, we can now focus our attention on the heart of our subject matter – the behavior *among* nations. As a first step in this larger analysis, we must devote some attention to that most crucial of all the concepts in the study of international relations, the concept of *power*.

THE NATURE OF POWER

The nature of a nation's power *vis-à-vis* other nations is one of the most elusive aspects of international relations. It is frequently suggested that a nation's *power* is simply the sum total of its *capabilities*. Yet such a definition fails to do the concept of power full justice. For though power always involves capabilities, it concerns other dimensions as well. Most importantly, while capabilities are objectively measurable, power must in every case be evaluated in more subtle psychological and relational terms.

The psychological aspect of power is crucial, since a nation's power may depend in considerable measure on what other nations think it is or even on what *it thinks* other nations think it is. The relational aspect of power can be illustrated as follows. Let us assume that two nations, for example the United States and the Soviet Union, are approximately balanced in their capabilities. To the extent that this condition prevails, the power of either nation *vis-à-vis* the other is almost nil, even though their capabilities might suffice to wipe each other from the face of the earth. Hence, because power is a relational thing, whereas capabilities are not, there may upon occasion be no correlation whatsoever between the two. Indeed, when capabilities are equal, as in a stalemate, power tends to disappear altogether. To put it crassly, when everybody is somebody, nobody may be anybody. By the same token, of course, even a small increase in the capabilities of one of the two nations might mean a really major advantage in terms of its power. [...]

Coming now to the analysis of the anatomy of power as a whole, including its tangible capability aspects, we find it frequently asserted that 'the most stable factor upon which the power of a nation depends is geography'. In the words of Hans J. Morgenthau:

> The fact that the continental territory of the United States is separated from other continents by bodies of water three thousand miles wide to the east and more than six thousand miles wide to the west is a permanent factor that determines the position of the United States in the world.[2]

In the opinion of other scholars, however, the advent of the atomic age and the development of intercontinental ballistic missiles have brought about the obsolescence of 'territoriality'. As John H. Herz has put it, 'now that power can destroy power from center to center, everything is different'.[3]

It would be difficult to agree with Morgenthau that *geography* is always and necessarily a crucial factor in the power of nations. No doubt the enormous land mass of the Soviet Union prevented that country from being conquered by three different invaders in three succeeding centuries. Yet there may also be circumstances in which geographical considerations are much less relevant. Thus the same Russia whose vast expanses proved the undoing of Charles XII of Sweden, Napoleon, and Hitler, was in 1904 brought low in a naval battle by tiny Japan. It would be misleading, however, to go all the way with Professor Herz and suggest that the role of geography has drastically declined. Even the coming of nuclear weapons and intercontinental missiles may be less significant in this regard than is often claimed. As many military strategists have pointed out, mutual nuclear deterrence on the part of the superpowers may result in the wars of the future being 'limited' to weapons and strategies not much different from those that have been used in the past. And to the extent that this might be the case, facts of national geography, location, and topography would continue to retain very considerable importance in the balancing of international power. [...]

A second major element in a nation's international power is usually considered to be its possession of *natural resources.* Yet though this factor is always significant, it, too, is in itself by no means decisive. For it is not primarily the possession of raw materials that makes a nation powerful; it is above all the *use* that nation is able to make of the resources it has available. Though the Arab states of the Middle East, for example, have grown rich and been extensively courted because of their large oil deposits, they have not, by virtue of this fact, become powerful nations.

What use a nation is able to make of the raw materials it possesses depends primarily on the extent of its economic and industrial development. To develop a powerful military establishment, nations today must first command an advanced technological base. How vital this requirement may be can be seen from the examples of Germany, Italy, and Japan in World War II. In the possession of strategic raw materials, all three of these countries are relatively poor. Yet because of their highly developed industry and technology, they proved able to build military machines that almost succeeded in bringing about an Axis victory. That the power of the Allies triumphed in the end is largely attributable to the fact that the latter possessed *both* an abundance of essential raw materials *and* an advanced industrial apparatus. [...]

The same point that has been noted in regard to geography and natural resources is also true of a third major element of national power, *population.* Once again, though a nation's population is certain always to be important as a factor in its power, the actual extent of its significance depends on many other considerations as well. Though both very populous, neither China nor India was in the past considered very powerful. Indeed, as the case of China illustrates, population is primarily *potential* power. As a result, it has been possible for nations with large populations to be weak, but impossible for nations without large populations to be powerful. Though the advent of atomic weapons may diminish the importance of manpower in warfare, the Vietnamese War would seem to have shown that the foot soldier has by no means been superseded. In the future as in the past, large populations are likely to remain an important military advantage. Hitler found it necessary to import slave labour from Eastern Europe to make up for manpower shortages in Germany. An armed conflict with a nation as populous as China would prove a struggle of the most overwhelming proportions. Even though it at the time had little else but its vast population, China was at the end of World War II accorded great-power status in the United Nations.

Population becomes most important of all as a power factor when it is combined with industrialization. It is common knowledge that those countries now going through the process of industrialization are also the ones that are growing most rapidly in population. This fact, known as the 'demographic transition', significantly affects a nation's power. Industrialization leads to an increase in population, which in turn may make possible further industrialization. As the case of China demonstrates once again, the potential power of population is actualized only when it is *used,* most profitably in the development of a modern industrial base which in turn makes possible a first-rate military establishment. In the view of many observers, once China succeeds in harnessing its immense population, it may in time become the most powerful nation on earth. [...]

A fourth element of national power, whose effects it is difficult to assess concerns the nature of a country's *government.* It is tempting to assume that a democratic form of government provides greater national strength than a dictatorship. Yet though the historical record does not invalidate this assumption, it certainly places it in question. The victory of Sparta over Athens is only one of many instances in which dictatorship emerged triumphant. But any analysis of this issue must remain inconclusive. There are simply too many imponderables involved to permit any easy conclusion. [...]

Many observers point out that democracy has a great advantage because it rests on the consent and voluntary support of the governed, where dictatorship requires coercion. While there is much truth in this oft-repeated assertion, it has been overdone. Modern totalitarianism has developed highly effective means of psychological indoctrination. Nazi Germany, Fascist Italy, the Soviet Union, and Communist China each developed a highly organized youth movement for this express purpose. In addition, 'brainwashing' – a kind of psychoanalysis in reverse – was widely applied to 'reactionary elements' in Communist China during the Cultural Revolution. These techniques, when coupled with the fact that modern totalitarianism deprives a population of standards of comparison in both time and space, have made possible the emergence of a new type of government: 'totalitarianism with the consent of the governed'; at times, totalitarian governments do not have to create popular support through these methods. The Nazi dictatorship, for example, enjoyed the fanatical support of most of the German population before 1941.

Hence, a broad base of popular support as a source of power is not a monopoly of the democracies. [...]

It appears from the above that the objective or 'capability' attributes of a nation's power depend, above all, on the *use* which its government makes of such physical factors as geography, population, and natural wealth. In the hands of a resourceful government, democratic or totalitarian, geography is turned to strategic advantage, and population and natural resources become twin pillars of power – military preparedness and industrialization. But as we have stated at the outset, despite their great importance these objective bases of national power are by no means the whole story. Of no less importance for a nation's power arsenal are its image of itself and, perhaps most crucial of all, the way it is viewed by other nations. To understand the latter dimension of power we must consider chiefly the factors of national character and morale, ideology, and national leadership.

We have seen earlier that the concept of *national character* is highly elusive, and that it refers to something that is constantly changing. Its relevance to power does not lie so much in its objective existence, which is still disputed by many scholars, but in the persistence of stereotypes that are imputed by one nation to another. The instability of these stereotypes themselves denies the permanence of national character. Yet that they vitally affect a nation's power nevertheless can be seen from the following situation. Before the United States had established any physical contact with Japan, the American image of the Japanese was that of a quaint, romantic, and picturesque society, almost rococo in its fragility. Hence when the Americans decided to 'open' Japan to the West in the mid-nineteenth century, they simply sent Commodore Perry and a few warships to force the door. Actually, the Japan of 1850 was a rigidly stratified society that had been ruled for over two hundred years by an authoritarian military clan, the Tokugawa. Under the Western impact, Japan modernized with astounding rapidity. [...]

Americans' image of Japan had also changed rapidly. The 'sweet and doll-like' Japanese of Perry's day had become 'leering, be-spectacled sadists' who raped and murdered innocent women and children. By the late 1930s, the Japanese image of the West, especially of the United States, became that of a decadent, corrupt, and spineless society which would disintegrate in the wake of a determined military attack. This distorted perception of America was matched by a Japanese self-image of absolute superiority and invincibility. In other words, a high *national morale* now became a major power factor. If the Japanese in 1941 had perceived themselves and the United States as they really were, there would have been no Pearl Harbor. It would have been obvious that Japan could not possibly win a war against the United States; that, in short, the objective fact of vastly superior capabilities was bound to overwhelm her. It was the power of an image that precipitated the Japanese attack. The incredible feats of little Japan during World War II cannot be explained in terms of its meager objective resources, but must be attributed above all to the existence of a self-image that was translated into superior national morale. This national morale became an immense storehouse of power. [...]

We have seen earlier that the very essence of nationalism is a nation's image of a common past and a common future. Hence it goes without saying that nationalism vitally affects a nation's power. Under certain conditions, moreover, the vision of a common future may become an *ideology*. This occurs when a nation's image of the future includes *the notion of a dynamic evolution toward some universal utopia.* Ideology has largely become the monopoly of totalitarian nations. Napoleon's vision of universal empire was rationalized by the ideology of the French '*mission civilisatrice*'. The ultimate vision of Nazi Germany was the enthronement of the 'Aryan race'. To accomplish this end, it became necessary for Germany to expand into ever wider areas of *Lebensraum* or 'living space'. The Japanese 'Co-Prosperity Sphere' was based on similar assumptions. The Communists, in turn, have their own blueprint for the world, which predicts the growing influence of the Soviet Union and China. In all these cases, the nation is seen as the dynamic instrument for world-wide dominion.

It would be too simple to assert, as does Morgenthau, that ideology is simply 'a flattering unction' for the concealment of imperialist expansion:

It is a characteristic aspect of all politics, domestic as well as international, that frequently its basic manifestations do not appear as what they actually are – manifestations of a struggle for power. Rather, the element of power as the immediate goal of the policy pursued is explained and justified in ethical, legal, or biological terms. That is to say: the true nature of the policy is concealed by ideological justifications and rationalizations....

Politicians have an ineradicable tendency to deceive themselves about what they are doing by referring to their policies not in terms of power but in terms of either ethical and legal principles or

biological necessities. In other words, while all politics is necessarily pursuit of power, ideologies render involvement in that
contest for power psychologically and morally acceptable to the
actors and their audience.[4]

Not only is it an exaggeration to claim that *all* politics is a pursuit of
power, but the relationship between power and ideology is a much
more complex and multifaceted one. In the first place, a widespread
belief in the 'truth' of an ideology may hasten its realization and thus
become a power factor. For example, the ideological conviction of
many Communists that the victory of Communism is ordained by
history has added immensely to the power of the Soviet Union and
Communist China. This faith in a metaphysical determinism has
tended to inspire Communism with a self-image of invincibility.
Second, ideology may assume an authority all its own, precisely
because its adherents are convinced of its metaphysical validity.
Power, in the last analysis, must rest on the capacity of physical force.
Authority, on the other hand, may attain similar compliance because
it is accepted as legitimate or 'true'. Ideology serves the peculiar
function of 'justifying power and transforming it into authority, thus
diminishing the amount of power which must be applied to achieve
compliance or to produce the desired effect'.[5] [...]
   Ideology as a source of power is largely a monopoly of totalitarianism. A democracy may have goals or ideals but not an ideology.
Since the very essence of a democracy is the principle of the right of
disagreement on substantive goals, such a nation lacks the fanaticism
and uniformity that lend an ideology its coherence and drive. The
citizens of the United States may disagree on America's 'national
purpose'. A totalitarian society, on the other hand, has only one
official ideology. This does not mean, of course, that democracy has
no resources to marshal against the aspirations of a universal
ideology. As we have seen, it has other great sources of power.
Besides, ideology is not *only* a source of power. It is the great
overreacher of international relations. By definition, its goals are
boundless and its horizons of conquest unlimited. The time must
come, as it always has, when the image of a universal ideology is
thwarted by an unyielding reality – when power encounters concerted
counter-power. Hence each ideology carries within itself the seed of
its own destruction, the hubristic assumption that power can expand
without limit.
   Finally, the quality of a nation's *leadership* and the image which it
projects upon the world are important sources of power. If leadership

is defective, all other resources may be to no avail. No amount of manpower or industrial and military potential will make a nation powerful unless its leadership *uses* these resources with maximum effect on the international scene. If the tangible resources are the body of power, and the national character its soul, leadership is its brains. It alone can decide how to apply its nation's resources. For example, the United States before World War II possessed virtually every single attribute of a powerful nation. But it played a relatively minor role in international relations because its leadership was committed to a policy of isolation. Hence as far as American power was concerned, the advantages of geography, natural resources, industrial and military potential, and size and quality of population might as well not have existed at all, for though they did in fact exist, American leadership proceeded as if they did not.

In concluding our analysis of power, we must take note of a striking paradox: while the power gap between big and small states has never been greater, never have big states been less able to impose their will upon lesser countries. The conflicts between the United States and North Vietnam, France and Algeria, and the Soviet Union and Yugoslavia are cases in point. Part of the reason for this is, of course, the fact that whenever one superpower is engaged against a lesser state, the other superpower tends to be arrayed on the other side. Yet, the French experience in Algeria and both the French and American experiences in Indochina demonstrate that power also has a great deal to do with a nation's willingness to accept punishment. American policy in Southeast Asia failed because the threshold of suffering for North Vietnam and the Vietcong was much higher than Washington had assumed, while the American threshold was considerably lower. The United States dropped more bombs on North Vietnam than she dropped on the Axis powers during the entire period of World War II. Yet that little nation virtually fought the United States to a standstill. It seems that, with the coming of the atomic age, the power of big states has diminished while the power of small states has increased. At any rate, power can no longer be calculated simply by adding up a nation's physical capabilities. Psychology and will must be given as much weight as resources and hardware.

Now that we have analyzed the anatomy of power, we may propose the following definition: *power in international relations is the capacity of a nation to use its tangible and intangible resources in such a way as to affect the behaviour of other nations.*

NOTES

1   Louis L. Snyder, *The Meaning of Nationalism* (Rutgers University Press, New Brunswick, NJ, 1954), p. 89.
2   Hans J. Morgenthau, *Politics Among Nations*, 4th edn (Knopf, New York, 1967), p. 106.
3   John H. Herz, *International Politics in the Atomic Age* (Columbia University Press, New York, 1959), p. 108.
4   Morgenthau, *Politics Among Nations*, pp. 83–4.
5   Zbigniew K. Brzezinski, *The Soviet Bloc; Unity and Conflict* (Harvard University Press, Cambridge, Mass., 1960), pp. 386–7.

1.2 The idea of the state and national security

Barry Buzan

Source: *People, States and Fear: The National Security Problem in International Relations* (Harvester-Wheatsheaf, Brighton, 1983), pp. 44–53.

Buzan argues that the state is an ambiguous component in world politics, reflecting a variety of forces and processes. In this extract, his central concern is with the purposes expressed by states, and in particular with the ways in which ideas and values provide a 'cement' for states and their identity. A specific manifestation of state purposes is the notion of national security, and much of Buzan's argument refers to this.

THE IDEA OF THE STATE

The notion of purpose is what distinguishes the idea of the state from its physical base and its institutions. The physical base simply exists, and has to be dealt with because of that fact. The institutions are created to govern, and to make the state work, but their functional logic falls a long way short of defining the totality of the state. Although institutions are, as we shall see, closely tied to aspects of the idea of the state, it is, as Kenneth Dyson points out, a 'category error' to conflate the idea of the state with its apparatus.[1] The European Community, for example, has institutions, but to the dismay of Mitrany-style functionalist theorists and others, these have failed by themselves to act as a gravitational core for the accretion of a European super-state. The missing element is a sense of purpose. No consensus exists about what the Community should be doing, how it should be doing it, or what it should, as an evolving political entity, be striving to become. With states, we should expect to find a clearer sense of both purpose and form, a distinctive idea of some sort which lies at the heart of the state's political identity. What does the state exist to do? Why is it there? What is its relation to the society which it contains? Why some particular size and form of state, when a glance at any historical atlas will reveal a variety of possible alternatives? In defining the idea of the state, reference to basic functions of providing civil order, collective goods and external defence does not take us very far. Although these functional considerations inevitably form part of the idea of the state, they indicate little about what binds the people into an entity which requires such services. Something more than a simple desire to escape the state of nature is at work in the creation and maintenance of states. Otherwise there would be no barrier to the founding of a universal state which would solve the state of nature problem without causing the troublesome intermediary of a fragmented international system of sovereign states.

A broad hint as to one direction worth exploring in search of the idea of the state is given by the term national security itself. Why *national* security? National security implies strongly that the object of security is the nation, and this raises questions about the links between nation and state. A nation is defined as a large group of people sharing the same cultural, and possibly the same racial, heritage, and normally living in one area. If the nation and the state coincide, then we can look for the purpose of the state in the protection and expression of an independently existing cultural entity: nation would define much of the relationship between state and society. This fact would give us some handles on what values might be at stake, and what priorities they might have, in the definition of national security. If the purpose of the state is to protect and express a cultural group, then life and culture must come high on the list of national security priorities. A pure modal of the nation-state would require that the nation precede the state, and in a sense give rise to it, as in the case of Japan, China, Germany and others. But it is obvious from a quick survey of the company of states that very few of them fit this model. Some nations have no state, like the Kurds, the Palestinians, the Armenians, and, before 1947, the Jews. Many nations are divided into more than one state, like the Koreans, the Germans, the Irish and the Chinese. And some states contain several nations, like India, the Soviet Union, Nigeria and the United Kingdom.

Given this evidence, either national security in a strict sense is a concept with only limited application to the state, or else the relationship between state and nation is more complex than that suggested by the primal model. The definition of nation imposes no condition of permanence, and since both culture and race are malleable qualities, there is no reason why states cannot create nations as well as be created by them. The United States provides an outstanding example of this process by which diverse territories and peoples can be forged into a self-regarding nation by the conscious action of the state. The possibility of state institutions being used to create nations, as well as just expressing them, considerably complicates and enriches the idea of nation. Since nations represent a pattern which covers the whole fabric of humanity, new nations cannot be created without destroying, or at least overlaying, old ones. The only exception to this rule is where new nations can be created on previously uninhabited territory, since mere emigration need not destroy the contributing nation(s). The United States benefited from this factor, though it destroyed the Indian nations in the process, but contemporary efforts at nation-building must take place in the more difficult context of *in situ* populations, there being no more large, habitable areas outside state control.

One obvious implication of this expanded view of the nation is that extensive grounds for conflict exist between natural nations and the attempts of states to create nations which coincide with their boundaries. The civil war in Nigeria, and the struggles of the Kurds, illustrate this problem, which provides an ironic level of contradiction in the meaning of national security. Clearly, from the point of view of efficient government, having state and nation coincide provides tremendous advantages in terms of unifying forces, ease of communication, definition of purpose, and such-like. The nation-state is therefore a powerful ideal, if not a widespread reality.

From this discussion we can conclude that the link between state and nation is not simple, and that the nation as the idea of the state, particularly in national security terms, will not be simple either. Several models of possible nation–state links suggest themselves. First is the primal *nation-state*, of which Japan is probably the strongest example. Here the nation precedes the state, and plays a major role in giving rise to it. The state's purpose is to protect and express the nation, and the bond between the two is deep and profound. The nation provides the state with both a strong identity in the international arena, and a solid base of domestic legitimacy – solid enough to withstand revolutionary upheavals, as in the case of France at the end of the eighteenth century, or defeat and occupation by foreign powers, as in the case of France and Japan during the 1940s.

The second model has been called the *state-nation*, since the state plays an instrumental role in creating the nation, rather than the other way around. The model is top-down rather than bottom-up. As suggested above, this process is easiest to perform when populations have been largely transplanted from elsewhere to fill an empty, or weakly held, territory. Thus the United States, Australia and many

Latin American countries provide the best models. The state generates and propagates uniform cultural elements like language, arts, custom and law, so that over time these take root and produce a distinctive, nation-like, cultural entity which identifies with the state. Citizens begin to attach their primary social loyalties to the state-nation, referring to themselves as Americans, Chileans, Australians, and such-like, and eventually, if all works well, an entity is produced which is similar in all respects except history to a primal nation-state. The state-nation model can also be tried in places where the state incorporates a multitude of nationalities, though here it requires the subordination of the indigenous nations on their own territory, a much tougher task than the incorporation of uprooted immigrants. Many African states, faced with complex tribal divisions, seem to look to the state-nation process as their salvation, and even a multi-nation state like India sometimes appears to lean in this direction.

While a mature state-nation like the United States will differ little from a nation-state in respect of the security implications of the state-nation link, immature state-nations like Nigeria will be highly vulnerable and insecure in this regard. The idea of the state as represented by the nation will be weakly developed and poorly established, and thus vulnerable to challenge and interference from within and without. Separatists may try to opt out, as the Ibos did in Nigeria. Or one domestic group may try to capture the nation-building process for its own advantage, as the whites tried to do in Rhodesia. Or the whole fragile process may be penetrated by stronger external cultures, as symbolised by the 'Coca-colaisation' of many Third World states, and the general complaint about western cultural imperialism. So long as such states fail to solve their nationality problem, they remain vulnerable to dismemberment, intervention, instability and internal conflict in ways not normally experienced by states in harmony with their nations.

The third model is the *part-nation-state*. This is where a nation is divided up among two or more states, and where the population of each state consists largely of people from that nation. Thus, the Korean, Chinese, and until 1973 the Vietnamese nations were divided into two states, while the German nation is split among three, though here some might argue that Austria, like Denmark and the Netherlands, is sufficiently distinctive to count as a nation in its own right. This model does not include nations split up among several states, but not dominant in any, like the Kurds. A variant of this model is where a nation-state exists, but a minority of its members fall outside its boundaries, living as minority groups in neighbouring states. Germany during the 1920s and 1930s, and Somalia today, illustrate this case. The mystique of the unified nation-state frequently exercises a strong hold on part-nation-states, and can easily become an obsessive and overriding security issue. Rival part-nation-states like East and West Germany, and North and South Korea, almost automatically undermine each other's legitimacy, and the imperative for reunification is widely assumed to be an immutable factor that will re-emerge whenever opportunity beckons. Germany's reunification drive during the 1930s, and Vietnam's epic struggle of nearly three decades, illustrate the force of this drive, and explain the intractable nature of what is still referred to as 'the German problem' in Europe. Part-nation-states frequently commit themselves to an intense version of the state-nation process in an attempt to build up their legitimacy by differentiating their part of the nation from the other parts. The frenzied competition between the two systems in North and South Korea provides perhaps the best contemporary illustration of this strategy, which, given time, has some prospects of success. Part-nation-states, then, can represent a severe source of insecurity both to themselves and to others. Their case offers the maximum level of contradiction in the idea of national security as applied to states, for it is precisely the nation that makes the idea of the state insecure.

The fourth model can be called the *multination-state*, and comprises those states which contain two or more substantially complete nations within their boundaries. Two sub-types exist within this model which are sufficiently distinct almost to count as models in their own right, and we can label these the *federative state* and the *imperial state*. Federative states, at least in theory, reject the nation-state as the ideal type of state. By federative, we do not simply mean any state with a federal political structure, but rather states which contain two or more nations without trying to impose an artificial state-nation over them. Separate nations are allowed, even encouraged, to pursue their own identities, and attempts are made to structure the state in such a way that no one nationality comes to dominate the whole state structure. Canada and Jugoslavia offer clear examples of this model, and countries like Czechoslovakia, the United Kingdom, New Zealand and India can be interpreted at least partly along these lines. Obviously, the idea of a federative state cannot be rooted in nationalism, and this fact leaves a dangerous political void at the heart of the state. The federative state has to justify itself by appeal to less emotive ideas like economies of scale – the argument that the component nations are too small by themselves to generate effective nation-states under the geopolitical circumstances in which they are located. Such states have no natural unifying principle, and consequently are more vulnerable to dismemberment, separatism and political interference than are nation-states. Nationality issues pose a constant source of insecurity for the state, as illustrated by Jugoslavia, and national security can be easily threatened by purely political action, as in the case of General de Gaulle's famous 1967 'Vive le Quebec libre' speech in Canada.

Imperial states are those in which one of the nations within the state dominates the state structures to its own advantage. The hegemony of the Great Russians within the Tsarist and Soviet states provides one example, the dominance of the Punjabis in Pakistan another. Several kinds of emphasis are possible within an imperial state. The dominant nation may seek to suppress the other nationalities by means ranging from massacre to cultural and racial absorption, with a view to transforming itself into something like a nation-state. It may seek simply to retain its dominance, using the machinery of the state to enforce its position without trying to absorb or eliminate other groups, or it may adopt the more subtle approach of cultivating a non-nationalist ideology which appears to transcend the national issue while in fact perpetuating the status quo. Imperial states contain possibilities of transformation into all the other types, and, like federative states, are vulnerable to threats aimed at their national divisions. Such states may be threatened by separatism, as in Ethiopia, by shifts in the demographic balance of the nations, as often mooted about the Soviet Union, or by dismemberment, as in the case of Pakistan. The stability of the imperial state depends on the ability of the dominant nation to retain its control. If its ability is weakened either by internal developments or external intervention, the state structure stands at risk of complete collapse, as in the case of Austria-Hungary after the First World War. Political threats are thus a key element in the national security problem of imperial states.

These models represent ideal types, and as with any such classification, not all real world cases fit smoothly into them. Numerous ambiguities occur on the boundaries of the models, and some minor 'special case' categories can be found. Switzerland, for example, contains fragments of three nations organised along federative lines, but has no distinctive or dominant national group of its own. France fits most closely into the nation-state mould, but Breton nationalists might claim with some justice that, from their minority viewpoint, the French state appears more imperial in nature. Similarly, French-Canadians might claim that Canada is more imperial than federative, just as smaller and weaker groups in Jugoslavia complain about

Serbian dominance. Conversely, imperial states like the Soviet Union may try to disguise themselves as federative ones. Appearances may also be deceptive in that periods of strength and prosperity may hide domestic rifts and give the appearance of a nation-state, only to give way to separatism when prosperity or central authority diminishes. The rise of regional nationalism in declining Britain illustrates this case.

Despite these difficulties, the models give us a useful framework within which to consider the links between state and nation. They make it clear that national security with regard to the nation can be read in several different ways, and that consequently different states will experience very different kinds of insecurity and security in relation to the nationality question. Some states may derive great strength from their link to the nation, whereas for others the links between state and nation might define their weakest and most vulnerable point. The importance of the nation as a vital component in the idea of the state has to be measured externally as well as internally. Unless the idea of the state is firmly planted in the minds of the population, the state as a whole has no secure foundation. Equally, unless the idea of the state is firmly planted in the 'minds' of other states, the state has no secure environment. Because the idea of national self-rule has a high legitimacy in the international system, a firmly established link between state and nation acts as a powerful moderator on the unconstrained operation of the international anarchy, and is therefore a vital element of national security. We shall explore this point in more detail when we come to look at international security. On that level, the confluence between the nation as a legitimising idea underpinning the state, and sovereignty, as the principal idea underpinning the anarchical society of the international system as a whole, becomes centrally important to developing a concept of international security.

While the concept of nation provides us with considerable insight into the idea of the state, it falls short of exhausting the subject. Nationalism adds a fundamental and ubiquitous demographic factor to the basic functions of the state, but it still leaves plenty of room for additional notions of purpose. There is great scope for variety in the way in which the state fulfils its responsibility to the nation, and there is even scope for higher ideological purposes aimed at transcending nationalism. These additional notions, however, differ from nationalism in that they tend to be less deeply-rooted, and therefore more vulnerable to disruption. A firmly established nation reproduces itself automatically by the transfer of culture to the young, and once established is extremely difficult to remove by measures short of obliteration. The well-founded nation is, in this sense, more stable and more secure than the state. What might be called the 'higher' ideas of the state, such as its principles of political organisation, are fragile by comparison, and thus more sensitive as objects of security. For example, fascism as an idea of the state was largely purged out of Germany, Japan and Italy by relatively brief and mild periods of foreign occupation. Similar measures would scarcely have dented the sense of nation in those countries.

The idea of the state can take many forms at this higher level, and our purposes here do not require us to explore these definitively. An indication of the types and range will suffice to give us an adequate sense of their security implication. Organising ideologies are perhaps the most obvious type of higher idea of the state. These can take the form of identification with some fairly general principle, like Islam or democracy, or some more specific doctrine, like republicanism. Many varieties of political, economic, religious and social ideology can serve as an idea of the state, and will be closely connected to the state's institutional structures. In some cases, an organising ideology will be so deeply ingrained into the state that change would have trans-formational, or perhaps fatal, implications. Democracy and capital-ism, for example, are so basic to the construction of the United States that it is hard to imagine the American state without them. In other cases, organising ideologies have only shallow roots, and large changes in official orientation occur frequently. Many Third World states display this tendency, as organising ideologies come and go with different leaderships, never having time to strike deeper roots among the population. Since these ideologies address the bases of relations between state and society they define the conditions for both harmony and conflict in domestic politics. If the ideas themselves are weak; or if they are weakly held within society; or if strongly held, but opposed, ideas compete within society; then the state stands on fragile foundations.

Different organising ideologies may represent different ends, as in the case of the Islamic state which emerged in Iran after the fall of the Shah, in comparison with the monarchist and materialist values which preceded it. But they may also represent different convictions about means, as in the liberal democratic versus the communist approaches to achieving material prosperity. They can also come in both positive and negative forms. The United States, for instance, pursues demo-cracy and capitalism as positive values, but at the same time gives anti-communism almost equal weight as a negative organising principle. Since organising ideologies are so closely tied to state institutions, we can deal with much of their security side when we discuss the institutional component of the state.

Other concepts can also serve as, or contribute to, the idea of the state. A sense of national purpose can spring from ideas about racial preservation, as in South Africa, or from ideas relating to a larger civilisation, as in pre-1917 Russian images of the Tsarist empire as a third Rome. Even simple fear or hatred of some external group might provide a substantial part of the idea of the state. One would expect to find this in a state occupying a highly exposed position, as, for example, in the Austrian empire at the height of the Ottoman expansions. Power [...] can also be seen as a purpose of the state. In a pure Realist view, states seek power not only as a means to protect or pursue other values, but also as a means of advancing themselves in the Social-Darwinistic universe of the international system. Power is thus the end, as well as the means, of survival, each state struggling to prove its superiority in the context of a ceaseless general competition. Each state will have its own unique idea, which in reality will be a compilation of many elements. In Japan, for example, the nation, and the values associated with national culture, would constitute a large slice of the idea of the state, but democratic and capitalist ideas would also weigh significantly. In the Soviet Union, nationalism would perhaps count for less, with pride of place going to the ideological foundations of the Soviet state.

The problem is how to apply a concept like security to something as ephemeral as an idea, or a set of ideas. Where the idea is firmly established, like that of an ancient nation, the problem of security is mitigated by the inherent difficulty of instigating change. But for higher ideas, even defining criteria for security is not easy, let alone formulating policies. Most organising ideologies are themselves essentially contested concepts, and therefore impossible to define with precision, and probably in a constant process of evolution by nature. Given this amorphous character, how is one to determine that the idea has been attacked or endangered? The classic illustration here is the old conundrum about democracy and free speech. If free speech is a necessary condition of democracy, but also a licence for anti-democratic propaganda, how does one devise a security policy for democracy? The component ideas which go to make up a concept like democracy change over time, as any history of Britain over the last two centuries will reveal. Even the cultural ideas which bind the nation do not remain constant, as illustrated by the 'generation gap' phenomena, in which older generations clash with younger ones about a wide range of cultural norms and interpretations. The natural ambiguity and flexibility of these ideas mean that security cannot be applied to them unless some criteria exist for distinguishing between acceptable and unacceptable sources and forms of change, a task beyond reasonable hope of complete fulfilment given, among other things, the weakness of our understanding of many of the cause-effect relationships involved. Ideas are, by their very nature, vulnerable to interplay with other ideas, which makes it extraordinarily difficult to apply a concept like security to them.

In part because of this indeterminate character of the ideas, it is possible to see them as potentially threatened from many quarters. Organising ideologies can be penetrated, distorted, corrupted, and eventually undermined by contact with other ideas. They can be attacked through their supporting institutions, and they can be suppressed by force. Even national cultures are vulnerable in this way, as illustrated on a small scale by French sensitivity to the penetration of the national language by English words and usages. Because of this broad spectrum vulnerability, an attempt to apply the concept of security to the idea of the state can lead to exceedingly sweeping criteria being set for attaining acceptable levels of security, a fact that can give rise to a dangerous streak of absolutism in national security policy. Making the idea of the state secure might logically be seen to require either a heavily fortified isolationism aimed at keeping out corrupting influences, or an expansionist imperial policy aimed at eliminating or suppressing threats at their source. Thus, one reading of German and Japanese expansionism up to the Second World War is that neither nation could make itself secure without dominating the countries around it. The Wilsonian idea of making the world safe for democracy by eliminating other forms of government has overtones of this theme about it, as does the idea common to many new revolutionary governments that they can only make their own revolution secure by spreading similar revolutions beyond their borders.

[...] it is worth considering who holds the idea of the state. An important undercurrent of the above discussion has been that a strong idea of some sort is a necessary component of a viable state, and the clear implication has been that the idea of the state must not only be coherent in its own right, but also widely held. Unless an idea is widely held, it cannot count as part of the idea of the state, but only as one of the ideas contained within the state, as in the distinction between a nation-state and a federative multi-nation state. From this perspective, it does not matter if ideas like nationalism and democracy stem from, and serve the interests of, particular groups or classes, so long as they command general support. Indeed, one of the advantages of an ambiguous idea like democracy is that its very looseness and flexibility allow it to attract a broad social consensus. Narrower ideas almost by definition imply greater difficulty in generating a popular base, and thus point to a larger role for institutions in underpinning the structure of the state. If the idea of the state is strong and widely held, then the state can endure periods of weak institutions, as France has done, without serious threat to its overall integrity. If the idea of the state is weakly held, or strongly contested, however, then a lapse in institutional strength might well bring the whole structure crashing down in revolution, civil war, or the disintegration of the state as a physical unit.

NOTE

1   K. Dyson, *The State Tradition in Western Europe* (Martin Robertson, Oxford, 1980), p. 3.

1.3 The national interest: normative foundations

W. David Clinton

Source: *The Review of Politics*. vol. 48, no. 4 (University of Notre Dame, Notre Dame, 1986), pp. 495–519.

Clinton argues that confusion over the meaning of 'national interest' and its use as a justification for state action arises from lack of conceptual clarity. He identifies two meanings of the concept: on the one hand, 'national interest' as the common good of the national society, and on the other, 'national interests' as the discrete objects of value over which states bargain in world politics. He goes on to argue that policies which are sensitive to both meanings can provide the best guide to ethical state conduct.

[Clinton begins by noting some of the many objections to the idea of 'national interest'.]

Whatever else they prove, the multifarious criticisms demonstrate that it is rare for the national interest to be regarded as a value-free tool of social science. Observers may praise the moral qualities of the concept: 'The choice is not between moral principles and the national interest, devoid of moral dignity, but between one set of moral principles divorced from political reality, and another set of moral principles derived from political reality.'[1] Or they may strongly condemn it: 'During periods of growing scarcity ... the temptation will be to secure resources and power for one national or regional segment of the species, while letting other segments of the species suffer or die. (This is, to a large extent, the operational definition given to the national interest by the superpowers.)'[2] Few, if any, profess themselves agnostics on its moral worth. The national interest *does* have normative implications.

To demonstrate that national interest is not only ethically significant, but also at least provisionally ethically valuable, it is necessary also to assert that for the foreseeable future states will continue to play the major role in international politics. Recognizing the effects of contemporary interdependence has shown us the inadequacy of any simple 'billiard ball' conception of unitary states monopolizing influence in the world arena. Reality should counteract the tendency to reify the state and to forget the crosscutting purposes pursued by other actors – individual and corporate, government and nongovernmental – who ignore and sometimes frustrate the wishes of putative leaders. There is more to be understood in international politics than the intentions of the foreign ministry.

Yet if states are not billiard balls, neither are they mothballs – objects that appear to be solid, but then dissolve into the thin air of interdependence without leaving a trace. The old agenda of 'high politics', which was deemed to be the special province of states, has not been pushed aside, if one sees the attention steadily focused on the breakoff and resumption of discussions on SALT–START, the introduction of new NATO missiles in Western Europe, or the dispute over the former Spanish Sahara. Does the heart of the modern era lie in the obsolescence of military force as a means of gaining what decision-makers and populations want most? Such does not seem to have been the case in the Falklands war or the [...] conflicts within Cambodia and between Iran and Iraq. Have states become so entangled in a web of international and transnational ties that they have lost the capacity for independent action in support of national objectives? The hypothesis must be squared with reports that OPEC is torn by dissension among members cheating on their assigned production quotas, or that the European Community is becalmed by the unwillingness of its members to accept majority voting as a complete substitute for unanimity.

What interdependence seems to have wrought is a world that is, to be sure, more complex – with more participants, not all of them states, seeking to press their claims, and new problems, many of which require cooperative solutions – but not one in which any other form of social organization has displaced the state from its central position or made it unable to act if it finds action necessary, by its lights and for its ends. It continues to be true, then, that improving the ethical standards of the international system means improving the conduct of states. Relying on their sovereignty, states may do unjust, harmful things, and the observer with normative concerns wishes to stop them from doing these things, through persuasion or deterrence. At times, states also do ethical, beneficial things, and they should be encouraged to do them more often. What seems unlikely to further world order or justice is an effort to assume states away or to define them simply as the cause of the problem of injustice rather than as one possible mechanism for its amelioration as well.

If world politics remains, in the last analysis, the politics of a society of independent (or even interdependent) states, then it remains important to know what the ends of states are. Understanding their goals is a necessary first step toward guiding their definition of their goals in morally satisfying ways. Rescuing national interest is not simply a gain for knowledge; it can also help to make the world of states more ethically tolerable than it otherwise might be. Promoting justice in world politics may not mean overcoming national interest, but rather working through it.

DEFINING NATIONAL INTEREST

To approach the normative issue, it is necessary first to separate two meanings of the term *national interest* that are frequently confused. The failure to distinguish between these two definitions – the tendency, indeed, to switch from one to the other without acknowledging the fact – accounts for some of the suspicion that *national interest* is an ambiguous and even dangerous term in discussing international relations.

First, 'the national interest' may be taken to mean the overall common good of an entire society. The definition of national interest proposed here rejects the view that society is simply a framework for the interaction – sometimes cooperative, more often competitive – of smaller interest groups, which form the real data of politics. Instead, it sees the national society as a community, with common standards of political ethics, with ties of mutual respect and appreciation (not only coinciding interests) binding its members together – and with a real common good that in the long run benefits all those within the community, in their role as members of the whole, if not always in their capacity of members of a subgroup. Individuals in society join together for purposes broader than convenience and the promotion of their own unshared aims. [...]

If the society as a whole is granted a reality other than that of the sum of its contending parts, then it becomes difficult to deny that the group defined by the society has its 'interest' just as the smaller, more particular groups have theirs. As they have their goals, so it has its own, more inclusive end – its preservation and improvement as the expression of the common life of its citizens and the means for promoting their common norms. Its interest is the common good.

The common good or common interest, then, is an end that is defined by rational consideration of what leads to the benefit of the

society, and by a normative choice of where the good of the whole
lies. It rests on a rejection of the position that public policy choices
are merely subjective 'values', and that no warrant exists for preferring
one set of values over another, because all preferences are equally
legitimate. The common interest assumes that society need not
maintain the sort of value neutrality that precludes an autonomous
public good and thereby makes public policy the resultant of an
interplay among private interests.

Many different agencies within the society can be means of
expressing the public good and of attempting to bring this goal closer
to reality. Recognition of the common good does not rule out
diversity or make scattered centers of power illegitimate or subject to
state control. However, the political arena is perhaps the most
important location for efforts to comprehend and further the
common good. The public interest or the national interest lies, in
part, in that which makes the state better able to fulfill its obligation
of protecting and promoting the good of the society. In the international realm, this includes the ability both to protect the society
from outside threats and to engage in mutually beneficial cooperation
with other societies. The national interest, as it relates to foreign
policy, is the end of maintaining the capacity of the state – that entity
delegated to speak and act for the society in matters of diplomacy –
to protect the society while it continues its search for its shared good.

This end of the community should not be reduced to the goals
pursued by policymakers. Nor can it be equated with a consensus in
public opinion. The common good is autonomous and forms the
standard by which to judge official actions and popular opinion. In
the goals they set, statesmen can attempt to approximate the common
good, and they may do so with some success. Still, the complex set of
aims they define by their decisions and actions is only an estimation
of the common interest; the interest is itself an objective reality that
does not depend on the aims selected by policymakers. If these
officials are skillful and wise, the national interest they define will be
quite close to the objective national good. But the two are not the
same.

'The national interest', then, refers to a general regulative principle
of diplomacy, which posits the common good of the society, in its
relations with other national units, as the end of diplomatic action.
The term *national interests*, by contrast, means a number of narrower
goals, which serve the broader end of 'the national interest' by
maintaining or increasing the power of the state. National interests
may include access to warm-water ports, rights to military bases on

foreign soil, friendly relations with a neighboring state, or any other goal that protects a state's diplomatic assets, which may take any of a large number of forms. To differentiate them from the overall common good, these particular national interests might be referred to as 'state interests'.

Each state has one overall national interest; it possesses many particular state interests, and it must pick and choose among them. Any one state interest is only part of the national interest. Of these particular interests, not all are of equal importance, not all can be pursued by any nation lacking infinite resources, and some may be mutually exclusive. Some must receive emphasis and attention, at the cost of postponing the pursuit of others or even of letting them drop by the wayside, and this choice ought to be made according to the guidance provided by the overall national interest. Moreover, the national interest cannot be equated with a list of state interests, any more than it can be reduced to the sum of demands by domestic groups. It may be necessary to the psychic health of a society that it choose to stand for principles as well as – and at times instead of – material interests in its foreign policy. It is one of the prime duties of statesmanship to know when and how to make such choices.

The goals that may increase the power of the state in its external relationships may vary widely among states and, within one state, across time. Circumstances may make any of a large number of aims a state interest of some state at some point. Yet, while these state interests display tremendous variety, they form a common thread that allows one to interpret much of international politics. Every state possesses interests and most states act on them. On the basis of trade-offs among these interests, compromises can be struck and diplomacy carried on. Despite their differences of regime, states can find in these interests a common language in which they may carry on diplomatic discourse.

On the other hand, because the overall national interest in the care of each state depends so heavily on the society's constitutive principles, it is likely to be unique to that society. Without de Gaulle's 'certain idea of France', it is unlikely that Michel Debré would ever have described the presidency of the Fifth Republic as 'le juge supérieur de l'intérêt national',[3] for the president's vision of France's mission gave meaning to the common good that France's citizens shared. The national interest of a community sets that community apart from the outside world; it necessarily looks to those bonds that are shared by the members of the community among themselves but not with others. As the leaders of other states who dealt with de

Gaulle might testify, the national interest of one society may be incomprehensible to a society of another type (although different societies may have regimes that are more or less similar, giving the national interest of one a greater or lesser resemblance to the national interest of another).

Individual state interests, despite their great variety and particularity, can nevertheless form the common ground on which states may meet to compose or at least confine their differences through self-interested bargains. The much more constant overall national interest, going to the heart of a society's self-definition and resting on what makes it distinctive as a national community, reminds states of their differences on questions of transcendent importance. It can be the subject of ideological disputes that worsen and prolong international conflict. An international politics of state interest, by contrast, focuses on the deals that states can strike and pushes into the background basic questions on which they will probably never be able to agree; it picks and chooses among a laundry list of particular interests and leaves unargued the fundamental issue of the national purpose that items on the list are intended to serve. Insofar as the United States and the Soviet Union have reached agreement in their uneasy common history, they have done so by concentrating on particular state interests – weapons systems, geographically defined spheres of influence, trading compacts – and not by debating their two over-arching national interests, which are grounded in opposing conceptions of the best regime and the place of the individual. Yet forgetting the national interest means losing hold of the very reason that state interests are important.

It is true that one can say only that 'most' states act on their interests. But while to say that most states act on their interests is to acknowledge that states do not always do so, it is also to claim that they are guided by their interests more often than by any other motive. Forced to cope with challenges through self-reliance (because they cannot call on a world government for assistance), members of the Western states system that developed during the past three centuries have by and large responded by taking actions that protected their ability for self-defense and independent action; that is, they have promoted their state interests. This pattern has not been altered by the great increase in the number and diversity of states in the twentieth century. Despite their very different cultural heritages, one Western idea that newly independent Third World states have apparently adopted is nationalism, coupled with an insistence on preserving independent sovereignty. The combination of the ASEAN states against the North Vietnamese occupation of Laos and Cambodia is an example of the balance of power and the protection of state interests that a Metternich or a Bolingbroke would have comprehended immediately. Most states seek to protect their power by following their interests because the exigencies of an ungoverned international system force them to it. No one person or state mandates that state interests will be generally valued; the impetus comes from the condition in which all states find themselves, although some may choose to resist it and act on other grounds. Statesmen are not always directed by their states' interests; they *are* so guided enough of the time to make the examination of state interests a significant part of the understanding of the national interest.

There is thus a reciprocal influence between the international environment and national interest. The picture is one of a broad but thin world community encompassing a number of much narrower but more potent national communities. Each particular community has its common good because the search for justice has an identifiable meaning for its members in their relations with one another. When one moves to the international level, the idea of a common interest becomes vastly paler and weaker as the community becomes less solid. Enough of a community exists, however, to prevent the rulers in each state from being the sole judges in their own cause when they assert various state interests to support their common or national interest. Rather, the entire world community – frail and divided though it may be – has the last word in defining the state's desire, either as a reasonable claim, supportable by justifying argument and compatible with prevailing ideas on the rights and duties of states, or as an unjustifiable grab for power. That many cases of juridically defined aggression succeed merely means that the international community's standards are loose, not that they are nonexistent. But they do supply some check on the excesses that can occur when the national interest of a particular state is invested with the aura of the highest good, from which there is no further appeal. And these standards may be strengthened when states act in a moderate, conservative way dictated by their state interests rather than attempting an ideological conversion of the world or acting on unlimited objectives that are said to serve 'the national interest' – and nothing else. [...]

Like the individual state's perception of its own interests, the international society's definition of a legitimate claim made in terms of state interests may alter. Under the pressure of circumstance, argument, or force, what had been unacceptable may become expected, and vice versa, a process that may or may not be codified in international law. 'Interests (material and ideal), not ideas, dominate directly the actions of men', noted Weber. He went on to add, however, 'Yet the "images of the world" created by these ideas have very often served as switches determining the tracks on which the dynamism of interests kept actions moving.'[4] F. H. Hinsley has applied this insight to international politics:

> In the existence of separate states we have a structure of power in which each state pursues its interests at all times. The historian of international relations is not concerned to show that they do this, still less to wish that they did not. His task is to show why they do it in different ways at different times – how and why interests themselves change.[5]

The very fact that the standards of international society change is evidence that they are not equivalent to ethical principles. Interest, for all its mitigating benefits, remains a provisional, prudential guide. The commands that prudence is to apply in concrete circumstances are to be found in prior standards of virtue, justice, and mercy. These guides are timeless, universal, and binding – but they are not unequivocal. Statesmanship brings them down to earth; yet, just as a leader may mistake where his state's real interest lies, the norms of the international community at any given moment in history 'may diverge widely from ultimate truth. At any step among the three levels – the state's conception of its own national interest and its important state interests, the consensus among states on what constitutes a legitimate interest claimed by any one of them, and the unchanging moral imperatives – disagreements can appear. One can only hope that the broader view of the world society, to the extent that it is free of national self-partiality, will approximate in some degree the best compromise between ethical aspirations and political practicality. [...]

There remains the question of the manner in which these two kinds of national interest interact and the normative implications of such interaction. At least six views may be identified on the link among the national interest, the international society that legitimates various state interests, and the demands of ethical conduct. One directs the attention of national leaders solely to their own national interest. A second advises these same leaders, in their capacity as international actors, to be concerned with the state interests of all actors and the international setting that supports them, but not with the common good within other societies. A third says attainment of any country's national interest requires the prior establishment of a solid international society governed on ethical principles; a fourth reverses that order. A fifth asks leaders and citizens alike to devote themselves to moral stands and the undifferentiated good of the world society, forsaking any obligation to the national interest or state interests. And a sixth believes a simultaneous attention to the national interest and state interests obtains the advantages of each and is perhaps the surest path to strengthening the world society and the observance of morality in international politics.

[Clinton goes on to examine these six possibilities in detail, and comes to the following overall conclusions.]

The contribution of national-interest thinking to the ethical dilemmas of today would seem to be primarily a negative one. Given a world of states accepting only a limited society among themselves, national interest generally prevents them from doing too much to one another, rather than chastising them for doing too little for one another. In the foreseeable future, states are not going to accord noncitizens all the rights and privileges of their nationals; international relations will not proceed as if state boundaries did not exist. The more immediate problem may be one of restraint, supported by a strengthened international consensus on the give-and-take of interests, or in other words an approach based on the sixth view, which makes use of both national interests and state interests.

To this endeavor, one might apply Tocqueville's description of 'interest rightly understood'. Tocqueville saw individual Americans pursuing their private interests within the framework of a larger system that allowed all citizens to do the same. Like theories of national interest on the international level, the doctrine of self-interest rightly understood did not attempt the avowedly futile task of persuading citizens to set aside their personal interests and devote themselves wholly to the common good. Instead, it sought to convince them of two things: (1) that diverting some of their resources to maintaining the system that gave them the freedom to pursue their own interests was itself in the long run also in their interests; and (2) that the preservation of the system depended to some extent on their willingness to moderate the demands of their private interests and to compromise their claims with those of others. Liberty would not survive a fixation on private affairs by 'practical' people who had no time for politics: 'Such folk think they are following the doctrine of self-interest, but they have a very crude idea thereof, and the better to guard their interests, they neglect the chief of them, that is, to remain their own masters.'[6] On the other hand, the spirit of a democratic age was inconsistent with expectations that the citizen would devote his complete attention to public and not private affairs (just as a system of sovereign states discourages an attitude of pure altruism on the part of any of them).

Tocqueville aimed for something less demanding – the recognition that the assertion of private interests had to be limited by the need to protect the liberal regime that made such assertions possible:

> The principle of interest rightly understood produces no great acts of self-sacrifice, but it suggests daily small acts of self-denial. By itself it cannot suffice to make a man virtuous, but it disciplines a number of citizens in habits of regularity, temperance, moderation, foresight, self-command; and, if it does not lead men straight to virtue by the will, it gradually draws them in that direction by their habits. If the principle of interest rightly understood were to sway the whole moral world, extraordinary virtues would doubtless be more rare; but I think that gross depravity would then also be less common.

Tocqueville may have underestimated the strength of community in even the individualistic American political culture and understated its ability to call forth self-sacrifice and the display of even 'extraordinary virtues'. But 'interest rightly understood' accurately describes the comparative frailty of the international community and the limited extent of the demands it can make on its members. It entails a measure of self-restraint on private demands so that the realm in which they are made can continue to exist. A willingness to devote some of one's time to preserving the polity and its liberties on the national level corresponds to a willingness to act according to interest and not sheer cupidity on the international. A policy grounded in the protection of state interests is not a 'lofty' doctrine, but if it teaches statesmen temperance, moderation, foresight, and self-command, it will have raised the ethical level of international behavior.

Interest rightly understood is applicable to international politics because it deals with citizens in their relations with one another, not with isolated individuals. Nor are states isolated from the outside world. Both internal and external circumstances determine a state's 'moral opportunity' – the leeway it enjoys to introduce ethical considerations into its actions. The scope of this opportunity depends on the extent to which it believes its political, military, and economic position is safe – that is, the extent to which its interests are secured. A stable international order regarded by its members as legitimate can be sustained by national policies directed toward concrete interests – knowable claims conforming to the expectations held by all of how states will act. At the same time, this order is a prerequisite for an international community that widens the moral opportunity of its participants, permitting their policy to move beyond the pure self-interest of Machiavelli to a self-interest softened by the obligations imposed by membership in a community. The mutual expectations of states are not equivalent to universal moral duties. They are maxims of prudence and applied political ethics; their strength and comprehensiveness depend on the degree to which the members of the system share in a common ethical framework.

And it is in these international assumptions of what constitutes a legitimate state interest that change *has* occurred in our era. At least since the Second World War, international society has been withdrawing its grant of legitimacy from state interests defined so as to include colonial possessions. 'National self-determination' for such dependencies has come to be regarded *a priori* as a justified claim; secession from an existing independent state, in general, has not. In 1973–74, the United States declined to test the general acceptance of a claim to the right to use armed force to secure continued access to Middle East oil. If statements by the General Assembly are a guide, racial discrimination by governments like South Africa has been defined as more unjust and a greater threat to international peace than other forms of tyranny. States have found they could successfully assert an interest in extending, for some purposes, their jurisdiction over the ocean floor from three to as much as two hundred miles from their coastline. The changing climate of opinion has made it easier for less-developed countries to assert control over foreign corporations within their territory, harder for any country to defend extraterritorial rights for its citizens abroad.

No one should argue that these changes are indistinguishable from disinterested justice. But they do show that international society evolves, even it if does not always progress. Because the ultimate power of effective action rests with states, national statesmen cannot abdicate their responsibility for moral choice to this world opinion. Sometimes, when the issue is vital, they must act even in the teeth of it. But they should be very sure of their ground before they do so. In not every case is the fallibility of the international community as clear as in the General Assembly's solemn declaration that Zionism is a form of racism. Policy founded on interests can counteract tendencies to national self-righteousness and give due weight to Madison's guide, 'the presumed or known opinion of the impartial world'.

Promoting justice in a world of states means, in part, working with their evolving national interests. It means seeking to nudge in desirable ways the shifting definition of a legitimate state interest – furthering restraints and throwing light on areas of common or shared interest as subjects for more positive cooperation; these could range from combating terrorism to lowering trade barriers against products from the Third World. Cast in these terms, national interest is inseparable from normative concerns. It does not promise great gains – only hard, slow work in making incremental changes in international expectations of state interest. Nor does it hope to replace power with morality in the determination of state policy. Nor can it be regarded as a substitute for the higher standards of ethics that ordinary conduct, both domestic and international, consistently flouts. It may, however, be the best application of practical wisdom to problems that will not yield to more ambitious designs.

NOTES

1   H. Morgenthau, *In Defense of the National Interest* (Knopf, New York, 1951), p. 33.
2   R. Johansen, *The National Interest and the Human Interest: An Analysis of U.S. Foreign Policy* (Princeton University Press, Princeton, 1980), p. 392.
3   Quoted in D. Thomson, *Democracy in France Since 1870*, 4th edn (Oxford University Press, New York, 1964), p. 271.
4   Quoted in H. Morgenthau, *Politics Among Nations: The Struggle for Power and Peace*, 5th edn, revised (Knopf, New York, 1978), p. 9.
5   F. Hinsley, *Power and the Pursuit of Peace* (Cambridge University Press, Cambridge, 1962), p. 197.
6   All quotations from Tocqueville are taken from *Democracy in America*, trans. Henry Reeve, 2 vols, 4th edn (Langley, New York, 1840), vol. II, bk 2, chs 8 and 14.

1.4 The formulation of foreign policy objectives

Keith R. Legg and James F. Morrison

Source: *Politics and the International System: An Introduction* (Harper and Row, New York, 1971), pp. 140–50.

Legg and Morrison discuss the requirements of a rational foreign policy. They suggest that it is the task of top decision makers to identify the political, economic and psychological needs of their country, to recognize the limitations involved in their pursuit and to work out 'a well-defined and well-ordered set of foreign policy objectives'.

Whatever the decision-making structure of a given state, some individual or institution must resolve conflict within the state, make collective decisions about the general needs and goals of the state and work out strategies for attaining them, including a determination of which goals can be attained only through interaction with other states in the international system. The process of formulating foreign policy objectives is by no means a simple one. In the first place, it is a fallacy to assume that a foreign policy decision – any more than a domestic policy one – affects all members of a state in the same way especially in the short run. The costs and benefits of most foreign policy decisions are unevenly distributed, and consequently, as noted, there is usually considerable internal conflict over what foreign policy should be. In the United States, for example, East European political refugees and those who profit from a high level of military expenditure are often less anxious to see a Soviet–American entente than are pacifists, businessmen who see opportunities to trade with Eastern Europe if agreement can be reached, or those who would prefer to see more money available for domestic welfare programs. Those of draft age or those who live in vulnerable cities may be less anxious to get involved in a war than those who live in rural areas and are in less danger of being directly involved. Manufacturers who sell to a domestic market and must compete with foreign imports are likely to be more favorable toward a protective tariff than those whose living depends on exports and who might suffer from retaliation. While all conflicting interests are not necessarily represented, the top decision-making authorities in a state must make some order out of the conflicting demands presented – integrating them with the decision-making elites' own beliefs about what is in their own interest and in the long-range interest of the state collectively. Although foreign policy goals in practice are seldom completely explicit, well-defined, stable, internally consistent, or ranked according to priority, a rational foreign policy model requires the decision-making authority of a state to work out such a well-defined and well-ordered set of foreign policy objectives as well as a strategy for attaining them.

A word must be said at this point about the relation between objectives and strategy (or between ends and means). In practice this distinction is largely analytical. In the first place, the distinction depends primarily on the objective on which one happens to be focusing. Few things we think of as objectives are ends in themselves, but are rather means, in turn, for the achievement of still more abstract or distant ends (e.g. happiness, security, success, prestige). The United States objective of winning the war in Korea or Vietnam, for example, is really only a means to contain communism. This in turn is only a means to protect the stability of the international system and to preserve a balance of power in the world favorable to the United States, and this, in turn, is a means to protect American security. In other words, there is no such thing as ends and means, only a complicated ends–means chain or an even more complicated intertwining ends–means net.

In the second place, objectives which originated entirely as a means of attaining some more distant end often take on a life of their own and become valued for their own sake, or because they become intertwining with other goals (originally not involved at all) such as prestige or self-respect. Although the objective of winning the war in Vietnam originated as a means of containing communism, in time winning became an end in itself – particularly for those most directly and emotionally involved in fighting or for those whose reputations as policy-makers depend on victory. The drive to win continued, despite growing doubts about whether it was possible or whether continuing to fight would in fact weaken and contain the communist movement and despite increasing evidence that continuing the fight might actually strengthen the communists and weaken the United States at home and her position in other parts of the world.

In the third place, experience and tradition over time – in combination with basic values and norms – create a set of relatively inflexible principles which also at least in part originated as means to achieving certain objectives. These principles, too, take on a life of their own and tend to persist even after they have ceased to serve as effective means, or principles. Examples of such general historical principles of United States foreign policy are the idea that communism must be contained at all costs, that the United States will never strike the first blow in a war, that only liberal-democratic states should be recognized or supported.

In the fourth place, there are often unintended consequences of the means one selects – i.e. the means may prove totally ineffective or even produce the opposite results than those intended, or they may produce both the desired ends and unintended consequences.

In the fifth place, every state, like every individual, has many objectives – and some of these objectives are bound to be in conflict with one another; therefore, the means necessary to achieve one objective may require a sacrifice of some other objective.

Despite these limitations, the distinction between ends and means is still useful. The rational foreign policy-making process to a large extent is the process of organizing clear and reliable (i.e. the means actually do lead to the desired end) means–ends chains, controlling the tendency of means to become ends in themselves and seeing that the original and more fundamental objectives are kept in perspective.

It is also important to remember that the goals or objectives of states – or even of each individual state – differ considerably not only in substance but also in a number of other ways:

1. The number, scope and mutual compatibility of the goals.
2. The intensity with which they are held, i.e. their relative importance *vis-à-vis* domestic goals and one another, and the cost the state is willing to pay in terms of the expenditure of capabilities or the sacrifice of other goals.
3. The urgency with which they must be achieved.
4. The flexibility with which they are pursued (i.e. the degree to which one goal can be substituted for another or modified in response to pressures for compromise, as long as the long-range goals are not impaired).
5. The risk the state is willing to run in the attempt to achieve its goals.
6. The state's expectations that the goals can actually be attained.

SOURCES OF FOREIGN POLICY OBJECTIVES

The most fundamental source of foreign policy objectives is perhaps the universally shared desire to insure the survival and territorial integrity of the community and state. Military security against invasion or bombardment is the minimum objective of every state's foreign policy. A related and also universal need is the preservation of the state's economy. These are usually purely defensive objectives, but under some circumstances internal or external conditions may require offensive action to insure the survival of the community and/ or the state.

Perhaps the single most important set of domestic sources of foreign policy are the economic needs of the community. These needs, however, are by no means static. Changing technology, growing population, economic development, new organizations and classes, changing values, beliefs, and expectations, and a changing political system will very much affect economic needs and their expression. At any given moment, however, the top decision-makers of a given state and the specialized foreign policy-making bureaucracy must consider a wide variety of factors: overpopulation and the consequent pressure for new cultivable land to increase food supplies, the need for industrial raw materials and investment capital as well as other imports necessary for the population's well-being and for economic development, the need for foreign markets for the goods produced in the state (particularly if the state must import to survive), the related need to preserve the state's balance of payments and to protect its currency, the need to protect or procure essential lines of communication and transportation, the need to protect investments in other states, ships and overseas installations, and one's citizens and nationals outside the country. (This latter need is often less an economic need than it is a matter of prestige or a cultural need.)

It is important to emphasize that economic needs are fundamental sources of a state's foreign policy. First, there are strong pressures generated in the state's political system to satisfy individual or group economic needs through foreign policy. Second, the economy of a state is fundamental to a state's capabilities and therefore to its power *vis-à-vis* other states, i.e. its ability to get other states to do what it desires. No top decision-maker in any state can be rational and ignore the problem of maintaining and, if possible, increasing capabilities to the point where they are adequate to achieve the state's objectives.

Another major domestic source of foreign policy is what we might call the political needs of a state and its leaders. If the state has serious internal political conflict or the political system has low legitimacy, the top decision-makers of the political system are likely to emphasize the foreign policy goals of preventing foreign intervention on the side of the dissenting or dissident groups and may seek aid in preserving the system or their own place in it (e.g. the USSR in 1918–24, South Vietnam at present [in the early 1970s]). Alternatively, the political leadership may take advantage of or even try to create foreign threats in order to distract the attention of a dissatisfied population from domestic problems or from the role of the elite in creating the problems. In general, even in stable political systems, the continued viability of the system rests on the ability of the top decision-makers to respond to politically significant domestic demands. This means that demands for foreign policy decisions from all quarters for any other cause also fall into this category.

Still another major domestic source of foreign policy is the cultural, psychological, and/or ideological needs of the state for prestige and status in the world: identity or meaning in life, needs for fulfilment of religious or sacred ideological imperatives, needs to follow moral principles or fulfill obligations (e.g. to come to the aid of victims of aggression or unjust oppression), and the like. Here we might also mention such psychological needs as relief for the population from tension, strain, uncertainty, anger, and frustration, which may generate strong pressures on foreign policy-makers to alter goals or even to take action immediately. Theoretically, this may not have a place in rational foreign policy-making, but it is clearly a fact of life in actual foreign policy-making and execution, and no national policy-maker can ignore such pressures completely.

One other domestic source of foreign policy might be termed the capability requirements of the state. Although most capability needs are met through decisions made in the area of domestic policy (e.g. decisions regarding investment rates, resource allocation, education, propaganda, government, military expenditures, draft calls), there is also an important area of capabilities determined by foreign policy decisions. Most obvious are decisions regarding the use of diplomacy to create alliances; acquire foreign air, naval, and other installations; to gain control over strategic land and waterways; or secure sources of raw materials. Decisions to recruit, train, and deploy intelligence-gathering units and clandestine operations teams and decisions to use force to increase one's capabilities are other examples. Somewhat less obvious are decisions regarding the recruitment and training of diplomats and career foreign service men. Least obvious, perhaps, is the long-range impact of the success or failure of foreign policy decisions on capabilities: if, for example, a diplomatic or military threat is made but not carried out (because of inadequate capabilities, planning, or willingness to run risks), then in the future when that state makes a similar threat, it is likely to go unheeded, even if the state has sufficient military capabilities or the will to act. In other words, a failure of foreign policy at one time may reduce the very important capability of credibility – a capability which, if successfully used, may avoid the expenditure of many irreplaceable capabilities in open warfare. Capability considerations of this kind are also important sources of foreign policy for rational decision-makers. On the other hand, the successful carrying out of a threat, though costly at the time, may increase one's credibility and increase the probability that making a similar threat in the future will itself be sufficient to achieve compliance.

Some writers (most notably Hans Morgenthau) have argued that capability considerations ('power' in Morgenthau's terminology) are the most important sources of foreign policy, and that states above all seek to increase their capabilities (power), as capabilities (power) are the key to all other objectives and therefore become the overriding objective for their own sake. This seems to us a very oversimplified theory, yet nevertheless one which contains more than a little truth.

There are also important external sources of foreign policy which the top foreign policy decision-makers and relevant general population alike must take into account. We have already mentioned external threats of military intervention and economic ruin. By implication, many of the domestic sources of foreign policy also have an external counterpart which has to be taken into account. If raw materials must be imported or foreign buyers found for one's products to pay for needed imports, the reality of the international economic and political system must be considered before policy is formulated. The external opportunities and limitations of trade are just as important determinants of a policy objective as are the actual domestic needs. The domestic needs are meaningless for foreign policy unless there is an external possibility of meeting those needs. Most foreign policies, in other words, involve a domestic need of one state which can be met only by enlisting active cooperation or at least the acquiescence of another state. The foreign policies of two states must interact to meet the domestic needs of each.

Nevertheless, there are also needs that arise primarily from external sources, such as a threat of invasion, subversion, or economic discrimination or blockade by another state. They create foreign policy needs for protection that can be met by alliance with a third state or by membership in a supranational or international organization. Likewise, by the very creation of a common market, or alliance, or international organization, neighboring states may create a threat to one's economic well-being or military security, if the activity is ignored, but it can also create an opportunity to cooperate and reap benefits otherwise unavailable. Another type of external source of foreign policy are opportunities created by events outside one's state: two neighboring states at war with one another; the disintegration of a neighboring empire; the discovery of new continents or mineral resources; two states on the verge of war in need of a mediator; and other similar changes create opportunities for a state to increase its power, size, wealth, or prestige by responding with a creative foreign policy. (In the same way that domestic sources of foreign policy have a foreign counterpart; likewise, such foreign sources of foreign policy require their domestic counterpart.)

Which of these various internal and external sources of foreign policy will be most important in a given case depends on the individual situation. By and large, among the domestic sources of foreign policy, the political system (the institutions and rules of the game) and the relative power of the contending groups will be among the major determinants.

THE LIMITATIONS OF THE FORMULATION OF OBJECTIVES

It is important to keep in mind that there are some important limitations which come into play in the rational formulation of foreign policy objectives. The internal limitations on goal formulation include limited capabilities or a limited ability to mobilize them for foreign policy objectives. This may mean an inability to mobilize adequate popular support or acquiescence for policies even among top decision-makers. There may also be cultural limits on policy objectives.

No rational attempt at foreign policy formulation can set forth serious objectives which exceed the ability of the state to achieve them. Every state's capabilities are limited, and one of the basic problems of rational foreign policy formulation is to keep the objectives of the state within the limits of the capabilities to achieve them. The possession of objective capabilities, of course, does not necessarily mean the ability to mobilize them for foreign policy purposes. The relevant population and institutions may be willing to utilize the capabilities which they control for some purposes (e.g. fighting off an invasion of home territory) but not for others (e.g. fighting in a distant land, for objectives that are not entirely clear).

Despite the best efforts of specialized foreign policy elites, it may simply prove impossible to persuade the domestic policy elites (or even the chief executive) to expend the necessary resources or run the risks necessary to achieve the objectives (or use the means) that the specialists think most desirable.

A failure to achieve announced objectives can be costly not only in terms of prestige, but can also be expensive in terms of the wasted economic and military capabilities which could have been put to better use. Moreover, failure also means a loss of political capabilities, such as reduced morale and loss of self-confidence and will. Even if one backs down from announced objectives, there is still the danger of lost prestige and credibility. All these things decrease the overall capabilities of a state and increase its vulnerability to other states. It is, of course, not easy to judge just how many capabilities one has available or what a given set of capabilities can accomplish. There are always unforeseen circumstances. Other states may suddenly join together to form a new alliance. There may be sudden advances in weapons technology (e.g. the atomic bomb). The weather may affect military operations unexpectedly (e.g. Napoleon's disastrous invasion of Russia). Internal economic or political crises may unexpectedly limit the ability to mobilize capabilities (e.g. the United States' experience in Vietnam). Moreover, there is no way to evaluate with any degree of precision the effects of given policies or weapons. Different types of weapons systems (e.g. armored weapons, airpower, guerrilla warfare tactics) are often used against one another and the effects of each against the others are not easy to measure accurately. In addition, there are factors of strategy, morale, and luck to consider even when opponents use similar weapons systems. At best, then, an evaluation of a given state's capabilities – even in relation to another state or a given set of objectives – is only a rough estimate. Incorrect analyses of the probable effectiveness of one's capabilities are among the important causes of war, e.g. World War II, Vietnam, the Arab–Israeli war of 1967.

For these reasons, rational decision-making requires the careful limitation of objectives to well within the range of state capabilities in order that possible errors of calculation can be sustained. Capabilities can also be underestimated and the state that is willing to run the greatest amount of risk – especially in relation to cautious states that are less willing to run risks – has a great advantage over adversaries because of the ability to bluff and force concessions. The irrational state in a world of rational states, in other words, often is at an advantage, at least in the short run and for limited gains that do not threaten what the other states consider to be their core values.

Another important domestic limit on foreign policy objectives is the need to mobilize sufficient support for a given objective. Enough people have to be persuaded that a given policy objective is worth the cost and risk involved. What constitutes adequate support, of course, depends on the nature of the political system, but even in highly authoritarian states the problem of mobilizing adequate support among the top decision-making elite remains. Lack of consensus over goals in either decentralized or highly centralized decision-making systems can lead to paralysis and an inability to take decisive action. It goes without saying that if a policy objective does not have adequate support it cannot be adopted. Problems of paralysis arise where there is a fairly even division between supporters and opponents of a given policy, a nearly even balance of support for different but conflicting policies, or where support is divided among three or more conflicting objectives with no single policy commanding adequate support. In such circumstances even if one faction is victorious over the others and a given policy is adopted, the lack of real consensus provides only precarious support for the decision, and there is always a good chance that the victorious faction or coalition will be overturned. Such continual crises not only make foreign policy irrational but also endanger the achievement of domestic goals and weaken the general capabilities of the state. Under such conditions objectives are often modified to accommodate enough individuals and groups to form a firmer base for the policy or the objectives are abandoned.

Finally there are domestic cultural limits on a state's objectives. Obviously the culture of a state affects the mobilization of support for objectives in general. It affects what people value and how much they are willing to pay or risk to achieve a given objective. Over and above this, however, there is another kind of limitation: namely, the body of norms and general principles which specify legitimate state objectives, strategies, and foreign policy instruments. A state holding to the norm of self-determination of peoples or anti-imperialism will find it more difficult to adopt an imperialist policy that states without such principles, even when great economic benefits could be derived from such a policy.

There are also important external limits to a state's goals, and in some ways these are also only counterparts of the domestic limitations. The capabilities of other states, for example, determine the probability that one's own will be sufficient to secure a given objective. The limits created by international organizations and norms operate effectively either because a state shares the norms itself (i.e. they are a part of its own cultural limitations) or because they are shared by others who consequently will be able to mobilize more capabilities to counter the initiatives of the state that does not share them.

1.5 The role of military power
John Garnett

Source: *Contemporary Strategy*, 2nd edn (Croom Helm, London, 1987), pp. 71–90.

Garnett, writing in the mid-1980s, identifies a series of arguments which suggest that military power is of declining relevance in world politics. He counters each argument, and reasserts the continuing importance of military power; the events of the 1980s are seen as a confirmation of this position, and Garnett's conclusion is that most political actors will continue to see military power as an essential ingredient of world politics.

THE MEANING OF MILITARY POWER

At its simplest, the term *military power* refers to the capacity to kill, maim, coerce, and destroy, and although occasionally this power may be possessed by individuals within the state – as the feudal barons did during the Middle Ages and as the IRA does today – nowadays military power tends to be monopolized by states and used primarily by *governments* to protect their countries from external aggression and internal subversion. Military power, therefore, is the legally sanctioned instrument of violence that governments use in their relations with each other, and, when necessary, in an internal security role.

Underlying the above definition is the assumption that military power is a purposive, functional thing – one of the many instruments in the orchestra of power that states use at an appropriate moment in the pursuit of their respective national interests. Since Clausewitz it has been fashionable to regard military power as but one of the many techniques of statecraft, taking its place alongside diplomacy, economic sanctions, propaganda, and so on. But of course even Clausewitz recognized that war is not always an instrument of policy, a purposive political act. Sometimes war is a kind of madness, an explosion of violence that erupts not as a result of political decisions but in spite of them.

69

[Garnett goes on to stress, however, that he is only concerned with the use of military power as a rational technique for pursuing foreign policy.]

Clearly, military power does not come into being by accident. It cannot be acquired without enormous effort in terms of manpower and industrial resources, and its very existence is a source of worry for the governments that control it. Democratically elected governments feel uneasy about military power for at least two reasons. First, because it is so incredibly expensive that its acquisition is bound to be unpopular with the electorate, particularly during a period of prolonged peace. In modern, welfare-oriented societies there is a tendency to see the acquisition of military power as a misallocation of resources. President Eisenhower spelled out the 'opportunity cost' of modern weapons very clearly when he said, 'The cost of one modern bomber is this: a modern brick school in more than thirty cities. It is two electric power plants each serving a town of 60,000 population. It is two fine, fully equipped hospitals. It is some fifty miles of concrete highway.'[1] In short, military power is regarded by many not as a means to economic well-being, but as an alternative to it. [...]

But there is an even more fundamental reason why democratic societies feel uneasy about the existence of large amounts of military power in their midst. Their unease stems from a real dilemma; while it is widely acknowledged that military power is necessary to protect democratic states from aggression and subversion, it is also recognized that the mere existence of this power in the hands of a few represents an inherent threat to the very democratic values it is supposed to protect. The problem of reconciling or striking a balance between the need to concentrate military power in the hands of a few and the need to preserve democratic values is a fundamental one for any democratic state.

The political control of the military is almost taken for granted in the United Kingdom, where there is a long tradition of political neutrality in the armed services, and where the threat of military rule is quite unreal. But not all states are as fortunate in their constitutional arrangements. In postwar years, even the United States has experienced growing tension between its large military establishment and its liberal democratic principles. The military–industrial complex, as President Eisenhower called it, is a very real symptom of this problem. Once big business and the military became inextricably entwined, an enormous and frightening pressure group was created that, according to some critics, is now so powerful that it dominates large areas of American life and is beyond democratic civilian control.

If military power is electorally unpopular and inherently difficult to control, one is tempted to ask why governments do not abolish it. And the answer, of course, is that the serious worries caused by the acquisition of military strength are quite dwarfed by the worries of trying to manage without it. Given the kind of world in which we live, military power is regarded by most statesmen as a prerequisite for national survival. Even neutral states, with no great ambitions, have found it necessary to remain armed, and many states have found that, over the years, their prosperity and influence have been directly related to their military power. In a world of independent sovereign states that, by definition, acknowledge no authority higher than themselves, and that are in constant and unceasing competition for scarce resources, military power has been an indispensable instrument of the national interest.

Life in international society has been likened to life in Hobbes's 'state of nature'. To survive in that tough, ruthless, ungoverned environment is a difficult business, and military power has proved a useful weapon. Its use frequently determines not who is right, but who is going to prevail in the constant jockeying for prosperity, prestige, and security. Its acquisition represents an attempt by statesmen to control as far as possible the dangerous and unpredictable environment in which they have to make their way, and it is difficult to imagine what international politics would be like in its absence. It is perfectly true that there are groupings of states within which war is unthinkable – the Common Market is one such 'security community' – but it is dangerous to assume either that relations between Common Market countries are unaffected by military power or that such relations could ever be extended to the world as a whole.

Michael Howard has suggested that 'the capacity of states to defend themselves, and their evident willingness to do so, provides the basic framework within which the business of international negotiations is carried on'. Military power is an intrinsic part of the rather fragile international order associated with the international system, and, as Howard says, 'It is not easy to see how international relations could be conducted and international order maintained, if it were totally absent.'[2] Until the world is radically transformed and the system of sovereign states replaced by a quite different international order, military power, and the capacity for violence it implies, are bound to play a significant part in international politics.

Because military power is an intrinsic part of a world of sovereign states, there is a sense in which criticism of it is irrelevant. Of course it would be nice if the world were ordered differently, but it is not, and schemes to change it invariably founder. Over the years there have been many proposals to rid the world of armed power, to disarm and to build a better-organized world community, but none of them have been practical politics. Henry IV's reputed comment on one such scheme is still appropriate: 'It is perfect,' the king said, 'perfect. I see no single flaw in it save one, namely, that no earthly prince would ever agree to it.' Hedley Bull has rightly condemned such solutions as 'a corruption of thinking about international relations and a distraction from its proper concerns'.[3] Constructive criticism accepts military power as a fact of life. It seeks not to abolish that which cannot be abolished, but to manage it successfully so that wars, both interstate and internal, become less rather than more frequent occurrences in international politics.

THE UTILITY OF MILITARY POWER

Traditionally, of course, neither statesmen nor political theorists have queried the utility of military power, and even today its value is self-evident in many parts of the world. It is very doubtful, for example, whether the Israelis or the Arabs or the Indians or the Chinese hold any illusions about the continuing importance of military power. Nor are there many signs of Soviet disenchantment. Many statesmen would consider it preposterous to question the value of military power given the dangerous world in which we all live and given the historical record of violence in the twentieth century. The authors of the recent volume of the *Cambridge Modern History*[4] dealing with the first half of the twentieth century entitled it *The Era of Violence*, and this grim description is perhaps some sort of indication of the importance of military power in contemporary international politics.

Nevertheless, in the late 1960s and early 1970s a number of American commentators – not all of them left-wing radicals – felt able to question the importance of military power. One of the reasons that they were able to do this with any degree of plausibility was that from the point of view of the United States and Western Europe, the international environment seemed less dangerous than at any time since the end of the Second World War. After all, by 1975 the United States had managed to extricate itself from Vietnam; the politics of the cold war had given way to the easier atmosphere of détente; there had been a rapprochement with China, and the various crises that threatened world peace in the 1950s and early 1960s had melted into history.

All this produced, in L. W. Martin's words, 'a diffused feeling of greater safety' in which military force seemed less necessary and, hence, less useful. As Martin put it, 'For many Western taxpayers, the military are on the way to becoming latter-day remittance men, given a small slice of the family income on condition that they go off and pursue their unsavoury activities quietly where they will not embarrass decent folk.' And, of course, Martin was not alone in thinking that with the coming of détente and a relaxation of tension in East–West relations, the utility of military power was diminishing. Klaus Knorr in his book *On the Uses of Military Power in the Nuclear Age* expressed similar sentiments and argued in a similar vein.[5]

Unfortunately, the passage of time has revealed that the optimistic climate of international relations suggested by the period of détente was not, as many believed, a permanent feature of the international environment, but a transient phenomenon, highly atypical of state relations. Indeed, in the more sober and worrying climate of the mid-1980s, speculation about the declining usefulness of military power has a decided anachronistic ring to it. [...]

Ten years ago, when the critics of military power were in the ascendancy and the strategists were very much on the defensive, it seemed easy to emphasize the uselessness of weapons of mass destruction for all practical purposes. American writers, soured by their country's experience in Vietnam, noted that those who were the most powerful militarily were not always the most politically successful. The critics were acutely aware that military preponderance cannot always be translated into political victory. The United States, for example, was not able to capitalize her virtual nuclear monopoly in the late 1940s and early 1950s by winning the cold war, and the Vietnam War must be the classic case of a superpower capable of destroying the entire world finding itself unable to defeat a guerrilla movement in what one writer described as a 'rice-based, bicycle-powered, economy'.

However, it is worth pointing out that it is dangerous to deduce from the American experience in Vietnam any general propositions about the utility or otherwise of military power. It may be that the American failure in Vietnam can be attributed to the incompetent way in which military power was used rather than any inherent defect in the military instrument itself. Hanson Baldwin, for example, has suggested that lack of success was not a result of using military power, but of not using enough of it early enough.[6] In other words, so his argument runs, rapid escalation might have induced the enemy to give up by presenting him with intolerable costs. The mistake the

Americans made was not fighting the war in the first place, but fighting it at a level that the enemy found tolerable, rather than escalating to a point where the North Vietnamese would find it unbearable.

CRITICISMS OF MILITARY POWER

Nevertheless, the critics of military power undoubtedly had a point. The relationship between military strength and political influence is certainly not the proportional one implied by Mao Tse-tung's famous dictum that 'political power grows out of the barrel of a gun'; but although it is not a straightforward connection, few would dispute that in general terms there is a relationship between military strength and political power. On the whole, those who wield the most military power tend to be the most influential; their wishes the most respected; their diplomacy the most heeded. Of all the great powers, only Japan appears to disprove the connection between military and political strength. As Ian Smart says, 'Japan is allegedly intent upon that alchemist's "grand experiment"; the transmutation of great economic into great political power without the use of any military catalyst.'[7] Whether Japan will succeed is highly problematic, and the fact that it is trying is not so much because it is confident of success as because it has no real alternative.

The connection between military strength and political power was clearly perceived by R. Chaput, when, commenting on the relative decline of British military strength in the 1930s, he wrote, 'The weight of Great Britain in diplomatic bargaining is, in the last resort, proportionate to the strength of her armaments, and her influence for peace is measurable in terms of the force she can muster to prevent the overthrow of the political equilibrium by armed force.'[8] It is undoubtedly a serious mistake to assume that political influence is proportional to military strength; but it is an even more serious error to deny any connection between the two.

A second arrow in the quiver of those who queried the utility of military power is the argument that in ideological quarrels it is an inappropriate weapon because ideas cannot be defeated by force of arms. It is sometimes claimed, for example, that the notion of a 'united Ireland', which gives point to IRA activity in Ulster, cannot be defeated by the British military presence, and, therefore, that a political solution must be found to the problems of that troubled province. It is also sometimes claimed that in so far as the West is engaged in an ideological struggle with communism, its concentration on military confrontation means that it is planning to fight the wrong war. It is, of course, debatable whether the IRA is much interested in a united Ireland or whether the East–West struggle is predominantly ideological, but even if they are, the proposition that ideas cannot be defeated by military force cannot be accepted without serious qualification.

It is perfectly true that ideas cannot be eradicated without destroying all the books where they are written down and killing all the people who have ever heard of them. In that sense the proposition that ideas cannot be destroyed by military force is probably true; but even though it may be impossible to *eliminate* ideas, it is certainly possible to render them politically ineffective by the use of military force. The ideas of Hitler and Mussolini live on in their writings, which are accessible to all, but the military defeat of the Axis powers in 1945 went a long way toward relegating fascism to the periphery of practical politics. Similarly, in Ireland one may speculate that the ruthless use of military power could make the idea of a united Ireland politically irrelevant for the foreseeable future. The word *ruthless* is important. If the Kremlin had the problem of Ulster to deal with, it is easy to believe that within a period of weeks rather than months the IRA would have been systematically destroyed, its sympathizers incarcerated, and the entire province subjected to military discipline. In other words, criticisms about the way in which the British government has used its military power in Ireland are not criticisms about the effectiveness of the military instrument per se; they are only criticisms about the halfhearted, squeamish way in which successive British governments, rightly or wrongly, have used it.

The argument that military power cannot defeat political ideas was, in the late 1960s and early 1970s, only part of a more general argument that queried the appropriateness of military power as an instrument of statecraft. It was suggested – with some plausibility given the general climate of détente prevailing at the time – that the real stakes of international politics were quite unrelated to such traditional uses of military power as the acquisition of territory and empire. It was claimed that, in the modern world, the goals of states were much more intangible; like, for example, improving trade relations, securing markets, gaining political friends, winning the favor of world opinion. And in the pursuit of these objectives military power was seen as at best irrelevant and at worst counterproductive.

At the time there seemed a good deal of sense in that view. There was plenty of evidence that the use of military power for territorial conquest was much less popular than it used to be – at least among advanced industrial states. It was felt that the appetite for conquest had become jaded partly because the military, moral, and political costs of unprovoked aggression had risen sharply, and partly because the expected value of conquest to advanced industrial states had fallen dramatically. Post-Second World War experience seemed to suggest that an industrial state bent on improving the material prosperity and standard of living of its citizens would be better advised to use its resources for increasing industrial investment and technological research rather than expending them in wars of conquest. In the 1970s the world contained many examples of states that had become wealthy and prosperous without military power. Japan and West Germany both spring to mind, and there were many who saw a direct connection between their impressive growth rates and their relatively low military expenditures.

CHANGING ATTITUDES TO MILITARY POWER IN THE 1980s

However, the world recession of the 1980s has demonstrated that neither Germany nor Japan are immune from the economic consequences of declining world demand, and the connection between strong economic growth and low military expenditure seems more tenuous than it used to seem. As for the claim that modern states are disinclined to use military power in the pursuit of their interests, that now has a very hollow ring to it in a world that has witnessed the Soviet invasion of Afghanistan, the British recapture of the Falklands, and American military involvement in Central America.

And it is not just the repeated use of military power over the past decade that has brought about a change in people's expectations about the likelihood of military violence. The entire moral climate has begun to change in such a way that military power is once again becoming an acceptable instrument of policy. In the years following the Second World War, and particularly in the aftermath of Vietnam, the use of force was, to quote Hedley Bull, 'inhibited by its growing illegitimacy'[9] and by the widespread feeling of revulsion toward its consequences, which was shared by all civilized people. Today there are indications that the public mood is hardening and that military force is once again becoming a tolerable instrument of policy. In Britain, for example, the fact that there is virtually no public hostility to defense spending, even in a period of economic recession when the very foundations of the welfare state are being threatened, perhaps bears witness to the growing public acceptability of military power.

And in the United States the same hardening of attitude on defense issues is suggested by record levels of defense expenditure and a very expensive 'Star Wars' research program. [...]

Bull makes the point that whereas in the late 1960s and early 1970s there was a widespread assumption of world resources readily available for the development of all states, it is now clear that this is unlikely to be true for the late 1980s and 1990s.[10] Third World demands for a 'New International Economic Order', the power of OPEC, and the scramble for sea and seabed resources have all highlighted the politics of scarcity and have suggested that in the future, far from being readily available, resources vital to civilized life may be accessible only to those who have the power to hold what they have and seize what they need. In that kind of world military power begins to look like an indispensable instrument for survival rather than a quaint anachronism. [...]

There are [also] powerful reasons why states may involve themselves in the internal affairs of foreign countries despite the risks and costs involved. First, because providing military assistance to a friendly government, however despotic and electorally unpopular that government is, may be the only way of preventing that state from falling into the hands of a foreign power or a new hostile regime. Second, because intervention in local conflicts provides the superpowers with an opportunity to pursue national and ideological goals without running the risks of mutual destruction, which are implicit in more direct confrontations. Third, because internal wars cause anxiety even in states not immediately affected by them. Internal wars constitute a form of social change that is fundamentally unpredictable, and 'no situation is more threatening to nations than one whose outcome has become so uncertain as to have moved beyond their control'.[11] In particular, civil violence is a contagious phenomenon, and what is not controlled in one country may, it is feared, spread to others. And the fourth reason why states may become militarily involved in the internal affairs of others is that few of them are immune from the moral pressure to throw their power behind a just cause even when so doing contravenes the principle of sovereign independence.

MILITARY POWER AND MILITARY FORCE

[Garnett notes that growing awareness of the need for military power, either for intervention or for power projection, cannot disguise its risks.]

One of the most persistent – though not the most intelligent – arguments against the continuing usefulness of military power is implied by the common assertion that modern weapons, particularly nuclear and thermonuclear weapons, are so destructive of life and property that they cannot reasonably be regarded as a usable instrument of policy. There are, so it is argued, no conceivable political objectives in the pursuit of which these devastating weapons could justifiably be used. In the public mind, at least, there is a widespread belief that any use of nuclear weapons is synonymous with Armaggedon. It is claimed, therefore, that we are in the incredible situation of spending vast amounts of money on a kind of armament that cannot be used rationally and that is therefore useless. Walter Millis put the case as well as it could be put:

> The great military establishments which exist are not practically usable in the conduct of international relations, and in general are not being so used today; and if it were possible to rid ourselves of the whole apparatus – the military establishments, and the war system they embody – international relations could be conducted far more safely, more efficiently, and more creatively in face of the staggering real problems facing humankind than is now the case.[12]

Though the argument is superficially attractive, it contains several serious flaws. First, and most obvious, it assumes that military power can only be useful if it is used physically, and it ignores the fact that a good deal of modern military power is most useful when it is not being used. Indeed, the most powerful weapons in the arsenals of the superpowers have been specifically acquired in order not to be used. The strategy of deterrence, which has come to dominate East–West relations and which provides the backdrop against which all East–West negotiations take place, is built on the assumption that it is the *possession*, not the *use*, of thermonuclear weapons that is sufficient to deter attack. Today, strategic power is designed to promote peace and security by preventing wars rather than by winning them. [...]

In this context it may be helpful to make the distinction between military power and military force. Military power may depend to a large extent on the availability of military force, but conceptually it is quite different; it emphasizes a political relationship between potential adversaries rather than a catalog of military capabilities. In a nutshell, the difference between the exercise of military force and military power is the difference between taking what you want and persuading someone to give it to you. In a sense, therefore, the use of military force represents the breakdown of military power. The physical use of deterrent power shows not how strong a country is but how impotent it has become.

One of the changes that has occurred since the Second World War is the increasing sophistication with which military power is exploited without military force being used. This is the age of brinkmanship, crisis management, and deterrence. These phenomena support the thesis that modern military force tends to be threatened and manipulated in peacetime rather than used in war. An example may reinforce the point. Think, for a moment, of the political attitude of Finland toward the Soviet Union. Though the sovereign independence of their state is not in question, the gross disparity in power between the two countries has forced the Finns into a relationship of reluctant deference toward the Soviet Union, which the latter must find very reassuring. Now Finlandization, as it is sometimes called, was brought about neither by Soviet threats nor any physical use of Soviet military power against Finland. It was simply an inevitable consequence of Soviet military preponderance in the area, an almost automatic payoff from the possession of powerful military forces. [...]

The second major flaw in the Millis thesis is that it is quite illogical to argue from the fact that using the most powerful military weapons is likely to be mutually destructive, that the use of *all* kinds of military force is equally pointless. At the moment of writing only six states have acquired any kind of nuclear capability at all, and although one may reasonably expect proliferation to continue, it seems clear that in the foreseeable future the vast majority of the world's states will not be able to avail themselves of this peculiarly destructive power. Hence in their relations with each other they are not likely to be much troubled by its terrible potential.

And, of course, it is also worth pointing out that the nuclear powers themselves have not renounced the physical use of all military power, not even all nuclear military power. Limited wars – that is, wars in which the belligerents exercise restraint in their use of military force – still make good political sense to nuclear powers. Indeed, it is not always recognized that limited wars are feasible precisely because total wars are not. The major incentive to keep limited wars limited is the fear that they may become total, and it therefore follows that the same terrible innovations in weapon technology that have taken total war out of the spectrum of rational options available to nuclear states have encouraged them to develop strategies of limited and sublimited war rather than give up the idea of war altogether. In short, though the advent of nuclear and thermonuclear weapons may have imposed new restraints upon those who control them, there is no evidence that they have seriously undermined the utility of military power.

What has happened, however, is that states have developed strategies that emphasize the *political* uses of military power even in war itself. It was never true that diplomacy ended when the shooting started, but in the prenuclear age there did seem some sense in the view that war was an alternative to diplomacy. But today the distinction is so fudged and blurred as to be almost meaningless. T. C. Schelling's definition of war as a 'bargaining process' or a sort of 'tough negotiation', and his telling phrase 'the diplomacy of violence'[13] all suggest that war, far from signifying the end of diplomacy, has become part of diplomacy itself.

Schelling has invented the terms *coercive warfare* and *compellance* to describe the use of military force for goals that are not strictly military at all and where 'the object is to make the enemy behave',[14] rather than to weaken or defeat him. The chief instrument of this vicious diplomacy and dirty bargaining is the power to hurt, to cause pain and suffering. Now all wars involve pain and suffering, and modern wars more than most, but traditionally the anguish caused by war has been no more than an incidental, almost regrettable, by-product of military action. What is being emphasized now is the strategy of using the power to hurt in a deliberate and conscious way to intimidate, demoralize, blackmail, and bargain to a position of advantage.

The use of nuclear weapons on Japan at the end of the Second World War is an interesting example of this technique. Though literally dropped on Hiroshima and Nagasaki, there is a sense in which these two atomic bombs were not really aimed at these cities at all. Their target was the decision makers in Tokyo, and the object of the exercise was not the military one of destroying the war-making capability of Japan, but the political one of inducing her leaders to surrender. In Schelling's words, 'The effect of the bombs and their purpose were not mainly the military destruction they accomplished but the pain and the shock and the promise of more.'[15] Military power, the power to hurt, was being used physically to intimidate an enemy and make him 'behave'. [...]

CONCLUSION

According to Lasswell and Kaplan, 'an arena is military when the expectation of violence is high; civic when the expectation is low'.[16] For hundreds of years it has been customary to regard the international system as a military arena in which interstate war was a more or less normal phenomenon, and the internal structure of states as a civic arena characterized by stability and order and a low expectation of violence. For a brief period in the late 1960s and early 1970s there were signs that this situation was changing; that is to say, that interstate violence was becoming comparatively rare, and domestic violence comparatively common. However, not even an optimistic commentator in the 1970s would have gone so far as to describe the modern international system as a *civic* arena, and no pessimistic commentator would have described the modern state as a *military* arena. However, fifteen years ago, strategic stability at the superpower level combined with political instability in many Afro-Asian states undoubtedly contributed to a shift of emphasis away from interstate violence toward the intrastate violence.

S. Huntington pointed out that between 1961 and 1968, 114 of the world's 121 major political units endured some significant form of violent conflict. And in 1966 Robert McNamara claimed that in the previous eight years out of 164 internationally significant outbreaks of violence only 15 were military conflicts between two states. The statistics may be queried in detail if only because of the ambiguity surrounding the terms, but the overall picture is clear. In many parts of the world, particularly in southern Asia, Latin America, Africa, and the Middle East, intrastate violence in which a nongovernmental body attempts to overthrow and replace an established government has become a common if not normal pattern of political change. Internal wars, described by H. Eckstein as 'any resort to violence within a political order to change its constitution, government or politics',[17] have become commonplace in the wake of decolonization, modernization, Westernization, and rapid economic development. In periods of rapid social, political, and economic change, many governments have been unable to control the tensions that simmer beneath the surface of political life before finally erupting in revolutionary violence. [...]

It has been estimated that since the Second World War there have been 135 armed conflicts.[18] Without confusing the continued use of military force with its usefulness, it is reasonable to believe that most of the states engaged in those wars regarded the use of military power as an appropriate and reasoned response to the international situation in which they found themselves. The frequency and persistence of military violence around the world provides prima facie evidence that large numbers of people continue to think that military power is a useful, perhaps even an indispensable, instrument of policy. The various qualifications that now have to be made to the once-fashionable thesis that military power has lost its utility go a long way toward undermining the theory completely.

In fact, few objective observers now dispute the utility of military power both as an instrument of change within and between states. In the terminology of Lasswell and Kaplan, today neither the state nor the international system can be described as *civic*. In significant areas of the world military violence seems endemic in both environments. Anyone who knows anything about Northern Ireland, for example, cannot dispute the useful role the army performs in keeping an uneasy peace between two hostile communities. Anyone who understands the role and record of the North Atlantic Alliance cannot dispute the defensive role of military power in the European theater. Anyone familiar with the strategic stalemate between the two superpowers will not need convincing that the 'balance of terror' depends very much on the existence of enormous military power in the arsenals of both the United States and the Soviet Union. Anyone cognizant of the political and social instability that disrupts so many countries of the world cannot doubt the usefulness of military power both for insurgents and those who seek to counter them.

The world around us is full of examples of military power being more or less effectively used. Hedley Bull has suggested that although Western societies are far from being militarized, 'the role of the military in them has become more comfortable than it was ... there is a greater willingness to shoulder defence burdens and to adopt military perspectives'.[19] We live in a military age, and there are few signs that either our children or grandchildren will experience anything else.

NOTES

1 Quoted by C. Hitch, *The Economics of Defense in the Nuclear Age* (Harvard University Press, Cambridge, Mass., 1961), p. 4.
2 M. Howard, 'Military Power and International Order', *International Affairs*, 40: 3 (July 1964), p. 405.
3 H. Bull, *The Control of the Arms Race* (Weidenfeld and Nicolson, London, 1961), pp. 26–7.
4 *The New Cambridge Modern History*, vol. 12, *The Era of Violence, 1898–1945* (Cambridge University Press, Cambridge, 1964).
5 L.W. Martin, 'The Utility of Military Force', in D. Thompson (ed.), 'Force in Modern Societies: Its Place in International Politics', *Adelphi Paper* no. 102 (International Institute for Strategic Studies, London, 1973), p. 15; ibid., p. 14; and K. Knorr, *On the Uses of Military Power in the Nuclear Age* (Princeton University Press, Princeton, NJ, 1966), chs 2 and 3.

6 H. Baldwin, 'The Cases for Escalation', *New York Times Magazine*, 22 February 1966, pp. 22–82.
7 I. Smart, 'Committee Discussions on the Utility of Military Force in Modern Societies: Report to the Conference', in Thompson (ed.), 'Force in Modern Societies', p. 22.
8 R. Chaput, *Disarmament in British Foreign Policy* (George Allen and Unwin, London, 1935), p. 372.
9 H. Bull, 'Force in International Relations', in R. O'Neill and D.M. Horner (eds), *New Directions in Strategic Thinking* (George Allen and Unwin, London, 1981), p. 28.
10 Ibid., pp. 22–4.
11 J.N. Rosenau, 'Internal War as an International Event', in J.N. Rosenau (ed.), *International Aspects of Civil Strife* (Princeton University Press, Princeton, NJ, 1964), p. 57.
12 W. Millis, 'The Uselessness of Military Power', in R.A. Goldwin (ed.), *America Armed* (Rand McNally, Chicago, 1961), p. 38.
13 T.C. Schelling, *Arms and Influence* (Yale University Press, New Haven and London, 1966), particularly ch. 1.
14 Ibid., pp. 69–71 and 173.
15 Ibid., p. 18.
16 H. Lasswell and M. Kaplan, *Power and Society* (Yale University Press, New Haven, 1950), p. 252.
17 S.P. Huntington, 'Civil Violence and the Process of Development', in 'Civil Violence and the International System', *Adelphi Paper* no. 83 (International Institute for Strategic Studies, London, 1971), p. 1; McNamara quoted by D. Wood, 'Conflict in the Twentieth Century', *Adelphi Paper* no. 48 (International Institute for Strategic Studies, London, 1968), p. 1; Eckstein quoted in R. Falk, *Legal Order in a Violent World* (Princeton University Press, Princeton, NJ, 1968), p. 132n.
18 R.A. Falk and S.S. Kim (eds), *The War System: An Interdisciplinary Approach* (Westview Press, Boulder, Colorado, 1980), p. 2.
19 H. Bull, 'Of Means and Ends', in O'Neill and Horner, *New Directions in Strategic Thinking*, p. 279.

1.6 The nature of national economic power

Klaus Knorr

Source: *Power and Wealth* (Basic Books, London, 1973), pp. 13–14 and 90.

Knorr distinguishes between 'putative' and 'actualized' power, the former representing power as a means that can be possessed and added to, the latter power as an effect that those means can be used to achieve. He goes on to use the distinction to discuss the capabilities which underpin the economic strength of a country and the mechanisms whereby those capabilities can be employed against another country.

The phenomenon of power lends itself to two sharply different conceptions. The inability to grasp this difference leads to inevitable misunderstanding and confusion. Since coercive influence limits the conduct of an actor subjected to it, power can be seen to reside in the capabilities that permit the power-wielder to make effective threats. But it can also be seen as identical with, and limited to, the influence on the actually achieved behavior of the threatened actor. On the first view, power is something that powerful states have and can accumulate; power is a *means*. On the second view, power is an *effect*, that is the influence actually enjoyed. It is generated in an interaction which is an encounter. On the first view, power is something that an actor can hope to bring into play in a range of future situations. On the second, power comes into being, is shaped, and enjoyed only in a specific situation; its measure is the amount of influence actually achieved.

Today, most theorists conceive of power as actually achieved influence, whereas most laymen see it as reposing in the capabilities that permit strong threats to be made. Both concepts catch a part of reality. But it is critically important that we know which one we have in mind when we speak of 'power'. In the following, we will call the one *putative* power and the other *actualized* power.

[Knorr goes on later in the book to examine this distinction in relation to the economic power of a nation. He begins by considering 'economic strength' as a basis of putative power and ends by noting how this putative power can be actualized.]

The sheer magnitude of a state's foreign economic transactions is one element of national economic strength. Obviously, a country accounting for thirty per cent of world exports and imports and of world exports of capital and technical assistance, tends to enjoy far greater leverage than a country accounting for only three per cent. However, it is not advantageous from this point of view that the state's trade and capital exports are also large in relation to GNP. If its trade is large in these terms as well, the country is also susceptible to economic pressure from the outside. In other words, while it provides leverage for application to other states, an important constituent of active economic power, a large volume of trade relative to GNP also tends to reduce passive economic power. Moreover, the larger trade is in relation to GNP, the more difficult will power-induced changes in exports and imports tend to be because of domestic economic disturbances experienced at home. From this point of view then, the United States is superior to the United Kingdom not only because American trade is larger, but also because American trade is much smaller than Britain's in relation to GNP.

Size of foreign trade varies mainly with size of population, degree of economic development, and the degree of international economic specialization. The implications of population size and stage of development are obvious. Even though India is a poor country, it has a larger foreign trade than Switzerland, which is rich; but Switzerland's foreign trade per capita is a multiple of India's. Clearly also, a country's foreign trade will tend to vary with the extent to which it is engaged in the international division of labor. This variable, in turn, is principally the consequence of trade policy (e.g. free trade versus protectionism), of breadth of endowment with natural and other resources, and of size of territory (i.e. internal transportation costs, like international transport costs, act like an equivalent import duty). A country's ability to acquire leverage from capital export is also in part a consequence of size (i.e. GNP, which reflects size of population and degree of economic development). If we assume funds for export to come from savings and taxes, or more generally speaking from economic surplus above private and public consumption and capital maintenance, the size of these funds, given the rate of savings and taxation, depends on the size of GNP.

Economic power, however, is a matter of structure as well as magnitude. Economic strength as a basis of national economic power is not the same as economic wealth, although wealth is an ingredient of it. Similarly, economic strength is not simply measured by the volume of a country's trade, even though such trade is another variable condition from which strength is derived. In order to serve the purposes of economic power, a country's economic capabilities and economy must have certain structural characteristics just as such a special (but different) economic structure is needed for the production of military strength. If we concentrate on the ability to alter international merchandise, service, and capital flows, a state would be equipped *structurally* with an ideal base for exercising economic power, if (1) it exported things in urgent demand abroad while importing things regarding which its own demand was highly elastic, and if (2) it held monopoly control over the supply of things demanded by foreign importing countries and monopsony control over the goods foreign countries have to export. Structural conditions also impinge on the ability of states to export capital. Whatever the size of GNP, the propensity to restrain consumption, public or private, is an important factor. In other words, national economic strength will tend to be the greater, the less the outside world can do without its exports and without its domestic market.

There are, of course, no states in the real world fully ideally meeting these structural descriptions. For a few years following World War II, the United States came closer to the ideal base than any other country has ever achieved. But this resulted from evidently exceptional circumstances. The bulk of the world was then impoverished and economically disorganized. To generalize with reference to the real world, the more a state's international economic position approximates the ideal construct, the stronger it will tend to be in terms of economic power. Conversely, the less it approximates the specified characteristics, the weaker a state will tend to be in these terms.

Since presumably no state is interested in exercising economic power *vis-à-vis* the entire outside world all at once, but rather *vis-à-vis* a particular state or group of states, the structural desiderata are not as exacting as the ideal type suggests. Even potential economic power depends then on particular actor relationships of conceivable interest. This is so also in the case of potential military power. There is, however, an important difference between the exercise of economic and military power. In the event of a military conflict between *A* and *B*, the number of other states supporting *A* or *B* is not usually large. Participation tends to be costly. In the event of a purely economic conflict, however, it is usually in the interest of most other states to provide the opponents with alternative markets and sources of supply. For instance, if *A* places an embargo on *B*'s exports, *B* will attempt to shift its exports to other markets. This would impose some difficulties of adjustment but no further ill effects if *A*, needing the type of goods it had imported from *B*, switches its purchases to other sources of supply. On the other hand, *B*'s position would be weaker, and *A*'s stronger, if *B* had an important high-cost export industry for which *A* had been the sole or principal outlet. In that case, *A*'s embargo would compel *B* either to export subsidized goods, or to suffer unemployment in its export industry, likewise with an income-depressing effect and with the consequent burden of shifting resources to other fields of production. This example, which can be paralleled by one involving *A*'s resort to an embargo of its own exports to *B*, points up the importance of structural factors and size of market. *A* holds a degree of economic power over *B* only if *A*'s trade is worth something to *B*, in that it is important in scale and irreplaceable, or hard to replace, and if *B* is more dependent economically on *A* than the other way round.

International currency reserves and gold are of some significance to national economic power. Governments require international monies in order to settle any net imbalance in their aggregate payments account with other countries. A country issuing an international key currency has an appreciable advantage from this point of view, as had the United States in the 1960s. Other governments normally maintain official reserves of foreign money to cover regularly or irregularly recurring deficits. Irregular imbalances can occur as a result of shifts in the demand for a state's exports or of sudden changes in capital movements, crop failures, war, or similar exogenous disturbances. (The other way round, similar factors can produce an accumulation of reserves.) Since the International Monetary Fund may help in the event of serious pressure, many governments tend to maintain smaller reserves of their own than caution requires.

In principle, copious foreign-exchange reserves (or gold) clearly can play a part in exerting or resisting economic pressure. *A*'s foreign-exchange hoard is important if it wants to sell *B*'s currency in order to put that currency under speculative pressure, or if it wants to shift imports from *B* to a higher-cost exporting country, or if it wants to cut exports to *B* while unable immediately to find substitute markets. Similarly, *B*'s international currency reserves are an important asset when *A* cuts off its imports from *B*, and *B* does not find satisfactory alternative markets, or if it must pay higher prices in order to replace imports embargoed by *A*. If *B* owns insufficient reserves under such circumstances, its industries depending on exports and imports will suffer with possibly multiplying consequences to employment and income; or *B* may have to borrow foreign currency from third countries on possibly unfavorable terms. Not rarely, a weak reserve position will curtail a government's capacity to engage in warfare at home or abroad. In 1956, when Great Britain and France, in collaboration with Israel, attempted to reoccupy the Suez Canal, a precipitate flight from sterling was important among the pressures that brought this military intervention to a quick end, especially since the United States government pointedly refused monetary assistance. In 1971, accumulating balance-of-payments deficits in the United States brought about a negotiated realignment of major currency values, depreciating that of the dollar *vis-à-vis* the surplus countries. This experience signaled a diminished international ability of the United States to finance the exercise of military power abroad, even though the currency negotiations also reflected the great economic power of the United States in that the results brought great short-term relief and advantage to it. On the other hand, accumulating large international reserves for various emergency purposes, or for strengthening a state's ability to wage economic warfare – contingent purposes that may not arise – is definitely expensive. Hoarding means foregoing the use of the sequestered funds for purchasing imports, and decreased imports mean either less consumption or less investment.

The foregoing analysis indicates how a state can increase its putative economic power generally and *vis-à-vis* particular countries. It can boost its general economic power by promoting its economic development relative to other states. Japan, which achieved exceptional growth rates throughout the 1960s, clearly had more such power at the end than at the beginning of the decade. However, the degree to which relative economic development enlarges economic power depends crucially on how it affects the structural conditions. Within limits (including costs) imposed by endowment with natural and other productive resources, a state can shift resources so as to lessen its economic dependence on other countries and to increase their economic dependence on itself. Within such limits, it can also cultivate monopolist and monopsonist market power. It can, for instance, develop superior technologies, giving it, at least temporarily, a degree of monopoly over the international supply of certain goods and services.

A state can also attempt to extend its control over resources and markets by forming monopolist or monopsonist arrangements with other states or by becoming the member of a regional bloc or customs union. Thus, states have in the past attempted joint regulation of the international supply of raw materials (e.g. rubber and tin) and are doing so now (e.g. the association of petroleum-exporting countries, sugar, and coffee). Alternatively, groups of private enterprises have set up private international cartels in order to control markets of manufactured products at home and abroad. A currently interesting development of market power is the European Economic Community (EEC) formed by France, Italy, West Germany, and the Benelux countries, which even prior to the entry of Great Britain constituted the world's largest territorial unit in international commerce. Such economic integration between states enlarges the size of international economic transactions, which is one determinant of economic power; and it also tends to extend the limits within which the structural requirements of such power can be promoted.

To the extent that schemes for concerting the economic policies of independent states provide a basis for enhanced economic power, this power is, of course, shared and has, as experience shows, a brittle foundation because the diverging interests of members impede cohesion. Member states frequently differ on the merits of particular policies. Cohesion tends to be especially weak when no one member has superior economic size and decisions are made, formally or informally, on the basis of unanimity, for such a configuration maximizes the veto power of each member. Cohesion will tend to be stronger if one member predominates in economic size *and* enjoys a position of leadership or domination based on political, military, or economic power over the other members. The predominant state may then be able to wield the bloc's economic power for its own or for more or less shared purposes. The leading state's ability to decide on this matter is the greater, the less it needs to bargain with (i.e. make concessions to) member states.

In addition to these measures apt to enhance a state's general economic power, it can do things designed to bolster its putative economic power *vis-à-vis* particular countries. Thus, *A* can concentrate more of its trade on *B*, making itself more important to *B* as an importer and exporter, by giving *B* preferential access to its market, by offering exports at preferential prices, or on attractive credit conditions, and by offering long-term trade contracts on favorable terms. In doing so, *A* may pay attention to qualitative factors, as by concentrating on exports for which it has a degree of monopoly power and *B*'s demand is very inelastic, and by concentrating on imports regarding which *A* enjoys or can build up a degree of monopsony power and for which its demand is elastic. Or *A* may be able to increase *B*'s dependence by bringing about and exploiting penetration of *B*'s economy by means of fostering direct investment, bribing officials and businessmen in *B*. Or *A* may export capital to *B* on favorable terms and induce a degree of international indebtedness in *B* that makes it unattractive to other exporters of capital. [...] Putative economic power, like putative military power, can become actualized in particular relationships through three mechanisms: (1) *A* applies economic power purposely for weakening *B* economically; (2) *A* applies economic power by threatening *B* with economic reprisals or by offering economic rewards for compliance with a request by *A*; (3) *B*'s behavior is influenced by the mere anticipation that, if he pursues actions detrimental to *A*'s interests, *A* might resort to the exercise of economic power. Clearly, economic domination occurs if *A* deliberately and regularly resorts to actions identified under (1) and (2). But *A*'s mere ability to take such measures does not involve *B*'s economic domination. The problem is trickier when it comes to the mechanism (3). Clearly, again, once *A* has had frequent recourse to mechanisms (1) and (2) *vis-à-vis B*, *B* may henceforth be dominated by the sheer anticipation of such further acts if he should cross *A*'s interests. This is how continued domination will normally operate. But if *B* has not been subjected to *A*'s economic power via mechanisms (1) and (2), it will be affected through mechanism (3) only if *A*, by repeated and recent power plays against other states, has displayed a strong predisposition to resort to its economic power. The less *A* has displayed such a propensity, the less *B* will be influenced and dominated by *A*'s economic power. Should *A* have no such propensity, no influence will occur. In any case, economic domination is strong if *A* deliberately cultivates the actualization of its economic power *vis-à-vis B*. Economic domination will be weaker if *A* has succeeded frequently in actualizing its economic power against *C* and *D*, but not against *B*. Economic domination does not arise at all if *A*, despite vastly superior 'economic strength' suitable as a basis of economic power, lacks any reputation for seeking to exploit this capacity, that is to say, for transforming it into economic power.

1.7 The spiral of international insecurity

Robert Jervis

Source: *Perception and Misperception in International Politics* (Princeton University Press, Princeton, 1976), pp. 63–76.

Jervis argues that the attempts of one state to achieve security precipitate a feeling of insecurity in other states. All states tend to assume the worst of others and respond accordingly. Their collective actions unintentionally generate a spiral of insecurity and, in a situation of anarchy, there can be no solution to this security dilemma. The dilemma is further exacerbated, according to Jervis, by the inflexible images that it generates in the minds of decision makers both of their own intentions and of those of their opposite numbers.

The lack of a sovereign in international politics permits wars to occur and makes security expensive. More far-reaching complications are created by the fact that most means of self-protection simultaneously menace others. Rousseau made the basic point well:

> It is quite true that it would be much better for all men to remain always at peace. But so long as there is no security for this, everyone, having no guarantee that he can avoid war, is anxious to begin it at the moment which suits his own interest and so forestall a neighbour, who would not fail to forestall the attack in his turn at any moment favourable to himself, so that many wars, even offensive wars, are rather in the nature of unjust precautions for the protection of the assailant's own possessions than a device for seizing those of others. However salutary it may be in theory to obey the dictates of public spirit, it is certain that, politically and even morally, those dictates are liable to prove fatal to the man who persists in observing them with all the world when no one thinks of observing them towards him.[1]

In extreme cases, states that seek security may believe that the best, if not the only, route to that goal is to attack and expand. Thus the tsars believed that 'that which stops growing begins to rot', the

Japanese decision-makers before World War II concluded that the alternative to increasing their dominance in Asia was to sacrifice their 'very existence', and some scholars have argued that German expansionism before World War I was rooted in a desire to cope with the insecurity produced by being surrounded by powerful neighbors.[2] After World War I France held a somewhat milder version of this belief. Although she knew that the war had left her the strongest state on the Continent, she felt that she had to increase her power still further to provide protection against Germany, whose recovery from wartime destruction might some day lead her to try to reverse the verdict of 1918. This view is especially likely to develop if the state believes that others have also concluded that both the desire for protection and the desire for increased values point to the same policy of expansionism.

The drive for security will also produce aggressive actions if the state either requires a very high sense of security or feels menaced by the very presence of other strong states. Thus Leites argues that 'the Politburo ... believes that its very life ... remains acutely threatened as long as major enemies exist. Their utter defeat is a sheer necessity of survival.' This view can be rooted in experience as well as ideology. In May 1944 Kennan wrote: 'Behind Russia's stubborn expansion lies only the age-old sense of insecurity of a sedentary people reared on an exposed plain in the neighborhood of fierce nomadic peoples.'[3]

Even in less extreme situations, arms procured to defend can usually be used to attack. Economic and political preparedness designed to hold what one has is apt to create the potential for taking territory from others. What one state regards as insurance, the adversary will see as encirclement. This is especially true of the great powers. Any state that has interests throughout the world cannot avoid possessing the power to menace others. For example, as Admiral Mahan noted before World War I, if Britain was to have a navy sufficient to safeguard her trading routes, she inevitably would also have the ability to cut Germany off from the sea. Thus even in the absence of any specific conflicts of interest between Britain and Germany, the former's security required that the latter be denied a significant aspect of great power status.

When states seek the ability to defend themselves, they get too much and too little – too much because they gain the ability to carry out aggression; too little because others, being menaced, will increase their own arms and so reduce the first state's security. Unless the requirements for offense and defense differ in kind or amount, a status quo power will desire a military posture that resembles that of an aggressor. For this reason others cannot infer from its military forces and preparations whether the state is aggressive. States therefore tend to assume the worst. The other's intentions must be considered to be co-extensive with his capabilities. What he can do to harm the state, he will do (or will do if he gets the chance). So to be safe, the state should buy as many weapons as it can afford.

But since both sides obey the same imperatives, attempts to increase one's security by standing firm and accumulating more arms will be self-defeating. [...]

These unintended and undesired consequences of actions meant to be defensive constitute the 'security dilemma' that Herbert Butterfield sees as that 'absolute predicament' that 'lies in the very geometry of human conflict.... [H]ere is the basic pattern for all narratives of human conflict, whatever other patterns may be superimposed upon it later.' From this perspective, the central theme of international relations is not evil but tragedy. States often share a common interest, but the structure of the situation prevents them from bringing about the mutually desired situation. This view contrasts with the school of realism represented by Hans Morgenthau and Reinhold Niebuhr, which sees the drive for power as a product of man's instinctive will to dominate others. As John Herz puts it, 'It is a mistake to draw from the universal phenomenon of competition for power the conclusion that there is actually such a thing as an innate "power instinct". Basically it is the mere instinct of self-preservation which, in the vicious circle [of the security dilemma], leads to competition for ever more power.'[4]

Arms races are only the most obvious manifestation of this spiral. The competition for colonies at the end of the nineteenth century was fueled by the security dilemma. Even if all states preferred the status quo to a division of the unclaimed areas, each also preferred expansion to running the risk of being excluded. The desire for security may also lead states to weaken potential rivals, a move that can create the menace it was designed to ward off. For example, because French statesmen feared what they thought to be the inevitable German attempt to regain the position she lost in World War I, they concluded that Germany had to be kept weak. The effect of such an unyielding policy, however, was to make the Germans less willing to accept their new position and therefore to decrease France's long-run security. Finally, the security dilemma can not only create conflicts and tensions but also provide the dynamics triggering war. If technology and strategy are such that each side believes that the state that strikes first will have a decisive advantage, even a state that is fully satisfied with the status quo may start a war out of fear that the alternative to doing so is not peace, but an attack by its adversary. And, of course, if each side knows that the other side is aware of the advantages of striking first, even mild crises are likely to end in war. This was one of the immediate causes of World War I, and contemporary military experts have devoted much thought and money to avoiding the recurrence of such destabilizing incentives. [...]

PSYCHOLOGICAL DYNAMICS

The argument sketched so far rests on the implications of anarchy, not on the limitations of rationality imposed by the way people reach decisions in a complex world. Lewis Richardson's path-breaking treatment of arms races describes 'what people would do if they did not stop to think'. Richardson argues that this is not an unrealistic perspective. The common analogy between international politics and chess is misleading because 'the acts of a leader are in part controlled by the great instinctive and traditional tendencies which are formulated in my description. It is somewhat as if the chessmen were connected by horizontal springs to heavy weights beyond the chessboard.'[5]

Contemporary spiral theorists argue that psychological pressures explain why arms and tensions cycles proceed as if people were not thinking. Once a person develops an image of the other – especially a hostile image of the other – ambiguous and even discrepant information will be assimilated to that image. [...] If they think that a state is hostile, behavior that others might see as neutral or friendly will be ignored, distorted, or seen as attempted duplicity. This cognitive rigidity reinforces the consequences of international anarchy.

Although we noted earlier that it is usually hard to draw inferences about a state's intentions from its military posture, decision-makers in fact often draw such inferences when they are unwarranted. They frequently assume, partly for reasons to be discussed shortly, that the arms of others indicate aggressive intentions. So an increase in the other's military forces makes the state doubly insecure – first, because the other has an increased capability to do harm, and, second, because this behavior is taken to show that the other is not only a potential threat but is actively contemplating hostile actions.

But the state does not apply this reasoning to its own behavior. A peaceful state knows that it will use its arms only to protect itself, not to harm others. It further assumes that others are not fully aware of this. As John Foster Dulles put it: 'Khrushchev does not need to be convinced of our good intentions. He knows we are not aggressors and do not threaten the security of the Soviet Union.' Similarly, in arguing that 'England seeks no quarrels, and will never give Germany cause for legitimate offence', Crowe assumed not only that Britain was benevolent but that this was readily apparent to others.[6] To take an earlier case, skirmishing between France and England in North America developed into the Seven Years' War partly because each side incorrectly thought the other knew that its aims were sharply limited. Because the state believes that its adversary understands that the state is arming because it sees the adversary as aggressive, the state does not think that strengthening its arms can be harmful. If the other is aggressive, it will be disappointed because the state's strengthened position means that it is less vulnerable. Provided that the state is already fairly strong, however, there is no danger that the other will be provoked into attacking. If the other is not aggressive, it will not react to the state's effort to protect itself. This means that the state need not exercise restraint in policies designed to increase its security. To procure weapons in excess of the minimum required for defense may be wasteful, but will not cause unwarranted alarm by convincing the other that the state is planning aggression.

In fact, others are not so easily reassured. As Lord Grey realized – after he was out of power:

> The distinction between preparations made with the intention of going to war and precautions against attack is a true distinction, clear and definite in the minds of those who build up armaments. But it is a distinction that is not obvious or certain to others ... Each Government, therefore, while resenting any suggestion that its own measures are anything more than for defense, regards similar measures of another Government as preparation to attack.

Herbert Butterfield catches the way these beliefs drive the spiral of arms and hostility:

> It is the peculiar characteristic of the ... Hobbesian fear ... that you yourself may vividly feel the terrible fear that you have of the other party, but you cannot enter into the other man's counter-fear, or even understand why he should be particularly nervous. For you know that you yourself mean him no harm, and that you want nothing from him save guarantees for your own safety; and it is never possible for you to realize or remember properly that since

he cannot see the inside of your mind, he can never have the same assurance of your intentions that you have. As this operates on both sides the Chinese puzzle is complete in all its interlockings and neither party can see the nature of the predicament he is in, for each only imagines that the other party is being hostile and unreasonable.[7]

Because statesmen believe that others will interpret their behavior as they intend it and will share their view of their own state's policy, they are led astray in two reinforcing ways. First, their understanding of the impact of their own state's policy is often inadequate – i.e. differs from the views of disinterested observers – and, second, they fail to realize that other states' perceptions are also skewed. Although actors are aware of the difficulty of making their threats and warnings credible, they rarely believe that others will misinterpret behavior that is meant to be more compatible with the other's interests. Because we cannot easily establish an objective analysis of the state's policy, these two effects are difficult to disentangle. But for many purposes this does not matter because both pressures push in the same direction and increase the differences between the way the state views its behavior and the perceptions of others.

The degree to which a state can fail to see that its own policy is harming others is illustrated by the note that the British foreign secretary sent to the Soviet government in March 1918 trying to persuade it to welcome a Japanese army that would fight the Germans: 'The British Government have clearly and constantly repeated that they have no wish to take any part in Russia's domestic affairs, but that the prosecution of the war is the only point with which they are concerned.' When reading Bruce Lockhart's reply that the Bolsheviks did not accept this view, Balfour noted in the margin of the dispatch: 'I have constantly impressed on Mr. Lockhart that it is *not* our desire to interfere in Russian affairs. He appears to be very unsuccessful in conveying this view to the Bolshevik Government.'[8] The start of World War I witnessed a manifestation of the same phenomenon when the tsar ordered mobilization of the Baltic fleet without any consideration of the threat this would pose even to a Germany that wanted to remain at peace. [...]

The same inability to see the implications of its specific actions limits the state's appreciation of the degree to which its position and general power make it a potential menace. As Klaus Epstein points out in describing the background to World War I, 'Wilhelmine Germany – because of its size, population, geographical location, economic dynamism, cocky militarism, and autocracy under a neurotic Kaiser – was feared by all other Powers as a threat to the European equilibrium; this was an objective fact which Germans should have recognized.'[9] Indeed even had Germany changed her behavior, she still would have been the object of constant suspicion and apprehension by virtue of being the strongest power in Europe. And before we attribute this insensitivity to the German national character, we should note that United States statesmen in the postwar era have displayed a similar inability to see that their country's huge power, even if used for others' good, represents a standing threat to much of the rest of the world. Instead the United States, like most other nations, has believed that others will see that the desire for security underlies its actions.

The psychological dynamics do not, however, stop here. If the state believes that others know that it is not a threat, it will conclude that they will arm or pursue hostile policies only if they are aggressive. For if they sought only security they would welcome, or at least not object to, the state's policy. Thus an American senator who advocated intervening in Russia in the summer of 1918 declared that if the Russians resisted this move it would prove that 'Russia is already Germanized'. This inference structure is revealed in an exchange about NATO between Tom Connally, the chairman of the Senate Foreign Relations Committee, and Secretary of State Acheson:

> Now, Mr. Secretary, you brought out rather clearly ... that this treaty is not aimed at any nation particularly. It is aimed only at any nation or any country that contemplates or undertakes armed aggression against the members of the signatory powers. Is that true?
>
> Secretary Acheson. That is correct, Senator Connally. It is not aimed at any country; it is aimed solely at armed aggression.
>
> The Chairman. In other words, unless a nation other than the signatories contemplates, meditates or makes plans looking toward, aggression or armed attack on another nation, it has no cause to fear this treaty.
>
> Secretary Acheson. That is correct, Senator Connally, and it seems to me that any nation which claims that this treaty is directed against it should be reminded of the Biblical admonition that 'The guilty flee when no man pursueth.'
>
> The Chairman. That is a very apt illustration.
>
> What I had in mind was, when a State or Nation passes a

criminal act, for instance, against burglary, nobody but those who are burglars or getting ready to be burglars need have any fear of the Burglary Act. Is that not true?

Secretary Acheson. Very true.

The Chairman. And so it is with one who might meditate and get ready and arm himself to commit a murder. If he is not going to indulge in that kind of enterprise, the law on murder would not have any effect on him, would it?

Secretary Acheson. The only effect it would have would be for his protection, perhaps, by deterring someone else. He wouldn't worry about the imposition of the penalties on himself, but he might feel that the statute added to his protection.[10]

[...] When the state believes that the other knows that is it not threatening the other's legitimate interests, disputes are likely to produce antagonism out of all proportion to the intrinsic importance of the issue at stake. Because the state does not think that there is any obvious reason why the other should oppose it, it will draw inferences of unprovoked hostility from even minor conflicts. [...] If, on the other hand, each side recognizes that its policies threaten some of the other's values, it will not interpret the other's reaction as indicating aggressive intent or total hostility and so will be better able to keep their conflict limited.

The perceptions and reactions of the other side are apt to deepen the misunderstanding and the conflict. For the other, like the state, will assume that its adversary knows that it is not a threat. So, like the state, it will do more than increase its arms – it will regard the state's explanation of its behavior as making no sense and will see the state as dangerous and hostile. When the Soviets consolidated their hold over Czechoslovakia in 1948, they knew this harmed Western values and expected some reaction. But the formation of NATO and the explanation given for this move were very alarming. Since the Russians assumed that the United States saw the situation the same way they did, the only conclusion they could draw was that the United States was even more dangerous than they had thought. As George Kennan put the Soviet analysis in a cable to Washington:

> It seemed implausible to the Soviet leaders, knowing as they did the nature of their own approach to the military problem, and assuming that the Western powers must have known it too, that defensive considerations alone could have impelled the Western governments to give the relative emphasis they actually gave to a program irrelevant in many respects to the outcome of the political

struggle in Western Europe (on which Moscow was staking everything) and only partially justified, as Moscow saw it, as a response to actual Soviet intentions.... The Kremlin leaders were attempting in every possible way to weaken and destroy the structure of the non-Communist world. In the course of this endeavor they were up to many things which gave plenty of cause for complaint on the part of Western statesmen. They would not have been surprised if these things had been made the touchstone of Western reaction. But why, they might ask, were they being accused precisely of the one thing they had *not* done, which was to plan, as yet, to conduct an overt and unprovoked invasion of Western Europe? Why was the imputation to them of this intention being put forward as the rationale for Western rearmament? Did this not imply some ulterior purpose ...?[11]

The Russians may have been even more alarmed if, as Nathan Leites has argued, they thought that we behaved according to the sensible proverb of 'whoever says A, says Z' and had knowingly assigned Czechoslovakia to the Russian sphere of influence during the wartime negotiations. 'How could, they must ask themselves, the elevation of an already dominant Czechoslovak Communist Party to full power in 1948 change the policies of Washington which had agreed to the presence of the Soviet Army in Czechoslovakia in 1945? Washington, after all, could hardly imagine that Moscow would indefinitely tolerate the presence of enemies ... within its domain!' The American protests over the takeover must then be hypocrisy, and the claim that this event was alarming and called for Western rearmament could only be a cover for plans of aggression.[12]
[...]
The explication of these psychological dynamics adds to our understanding of international conflict, but incurs a cost. The benefit is in seeing how the basic security dilemma becomes overlaid by reinforcing misunderstandings as each side comes to believe that not only is the other a potential menace, as it must be in a setting of anarchy, but that the other's behavior has shown that it is an active enemy. The inability to recognize that one's own actions could be seen as menacing and the concomitant belief that the other's hostility can only be explained by its aggressiveness help explain how conflicts can easily expand beyond that which an analysis of the objective situation would indicate is necessary. But the cost of these insights is the slighting of the role of the system in inducing conflict and a tendency to assume that the desire for security, rather than expan-

sion, is the prime goal of most states. [...]

Both the advantages and pitfalls of this elaboration of the security dilemma are revealed in Kenneth Boulding's distinction between

> two very different kinds of incompatibility.... The first might be called 'real' incompatibility, where we have two images of the future in which realization of one would prevent the realization of the other.... The other form of incompatibility might be called 'illusory' incompatibility, in which there exists a condition of compatibility which would satisfy the 'real' interests of the two parties but in which the dynamics of the situation or illusions of the parties create a situation of perverse dynamics and misunderstandings, with increasing hostility simply as a result of the reactions of the parties to each other, not as a result of any basic differences of interest.[13]

This distinction can be very useful but it takes attention away from the vital kind of system-induced incompatibility that cannot be easily classified as either real or illusory. If both sides primarily desire security, then the two images of the future do not clash, and any incompatibility must, according to one reading of the definition, be illusory. But the heart of the security dilemma argument is that an increase in one state's security can make others less secure not because of misperception or imagined hostility, but because of the anarchic context of international relations.

Under some circumstances, several states can simultaneously increase their security. But often this is not the case. For a variety of reasons, many of which have been discussed earlier, nations' security requirements can clash. While an understanding of the security dilemma and psychological dynamics will dampen some arms-hostility spirals, it will not change the fact that some policies aimed at security will threaten others. To call the incompatibility that results from such policies 'illusory' is to misunderstand the nature of the problem and to encourage the illusion that if the states only saw themselves and others more objectively they could attain their common interest.

NOTES

1 Rousseau, *A Lasting Peace through the Federation of Europe*, translated by C.E. Vaughan (Constable, London, 1917), pp. 78–9.
2 Quoted in Adam Ulam, *Expansion and Coexistence* (Praeger, New York, 1968), p. 5; quoted in Butow, *Tojo and the Coming of the War* (Princeton University Press, NJ, 1961), p. 203; Klaus Epstein, 'Gerhard

Ritter and the First World War', in H.W. Koch (ed.), *The Origins of the First World War* (Macmillan, London, 1972), p. 290.

3 Nathan Leites, *A Study of Bolshevism* (Free Press, Glencoe, Illinois, 1953), p. 31; quoted in Arthur Schlesinger Jr, 'The Origins of the Cold War', *Foreign Affairs*, 46 (October 1967), p. 30.

4 Herbert Butterfield, *History and Human Relations* (Collins, London, 1951), pp. 19–20; John Herz, *Political Realism and Political Idealism* (University of Chicago Press, Chicago, 1959), p. 4.

5 Lewis Richardson, *Statistics of Deadly Quarrels* (Boxwood Press, Pittsburgh; Quadrangle, Chicago, 1960), p. xxiv; Lewis Richardson, *Arms and Insecurity* (Boxwood Press, Pittsburgh; Quadrangle, Chicago, 1960), p. 227.

6 Quoted in Richard Nixon, *Six Crises* (Doubleday, Garden City, NY, 1962), p. 62; Eyre Crowe, 'Memorandum on the Present State of Relations with France and Germany, January 1907' in G.P. Gooch and H. Temperley (eds), *British Documents on the Origins of the War, 1898–1914*, vol. 3 (HMSO, London, 1928).

7 Edward Grey, *Twenty-five Years*, vol. 1 (Hodder and Stoughton, London, 1925), p. 91; Butterfield, *History and Human Relations*, pp. 19–20.

8 Quoted in John Wheeler-Bennett, *Brest-Litovsk* (Norton, New York, 1971), pp. 295–6.

9 Epstein, 'Gerhard Ritter and the First World War', p. 293.

10 Quoted in Peter Filene, *Americans and the Soviet Experiment 1917–1933* (Harvard University Press, Cambridge, Mass., 1967), p. 43; Senate Committee on Foreign Relations, *Hearings, North Atlantic Treaty*, 81st Congress, 1st Session, p. 17.

11 George Kennan, *Memoirs*, vol. 2, *1950–1963* (Little, Brown, Boston, 1972), pp. 335–6.

12 Leites, *A Study of Bolshevism*, pp. 42, 34.

13 Kenneth Boulding, 'National Images and International Systems', *Journal of Conflict Resolution*, 3 (June 1959), p. 130.

1.8 Cooperation and international regimes

Robert O. Keohane

Source: *After Hegemony: Cooperation and Discord in the World Political Economy* (Princeton University Press, Princeton, 1984), pp. 51–63.

Keohane's aim is to identify ways in which states will cooperate in the absence of a hegemonial power able to impose its will on others. In this extract, he focuses on two central aspects of the problem: first, the nature of cooperation, which arises out of the need to manage conflicting or discordant interests, and second, the role played by international regimes in conditioning cooperation. In all of this, Keohane argues, 'sovereignty remains a constitutive principle' and state authorities play a crucial role.

Cooperation must be distinguished from harmony. Harmony refers to a situation in which actors' policies (pursued in their own self-interest without regard for others) *automatically* facilitate the attainment of others' goals. The classic example of harmony is the hypothetical competitive-market world of the classical economists, in which the Invisible Hand ensures that the pursuit of self-interest by each contributes to the interest of all. In this idealized, unreal world, no one's actions damage anyone else; there are no 'negative externalities', in the economists' jargon. Where harmony reigns, cooperation is unnecessary. It may even be injurious, if it means that certain individuals conspire to exploit others. Adam Smith, for one, was very critical of guilds and other conspiracies against freedom of trade. Cooperation and harmony are by no means identical and ought not to be confused with one another.

Cooperation requires that the actions of separate individuals or organizations – which are not in pre-existent harmony – be brought into conformity with one another through a process of negotiation, which is often referred to as 'policy coordination'. Charles E. Lindblom has defined policy coordination as follows:[1]

A set of decisions is coordinated if adjustments have been made in them, such that the adverse consequences of any one decision for other decisions are to a degree and in some frequency avoided, reduced, or counterbalanced or overweighed.

Cooperation occurs when actors adjust their behavior to the actual or anticipated preferences of others, through a process of policy coordination. To summarize more formally, *intergovernmental cooperation takes place when the policies actually followed by one government are regarded by its partners as facilitating realization of their own objectives, as the result of a process of policy coordination.*

With this definition in mind, we can differentiate among cooperation, harmony, and discord, as illustrated by Figure 1. First, we ask whether actors' policies automatically facilitate the attainment of others' goals. If so, there is harmony: no adjustments need to take place. Yet harmony is rare in world politics. Rousseau sought to account for this rarity when he declared that even two countries guided by the General Will in their internal affairs would come into conflict if they had extensive contact with one another, since the General Will of each would not be general for both. Each would have a partial, self-interested perspective on their mutual interactions. Even for Adam Smith, efforts to ensure state security took precedence over measures to increase national prosperity. In defending the Navigation Acts, Smith declared: 'As defence is of much more importance than opulence, the act of navigation is, perhaps, the wisest of all the commercial regulations of England.'[2] Waltz summarizes the point by saying that 'in anarchy there is no automatic harmony'.[3]

Yet this insight tells us nothing definitive about the prospects for cooperation. For this we need to ask a further question about situations in which harmony does not exist. Are attempts made by actors (governmental or nongovernmental) to adjust their policies to each others' objectives? If no such attempts are made, the result is discord: a situation in which governments regard each others' policies as hindering the attainment of their goals, and hold each other responsible for these constraints.

Discord often leads to efforts to induce others to change their policies; when these attempts meet resistance, policy conflict results. Insofar as these attempts at policy adjustment succeed in making policies more compatible, however, cooperation ensues. The policy coordination that leads to cooperation need not involve bargaining or negotiation at all. What Lindblom calls 'adaptive' as opposed to 'manipulative' adjustment can take place: one country may shift its

Figure 1 Harmony, cooperation, and discord

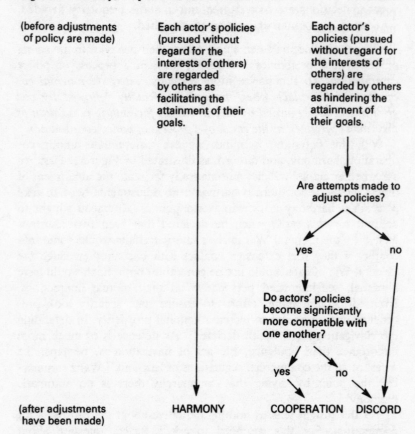

(before adjustments of policy are made)

Each actor's policies (pursued without regard for the interests of others) are regarded by others as facilitating the attainment of their goals.

Each actor's policies (pursued without regard for the interests of others) are regarded by others as hindering the attainment of their goals.

Are attempts made to adjust policies?

yes   no

Do actors' policies become significantly more compatible with one another?

yes   no

(after adjustments have been made)   HARMONY   COOPERATION   DISCORD

policy in the direction of another's preferences without regard for the effect of its action on the other state, defer to the other country, or partially shift its policy in order to avoid adverse consequences for its partner. Or nonbargained manipulation – such as one actor confronting another with a *fait accompli* – may occur.[4] Frequently, of course, negotiation and bargaining indeed take place, often accompanied by other actions that are designed to induce others to adjust their policies to one's own. Each government pursues what it perceives as its self-interest, but looks for bargains that can benefit all parties to the deal, though not necessarily equally.

Harmony and cooperation are not usually distinguished from one another so clearly. Yet, in the study of world politics, they should be. Harmony is apolitical. No communication is necessary, and no influence need be exercised. Cooperation, by contrast, is highly political: somehow, patterns of behavior must be altered. This change may be accomplished through negative as well as positive inducements. Indeed, studies of international crises, as well as game-theoretic experiments and simulations, have shown that under a variety of conditions strategies that involve threats and punishments as well as promises and rewards are more effective in attaining cooperative outcomes than those that rely entirely on persuasion and the force of good example.

Cooperation therefore does not imply an absence of conflict. On the contrary, it is typically mixed with conflict and reflects partially successful efforts to overcome conflict, real or potential. Cooperation takes place only in situations in which actors perceive that their policies are actually or potentially in conflict, not where there is harmony. Cooperation should not be viewed as the absence of conflict, but rather as a reaction to conflict or potential conflict. Without the specter of conflict, there is no need to cooperate.

The example of trade relations among friendly countries in a liberal international political economy may help to illustrate this crucial point. A naive observer, trained only to appreciate the overall welfare benefits of trade, might assume that trade relations would be harmonious: consumers in importing countries benefit from cheap foreign goods and increased competition, and producers can increasingly take advantage of the division of labor as their export markets expand. But harmony does not normally ensue. Discord on trade issues may prevail because governments do not even seek to reduce the adverse consequences of their own policies for others, but rather strive in certain respects to increase the severity of those effects. Mercantilist governments have sought in the twentieth century as well as the seventeenth to manipulate foreign trade, in conjunction with warfare, to damage each other economically and to gain productive resources themselves. Governments may desire 'positional goods', such as high status, and may therefore resist even mutually beneficial cooperation if it helps others more than themselves. Yet even when neither power nor positional motivations are present, and when all participants would benefit in the aggregate from liberal trade, discord tends to predominate over harmony as the initial result of independent governmental action.

This occurs even under otherwise benign conditions because some groups or industries are forced to incur adjustment costs as changes in comparative advantage take place. Governments often respond to the ensuing demands for protection by attempting, more or less effectively, to cushion the burdens of adjustment for groups and industries that are politically influential at home. Yet unilateral measures to this effect almost always impose adjustment costs abroad, and discord continually threatens. Governments enter into international negotiations in order to reduce the conflict that would otherwise result. Even substantial potential common benefits do not create harmony when state power can be exercised on behalf of certain interests and against others. In world politics, harmony tends to vanish: attainment of the gains from pursuing complementary policies depends on cooperation.

Observers of world politics who take power and conflict seriously should be attracted to this way of defining cooperation, since my definition does not relegate cooperation to the mythological world of relations among equals in power. Hegemonic cooperation is not a contradiction in terms. Defining cooperation in contrast to harmony should, I hope, lead readers with a Realist orientation to take cooperation in world politics seriously rather than to dismiss it out of hand. To Marxists who also believe in hegemonic power theories, however, even this definition of cooperation may not seem to make it relevant to the contemporary world political economy. From this perspective, mutual policy adjustments cannot possibly resolve the contradictions besetting the system because they are attributable to capitalism rather than to problems of coordination among egoistic actors lacking common government. Attempts to resolve these contradictions through international cooperation will merely transfer issues to a deeper and even more intractable level. Thus it is not surprising that Marxian analyses of the international political economy have, with few exceptions, avoided sustained examinations of the conditions under which cooperation among major capitalist countries can take place. Marxists see it as more important to expose relationships of exploitation and conflict between major capitalist powers on the one hand and the masses of people in the periphery of world capitalism on the other. And, from a Leninist standpoint, to examine the conditions for international cooperation without first analyzing the contradictions of capitalism, and recognizing the irreconcilability of conflicts among capitalist countries, is a bourgeois error.

This is less an argument than a statement of faith. Since sustained international coordination of macroeconomic policies has never been tried, the statement that it would merely worsen the contradictions facing the system is speculative. In view of the lack of evidence for it, such a claim could even be considered rash. Indeed, one of the most perceptive Marxian writers of recent years, Stephen Hymer, recognized explicitly that capitalists face problems of collective action and argued that they were seeking, with at least temporary prospects of success, to overcome them. As he recognized, any success in internationalizing capital could pose grave threats to socialist aspirations and, at the very least, would shift contradictions to new points of tension.[5] Thus even were we to agree that the fundamental issue is posed by the contradictions of capitalism rather than the tensions inherent in a state system, it would be worthwhile to study the conditions under which cooperation is likely to occur.

INTERNATIONAL REGIMES AND COOPERATION

One way to study cooperation and discord would be to focus on particular actions as the units of analysis. This would require the systematic compilation of a data set composed of acts that could be regarded as comparable and coded according to the degree of cooperation that they reflect. Such a strategy has some attractive features. The problem with it, however, is that instances of cooperation and discord could all too easily be isolated from the context of beliefs and behavior within which they are embedded. This book does not view cooperation atomistically as a set of discrete, isolated acts, but rather seeks to understand patterns of cooperation in the world political economy. Accordingly, we need to examine actors' expectations about future patterns of interaction, their assumptions about the proper nature of economic arrangements, and the kinds of political activities they regard as legitimate. That is, we need to analyze cooperation within the context of international institutions, broadly defined, [. . .] in terms of practices and expectations. Each act of cooperation or discord affects the beliefs, rules, and practices that form the context for future actions. Each act must therefore be interpreted as embedded within a chain of such acts and their successive cognitive and institutional residues.

This argument parallels Clifford Geertz's discussion of how anthropologists should use the concept of culture to interpret the societies they investigate. Geertz sees culture as the 'webs of significance' that people have created for themselves. On their surface, they are enigmatical; the observer has to interpret them so that they make sense. Culture, for Geertz, 'is a context, something within which [social events] can be intelligibly described'.[6] It makes little sense to describe naturalistically what goes on at a Balinese cock-fight unless one understands the meaning of the event for Balinese culture.

There is not a world culture in the fullest sense, but even in world politics, human beings spin webs of significance. They develop implicit standards for behavior, some of which emphasize the principle of sovereignty and legitimize the pursuit of self-interest, while others rely on quite different principles. Any act of cooperation or apparent cooperation needs to be interpreted within the context of related actions, and of prevailing expectations and shared beliefs, before its meaning can be properly understood. Fragments of political behavior become comprehensible when viewed as part of a larger mosaic.

The concept of international regime not only enables us to describe patterns of cooperation; it also helps to account for both cooperation and discord. Although regimes themselves depend on conditions that are conducive to interstate agreements, they may also facilitate further efforts to coordinate policies. To understand international cooperation, it is necessary to comprehend how institutions and rules not only reflect, but also affect, the facts of world politics.

Defining and identifying regimes

When John Ruggie introduced the concept of international regimes into the international politics literature in 1975, he defined a regime as 'a set of mutual expectations, rules and regulations, plans, organizational energies and financial commitments, which have been accepted by a group of states'.[7] More recently, a collective definition, worked out at a conference on the subject, defined international regimes as 'sets of implicit or explicit principles, norms, rules and decision-making procedures around which actors' expectations converge in a given area of international relations. Principles are beliefs of fact, causation, and rectitude. Norms are standards of behavior defined in terms of rights and obligations. Rules are specific prescriptions or proscriptions for action. Decision-making procedures are prevailing practices for making and implementing collective choice.'[8]

This definition provides a useful starting-point for analysis, since it begins with the general conception of regimes as social institutions and explicates it further. The concept of norms, however, is ambiguous. It is important that we understand norms in this definition simply as standards of behavior defined in terms of rights and obligations. Another usage would distinguish norms from rules and principles by stipulating that participants in a social system regard norms, but not rules and principles, as morally binding regardless of considerations of narrowly defined self-interest. But to include norms, thus defined, in a definition of necessary regime characteristics would be to make the conception of regimes based strictly on self-interest a contradiction in terms. [...] I will maintain a definition of norms simply as standards of behavior, whether adopted on grounds of self-interest or otherwise. [...]

The principles of regimes define, in general, the purposes that their members are expected to pursue. For instance, the principles of the postwar trade and monetary regimes have emphasized the value of open, nondiscriminatory patterns of international economic transactions; the fundamental principle of the nonproliferation regime is that the spread of nuclear weapons is dangerous. Norms contain somewhat clearer injunctions to members about legitimate and illegitimate behavior, still defining responsibilities and obligations in relatively general terms. For instance, the norms of the General Agreement on Tariffs and Trade (GATT) do not require that members resort to free trade immediately, but incorporate injunctions to members to practise nondiscrimination and reciprocity and to move toward increased liberalization. Fundamental to the nonproliferation regime is the norm that members of the regime should not act in ways that facilitate nuclear proliferation.

The rules of a regime are difficult to distinguish from its norms; at the margin, they merge into one another. Rules are, however, more specific: they indicate in more detail the specific rights and obligations of members. Rules can be altered more easily than principles or norms, since there may be more than one set of rules that can attain a given set of purposes. Finally, at the same level of specificity as rules, but referring to procedures rather than substances, the decisionmaking procedures of regimes provide ways of implementing their principles and altering their rules.

An example from the field of international monetary relations may be helpful. The most important principle of the international balance-of-payments regime since the end of World War II has been that of liberalization of trade and payments. A key norm of the regime has been the injunction to states not to manipulate their exchange rates unilaterally for national advantage. Between 1958 and 1971 this norm was realized through pegged exchange rates and procedures for consultation in the event of change, supplemented with a variety of devices to help governments avoid exchange-rate changes through a combination of borrowing and internal adjustment. After 1973 governments have subscribed to the same norm, although it has been implemented more informally and probably less effectively under a system of floating exchange rates. Ruggie has argued that the abstract principle of liberalization, subject to constraints imposed by the acceptance of the welfare state, has been maintained throughout the postwar period: 'embedded liberalism' continues, reflecting a fundamental element of continuity in the international balance-of-payments regime. The norm of nonmanipulation has also been maintained, even though the specific rules of the 1958–71 system having to do with adjustment have been swept away.[9]

The concept of international regime is complex because it is defined in terms of four distinct components: principles, norms, rules, and decisionmaking procedures. It is tempting to select one of these levels of specificity – particularly, principles and norms or rules and procedures – as *the* defining characteristic of regimes. Such an approach, however, creates a false dichotomy between principles on the one hand and rules and procedures on the other. As we have noted, at the margin norms and rules cannot be sharply distinguished from each other. It is difficult if not impossible to tell the difference between an 'implicit rule' of broad significance and a well-understood, relatively specific operating principle. Both rules and principles may affect expectations and even values. In a strong international regime, the linkages between principles and rules are likely to be tight. Indeed, it is precisely the linkages among principles, norms, and rules that give regimes their legitimacy. Since rules, norms, and principles are so closely intertwined, judgements about whether changes in rules constitute changes *of* regime or merely changes *within* regimes necessarily contain arbitrary elements.

Principles, norms, rules, and procedures all contain injunctions about behavior: they prescribe certain actions and proscribe others. They imply obligations, even though these obligations are not enforceable through a hierarchical legal system. It clarifies the definition of regime, therefore, to think of it in terms of injunctions of greater or lesser specificity. Some are far-reaching and extremely important. They may change only rarely. At the other extreme, injunctions may be merely technical, matters of convenience that can be altered without great political or economic impact. In-between are injunctions that are both specific enough that violations of them are in principle identifiable and that changes in them can be observed, and sufficiently significant that changes in them make a difference for the behavior of actors and the nature of the international political economy. It is these intermediate injunctions – politically consequential but specific enough that violations and changes can be identified – that I take as the essence of international regimes.

A brief examination of international oil regimes, and their injunctions, may help us clarify this point. The pre-1939 international oil regime was dominated by a small number of international firms and contained explicit injunctions about where and under what conditions companies could produce oil, and where and how they should market it. The rules of the Red Line and Achnacarry or 'As-Is' agreements of 1928 reflected an 'anti-competitive ethos': that is, the basic principle that competition was destructive to the system and the norm that firms should not engage in it.[10] This principle and this norm both persisted after World War II, although an intergovernmental regime with explicit rules was not established, owing to the failure of the Anglo-American Petroleum Agreement. Injunctions against price-cutting were reflected more in the practices of companies than in formal rules. Yet expectations and practices of major actors were strongly affected by these injunctions, and in this sense the criteria for a regime – albeit a weak one – were met. As governments of producing countries became more assertive, however, and as formerly domestic independent companies entered international markets, these arrangements collapsed; after the mid-to-late 1960s, there was no regime for the issue-area as a whole, since no injunctions could be said to be accepted as obligatory by all influential actors. Rather, there was a 'tug of war' in which all sides resorted to self-help. The Organization of Petroleum Exporting Countries (OPEC) sought to create a producers' regime based on rules for prorationing oil production, and consumers established an emergency oil-sharing system in the new International Energy Agency to counteract the threat of selective embargoes.

If we were to have paid attention only to the principle of avoiding competition, we would have seen continuity: whatever the dominant actors, they have always sought to cartelize the industry one way or another. But to do so would be to miss the main point, which is that momentous changes have occurred. At the other extreme, we could have fixed our attention on very specific particular arrangements, such as the various joint ventures of the 1950s and 1960s or the specific provisions for controlling output tried by OPEC after 1973, in which case we would have observed a pattern of continual flux. The significance of the most important events – the demise of old cartel arrangements, the undermining of the international majors' positions in the 1960s, and the rise of producing governments to a position of influence in the 1970s – could have been missed. Only by focusing on the intermediate level of relatively specific but politically consequential injunctions, whether we call them rules, norms, or principles, does the concept of regime help us identify major changes that require explanation.

As our examples of money and oil suggest, we regard the scope of international regimes as corresponding, in general, to the boundaries of issue-areas, since governments establish regimes to deal with problems that they regard as so closely linked that they should be dealt with together. Issue-areas are best defined as sets of issues that are in fact dealt with in common negotiations and by the same, or closely coordinated, bureaucracies, as opposed to issues that are dealt with separately and in uncoordinated fashion. Since issue-areas depend on actors' perceptions and behavior rather than on inherent qualities of the subject-matters, their boundaries change gradually over time. Fifty years ago, for instance, there was no oceans issue-area, since particular questions now grouped under that heading were dealt with separately; but there was an international monetary issue-area even then. Twenty years ago trade in cotton textiles had an international regime of its own – the Long-Term Agreement on Cotton Textiles – and was treated separately from trade in synthetic fibers. Issue-areas are defined and redefined by changing patterns of human intervention; so are international regimes.

Self-help and international regimes

The injunctions of international regimes rarely affect economic transactions directly: state institutions, rather than international organizations, impose tariffs and quotas, intervene in foreign exchange markets, and manipulate oil prices through taxes and subsidies. If we think about the impact of the principles, norms, rules, and decisionmaking procedures of regimes, it becomes clear that insofar as they have any effect at all, it must be exerted on national controls, and especially on the specific interstate agreements that affect the exercise of national controls. International regimes must be distinguished from these specific agreements; [...] a major function of regimes is to facilitate the making of specific cooperative agreements among governments.

Superficially, it could seem that since international regimes affect national controls, the regimes are of superior importance – just as federal laws in the United States frequently override state and local legislation. Yet this would be a fundamentally misleading conclusion. In a well-ordered society, the units of action – individuals in classic liberal thought – live together within a framework of constitutional principles that define property rights, establish who may control the state, and specify the conditions under which subjects must obey governmental regulations. In the United States, these principles establish the supremacy of the federal government in a number of policy areas, though not in all. But world politics is decentralized rather than hierarchic: the prevailing principle of sovereignty means that states are subject to no superior government. The resulting system is sometimes referred to as one of 'self-help'.

Sovereignty and self-help mean that the principles and rules of international regimes will necessarily be weaker than in domestic society. In a civil society, these rules 'specify terms of exchange' within the framework of constitutional principles. In world politics, the principles, norms, and rules of regimes are necessarily fragile because they risk coming into conflict with the principle of sovereignty and the associated norm of self-help. They may promote cooperation, but the fundamental basis of order on which they would rest in a well-ordered society does not exist. They drift around without being tied to the solid anchor of the state.

Yet even if the principles of sovereignty and self-help limit the degree of confidence to be placed in international agreements, they do not render cooperation impossible. Orthodox theory itself relies on mutual interests to explain forms of cooperation that are used by states as instruments of competition. According to balance-of-power theory, cooperative endeavors such as political–military alliances necessarily form in self-help systems. Acts of cooperation are accounted for on the grounds that mutual interests are sufficient to enable states to overcome their suspicions of one another. But since even orthodox theory relies on mutual interests, its advocates are on weak ground in objecting to interpretations of system-wide cooperation along these lines. There is no logical or empirical reason why mutual interests in world politics should be limited to interests in combining forces against adversaries. As economists emphasize, there can also be mutual interests in securing efficiency gains from voluntary exchange or oligopolistic rewards from the creation and division of rents resulting from the control and manipulation of markets.

International regimes should not be interpreted as elements of a new international order 'beyond the nation-state'. They should be comprehended chiefly as arrangements motivated by self-interest: as components of systems in which sovereignty remains a constitutive principle. This means that, as Realists emphasize, they will be shaped largely by their most powerful members, pursuing their own interests. But regimes can also affect state interests, for the notion of self-interest is itself elastic and largely subjective. Perceptions of self-

interest depend both on actors' expectations of the likely
consequences that will follow from particular actions and on their
fundamental values. Regimes can certainly affect expectations and
may affect values as well. Far from being contradicted by the view
that international behavior is shaped largely by power and interests,
the concept of international regime is consistent both with the
importance of differential power and with a sophisticated view of self-
interest. Theories of regimes can incorporate Realist insights about
the role of power and interest, while also indicating the inadequacy of
theories that define interests so narrowly that they fail to take the role
of institutions into account.

Regimes not only are consistent with self-interest but may under
some conditions even be necessary to its effective pursuit. They
facilitate the smooth operation of decentralized international political
systems and therefore perform an important function for states. In a
world political economy characterized by growing interdependence,
they may become increasingly useful for governments that wish to
solve common problems and pursue complementary purposes
without subordinating themselves to hierarchical systems of control.

NOTES

1 C. Lindblom, *The Intelligence of Democracy* (Free Press, New York,
   1965), p. 227.
2 A. Smith, *The Wealth of Nations* (Chicago University Press, Chicago,
   1976 edn), p. 487.
3 K. Waltz, *Man, The State and War* (Columbia University Press, 1959),
   p. 182.
4 Lindblom, *The Intelligence of Democracy*, pp. 33–4 and ch. 4.
5 S. Hymer, 'The Internationalization of Capital', *Journal of Economic
   Issues*, 6: 1 (March 1972).
6 C. Geertz, *The Interpretation of Cultures* (Basic Books, New York,
   1973), p. 14.
7 J. Ruggie, 'International Responses to Technology: concepts and trends',
   International Organization, 29: 3 (Summer 1975), pp. 557–84, at
   p. 570.
8 S. Krasner (ed.), *International Regimes* (Cornell University Press, Ithaca,
   1983), p. 2.
9 J. Ruggie, 'International Regimes, Transactions and Change', in Krasner
   (ed.), *International Regimes*, pp. 195–232.
10 L. Turner, *Oil Companies in the International System* (George Allen and
   Unwin, London, 1978), p. 30.

1.9 The balance of power and international order

Hedley Bull

Source: *The Anarchical Society: A Study of Order in World Politics* (Macmillan, London, 1977), pp. 106-17.

In this extract, Hedley Bull is concerned to identify the ways in which a balance of power in the international system might contribute to the maintenance of international order. He examines both the historical and the contemporary relevance of the notion of balance of power, and replies to a number of criticisms which have been levelled at it.

[Bull begins by outlining the characteristics of the balance of power, which he takes as meaning 'a state of affairs such that no one power is in a position where it is preponderant and can lay down the law to others'. Four dimensions of comparison between balances are identified by Bull: simplicity or complexity, general or local scope, subjective or objective manifestations, fortuitous or contrived nature. He then goes on to relate the balance to the problem of international order.]

FUNCTIONS OF THE BALANCE OF POWER

Preservation of a balance of power may be said to have fulfilled three historic functions in the modern states system:

(1) the existence of a general balance of power throughout the international system as a whole has served to prevent the system from being transformed by conquest into a universal empire;

(ii) the existence of local balances of power has served to protect the independence of states in particular areas from absorption or domination by a locally preponderant power;

(iii) both general and local balances of power, where they have existed, have provided the conditions in which other institutions on which international order depends (diplomacy, war, international law, great power management) have been able to operate.

115

The idea that balances of power have fulfilled positive functions in relation to international order, and hence that contrivance of them is a valuable or legitimate object of statesmanship, has been subject to a great deal of criticism in this century. At the present time criticism focuses upon the alleged obscurity or meaninglessness of the concept, the untested or untestable nature of the historical generalisations upon which it rests, and the reliance of the theory upon the notion that all international behavior consists of the pursuit of power. Earlier in the century, especially during and after the First World War, critics of the doctrine of the balance of power asserted not that it was unintelligible or untestable, but that pursuit of the balance of power had effects upon international order which were not positive, but negative. In particular, they asserted that the attempt to preserve a balance of power was a source of war, that it was carried out in the interests of the great powers at the expense of the interests of the small, and that it led to disregard of international law. I shall deal with these latter criticisms first.

Attempts to contrive a balance of power have not always resulted in the preservation of peace. The chief function of the balance of power, however, is not to preserve peace, but to preserve the system of states itself. Preservation of the balance of power requires war, when this is the only means whereby the power of a potentially dominant state can be checked. It can be argued, however, that the preservation of peace is a subordinate objective of the contrivance of balances of power. Balances of power which are stable (that is, which have built-in features making for their persistence) may help remove the motive to resort to preventive war.

The principle of preservation of the balance of power has undoubtedly tended to operate in favour of the great powers and at the expense of the small. Frequently, the balance of power among the great powers has been preserved through partition and absorption of the small: the extraordinary decline in the number of European states between 1648 and 1914 illustrates the attempt of large states to absorb small ones while at the same time following the principle of compensation so as to maintain a balance of power. This has led to frequent denunciation of the principle of the balance of power as nothing more than collective aggrandisement by the great powers, the classic case being the partition of Poland in 1772 by Austria, Russia and Prussia. [...]

From the point of view of a weak state sacrificed to it, the balance of power must appear as a brutal principle. But its function in the preservation of international order is not for this reason less central. It is part of the logic of the principle of balance of power that the needs of the dominant balance must take precedence over those of subordinate balances, and that the general balance must be prior in importance to any local or particular balance. If aggrandisement by the strong against the weak must take place, it is better from the standpoint of international order that it should take place without a conflagration among the strong than with one.

It is a paradox of the principle of balance of power that while the existence of a balance of power is an essential condition of the operation of international law, the steps necessary to maintain the balance often involve violation of the injunctions of international law. It is clear that situations in which one state has a position of preponderance are situations in which that state may be tempted to disregard rules of law; preponderant powers are, as Vattel perceives, in a position to 'lay down the law to others'. The most basic of the rules of international law – those dealing with sovereignty, non-intervention, diplomatic immunity and the like – depend for their effectiveness on the principle of 'reciprocity'. Where one state is preponderant, it may have the option of disregarding the rights of other states, without fear that these states will reciprocate by disregarding their rights in turn. [...]

But while international law depends for its very existence as an operating system of rules on the balance of power, preservation of the latter often requires the breaking of these rules. Rules of international law where they allow the use or threat of force at all do so only, in Grotius's phrase, 'to remedy an injury received'. Before a state may legitimately resort to force against another state there must first be a violation of legal rights which can then be forcibly defended. Preservation of the balance of power, however, requires the use or threat of force in response to the encroaching power of another state, whether or not that state has violated legal rules. Wars initiated to restore the balance of power, wars threatened to maintain it, military interventions in the internal affairs of another state to combat the encroaching power of a third state, whether or not that state has violated legal rules, bring the imperatives of the balance of power into conflict with the imperatives of international law. The requirements of order are treated as prior to those of law, as they are treated also as prior to the interests of small powers and the keeping of peace.

It is noticeable that while, at the present time, the term 'balance of power' is as widely used as at any time in the past in the everyday discussion of international relations, in scholarly analyses of the subject it has been slipping into the background. This reflects impatience with the vagueness and shifting meaning of what is undoubtedly a current cant word; doubts about the historical generalisations that underlie the proposition that preservation of a balance of power is essential to international order; and doubts about its reliance on the discredited notion that the pursuit of power is the common denominator to which all foreign policy can be reduced.

The term 'balance of power' is notorious for the numerous meanings that may be attached to it, the tendency of those who use it to shift from one to another and the uncritical reverence which statements about it are liable to command. It is a mistake, however, to dismiss the notion as a meaningless one, as von Justi did in the eighteenth century and Cobden in the nineteenth, and some political scientists are inclined to do now.[1] The term is not unique in suffering abuses of this kind, and as with such other overworked terms as 'democracy', 'imperialism' and 'peace', its very currency is an indication of the importance of the ideas it is intended to convey. We cannot do without the term 'balance of power' and the need is to define it carefully and use it consistently.

But if we can make clear what we mean by the proposition that preservation of the balance of power functions to preserve international order, is it true? Is it the case that a state which finds itself in a position of preponderant power will always use it to 'lay down the law to others'? Will a locally preponderant state always be a menace to the independence of its neighbours, and a generally preponderant state to the survival of the system of states?

The proposition is implicitly denied by the leaders of powerful states, who see sufficient safeguard of the rights of others in their own virtue and good intentions. Franklin Roosevelt saw the safeguard of Latin America's rights in US adherence to the 'good-neighbour policy'. The United States and the Soviet Union now each recognise a need to limit the power of the other, and assert that this is a need not simply of theirs but of international society at large. But they do not admit the need for any comparable check on their own power.

One form of this view is Kant's idea that the constitutional state or *Rechtsstaat*, which has its own internal checks on the power of rulers, is capable of international virtue in a way in which the absolutist state is not. Thus he is able to recommend the formation of a coalition of *Rechtsstaaten*, which through accretion may come eventually to dominate international politics, without any sense that this coalition will abuse its power.[2] In the early 1960s doctrines of an Atlantic Community, built upon the coalition of North American and West European power, followed the Kantian pattern: they were put forward without any sense that such a coalition would seem or would be menacing to other states, or that these latter would have a legitimate interest in developing a counterpoise to it.

Against this we have to set Acton's view that power itself corrupts, that no matter what the ideology or the institution or the virtue or good intentions of a state in a position of preponderance, that position itself contains a menace to other states which cannot be contained by agreements or laws but only by countervailing power.[3] States are not prevented from falling foul of this by constitutional systems of checks and balances; the corrupting effects of power are felt not merely by the rulers but by the political system as a whole. [...]

Criticism of the doctrine that the balance of power functions to maintain international order sometimes derives from the idea that this is part of a theory of 'power politics', which presents the pursuit of power as the common and overriding concern of all states in pursuing foreign policy. On this view the doctrine we have been discussing involves the same fallacies as the 'power-political' theory of which it is part.

Doctrines which contend that there is, in any international system, an automatic tendency for a balance of power to arise do derive from a 'power-political' theory of this kind. The idea that if one state challenges the balance of power, other states are bound to seek to prevent it, assumes that all states seek to maximise their relative power position. This is not the case. States are constantly in the position of having to choose between devoting their resources and energies to maintaining or extending their international power position, and devoting these resources and energies to other ends. The size of defence expenditure, the foreign-aid vote, the diplomatic establishment, whether or not to play a role in particular international issues by taking part in a war, joining an alliance of an international organisation, or pronouncing about an international dispute – these are the matters of which the discussion of any country's foreign policy consists, and proposals that have the effect of augmenting the country's power position can be, and frequently are, rejected. Some states which have the potential for playing a major role – one thinks of the United States in the interwar period and Japan since her economic recovery after the Second World War – prefer to play a relatively minor one. But the doctrine I have been expounding does not assert any inevitable tendency for a balance of power to arise in the international system, only a need to maintain one if international order is to be preserved. States may and often do behave in such a way as to disregard the requirements of a balance of power.

THE PRESENT RELEVANCE OF THE BALANCE OF POWER

[...] There clearly does now exist a general balance of power in the sense that no one state is preponderant in power in the international system as a whole. The chief characteristic of this general balance is that whereas in the 1950s it took the form of a simple balance (though not a perfectly simple one), and in the 1960s was in a state of transition, in the 1970s it takes the form of a complex balance. At least in the Asian and Pacific region China has to be counted as a great power alongside the United States and the Soviet Union; while Japan figures as a potential fourth great power and a united Western Europe may in time become a fifth. However, the statement that there is now a complex or multilateral balance of power has given rise to a number of misunderstandings, and it is necessary to clear these away.

To speak of a complex or multiple balance among these three or four powers is not to imply that they are equal in strength. Whereas in a system dominated by two powers a situation of balance or absence of preponderance can be achieved only if there is some rough parity of strength between the powers concerned, in a system of three or more powers balance can be achieved without a relationship of equality among the powers concerned because of the possibility of combination of the lesser against the greater.

Moreover, to speak of such a complex balance of power is not to imply that all four great states command the same kind of power or influence. Clearly, in international politics moves are made on 'many chess-boards'. On the chess-board of strategic nuclear deterrence the United States and the Soviet Union are supreme players, China is a novice and Japan does not figure at all. On the chess-board of conventional military strength the United States and the Soviet Union, again, are leading players because of their ability to deploy non-nuclear armed force in many parts of the world, China is a less important player because the armed force it has can be deployed only in its own immediate vicinity, and Japan is only a minor player. On the chess-boards of international monetary affairs and international trade and investment the United States and Japan are leading players, the Soviet Union much less important and China relatively unimportant. On the chess-board of influence derived from ideological appeal it is arguable that China is the pre-eminent player.

However, the play on each of these chess-boards is related to the play on each of the others. An advantageous position in the international politics of trade or investment may be used to procure advantages in the international politics of military security; a weak position on the politics of strategic nuclear deterrence may limit and circumscribe the options available in other fields. It is from this interrelatedness of the various chess-boards that we derive the conception of over-all power and influence in international politics, the common denominator in respect of which we say that there is balance rather than preponderance. Over-all power in this sense cannot be precisely quantified: the relative importance of strategic, economic and politico-psychological ingredients in national power (and of different kinds of each of these) is both uncertain and changing. But the relative position of states in terms of over-all power nevertheless makes itself apparent in bargaining among states, and the conception of over-all power is one we cannot do without.

Furthermore, to speak of the present relations of the great powers as a complex balance is not to imply that they are politically equidistant from one another, or that there is complete diplomatic mobility among them. At the time of writing a *détente* exists between the United States and the Soviet Union, and between the United States and China, but not between the Soviet Union and China. Japan, while it has asserted a measure of independence of the United States and improved its relations with both the Soviet Union and China, is still more closely linked both strategically and economically to the United States than to any of the others. While, therefore, the four major powers have more diplomatic mobility than they had in the period of the simple balance of power, their mobility is still limited, especially by the persistence of tension between the two communist great powers so considerable as to preclude effective collaboration between them.

We have also to note that the complex balance of power that now exists does not rest on any system of general collaboration or concert among the great powers concerned. There is not any general agreement among the United States, the Soviet Union, China and Japan on the proposition that the maintenance of a general balance of power is a common objective as in the proposition proclaimed by the European great powers in the Treaty of Utrecht. Nor is there any general agreement about a system of rules for avoiding or controlling crises, or for limiting wars.

The present balance of power is not wholly fortuitous in the sense defined above, for there is an element of contrivance present in the 'rational' pursuit by the United States, the Soviet Union and China of policies aimed at preventing the preponderance of any of the others. It may be argued also that there is a further element of contrivance in the agreement between the United States and the Soviet Union on the common objective of maintaining a balance between themselves, at least in the limited sphere of stategic nuclear weapons. There is not, however, a contrived balance of power in the sense that all three or four great powers accept it as a common objective – indeed, it is only the United States that explicitly avows the balance of power as a goal. Nor is there any evidence that such a balance of power is generally thought to imply self-restraint on the part of the great powers themselves, as distinct from the attempt to restrain or constrain one another.

The United States and the Soviet Union have developed some agreed rules in relation to the avoidance and control of crises and the limitation of war. There is not, however, any general system of rules among the great powers as a whole in these areas. Neither in the field of Sino-Soviet relations nor in that of Sino-American relations does there exist any equivalent of the nascent system of rules evolving between the two global great powers. In the absence of any such general system of rules, we cannot speak of there being, in addition to a balance among the great powers, a concert of great powers concerned with the management of this balance.

Finally, the present complex balance of power does not rest on a common culture shared by the major states participating in it, comparable with that shared by the European great powers that made up the complex balances of the eighteenth and nineteenth centuries. In the European international system of those centuries one factor that facilitated both the maintenance of the balance itself and co-operation among the powers that contributed to it was their sharing of a common culture, both in the sense of a common intellectual tradition and stock of ideas that facilitated communication, and in the sense of common values, in relation to which conflicts of interest could be moderated. Among the United States, the Soviet Union, China and Japan there does exist some common stock of ideas, but there is no equivalent of the bonds of common culture among European powers in earlier centuries.

All five of the misunderstandings that have been mentioned arise from the fact that in present-day thinking the idea of a balance of power tends to be confused with the European balance-of-power system, particularly that of the nineteenth century. The latter system is commonly said to have been characterised by rough equality among the five principal powers (Britain, France, Austria-Hungary, Russia and Prussia-Germany); by comparability in the kind of power available to each, which could be measured in terms of numbers of troops; by political equidistance among the powers and maximum diplomatic mobility; by general agreements as to the rules of the game; and by an underlying common culture.

Whether or not the European system of the last century in fact possessed all these qualities might be disputed. Thus there were substantial inequalities between the five powers at different times. It was never possible to reduce British sea power and financial power, and continental land power, to a common denominator. There were ideological inhibitions to diplomatic mobility arising from associations such as the Holy Alliance, the *Dreikaiserbund* and the 'Liberal Alliance' of Britain and France. We do have to recognise, however, that the European balance of the nineteenth century was only one historical manifestation of a phenomenon that has occurred in many periods and continents, and that in asserting that there exists a complex balance of power at the present time we are not contending that this embodies every feature of the European model of the last century.

This presently existing balance of power appears to fulfil the same three functions in relation to international order that it has performed in earlier periods, and that were mentioned in the last section. First, the general balance of power serves to prevent the system of states from being transformed by conquest into a universal empire. While the balance continues to be maintained, no one of the great powers has the option of establishing a world government by force.

Second, local balances of power – where they exist – serve to protect the independence of states in particular areas from absorption or domination by a locally preponderant power. [...] It would be going too far to assert that the existence of a local balance of power is a necessary condition of the independence of states in any area. To assert this would be to ignore the existence of the factor of a sense of political community in the relations between two states, the consequence of which may be that a locally preponderant state is able, up to a point, to respect the independence of a weaker neighbour, as the United States respects the independence of Canada, or Britain respects the independence of Eire. We have also to recognise that the independence of states in a particular area may owe less to the existence or non-existence of a balance among the local powers than to the part played in the local equilibrium by powers external to the region: if a balance exists at present between Israel and her Arab neighbours, for example, this balance owes its existence to the role played in the area by great powers external to it.

Third, both the general balance of power, and such local balances

124   *Hedley Bull*

as exist at present, help to provide the conditions in which other institutions on which international order depends are able to operate. International law, the diplomatic system, war and the management of the international system by the great powers assume a situation in which no one power is preponderant in strength. All are institutions which depend heavily on the possibility that if one state violates the rules, others can take reciprocal action. But a state which is in a position of preponderant power, either in the system as a whole or in a particular area, may be in a position to ignore international law, to disregard the rules and procedures of diplomatic intercourse, to deprive its adversaries of the possibility of resort to war in defence of their interests and rights, or to ignore the conventions of the comity of great powers, all with impunity.

NOTES

1 J.H. von Justi, *Die Chimare des Gleichgewichts in Europa* (Altona, 1758); and Richard Cobden, 'Russia', in *Political Writings* (Ridgeway, London, 1867, and Cassell, London, 1886).
2 Kant, *Perpetual Peace*, translated by H. O'Brien (Liberal Arts Press, 1957).
3 Lord Acton, *Lectures on Modern History*, edited by J.N. Figgis and R.V. Laurence (Macmillan, London, 1910).

1.10 State power and the structure of international trade

Stephen D. Krasner

Source: *World Politics*, vol. XXVIII, no. 3 (Princeton University Press, Ithaca, 1976), pp. 317–47.

Krasner sets out to reassert the power of states to determine the character of the international system. He takes the structure of international trade in the nineteenth and twentieth centuries as an example and demonstrates that the degree of 'openness' in that structure can be partially explained by the distribution of economic power among states. In particular, he argues that the existence of a hegemonic state leads to a higher level of free trade than that found when the distribution of power is more equal.

INTRODUCTION

In recent years, students of international relations have multinationalized, transnationalized, bureaucratized, and transgovernmentalized the state until it has virtually ceased to exist as an analytic construct. Nowhere is that trend more apparent than in the study of the politics of international economic relations. The basic conventional assumptions have been undermined by assertions that the state is trapped by a transnational society created not by sovereigns, but by nonstate actors. Interdependence is not seen as a reflection of state policies and state choices (the perspective of balance-of-power theory), but as the result of elements beyond the control of any state or a system created by states.

This perspective is at best profoundly misleading. It may explain developments within a particular international economic structure, but it cannot explain the structure itself. That structure has many institutional and behavioral manifestations. The central continuum along which it can be described is openness. International economic structures may range from complete autarky (if all states prevent movements across their borders), to complete openness (if no restrictions exist). In this paper I will present an analysis of one aspect of the international economy – the structure of international trade: that is, the degree of openness for the movement of goods as opposed to capital, labor, technology, or other factors of production.

Since the beginning of the nineteenth century, this structure has gone through several changes. These can be explained, albeit imperfectly, by a state-power theory: an approach that begins with the assumption that the structure of international trade is determined by the interests and power of states acting to maximize national goals. [...]

THE CAUSAL ARGUMENT: STATE INTERESTS, STATE POWER, AND INTERNATIONAL TRADING STRUCTURES

Neoclassical trade theory is based upon the assumption that states act to maximize their aggregate economic utility. This leads to the conclusion that maximum global welfare and Pareto optimality are achieved under free trade. While particular countries might better their situations through protectionism, economic theory has generally looked askance at such policies. [...]

State preferences

Historical experience suggests that policy makers are dense, or that the assumptions of the conventional argument are wrong. Free trade has hardly been the norm. Stupidity is not a very interesting analytic category. An alternative approach to explaining international trading structures is to assume that states seek a broad range of goals. At least four major state interests affected by the structure of international trade can be identified. They are: political power, aggregate national income, economic growth, and social stability. The way in which each of these goals is affected by the degree of openness depends upon the potential economic power of the state as defined by its relative size and level of development.

Let us begin with aggregate national income because it is most straightforward. Given the exceptions noted above, conventional neoclassical theory demonstrates that the greater the degree of openness in the international trading system, the greater the level of aggregate economic income. This conclusion applies to all states regardless of their size or relative level of development. The static economic benefits of openness are, however, generally inversely related to size. Trade gives small states relatively more welfare benefits than it gives large ones. Empirically, small states have higher ratios of trade to national product. They do not have the generous factor endowments or potential for national economies of scale that are enjoyed by larger – particularly continental – states.

The impact of openness on social stability runs in the opposite direction. Greater openness exposes the domestic economy to the exigencies of the world market. That implies a higher level of factor movements than in a closed economy, because domestic production patterns must adjust to changes in international prices. Social instability is thereby increased, since there is friction in moving factors, particularly labor, from one sector to another. The impact will be stronger in small states than in large, and in relatively less developed than in more developed ones. Large states are less involved in the international economy: a smaller percentage of their total factor endowment is affected by the international market at any given level of openness. More developed states are better able to adjust factors: skilled workers can more easily be moved from one kind of production to another than can unskilled laborers or peasants. Hence social stability is, *ceteris paribus*, inversely related to openness, but the deleterious consequences of exposure to the international trading system are mitigated by larger size and greater economic development.

The relationship between political power and the international trading structure can be analyzed in terms of the relative opportunity costs of closure for trading partners. The higher the relative cost of closure, the weaker the political position of the state. Hirschman has argued that this cost can be measured in terms of direct income losses and the adjustment costs of reallocating factors.[1] These will be smaller for large states and for relatively more developed states. Other things being equal, utility costs will be less for large states because they generally have a smaller proportion of their economy engaged in the international economic system. Reallocation costs will be less for more advanced states because their factors are more mobile. Hence a state that is relatively large and more developed will find its political power enhanced by an open system because its opportunity costs of closure are less. The large state can use the threat to alter the system to secure economic or noneconomic objectives. Historically, there is one important exception to this generalization – the oil-exporting states. The level of reserves for some of these states, particularly Saudi Arabia, has reduced the economic opportunity costs of closure to a very low level despite their lack of development.

The relationship between international economic structure and economic growth is elusive. For small states, economic growth has generally been empirically associated with openness.[2] Exposure to the international system makes possible a much more efficient allocation of resources. Openness also probably furthers the rate of growth of large countries with relatively advanced technologies because they do not need to protect infant industries and can take advantage of expanded world markets. In the long term, however, openness for capital and technology, as well as goods, may hamper the growth of large, developed countries by diverting resources from the domestic economy, and by providing potential competitors with the knowledge needed to develop their own industries. Only by maintaining its technological lead and continually developing new industries can even a very large state escape the undesired consequences of an entirely open economic system. [...]

From state preferences to international trading structures

The next step in this argument is to relate particular distributions of potential economic power, defined by the size and level of development of individual states, to the structure of the international trading system, defined in terms of openness.

Let us consider a system composed of a large number of small, highly developed states. Such a system is likely to lead to an open international trading structure. The aggregate income and economic growth of each state are increased by an open system. The social instability produced by exposure to international competition is mitigated by the factor mobility made possible by higher levels of development. There is no loss of political power from openness because the costs of closure are symmetrical for all members of the system.

Now let us consider a system composed of a few very large, but unequally developed states. Such a distribution of potential economic power is likely to lead to a closed structure. Each state could increase its income through a more open system, but the gains would be modest. Openness would create more social instability in the less developed countries. The rate of growth for more backward areas might be frustrated, while that of the more advanced ones would be enhanced. A more open structure would leave the less developed states in a politically more vulnerable position, because their greater factor rigidity would mean a higher relative cost of closure. Because of these disadvantages, large but relatively less developed states are unlikely to accept an open trading structure. More advanced states cannot, unless they are militarily much more powerful, force large backward countries to accept openness.

Finally, let us consider a hegemonic system – one in which there is a single state that is much larger and relatively more advanced than its trading partners. The costs and benefits of openness are not symmetrical for all members of the system. The hegemonic state will have a preference for an open structure. Such a structure increases its aggregate national income. It also increases its rate of growth during its ascendency – that is, when its relative size and technological lead are increasing. Further, an open structure increases its political power, since the opportunity costs of closure are least for a large and developed state. The social instability resulting from exposure to the international system is mitigated by the hegemonic power's relatively low level of involvement in the international economy, and the mobility of its factors.

What of the other members of a hegemonic system? Small states are likely to opt for openness because the advantages in terms of aggregate income and growth are so great, and their political power is bound to be restricted regardless of what they do. [...] The potentially dominant state has symbolic, economic, and military capabilities that can be used to entice or compel others to accept an open trading structure.

At the symbolic level, the hegemonic state stands as an example of how economic development can be achieved. Its policies may be emulated, even if they are inappropriate for other states. Where there are very dramatic asymmetries, military power can be used to coerce weaker states into an open structure. [...]

Most importantly, the hegemonic state can use its economic resources to create an open structure. In terms of positive incentives, it can offer access to its large domestic market and to its relatively cheap exports. In terms of negative ones, it can withhold foreign grants and engage in competition, potentially ruinous for the weaker state, in third-country markets. The size and economic robustness of the hegemonic state also enable it to provide the confidence necessary for a stable international monetary system, and its currency can offer the liquidity needed for an increasingly open system.

In sum, openness is most likely to occur during periods when a hegemonic state is in its ascendancy. Such a state has the interest and the resources to create a structure characterized by lower tariffs, rising trade proportions, and less regionalism. There are other distributions of potential power where openness is likely, such as a system composed of many small, highly developed states. But even here, that potential might not be realized because of the problems of creating confidence in a monetary system where adequate liquidity would have to be provided by a negotiated international reserve asset or a group of national currencies. Finally, it is unlikely that very large states, particularly at unequal levels of development, would accept open trading relations.

These arguments, and the implications of other ideal typical configurations of potential economic power for the openness of trading structures, are summarized in Figure 1.

Figure 1 Probability of an open trading structure with different distributions of potential economic power

		SIZE OF STATES		
		RELATIVELY EQUAL		VERY UNEQUAL
		Small	Large	
Level of development of states	Equal	Moderate–high	Low–moderate	High
	Unequal	Moderate	Low	Moderate–high

THE DEPENDENT VARIABLE: DESCRIBING THE STRUCTURE OF THE INTERNATIONAL TRADING SYSTEM

The structure of international trade has both behavioral and institutional attributes. The degree of openness can be described both by the *flow* of goods and by the *policies* that are followed by states with respect to trade barriers and international payments. The two are not unrelated, but they do not coincide perfectly.

In common usage, the focus of attention has been upon institutions. Openness is associated with those historical periods in which tariffs were substantially lowered: the third quarter of the nineteenth century and the period since the Second World War.

Tariffs alone, however, are not an adequate indicator of structure. They are hard to operationalize quantitatively. Tariffs do not have to be high to be effective. If cost functions are nearly identical, even low tariffs can prevent trade. Effective tariff rates may be much higher than nominal ones. Non-tariff barriers to trade, which are not easily compared across states, can substitute for duties. An undervalued exchange rate can protect domestic markets from foreign competition. Tariff levels alone cannot describe the structure of international trade.

A second indicator, and one which is behavioral rather than institutional, is trade proportions – the ratios of trade to national income for different states. Like tariff levels, these involve describing the system in terms of an agglomeration of national tendencies. A period in which these ratios are increasing across time for most states can be described as one of increasing openness.

A third indicator is the concentration of trade within regions composed of states at different levels of development. The degree of such regional encapsulation is determined not so much by comparative advantage (because relative factor endowments would allow almost any backward area to trade with almost any developed one), but by political choices or dictates. Large states, attempting to protect themselves from the vagaries of a global system, seek to maximize their interests by creating regional blocs. Openness in the global economic system has in effect meant greater trade among the leading industrial states. Periods of closure are associated with the encapsulation of certain advanced states within regional systems shared with certain less developed areas.

A description of the international trading system involves, then, an exercise that is comparative rather than absolute. A period when tariffs are falling, trade proportions are rising, and regional trading patterns are becoming less extreme will be defined as one in which the structure is becoming more open.

[Krasner goes on to investigate the evidence available for the period 1820–1970, using these three indicators, and comes to the following conclusions.]

If we put all three indicators – tariff levels, trade proportions, and trade patterns – together, they suggest the following periodization:

Period I (1820–79): Increasing openness – tariffs are generally lowered; trade proportions increase. Data are not available for trade patterns. However, it is important to note that this is not a universal pattern. The United States is largely unaffected: its tariff levels remain high (and are in fact increased during the early 1860s) and American trade proportions remain almost constant.

Period II (1879–1900): Modest closure – tariffs are increased;

trade proportions decline modestly for most states. Data are not available for trade patterns.

Period III (1900–13): Greater openness – tariff levels remain generally unchanged; trade proportions increase for all major trading states except the United States. Trading patterns become less regional in three out of the four cases for which data are available.

Period IV (1918–39): Closure – tariff levels are increased in the 1920s and again in the 1930s; trade proportions decline. Trade becomes more regionally encapsulated.

Period V (1945–c.1970): Great openness – tariffs are lowered; trade proportions increase, particularly after 1960. Regional concentration decreases after 1960. However, these developments are limited to non-communist areas of the world.

THE INDEPENDENT VARIABLE: DESCRIBING THE DISTRIBUTION OF POTENTIAL ECONOMIC POWER AMONG STATES

Analysts of international relations have an almost *pro forma* set of variables designed to show the distribution of potential power in the international *political* system. It includes such factors as gross national product, per capita income, geographical position, and size of armed forces. A similar set of indicators can be presented for the international *economic* system.

Statistics are available over a long period of time for per capita income, aggregate size, share of world trade, and share of world investment. They demonstrate that, since the beginning of the nineteenth century, there have been two first-rank economic powers in the world economy – Britain and the United States. The United States passed Britain in aggregate size sometime in the middle of the nineteenth century and, in the 1880s, became the largest producer of manufactures. America's lead was particularly marked in technologically advanced industries turning out sewing machines, harvesters, cash registers, locomotives, steam pumps, telephones, and petroleum. Until the First World War, however, Great Britain had a higher per capita income, a greater share of world trade, and a greater share of world investment than any other state. The peak of British ascendance occurred around 1880, when Britain's relative per capita income, share of world trade, and share of investment flows reached their highest levels. Britain's potential dominance in 1880 and 1900 was particularly striking in the international economic system, where her share of trade and foreign investment was about twice as large as that of any other state.

It was only after the First World War that the United States became relatively larger and more developed in terms of all four indicators. This potential dominance reached new and dramatic heights between 1945 and 1960. Since then, the relative position of the United States has declined, bringing it quite close to West Germany, its nearest rival, in terms of per capita income and share of world trade. The devaluations of the dollar that have taken place since 1972 are reflected in a continuation of this downward trend for income and aggregate size.

The relative potential economic power of Britain and the United States is shown in Tables 1 and 2.

Table 1 Indicators of British potential power (ratio of British value to next highest)

	Per capita income	Aggregate size	Share of world trade	Share of world investment[a]
1860	.91 (US)	.74 (US)	2.01 (FR)	n.a.
1880	1.30 (US)	.79 (1874–83 US)	2.22 (FR)	1.93 (FR)
1900	1.05 (1899 US)	.58 (1899 US)	2.17 (1890 GERM)	2.08 (FR)
1913	.92 (US)	.43 (US)	1.20 (US)	2.18 (1914 FR)
1928	.66 (US)	.25 (1929 US)	.79 (US)	.64 (1921–29 US)
1937	.79 (US)	.29 (US)	.88 (US)	.18 (1930–38 US)
1950	.56 (US)	.19 (US)	.69 (US)	.13 (1951–55 US)
1960	.49 (US)	.14 (US)	.46 (1958 US)	.15 (1956–61 US)
1972	.46 (US)	.13 (US)	.47 (1973 US)	n.a.

[a]Stock 1870–1913; Flow 1928–50.
Years are in parentheses when different from those in first column.
Countries in parentheses are those with the largest values for the particular indicator other than Great Britain.

Table 2 Indicators of US potential power (ratio of US value to next highest)

	Per capita income	Aggregate size	Share of world trade	Share of world investment flows
1860	1.10 (GB)	1.41 (GB)	.36 (GB)	Net debtor
1880	.77 (GB)	1.23 (1883 GB)	.37 (GB)	Net debtor
1900	.95 (1899 GB)	1.73 (1899 GB)	.43 (1890 GB)	n.a.
1913	1.09 (GB)	2.15 (RUS)	.83 (GB)	Net debtor
1928	1.51 (GB)	3.22 (USSR)	1.26 (GB)	1.55 (1921–30 UK)
1937	1.26 (GB)	2.67 (USSR)	1.13 (GB)	5.53 (1930–38 UK)
1950	1.78 (GB)	3.15 (USSR)	1.44 (GB)	7.42 (1951–55 UK)
1960	2.05 (GB)	2.81 (USSR)	2.15 (1958 GB)	6.60 (1956–61 UK)
1972	1.31 (GERM)	n.a.	1.18 (1973 GERM)	n.a.

Years are in parentheses when different from those in first column.
Countries in parentheses are those with the largest values for the particular indicator other than the United States.

In sum, Britain was the world's most important trading state from the period after the Napoleonic Wars until 1913. Her relative position rose until about 1880 and fell thereafter. The United States became the largest and most advanced state in economic terms after the First World War, but did not equal the relative share of world trade and investment achieved by Britain in the 1880s until after the Second World War.

TESTING THE ARGUMENT

The contention that hegemony leads to a more open trading structure is fairly well, but not perfectly, confirmed by the empirical evidence presented in the preceding sections. The argument explains the periods 1820 to 1879, 1880 to 1900, and 1945 to 1960. It does not fully explain those from 1900 to 1913, 1919 to 1939, or 1960 to the present.

[Krasner goes on to examine evidence for the fluctuations in British and American influence, and especially for the fact that there appear to be 'time-lags' in adaptations to a changed power distribution. He concludes thus:]

In sum, although the general pattern of the structure of international trade conforms with the predictions of a state-power argument – two periods of openness separated by one of closure – corresponding to periods of rising British and American hegemony and an inter-regnum, the whole pattern is out of phase. British commitment to openness continued long after Britain's position had declined. American commitment to openness did not begin until well after the United States had become the world's leading economic power and has continued during a period of relative American decline. The state-power argument needs to be amended to take these delayed reactions into account.

AMENDING THE ARGUMENT

The structure of the international trading system does not move in lockstep with changes in the distribution of potential power among states. Systems are initiated and ended, not as a state-power theory would predict, by close assessments of the interests of the state at every given moment, but by external events – usually cataclysmic ones. The closure that began in 1879 coincided with the Great

Depression of the last part of the nineteenth century. The final dismantling of the nineteenth-century international economic system was not precipitated by a change in British trade or monetary policy, but by the First World War and the Depression. The potato famine of the 1840s prompted abolition of the Corn Laws; and the United States did not assume the mantle of world leadership until the world had been laid bare by six years of total war. Some catalytic external event seems necessary to move states to dramatic policy initiatives in line with state interests.

Once policies have been adopted, they are pursued until a new crisis demonstrates that they are no longer feasible. States become locked in by the impact of prior choices on their domestic political structures. The British decision to opt for openness in 1846 corresponded with state interests. It also strengthened the position of industrial and financial groups over time, because they had the opportunity to operate in an international system that furthered their objectives. That system eventually undermined the position of British farmers, a group that would have supported protectionism if it had survived. Once entrenched, Britain's export industries, and more importantly the City of London, resisted policies of closure. In the interwar years, the British rentier class insisted on restoring the prewar parity of the pound – a decision that placed enormous deflationary pressures on the domestic economy – because they wanted to protect the value of their investments.

Institutions created during periods of rising ascendancy remained in operation when they were no longer appropriate. For instance, the organization of British banking in the nineteenth century separated domestic and foreign operations. The Court of Directors of the Bank of England was dominated by international banking houses. Their decisions about British monetary policy were geared toward the international economy. Under a different institutional arrangement more attention might have been given after 1900 to the need to revitalize the domestic economy. The British state was unable to free itself from the domestic structures that its earlier policy decisions had created, and continued to follow policies appropriate for a rising hegemony long after Britain's star had begun to fall.

Similarly, earlier policies in the United States begat social structures and institutional arrangements that trammeled state policy. After protecting import-competing industries for a century, the United States was unable in the 1920s to opt for more open policies, even though state interests would have been furthered thereby. Institutionally, decisions about tariff reductions were taken primarily in congressional committees, giving virtually any group seeking protection easy access to the decision-making process. When there were conflicts among groups, they were resolved by raising the levels of protection for everyone. It was only after the cataclysm of the Depression that the decision-making processes for trade policy were changed. The Presidency, far more insulated from the entreaties of particular societal groups than congressional committees, was then given more power. Furthermore, the American commercial banking system was unable to assume the burden of regulating the international economy during the 1920s. American institutions were geared toward the domestic economy. Only after the Second World War, and in fact not until the late 1950s, did American banks fully develop the complex institutional structures commensurate with the dollar's role in the international monetary system.

Having taken the critical decisions that created an open system after 1945, the American Government is unlikely to change its policy until it confronts some external event that it cannot control, such as a worldwide deflation, drought in the great plains, or the malicious use of petro-dollars. In America perhaps more than in any other country 'new policies', as E.E. Schattschneider wrote in his brilliant study of the Smoot-Hawley Tariff in 1935, 'create new politics',[3] for in America the state is weak and the society strong. State decisions taken because of state interests reinforce private societal groups that the state is unable to resist in later periods. Multinational corporations have grown and prospered since 1950. International economic policy making has passed from the Congress to the Executive. Groups favoring closure, such as organized labor, are unlikely to carry the day until some external event demonstrates that existing policies can no longer be implemented.

The structure of international trade changes in fits and starts; it does not flow smoothly with the redistribution of potential state power. Nevertheless, it is the power and the policies of states that create order where there would otherwise be chaos or at best a Lockian state of nature. The existence of various transnational, multinational, transgovernmental, and other nonstate actors that have riveted scholarly attention in recent years can only be understood within the context of a broader structure that ultimately rests upon the power and interests of states, shackled though they may be by the societal consequences of their own past decisions.

NOTES

1   Albert O. Hirschman, *National Power and the Structure of Foreign Trade* (University of California Press, Berkeley, 1945), pp. 13–34.
2   Simon Kuznets, *Modern Economic Growth: Rate, Structure and Spread* (Yale University Press, New Haven, 1966), p. 302.
3   E.E. Schattschneider, *Politics, Pressure and the Tariff: A Study of Free Enterprise in Pressure Politics as Shown in the 1929–1930 Revision of the Tariff* (Prentice-Hall, New York, 1935).

Part II

The politics of interdependence and transnational relations

INTRODUCTION

The extracts in this part reflect the dissatisfaction which emerged during the 1970s with the precepts of realism and the traditional state-centric approach to world politics. As it developed, the critique of realism was based on three central arguments. In the first place, critics disputed the claim that states are necessarily the dominant actors in world politics, and the accompanying assumption that states act in a unitary fashion on behalf of their citizens. Second, there was an attack on the assumption that the dictates of national security always formed the mainsprings of national action, and that the hierarchy of issues in world politics would inevitably be dominated by the 'high politics' of the competition for power between states. Finally, the critics of realism disputed the notion that competition, insecurity and potential violence were the central components of the political process in the world arena. The selections that follow can all be seen as expressions of these challenges, and as the foundation of a more differentiated perspective on world politics. In general, the perspective can be described in terms of a kind of international pluralism, through which actors, processes and outcomes are perceived in much less stark and clearcut ways than those encapsulated in the realist vision. As will be seen, this does not mean that states become unimportant; rather, their position, their concerns and their methods of action need to be evaluated in a changed context.

The first three selections all address the problem of the state as an actor in a changing world, and attempt to assess the ways in which states can adapt to the new context. Hanrieder (2.1) is at pains to demonstrate the continuing vigour of the state, but also to emphasize the new and growing constraints of interdependence and the declining self-sufficiency of purely national political and economic

139

systems. In his argument, it becomes clear that the realists' traditional distinction between domestic and international politics is breaking down, and that world politics has become in many respects 'domesticated', with new institutions and procedures playing a major role. Although the rhetoric of nationalism and independence still flourishes, this is often at odds with the reality of coordination and collaboration between national authorities, particularly in the area of 'distributive politics' concerned with welfare and prosperity. Ikenberry (2.2) pays particular attention to the ways in which this affects the position of governing elites, who act on behalf of national states. He sees them as engaged in a continuous process of adjustment, in which they have to mediate the demands of domestic and international activities, and in which the dominant form of relations is one of bargaining rather than competition. As already noted, this does not render states and national governments redundant, but it does change their concerns and patterns of policy. Morse (2.3) takes up the policy making theme, and relates it strongly to the impact of 'modernization' in advanced industrial societies. He argues that foreign policy has been transformed by the growth of interdependence: the goals pursued by policy makers are increasingly those of prosperity and welfare rather than military and diplomatic power of the traditional kind, and this implies both new processes of policy formulation and new types of policy instrument.

Another challenge to the entrenched position of the state in world politics is expressed by Destler (2.4) and Alger (2.5). The former draws attention to the ways in which the complexity of governmental bureaucracy and the competition between members of different agencies can undermine the apparent rationality of policy making, whilst the latter points to the growing fragmentation of national populations and to the major role that interest groups especially can play in the formulation of foreign as well as domestic policies. Both bear witness to the ways in which interdependence generates new types of policy issues and new types of participants in the policy process, undermining the realist assumption of national interests expressed by authoritative national governments.

Besides the challenge to the position and authority of national states and governments, the 'politics of interdependence and transnational relations' mounted a critique based on the emergence of new actors and processes in world politics. Huntington (2.6) focuses on the transnational organization – in particular, the multinational corporation – and argues that it is very far from being simply the creature of the nation-state: on the contrary, it can play an independent role on the world stage, pursuing the aim of economic advantage and assisted by its mobility and technical expertise. Keohane and Nye (2.7) extend the argument by pointing to the ways in which national governmental officials can themselves play a relatively independent role, forming transgovernmental coalitions with their colleagues in other societies and at times defeating the purposes of their national authorities. A key role in this process is played by international organizations, which provide a forum for the development of new alliances and a channel for policy formation at the international level. Pentland (2.8) develops this point by assessing the different roles played by international organizations: they are not to be seen simply as the passive instrument of state policies, or as the first elements of world government, but perhaps more importantly as major modifying elements in world politics, changing the calculations of both states and other actors.

The world produced by these new forces and processes is a very different one from that reflected in traditional realist thinking. In the first place, as already noted, the state is surrounded by a changing context, with consequent need for adjustment and new forms of behaviour. Puchala (2.9) points out that particularly in Western Europe, the growth of regional integration has produced a kind of 'learning process' in which governments and other groupings expect to collaborate and to build new structures. This does not preclude conflict and competition, but it does divert it into new channels and direct it at areas of economic and social policy. For Brown (2.10) this is one of the tests for the nation-state system as a source of order and authority, and one which it fails. In a number of areas, states are no longer adequate to the tasks of ensuring security and prosperity, allocating resources and reconciling social justice with cultural diversity. As a result, the emergent world polity is best described as a 'polyarchy', in which each region or area of activity generates its own structures of authority and mechanisms for management.

It should not be assumed, though, that all authors who stress the importance of interdependence and transnational relations subscribe to a uniform version of pluralism in world politics. Among the selections can be found very different versions of the role of the state (cf. Hanrieder and Brown, for example), or of international organization (Huntington as against Keohane and Nye). A second point relates to this: that not all of these authors would totally reject the realist perspective. As has been noted, the role of the national state remains important for many if not all of the authors, and much of the interest lies in the adaptation of states to a more pluralistic world.

Finally, it is apparent that all of the selections draw much of their inspiration from the industrialized world, and particularly from the United States and Western Europe. Although they project the image of a diverse and pluralistic world, their evidence and their conclusions relate best to one part of that world. The orientation is generally reformist, and reflects essentially a view of the world 'from the top down'. In this sense, it shares many of the assumptions of the realist perspective, assumptions that are vigorously challenged in the final perspective with its view of world politics 'from the bottom up'.

2.1 Dissolving international politics: reflections on the nation-state

Wolfram F. Hanrieder

Source: *The American Political Science Review*, vol. 72, no. 4 (American Political Science Association, 1978), pp. 1276–87.

Hanrieder contrasts the dramatic increase in the role and power of the state in the domestic arena with the growth in restraints imposed upon state activity in the international arena. He suggests that the result has been a domestication of international politics, in which security issues have diminished in salience and economic issues have increased in frequency and intensity. This has not, however, undermined the nation-state but served to underline its continuing vitality.

Two distinctive forces act on the modern nation-state, and through it, on contemporary international politics. On the one hand, the welfare demands of its citizens have pushed the modern nation-state toward a peak of power and activity unprecedented in its 300-year history. Whatever a country's institutional arrangements, stages of economic growth, or ideological preferences may be, remedies for the economic and social problems of the individual are sought in public policy and collective action. Politics has become the primary arena for the redistribution of income, status and other public satisfactions. Politics everywhere extends into wider areas, touching upon aspects of public and private life that in the past have escaped governmental scrutiny as well as governmental solicitude. The modern state is pervasive in its activities; assertive of its prerogatives; and powerful in what it can give, take or withhold.

On the other hand, the power of the state, although obtrusive and dominant in its domestic context, appears compromised in rather novel ways in its international context – in part because of the restraints imposed by the nuclear balance of terror, and in part because the domestic power of the state can be sustained only through international economic cooperation and political accommodation. In order to meet its responsibilities for mass social and economic welfare, the modern state is compelled to interact with other states in ways which, although not lacking in conflict and competition, demand cooperation, acceptance of the logic of interdependence and a willingness to condone restraints on state behavior and sovereign prerogatives. Internal state power is sustained by external cooperation.

These two forces acting on the nation-state carry with them conflicting as well as complementary implications about the nature of the contemporary international system; and they lead to questions about the balance between independent and interdependent state activities, between security concerns and welfare concerns, between conflict and cooperation, and between domestic and international politics.

NATIONALISM AND THE CONTEMPORARY INTERNATIONAL SYSTEM

The assertive character of the nation-state is reflected in a 'new nationalism', a phenomenon that has a deep impact on global politics. The forces of nationalism, aside from the inhibitions created by the nuclear balance, have proved to be the major restraint placed upon the conduct of the superpowers in the period after World War II. In their attempt to create a world order congenial to their ideological preferences or to their national interests, both the United States and the Soviet Union have had to contend with the stubborn appeal of nationalism, inside as well as outside of their respective alliances. The fissures appearing in both the North Atlantic Treaty Organization and the Warsaw Treaty Organization during the last two decades are in large part attributable to the resistance of secondary alliance members to making their policies conform to the guidelines set forth by their alliance superpower. In many instances, this resistance is based not so much on ideological grounds – nationalism as a counter-ideology to international ideologies – but on pragmatic considerations which suggest that differences among national socioeconomic, cultural and political circumstances warrant different definitions of the public good and require divergent paths toward its realization. The 'new nationalism', although not lacking in emotional overtones, is supported by rational calculations on how to further the national interest within global and regional configurations of power in which the superpowers still exert an overwhelming measure of influence. Nor are these calculations directed solely toward the superpowers. Secondary powers engage in competitive nationalism among themselves, especially in regional ventures such as the European Economic Community where conflicting interests rub against one another abrasively precisely because they are packed together closely.

National divergencies continue to resist attempts to streamline and coordinate policies within alliances. Both the United States and the Soviet Union have responded to 'deviationists' within their alliances with a good deal of exasperation; and both have sought to contain the centrifugal forces within their spheres of influence as much as possible, although in practical terms they have dealt differently with challenges to their hegemony. [...]

THE DOMESTICATION OF INTERNATIONAL POLITICS

Nationalism, then, is alive and well. Far from being secondary or obsolete, the nation-state, nationalism, and the idea of the national interest are central elements in contemporary world politics. The international system has remained an interstate system in many of its essential features. At the same time equally powerful forces are at work which have modified the role of the nation-state, broadening its capacity to shape events in some respects, narrowing it in others. These forces are in part the result of the changing nature of the nation-state itself and in part the result of new ways in which nation-states interact. They are developments which go to the roots of the perennial preoccupations of the state: welfare and security.

The meaning of national welfare and the approaches toward its achievement are profoundly affected by the major change in the nation-state that I mentioned at the beginning: its growing responsiveness to the revolution of rising expectations or, as Daniel Bell calls it in a somewhat sharper term, the 'revolution of rising entitlement'.[1] Modern governments have become increasingly sensitive to demands for a wide variety of welfare services and have taken on responsibility for mass social and economic welfare. The improvement through state intervention of the material (and perhaps even psychological) well-being of its citizens has become one of the central functions of state activity. The satisfaction of rising claims by citizens has become a major source of the state's legitimation and of a government's continuance in office.

This has led to an intensive flow of interactions, of social demand-and-supply communications between the state and society, through which politics and the bureaucracy rather than the market have become the major agents for social change and the redistribution of wealth and power. But the demands which are generated and processed through these 'vertical' interactions on the domestic level

can be satisfied only by extensive commercial, monetary and technological interactions on the international level. Three types of
processes are available for this purpose. There are the 'horizontal'
interactions among the units of world politics, on the government-to-
government level, which take place in bilateral as well as multilateral
settings. This is the stuff of traditional international politics. There are
'lateral' interactions, also called 'transnational', which are the society-
to-society dealings across national boundaries among subnational
groups and organizations, such as multinational corporations, international banks, export–import firms, professional organizations,
coordinating and consultative arrangements among national political
parties, labor unions, guerrilla organizations, and so forth. (Although
the participants in this type of transaction are 'private' or 'semi-
public', their juridical and political status differs from country to
country – a point to which I shall return later.) Another type of
interaction is 'integrative', involving supranational processes (such as
those of the European Economic Community) which are institutionalized and have to some extent diminished national prerogatives. [...]

These processes of interaction are interdependent – that is to say
they are a system – and they perform a variety of functions, most
prominently those of welfare and security. They are the structures
through which governments perform a variety of functions; they are
the ways in which state and society seek to arrange their domestic and
foreign environment. But even in a highly interdependent global
system national governments have ample discretion as to what
structures, what types of interactions, they wish to employ for
performing certain functions. To put it more precisely: the choice of
one structure over another is determined as much by internal
ideological, institutional, and political orthodoxies as it is by external
necessities. Most trading relationships in the industrialized noncommunist parts of the world are handled in transnational processes, with
national governments deciding how 'private' the enterprise system is
allowed to be; in communist countries international trade is a state
activity. Security issues everywhere are traditionally processed on the
international, government-to-government level; as are such important
economic issues as formal currency devaluations and tariff policies.
Supranational processes, as exemplified in the European Economic
Community, tend to be limited to essentially economic interactions.

In what follows, I shall try to demonstrate that the bulk of today's
global political processes are of a kind that are typical of and
approximate domestic political processes, leading to the 'domestication' of international politics; and that, contrary to the expect-

ations of functionalists and other theorists, it is not a new type of international politics which is 'dissolving' the traditional nation-state but a new nation-state which is 'dissolving' traditional international politics.

Five aspects of the contemporary global political system have a bearing on my argument. First, interdependence requires a permissive context; it is possible only in a type of international system that allows it. 'Liberalization' of trade and money flows, minimal interference with transnational investment activities, absence of protectionism, and other 'liberal' economic preferences – as well as the political purposes and ideological justifications connected with them – are prerequisites for a highly interdependent political and economic system. Although it is technology that has shrunk the world, politics has kept it that way. International economic systems, as much as military-strategic and political systems, reflect the influence and interests of their predominant members. [...]

Second, although domestic demands can be satisfied only by intense participation in international or transnational activities – providing governments with powerful incentives to cooperate with one another – nationalism nonetheless can thrive in a context of interdependence just as interdependence can survive competing nationalisms. Richard Rosecrance and Arthur Stein suggest that

> under the stimulus of economic nationalism ... nations may occasionally act against the multilateral framework.... Nationalism might have been expected to reduce interdependence. It might be argued that, if nations seek only to achieve their own goals without reference to the rest of the system, the linkage between units must decline. If nationalistic goals depend on supportive actions by other members of the international community, however, nationalism cannot be achieved in isolation. Not only does interdependence not decline in such circumstances, aggressive nationalism may lead to higher negative interdependence. The greater nationalism of the twentieth century therefore need not entail a reduction of interdependence.[2]

A third point is that in an interdependent system, whether global or regional, domestic political conflicts over the redistribution of wealth and power may extend into the transnational, supranational, or international context. This affects the disposition of issues. Schattschneider says: 'The outcome of all conflict is determined by the *scope* of its contagion. The number of people involved in any conflict determines what happens; every change in the number of participants, every increase or reduction in the number of participants affects the result.'[3] Whether the constituency for conflict resolution is enlarged in an interdependent system depends on the extent to which national governments permit transnational and supranational processes to take place. If these processes are curtailed by governmental restrictions, the scope of conflict remains localized, with the government acting as the gatekeeper between internal and external demand flows.

The same process can work in reverse. Political conflict may be projected not only from the domestic onto the international scene but international conflicts over redistribution of income may be projected onto domestic political scenes. National governments have always been at the fulcrum where foreign and domestic politics meet, where conflicting pressures have to be weighed and adjusted, where the perennial scarcity of resources requires hard choices and rank-ordering of priorities. Governments have to manage two interlocking processes of redistribution of power, influence, and wealth. In most contemporary societies, the government engages in a continuing process of redistributing domestic power and wealth. It does so whether it is an 'activist' government or whether it is content to let 'market forces' make the redistribution. A redistribution takes place in either case. By not acting, the government also acts. At the same time a national government is confronted with a continuous redistributive process in the international system, a constantly shifting configuration of power. In states where the national government allows or encourages a wide range of transnational 'private' interactions – where the government partially forswears the role of gatekeeper between internal and external environment – international redistributive processes reach into national redistributive processes more easily because they are not checked by governmental interposition.

As a result, and this is my fourth point, a new convergence of international and domestic political processes is under way in the industrialized noncommunist parts of the world, with consequences that are most likely irreversible but are neither fully understood nor perhaps fully acceptable. In some major respects, governments find it increasingly difficult, or meaningless, to distinguish between foreign policy and domestic policy. Nowhere is this more clearly visible and institutionalized than in the operations of regional international organizations that are endowed with some measure of supranational authority, however limited. It is difficult to distinguish between domestic and foreign policy in an institution whose policies have consequences that cannot be assessed in terms of either purely external or purely internal consequences. But the fusion of domestic and foreign policy takes place even in the absence of supranational processes; it reflects a process in which the traditional boundaries separating the nation-state from the environing international system are becoming increasingly obscured and permeable.

The fifth point, which is of central importance, is that security issues have diminished in salience relative to economic issues. Although security can become a question of national survival in the nuclear age – and in that sense is unsurpassed in importance – a noticeable shift of emphasis has taken place in world politics, away from the primacy of military-strategic elements of power toward the primacy of economic elements. For one, the likelihood of invasions and direct military aggression has receded, especially in areas which are basically unattractive objects of physical aggression and territorial occupation. Except in parts of the non-industrialized world and in the Middle East, territorial revisions are not a pressing issue in modern international politics. A number of years ago, John Herz argued that for centuries the major attribute of the nation-state was its 'territoriality': its identification with an area that was surrounded by a 'wall of defensibility' and hence relatively impermeable to outside penetration. This territoriality was bound to vanish, so Herz argued, largely because of developments in the means of destruction, such as nuclear weapons, which made even the most powerful nation-state subject to being permeated.[4] Although Herz later modified his views on the future of the nation-state,[5] his argument on the changed meaning and importance of territoriality was clearly valid.

The diminishing salience of territorial issues, the restraints imposed by the nuclear balance, and the day-to-day realities of economic interdependence have changed the meaning of power in global politics. Access rather than acquisition, presence rather than rule, penetration rather than possession have become the important issues. Often one gains the impression that negotiations over such technical questions as arms control, trade agreements, technology transfers, and monetary reform are not only attempts at problem-solving but also re-examinations of the meaning and sources of power in the last third of this century. Many military-strategic and economic issues are at bottom political issues couched in technical terms.

This has led a number of analysts to argue that 'low politics' has replaced 'high politics' as the stuff of international politics. There is a good deal of truth in this; and the distinction is a useful one although it should be sharpened. For one, the dichotomy between 'high' and 'low' politics, between the pursuit of security and power (the dramatic–political–intangible) and the pursuit of welfare and affluence (the economic–incremental–tangible) can be overdrawn. Karl Kaiser was correct when he suggested a number of years ago that what political actors view as either high or low politics depends on specific circumstances, changes over time, and in any case may be different from country to country.[6] Also, there is a difference between high and low politics that has not been sufficiently stressed and that is pertinent to my argument: power, security and defense commodities are indivisible, and hence less subject to the redistributive aspects of political processes, whereas welfare issues are divisible and at the very core of redistribution politics. Goals such as power and security are public goods and subject to the calculus of relative gain. Goals pertaining to welfare, economics and 'profit' are private goods and can be assessed with respect to absolute gain. To put it another way: high politics pertains to indivisible collective goods whereas low politics pertains to divisible private goods.

In combination, the five features of global politics that I have enumerated suggest that international politics is subject to a process of 'domestication'. In particular, the more international political processes concentrate on activities that are distributive the more they resemble traditional domestic political processes. This development is fed from two sources, as I have tried to demonstrate. On the one hand, the diminishing salience of security issues relative to economic issues narrows the area of 'high' nondistributive politics and enlarges the area of 'low' distributive politics. At the same time, distributive processes have increased in frequency as well as in intensity – nationally as well as internationally and transnationally. It isn't so much that welfare issues have emerged as high politics, as some authors would suggest, but rather that distributive political processes have gained in relative importance, and that the mounting demands generated within a society cannot be satisfied without recourse to international and transnational processes. As governments rely on external transactions to meet domestic demands, distributive politics on the international and national levels have become intermingled, leading to a fusion of domestic and foreign policy in the area of distributive politics. In order for this to happen, both international and domestic circumstances must be appropriate. The international system must be sufficiently stable, predictable, and permissive for extensive transnational processes to take place; and national political systems must feature political, institutional, and ideological attitudes that accept these processes.

It is precisely the domestication of international politics which sustains (and demonstrates) the vitality of the nation-state. By extending domestic political processes and their corresponding attitudes into the international environment, the nation-state has eroded traditional aspects of international politics. Many analysts in the postwar period perceived the major change in international political, economic, and strategic processes to come from a gradual weakening of the nation-state. Transnational and international processes were expected to modify the nation-state. Modern international politics was to dissolve the nation-state. What has happened, however, is that the modern nation-state has 'dissolved' a certain type of international politics as the importance of nondistributive processes diminished relative to distributive processes.

This is not to deny the continuing importance of security issues and the extensive residual of traditional international politics that is still visible in global processes. The contemporary international system is a mix of traditional and novel processes, and its essence lies in the dialectic relationship between the old and the new. This dialectic is reflected in what has happened to the idea of the 'national interest'. The concept of the national interest is, practically by definition, an idea based on nondistributive, indivisible values, enjoyed by society as a whole: security, prestige, territoriality, political advantages sought in manipulating the balance of power, and so forth. In short: the idea of the national interest is synonymous with 'high' politics. As international politics becomes more 'domesticated', the policy areas covered by the concept of the national interest become more narrow and ambiguous. Distributive values, unlike nondistributive values, are not shared equally by all segments of society. Since the idea of the nation-state and the national interest have been used in an almost symbiotic sense, at least in traditional parlance, it seems ironic that while the salience of the nation-state has been enhanced, for the reasons enumerated, the analytical usefulness of the term 'national interest' has been seriously diminished.

[Hanrieder suggests that the 'domesticated' international system does not correspond to either the Chinese or the Soviet view of the state, nor to the type of domestic politics found in the Third World. Rather, it matches the kind of politics that operate within the Western industrialized societies. To illustrate this point, he considers the case of European integration and the relation between the United States and her partners in Western Europe.]

COORDINATION OF POLITICS AND THE NATION-STATE

From the beginning of European integration and of the coordinating features of the Atlantic alliance, two contradictory processes (at times of unequal intensity) have been visible: a process of divergence and a process of integration. These contradictory trends have been analyzed in a long series of academic publications, and a review of this literature, as well as of the public debate about the issues themselves, need not detain us here. One might suggest, however, that the processes of 'coordination' of policies among nation-states in the European and Atlantic communities occupy a middle ground between the tendencies toward divergence and the tendencies toward integration. A spectrum of policies and attitudes emerges that goes from divergence to 'parallelism' to coordination to integration, ranging from minimal cooperation to maximal institutional collaboration.

All members of the European and Atlantic communities have at different times, for different reasons, and on different issues, pursued all four categories of policies. There are a number of well-known examples of policy divergencies as well as of integrative processes: de Gaulle's decision to remove France from the unified command structure of NATO (as well as other Gaullist foreign policy projects) is an example of policy divergence, whereas the establishment of the European Community is an example of an integrative type of policy.

Located as they are at the two extremes of the divergence–parallelism–coordination–integration spectrum, such examples tend to be the most dramatic. It seems to me, however, that the more pressing issues in transatlantic and intra-European processes are located in the middle ground of the spectrum, in the areas of parallelism and coordination.

There is no question that in many important respects the political systems of Western Europe have become more and more alike. But parallelism has not impelled them toward more integrative structures but, at best, toward more coordination of national policies. This is so not only because of internal domestic obstacles but also because each member of the European Community has a distinctly different relationship with the United States.

But at the same time governments must employ horizontal and encourage lateral transactions in order to satisfy the vertical demands pressed upon them by their electorates, which can be ignored only at the risk of being removed from office. It is primarily for this reason that the coordination of policies has become a central issue in intra-

European as well as transatlantic relationships. Parallel developments, the similarity of domestic problems and of public demands,
require some measure of international and transnational cooperation.
But since the intensification of integration is unacceptable to many
members of the European Community for a variety of reasons,
coordination appears to be the only alternative. Policy coordination
has become a substitute for integration.

Should the Community be enlarged in the next few years, the
prospects for deeper integration become even more remote. But there
is a question right now whether there exist compelling economic and
monetary reasons for giving community institutions more power, or
whether it is sufficient to solidify and streamline them. As Leon
Lindberg and Stuart Scheingold have pointed out several years ago,[7]
important industrial and commercial interests in the Community are
interested primarily in sustaining the present level of integration,
seeing their interests adequately served by the status quo and shying
away from the uncertainties and readjustments which attend changes
in the scope and intensity of supranational arrangements. Solidifi-
cation and rationalization rather than intensification is the key phrase
here – and the trend is as pronounced now as it was years ago. The
'expansive logic of sector integration', as Ernst Haas called it, seems
to have turned into the 'status quo logic of sector integration', a logic
which welcomes the existing measure of integration but turns to
coordination for solving new problems rather than go beyond it. [...]

The possibilities for coordination are uneven in the area of
indivisible goods, such as security issues and 'high politics' foreign
policy issues. The Western stance at the European Security Conference was fairly well coordinated, but this was so in large part
because West Germany's *Ostpolitik* and the resulting treaty arrangements had already resolved issues that were vital to the Soviet Union
and Eastern Europe. A coordinated European foreign policy is as
remote now as it has ever been; and it is difficult to imagine events
that would push the Community in that direction, especially in a
decade in which governments are less inclined to pursue grandiose
schemes for global and regional power rearrangements than in the
1960s.

Coordination on security issues is a particularly instructive
example, for here one must distinguish between security as an end –
which may be an 'indivisible' product for an alliance as well as for a
nation-state – and the means with which that end is achieved (say,
weapons procurement) which can be a highly divisible commodity.
Whether security is indivisible in the Western alliance, and in its

regional European NATO component, is an uncertainty that has plagued NATO for almost two decades. With the institutionalization of strategic nuclear 'parity' and 'equivalence' in the SALT accords, Washington's European NATO partners (and especially the Federal Republic) can hardly feel reassured about the willingness of the United States to meet a conventional attack with a nuclear response. It is still the central paradox of NATO strategy that in dealing with the Soviet Union the United States must implicitly recognize strategic parity whereas a convincing extension of American nuclear protection to Europe implies American superiority. Were it not for the fact that direct military aggression is highly unlikely, the fissures within NATO would be wider and deeper than they are. As it is, the issue has been swept under the rug, and when it tends to reappear – which happens whenever the Europeans see or imagine reasons to question American resolve – the rug is simply moved to cover it up again. [...]

Highly divisible aspects of security policy – weapons procurement, weapons standardization, cost-sharing arrangements, and so forth – make coordination much more difficult. The same is true in energy policy and raw materials policy, because high politics tends to mingle with low politics along the lines I have redefined these terms earlier.

Aside from conflicting interests, the obstacles to policy coordination stem from differences among national styles of problem solving and decision making. Even if the problems and their apparent solutions were the same in different countries (which they are not), there would be different ways of approaching them. In each country there are entrenched administrative practices that are unique and that resist international or transnational coordination. While the bureaucratic instinct may be universal and timeless, it cannot be stripped totally of its local historical and institutional context. Equally important, in each country powerful juridical, political and ideological traditions have developed which circumscribe the proper role of government in the economy and society – to use a simple phrase for a highly complex reality. These traditions, and their structural manifestations, are different in different countries. The differences are especially pertinent in policy processes that are distributive rather than nondistributive; they appear in their starkest form in welfare concerns rather than in security concerns. Although governments everywhere are pressured to direct the solution of economic and social problems, their impulses and capacities to act are energized and inhibited in different ways. [...]

NATIONALISM AND INTERDEPENDENCE

The processes I have described reflect a dialectic of independence and interdependence. In advancing their interests, governments and subgovernmental groups, society as well as the state, have brought about interdependence. Interdependence is sustained because these interest calculations do not allow the disintegration of interdependence toward a more fragmented and contentious international system but neither propel it toward more integration and supranationality. Interdependence, and the coordination required for its operation, is a halfway house between disintegration and integration of political and economic processes. Interdependence is the prototypical phenomenon of an international system that derives its dynamics from the pursuit of the national interest as well as of interests that are narrower and larger than the national interest.

It must be stressed again that the term 'national interest' in this context is ambiguous and can be misleading. Distributive goods, which are the bulk of interdependence processes, are not shared equally by all segments of society as is the case with nondistributive goods, such as security. If we cannot even properly apply the term 'national interest', with its rationalistic overtones, it would appear to be even more misleading to use the term 'nationalism', with its emotive, irrational and atavistic implications – implications that correspond much more to the nation-state concept that we see as being eroded by various permeative processes. The concept of nationalism is analytically outdated, focusing as it does on an irrelevant view of territoriality and carrying with it the assumption that the nation, incorporated by its people, represents an organic whole. In short, the terminology of nationalism is inappropriate precisely because it rests on the notion of indivisible values and the corresponding idea of 'high politics', at a time when most day-to-day political and economic processes are of the divisible kind.

I am aware of the paradox of having stated earlier that 'nationalism is alive and well', and suggesting now the inapplicability of the term itself. But there is a difference between a concept and a sentiment. The idea of the 'nation' as a communal organization still elicits feelings of commitment and hence enriches public life. This 'psychological' nationalism should perhaps be viewed as a quest for continuity when traditional values are changing and the possibilities for identification with a larger purpose are diminishing. The secularization of both theological and political ideologies brings with it an agnostic pragmatism which provides little more than a utilitarian view of public life. The theme of the 'end of ideology', tattered as it is, still explains a good deal.

Interdependence also narrows the opportunities for national self-identification. The contours of a national identity become nebulous precisely because the interests and values advanced in processes of interdependence cannot be unequivocally defined and experienced in national terms. In part they continue to be national, but they are at the same time larger and smaller – global as well as municipal, cosmopolitan as well as provincial. The nation-state, the social and cultural environment within which most citizens continue to define their spiritual and material well-being, has become deficient in providing that well-being – at the very least in its material sense, but most likely in a spiritual sense as well. Governments, in seeking to meet the demands pressed upon them by their electorates, are compelled to turn to external sources in order to meet these demands. But their reluctance to opt either for divergence or for integration places them in an area of ambiguity where coordination appears as the reasonable as well as the necessary course of action. And yet the obstacles to coordination arise from the differences among industrialized societies and their governmental structures, although the needs that coordination is intended to meet are common and widely shared.

NOTES

1   Daniel Bell, 'The Future World Disorder: The Structural Context of Crises', *Foreign Policy*, 27 (1977), pp. 109–35.
2   R. Rosecrance and A. Stein, 'Interdependence: myth or reality?', *World Politics*, XXVI (1973), pp. 1–27.
3   E.E. Schattschneider, *The Semi-Sovereign People* (Holt, Rinehart and Winston, New York, 1964), p. 2.
4   John H. Herz, 'The Rise and Demise of the Territorial State', *World Politics*, IX (1957), pp. 473–93.
5   John H. Herz, 'The Territorial State Revisited – Reflections on the Future of the Nation-State', *Polity*, 1 (1968), pp. 11–34.
6   Karl Kaiser, 'The U.S. and the EEC in the Atlantic System: The Problem of Theory', *Journal of Common Market Studies*, 5 (1967), pp. 338–425.
7   Leon N. Lindberg and Stuart A. Scheingold, *Europe's Would-Be Polity* (Prentice-Hall, Englewood Cliffs, NJ, 1970).

2.2 The state and strategies of international adjustment

G. John Ikenberry

Source: *World Politics*, vol. 39, no. 1 (Princeton University Press, Princeton, 1986), pp. 53–77.

Ikenberry takes as his starting point the interaction of domestic and international political economy, and the constant attempts by state authorities to adjust to change in both these domains. He sees the state (or the state elite) as the crucial actor in this adjustment process, and goes on to develop a framework within which state strategies can be evaluated. Crucially, he sees state elites as engaged in a constant bargaining relationship with their societies – a relationship which is closely connected with international pressures, and influenced by international structures.

States participate in both domestic and international political economic systems. Constituted of different organizational capacities and styles of maneuver, states occupy a unique position to mediate internal and external change. Nettl's 'gatekeeper' is an apt image.[1]

As administrative and coercive organizations, states are embedded in complex political and economic environments and have a monopoly on the legitimate use of violence. Although they vary considerably, they have several elements in common. All states make exclusive claims to the coercive and juridical control of particular territories, and they also make special claims to the definition and representation of broad national interests.

States are also organizations that are staffed by officials whose positions are ultimately insecure. The claim of these officials to office and legitimacy is fundamentally tied up with the state's *sui generis* position in the international system: it acts to protect security interests and property rights. But the legitimacy of the state is always conditional; incumbents are merely stewards of the national economy. Performance and success, however they are measured, are always problematic. All states exist within these enduring national and international contexts.

Finally, states are organizations that, given the alternatives, would like to survive. Consequently, they must change and adapt. They must also bargain with societal and economic actors. This notion – of the state separate from but in a constant bargaining relationship with society – is captured most effectively in historical analyses of states at their moments of birth. In a recent essay, Charles Tilly has sketched a series of relationships between warmaking, capital accumulation, extraction, and European statemaking. Tilly notes that leaders of nascent states, engaged in war with adjacent powerholders, needed to extract resources from local producers and traders. 'The quest inevitably involved them in establishing regular access to capitalists who could supply and arrange credit, and to imposing one form of regular taxation or another on the people and activities within their sphere of control.'[2] But capitalists were capable of movement (they had what Hirschman calls 'movable wealth'),[3] and therefore it was important for state officials to form alliances with various social classes and to foster capital accumulation. At the earliest moment of European state building, state leaders were confronted with a double-edged imperative: to harness domestic wealth so as to strengthen the state's foreign position, and to do so in a way that would not scare off capitalists or diminish economic growth.

Even when mobility of productive resources is low, state intervention can stifle economic growth and diminish state revenue. International competition, and the resulting need of the state to extract societal resources, may constrain states even in relatively closed national economies. Indeed, the logic of a state's bargaining with society extends beyond considerations of economic growth. Tilly notes that

> the process of bargaining with ordinary people for their acquiescence and their surrender of resources – money, goods, labor power – engaged the civilian managers of the state in establishing limits to state control, perimeters to state violence, and mechanisms for eliciting the consent of the subject population.[4]

This underlying dilemma and the continuing structural necessity for the state to bargain with its own society – so pressing for early modern state builders – is no less relevant for an analysis of the contemporary state.

Of the many international and domestic forces that set states in motion, none is more important than the constant pressure for national adjustment to international change produced by constant differential change between national and international systems.

Gilpin notes:

> In every international system there are continual occurrences of
> political, economic, and technological changes that promise gains
> and losses for one or another actor ... In every system, therefore, a
> process of disequilibrium and adjustment is constantly taking
> place.[5]

This differential change may involve system-wide economic upheavals such as the Depression of the 1930s or the oil price revolution of
the 1970s. It may be more gradual – as in the changing competitive
position of particular industrial sectors in advanced industrial countries. It will either generate new opportunities for aggressive domestic
response to international change, or it will generate pressure for
defensive action to preserve existing domestic arrangements.

Adjustment processes can and do take place in the absence of (or
in spite of) state policy and strategy. International financial markets,
for example, responded to the petrodollar recycling process much
more effectively than had been anticipated by Western officials.
(Also, a portion of the oil price increases of the 1970s was absorbed
in the inflation of American dollars.) International market processes
such as these can autonomously provide the forces that re-equilibrate
or adjust national economies to prevailing international conditions.
Even if a state's adjustment policy were directed primarily at the
margin of larger international processes, it would be a mistake to
diminish its significance. The stability and security of nations may
hinge on actions taken within that margin. What may appear to be of
marginal importance in the long term may be of powerful significance
for political and economic actors in the short term. And marginal
actions stretched over extended periods can result in profound
political and economic change.

The maneuvering of states within national and international arenas
can be conceived of as controlled by strategies that states develop to
cope with adjustment problems. Adjustment strategy may be directed
outward at international regimes, or inward at transforming domestic
structures, or somewhere in between in order to maintain existing
relationships. Which strategy is chosen will depend in large part on
the gross structural circumstances within which the state finds itself –
defined in terms of state-society relations on the one hand, and
position within the international system on the other. In this paper, I
seek to explore the bases on which these choices are made, and to
specify the interconnections between domestic and international
political economy.

ADJUSTMENT STRATEGIES

The logical possibilities for solving adjustment problems fall along two dimensions – the location of adjustment (international or domestic) and the objective of the adjustment initiative. The latter either consists of actions seeking to transform the (national or international) system or of actions seeking to preserve existing arrangements. This two-dimensional typology, as summarized in Figure 1, indicates the four possibilities that exist for states seeking to address adjustment problems.

Figure 1 Adjustment strategies

	International	Domestic
Offensive	Create new international regime	Change domestic structure
Defensive	Maintain or protect regime	Protect domestic structure

One dimension is adjustment conducted within international arenas. The strategy behind the use of international regime agreements is to avoid difficult domestic adjustments, either by creating new international regimes (offensive international adjustment) or by using international regimes or more temporary agreements to protect existing arrangements (defensive international adjustment). Adjustment within national borders – adapting to new international realities – either changes domestic economic and social structures (offensive domestic adjustment) or it protects those structures by means such as subsidies or tariffs (defensive domestic adjustment).

Offensive international adjustment is the more ambitious type of response. The strategy involves the creation of new 'rules of the game' for international interactions, and the number of states necessary to create an international regime and the level of adherence to rules and procedures is considerably greater than in the other strategies. The GATT trade regime, the Bretton Woods monetary system, and the proposed rules embodied in the New International

Economic Order are the most ambitious and far-reaching examples of this type of international system of rules and obligations.

For defensive international adjustment, the international arrangements are more limited. Rather than creating new international rules and procedures, the strategy here involves drawing on international agreements to protect existing domestic industries and institutions. In this response, a number of countries cooperate to protect domestic institutions within the prevailing international rules by such means as negotiated trade quotas and orderly marketing agreements. While international offensive adjustment seeks agreements to rewrite the rules of the game, international defensive adjustment seeks agreement on more narrow steps in order to mitigate the effects of adverse international economic change.

Domestic offensive and domestic defensive strategies mirror this distinction. In domestic offensive strategy, the structure of national industries and institutions is changed in an effort to cope with new international realities. This may involve phasing out or encouraging the growth of particular industries, or creating new institutions and arrangements that facilitate domestic economic adjustment. Efforts are focused inward at adapting institutions and redeploying domestic resources. One form of this strategy may involve vigorous and anticipatory government action to gain an edge over competitors. Investment in research and development, rationalization of corporate investment decision making, and other government devices may be used to encourage or coerce private firms to alter their behavior. Alternatively, the government may simply stand aside and let market forces do the work. Here the state acts by abstaining from intervention; put differently, the state acting as 'gatekeeper', keeping the gate open.

Domestic defensive adjustment is protective and seeks to avoid change altogether. A strategy of this sort typically culminates in the erection of barriers to new international economic competition or to other forms of change. The tariff is the most obvious example; less obvious state actions, such as subsidies and other non-tariff barriers, have increasingly emerged in contemporary trade relations.

EXPLAINING STATE PREFERENCES

How does one explain in which cases these various adjustment strategies will be pursued by states? An explanation of states' preferences must be a layered exercise. At one level, we must investigate what states would like if multiple possibilities for action existed.

That is essentially an exercise in specifying states' interests. At a second level, we must explore the constraints that delimit how those interests may be realized – in other words, the structural bases of states' actions.

In a useful analysis of these two types of explanation, Steven Lukes makes a distinction between 'rational' and 'structural' constraints.[6] The term 'rational constraints' refers to the array of economic costs that attach to particular policy options; decisions are based on a rational calculation of the differential costs and advantages of each choice. Rational constraints are not concerned with the availability of opportunities for action, but with their expense. The term 'structural constraints' refers to the institutional obstacles to action. Even if he is willing to pay the costs, the actor may either not be able to pursue an option, or structural obstacles may limit his knowledge of it.

In exploring rational constraints on state action, I will develop a model of adjustment politics. To start with, there are several assumptions about the interests of states that must be related to the strategies sketched above.

Assumption 1: *States seek to minimize the costs of governance and to maximize national competitiveness; when there are conflicts, they will prefer the former over the latter.*

In this model, states have only two interests. *The first is to minimize the domestic political costs of changes.* Because they are fundamentally political organizations, even autonomous and powerful states are enmeshed in a complex political and economic environment – an environment that rewards and punishes state action. In the present analysis, I shall assume that state action which seeks to change the behavior of specific societal groups is costly; how costly it is, and whether the state is willing to bear that cost, must be weighed against the availability of alternative options and the gains to be found in meeting adjustment goals themselves.

The state's second interest, that of *maximizing national competitiveness,* is essentially an efficiency value which is important because it reflects the competitiveness and productivity of the national economy. Where competitiveness is maximized, the national economy is based on a sound and efficient footing. In making the adjustment, it may be necessary to discourage uncompetitive industry and to encourage promising industry; or societal behavior that bears on national economic performance may have to be influenced.

The two state interests may conflict with each other when added measures of efficiency cannot be gained without incurring additional political costs. Ultimately, however, they may complement each other: because full competitiveness is a measure of economic health, the state should reap the political rewards.

The two interests may diverge temporally, however. The long-term value of competitiveness or efficiency may require state action that is quite costly in the short term. Consequently, the model assumes that, when serious conflict does emerge, the state will choose to forgo long-term adjustment gains in order to conserve short-term political costs. Implicit in this assumption is that the state is a political organization which seeks to protect itself *qua* organization. Its officials hold positions that are ultimately insecure. Because of its uniquely constituted position at the intersection of domestic and international systems, the state is a steward of both the national economy and society; but when push comes to shove, it will choose organizational over national goals.

Assumption 2: *International policies have lower costs of governance than domestic policies.*

As noted above, adjustment can be achieved by making either domestic or international changes. By this second assumption, the state will bear fewer political costs if the changes come at the international rather than the domestic level. If the relevant international regime is arranged to accommodate domestic patterns of societal behavior or industrial performance, the internal costs of change will be negligible. Therefore, wherever possible, states will seek international solutions to problems of adjustment.

When adjustment takes place in the international system, the costs are shared among a number of countries. International solutions are likely to take the form of regimes – rules and procedures of a general sort that can be used to solve individual problems of adjustment. [...] States are most likely to seek international regime arrangements when they cannot control their environments effectively. Successful regimes will emerge where a number of states share similar risks, but where events do not impinge uniformly on all the states at the same moment.

For example, a state with a national steel industry facing a major international competitive challenge and diminished markets would rather set up international agreements limiting surplus capacity than engage in wholesale industrial restructuring. The international agreement limits the pressure on the domestic industry; the cost of surplus capacity and competitive threat is shouldered by a number of producing countries rather than the single national industry. Thus, the state conserves the governance costs of the political pressure generated by displaced workers and the turmoil surrounding the insecurity of other domestic constituencies that would suffer from temporary or long-term unemployment or industrial disruption.

Another example would be countries with national economies that are highly dependent on the export of a unique or limited set of commodities. Here the adjustment problem often centers on fluctuating demand and prices in international markets. Adjustment could be achieved by the frequent though painful expansion and contraction of the national economy; domestically, offensive adjustment would entail restructuring and diversifying export goods, while defensive measures at the national level might involve steps to cushion labor and capital from international fluctuations. International arrangements to stabilize those external markets would thus be preferable. Efforts to achieve these sorts of international solutions can be found in proposals tendered by third-world, commodity-exporting nations in UNCTAD and in regional groupings such as the Lomé Convention. From the perspective of the state, the international redress of adjustment dilemmas is more attractive because the costs are shouldered by an enlarged set of actors.

The state experiences governance costs because internal change can jeopardize state coherence and control. International redress of adjustment problems shifts the burden of change or at least distributes it more broadly. In other words, international solutions to adjustment problems tend to preserve the stability of domestic political institutions – a stability that is valued by the state. As one analyst notes:

> The state's personnel ordinarily have a strong interest in maintaining the stability of institutions which stand between the society and the collapse into civil war; the ease of their own jobs, the prestige of the institutions with which they are identified, ultimately perhaps their physical safety and (in the case of elected politicians and those about them) their survival in office, all depend on continuing social stability. It is that pursuit of stability which provides the clues to the ultimate motivation of state action.[7]

Assumption 3: *Offensive policies have higher competitive gains than defensive policies.*

This assumption addresses the maximization of competitiveness. Offensive policies, either domestic or international, further adjustment processes more completely than defensive policies. While defensive policies seek to preserve the old order in some fashion, offensive policies seek to create new conditions that establish efficient or competitive relationships between domestic and international systems. Thus, offensive policies either create new regimes or new and favorable competitive positions within old regimes; defensive policies create protective blocks within old regimes or within underlying competitive positions. For this reason, I argue that offensive policies do more to promote further adjustment than defensive policies.

In effect, offensive policies are more efficient because they re-establish an international equilibrium. (I am here accepting the neoclassical assumptions concerning the efficiency and productivity of self-sustaining economic relations.) But the perspective is decidedly state-centered. The argument is that the state benefits from, and therefore comes to have an interest in, more rather than less economic efficiency. In other words, if the political costs are equal among available options, the state will support the option that furthers national economic efficiency and competitiveness.

From the foregoing assumptions, we can spell out the relevant state preference function:

Governance $(G)_{Low}$/Competition $(C)_{High} > G_L/C_L > G_H/C_H > G_H/C_L$

These preferences could be expanded upon, but it is more useful to recast the preference ranking in terms of the four strategies specified above. In accordance with our assumptions, the strategies may be ranked as follows:

1. Offensive international strategy.
2. Defensive international strategy.
3. Offensive domestic strategy.
4. Defensive domestic strategy.

If a state can change the international regime to facilitate adjustment, that will be the preferred strategy because it maximizes competitiveness (more than the defensive international strategy) and it has lower governance costs than the domestic alternatives. If that strategy is not possible, the next likely one is defensive international adjustment. It does not achieve more adjustment than the domestic offensive strategy, but it has fewer governance costs. By the first assumption of the model, the state will exchange adjustment gains for fewer governance costs when it has to make the choice. Where competitive gains from domestic offensive adjustment are exceptional and governance costs minimal, the ordering of the middle two strategies may be reversed. For present purposes, the model leaves this possible indeterminacy to empirical applications. Thus, domestic offensive strategy ranks third because it allows more adjustment than the international defensive alternative; it will be chosen if the costs of governance remain equal between them. The lowest-ranking strategy is defensive domestic adjustment, which does not have the adjustment-maximizing possibilities of either international strategies or the domestic offensive strategy.

STRUCTURAL CONSTRAINTS ON STRATEGIES

The above rankings predict the strategy that a state will adopt where choices are available. But the larger argument is that these choices are made in the context of domestic and international structural constraints, which radically delimit their range. The preference function predicts what states will seek to achieve; structural constraints will determine what is possible.

At this point, the specification of structural constraints remains crude. The term is used to refer to both domestic and international institutional conditions that remain relatively stable over time and constrain policy choice. Structure is defined from the perspective of the actor itself: domestic structure determines the ability of the state to alter the behavior of domestic actors, and international structure defines the access of the state to international rules and norms. Structure may be different for different states: a small state with few resources will find structures at the international level more inflexible than a larger state with resources capable of changing international regimes and arrangements.

Domestic structures also differ. Some states will find their domestic institutions and groups less tractable than others. Structural properties attached to these differences in the configuration of their domestic economic and political institutions – which are often summarized in terms of state and society relationships – provide powerful constraints on the exercise of state action. A recent study of crossnational differences in industrial adjustment capacity points precisely to those gross configurations of domestic organizational structures that are summarized in terms of 'industry-institutional' relationships.

States differ in their capacity to reach out into international structures and influence rules and regimes to mediate adjustment. Only certain states, perhaps only a single hegemonic actor, can create a new regime for the purpose of its adjustment. Other international strategies, however, exist without regime-creating power. These strategies are more unilateral; in a sense, they externalize domestic problems. In each case, however, structure ultimately limits adjustment strategy.

The analysis comes to a juncture at this point. One method of discussing the structural determinants of adjustment is to work inductively from the strategies to the structure without directly specifying structural conditions. Rather, one would look at the strategies themselves and assume that they *reveal* the structures. This approach would not provide a test of the model. In effect, the strategies, assuming the veracity of the preference ranking, are a window into the structural world. In this approach, the strength of the model lies in accepting the robustness of the assumptions and using them heuristically to uncover the international and domestic structural constraints on state adjustment.

In an alternative approach, the structures themselves would be specified more precisely, thus setting up deductive propositions about the likely adoption of an adjustment strategy. With a stronger *a priori* identification of relevant structural variables, this approach would predict outcomes based on the presence or absence of those variables.

Although these are valid alternative methods of elaborating the adjustment model, a clear-cut choice would not be constructive at the present state of research. The problem with adopting the first method is that it does not provide a basis for predicting (and therefore falsifying) the propositions. The problem with the second method is that at this stage it is difficult to specify structure, whether domestic or international, in completely formal terms. Furthermore, structure is not, strictly speaking, a source of *causation*. The structures provide *limits on and possibilities for* state action; the state's interests themselves are not determined by structure. They emerge through the interplay of a state elite that is adapting and strategizing in the context of those structures. More precisely, the *formal* interests of states stem from the obdurate organizational predicament of the state's geopolitical and spatial position. The *substantive* interests – in this case, the type of adjustment strategy – emerge in the struggle to find ways for the state to assert itself in the adjustment process.

168   *G. John Ikenberry*

NOTES

1   J.P. Nettl, 'The State as a Conceptual Variable', *World Politics*, 20 (July 1968), pp. 559–92.
2   C. Tilly, 'Warmaking and Statemaking as Organized Crime', in P. Evans, D. Rueschmeyer and T. Skocpol (eds), *Bringing the State Back In* (Cambridge University Press, New York, 1985), pp. 169–91, at p. 172.
3   A. Hirschman, 'Exit, Voice, and the State', *World Politics*, 31 (October 1978), pp. 90–107.
4   C. Tilly, *Big Structures, Large Processes, Huge Comparisons* (Russell Sage Foundation, New York, 1985).
5   R. Gilpin, *War and Change in World Politics* (Cambridge University Press, New York, 1981), p. 13.
6   S. Lukes, 'Power and Structure', in *Essays in Social Theory* (Columbia University Press, New York, 1977), pp. 12–13.
7   C. Crouch, 'The State, Capital and Liberal Democracy', in C. Crouch (ed.), *State and Economy in Contemporary Capitalism* (Macmillan, New York, 1979), p. 40.

2.3 The transformation of foreign policies: modernization, interdependence and externalization

Edward L. Morse

Source: *World Politics*, vol. XXII, no. 3 (Princeton University Press, Princeton, 1970), pp. 371–92.

Morse argues that the process of modernization has altered the character of foreign policy in three ways. It has effectively broken down the classical distinction between foreign and domestic policy; it has changed the balance between 'high' and 'low' policies in favour of the latter; and it has significantly reduced the level of control that any state can exercise in the domestic or the international arena.

Foreign policy has been radically transformed by the revolutionary processes of modernization not only in the societies composing the Atlantic region, but wherever high levels of modernization exist. There is a quality about modernization that dissolves the effects of what have generally been considered the major determinants of foreign policy, whether these determinants are based on ideology and type of political system (democratic versus totalitarian foreign policies, for example), or power and capability (great-power versus small-power policies). Wherever modernized societies exist, their foreign policies are more similar to each other than they are to the foreign policies of nonmodernized societies, regardless of the scale of the society or its type of government.

Both the international and the domestic settings in which foreign policies are formulated and conducted are subjected to continual and revolutionary transformation once high levels of modernization exist. Internationally, modernization is accompanied by increased levels and types of interdependencies among national societies. Domestically, it is associated with increased centralization of governmental institutions and governmental decision-making as well as with increased priorities for domestic rather than for external needs.

As a result of these transformations, three general sets of conditions have developed. First, the ideal and classical distinctions between foreign and domestic affairs have broken down, even though the myths associated with sovereignty and the state have not. Second, the distinction between 'high policies' (those associated with security and the continued existence of the state) and 'low policies' (those pertaining to the wealth and welfare of the citizens) has become less important as low policies have assumed an increasingly large role in any society. Third, although there have been significant developments in the instrumentalities of political control, the actual ability to control events either internal or external to modernized societies – even those that are Great Powers – has decreased with the growth of interdependence, and is likely to decrease further.

MODERNIZATION AND FOREIGN POLICY

[...] The general characteristics of modernized societies include the growth of knowledge about and control over the physical environment; increased political centralization, accompanied by the growth of specialized bureaucratic organizations and by the politicization of the masses; the production of economic surpluses and wealth generalized over an entire population; urbanization; and the psychological adjustment to change and the fleeting, rather than acceptance of the static and permanent.

The achievement of high levels of modernization has also been associated with the growth of nationalism and the idealization of the nation-state as the basic political unit. The consolidation of the nation-state, however, is the central political enigma of contemporary international affairs, for modernization has also been accompanied by transnational structures that cannot be subjected to the control of isolated national political bodies. These structures exist in the military field, where security in the nuclear age has everywhere become increasingly a function of activities pursued outside the state's borders. They also exist in the economic field, where the welfare not only of the members of various societies, but of the societies themselves, increasingly relies upon the maintenance of stable commercial and monetary arrangements that are independent of any single national government.

The confrontation of the political structures that have developed along the lines of the nation-state with these transnational activities is one of the most significant features of contemporary international politics. Modernization has resulted in the integration of individual national societies, which face problems that can be solved in isolation with decreasing reliability. In other words, modernization has transformed not only the domestic setting in which foreign policy is formulated; by creating higher levels of interdependence among the diverse national societies, it has also transformed the general structures of international society.

Foreign and domestic politics

The fundamental distinction that breaks down under modernization is between foreign and domestic policies, at least in ideal terms. This distinction is much more characteristic of the foreign policies of nonmodernized societies in both ideal and actual terms than it is of modernized states. In modernized societies, it is difficult to maintain because both predominantly political and predominantly nonpolitical interactions take place across societies at high levels, and because transnational phenomena are so significant that either territorial and political or the jurisdictional boundaries are extremely difficult to define. The whole constellation of activities associated with modernization blurs the distinction so that an observer must analyze carefully any interaction in order to ascertain in what ways it pertains to foreign and domestic affairs.

[...] Foreign policy has been thought to differ from domestic policy in its ends (the national interest as opposed to particular interests), its means (any means that can be invoked to achieve the ends, as opposed to domestically 'legitimate' means), and its target of operation (a decentralized, anarchic milieu over which the state in question maintains little control, as opposed to a centralized domestic order in which the state has a monopoly of the instruments of social order). Whether the substance of the distinction stresses domestic or foreign affairs, the separation of the two has a strong empirical foundation. Levels of interdependence among all nonmodernized societies were generally so low that governments could take independent actions either domestically or abroad with fairly little likelihood that much spillover between them would take place. The instruments used to implement either domestic or foreign policies had effects on either that were in normal terms negligible. The 'externalities' generated by either domestic or foreign policies did not significantly alter policies in other fields.

This is not to say that domestic factors did not affect foreign policy at all, nor that the general international setting did not affect the substance of policies. What it does suggest is that the normative distinction between foreign and domestic activities was quite well matched by actual conditions. The degrees to which they did not coincide led to debates about ways to improve the efficacy of foreign or domestic policies, or about their goals. But the degree of divergence was not so great as to call the distinction into question.

Regardless of how the distinction is made, it breaks down once societies become fairly modernized. This does not mean, as Friedrich has argued, that 'foreign and domestic policy in developed Western systems constitutes today a seamless web'.[1] Distinctions along the analytic lines I have suggested above still obtain, and governments still formulate policies with a predominant external or internal orientation. But foreign and other policies formulated under modern conditions affect each other in ways that are not salient in non-modernized or premodernized societies and that derive from both the domestic and international interdependencies associated with modernization. They also derive from the increased scope of governmental activities under modern conditions. Before the Western societies became highly modernized, for example, the major part of government expenditures was devoted to foreign affairs, which was the central concern of government. As the role of the government in the economy and in domestic social life increases, concern for foreign affairs must decrease relative to concern for domestic affairs. In addition, as a result of growing international interdependencies, the external and internal consequences of domestic and foreign policies become more significant, and consequences that are not intended and that may or may not be recognized tend also to increase. Therefore, undesirable policy-consequences also increase. [...]

The linkages between domestic and foreign policies constitute the basic characteristic of the breakdown in the distinction between foreign and domestic affairs in the modernized, interdependent international system. This statement does not imply that foreign and domestic policies are indistinguishable; for with regard to articulated goals and problems of implementation, they remain separate. Rather, it is suggestive of the ways in which foreign policies are transformed by the processes of modernization and the development of high levels of interdependence. These processes have put an end to the normative distinctions asserting the primacy of the one or the other. They also overshadow the empirical distinction according to which foreign policies vary in type with the political institutions in which they are formulated.

The dynamics of foreign policies in modernized societies

[...]

The transformation of policy objectives

Preoccupation with high policies and traditional foreign policy objectives and instrumentalities has drawn the attention of scholars away from the changes in policy goals that have accompanied modernization, and specifically from the increased salience of low policies and the merging of goals of power and goals of plenty.

Two general transformations associated with high levels of modernization are responsible for this change. One pertains to the classical instruments of policy, armaments and weapons, and the changes brought about in external goals by the development of nuclear weapons and their delivery systems. The other is related to more general transformations of domestic society.

The effects of nuclear weapons on national external goals have received far greater attention than have the effects of the transformation of domestic society. This one-sided attention is a result of the preoccupation with high policies and serves to obscure more radical changes in policy objectives. It is also related to the assumption that even with the development of nuclear weapons systems *plus ça change, plus c'est la même chose,* or that neither military nor economic interdependence has grown in recent years, but that they may even have diminished considerably. The development of nuclear weapons has had a cross-cutting effect. On the one hand, it makes the territorial state incapable of providing defense and security, by creating the first truly global international system unified by the possibility of generating unacceptable levels of human destruction. On the other hand, nuclear weapons are also said to reaffirm the viability of the nation-state as a political unit, by providing its absolute defense by deterrence.[2]

In any case, the key to the obsolescence of territorial goals that accompanied the development of nuclear weapons is the increased cost of territorial accretion. No modernized state can afford it. It is therefore no accident that major territorial disputes have disappeared from relations among the highly modernized states and now can occur where there is no danger that nuclear weapons will be used and, therefore, accompany nation-building efforts only in the nonmodernized societies. Modernized societies are involved in major territorial disputes only when these disputes also involve a nonmodernized society as well, as in the case of the Sino-Soviet border. Territoriality decreases in importance even further as alliances become less useful. Requisites for American security, once consisting of territorial bases encircling the Soviet bloc, have changed tremendously with the hardening of missiles and the development of Polaris and Poseidon submarines. [...]

Rapid domestic economic growth, one of the prime indices of modernization, has a profound effect on both the relative priority of domestic and foreign goals and on the substance of each. Once economic growth sets in as a continuous, dynamic process, the value of accretion of territory and population dwindles and the 'domestic savings and investment and advancement of education, science, and technology are [seen as] the most profitable means and the most secure avenues to the attainment of wealth and welfare'.[3] The logic of economic growth, in other words, turns men's minds away from the external goals associated with the ruling groups of early modern Europe and toward the further development of domestic wealth by domestic means and under conditions of peace.

Domestic economic growth, like the creation of nuclear weapons, offers only a partial explanation of the transformation of foreign policy goals. In addition, the salience of low policies and the expansion of conflictual, zero-sum relations to cooperative strategies result also from transnational structures associated with the modernization and the interdependencies that have developed among the modernized states. Low policies, in this sense, derive from the interactions of citizens in various states and from the actions of governments in the interests of their citizens or their responses to private group behavior in order to assure general stability and the achievement of other goals. These goals are themselves undermined by the scope of nongovernmental transnational and international interchanges and may also be predominantly domestic and pertain to welfare and social services.

Another aspect of the increased salience of low policies pertains to the interests of governments in building new transnational structures in order to achieve both international and domestic goals. For example, one of the motivations for creating a common market in Europe has been the increased wealth it would bring to the citizens of each member-state as a result of increased levels of trade. It is for this reason that one principal characteristic of foreign policies under modernized conditions is that they approach the pole of cooperation rather than the pole of conflict. Conflictual or political activities, therefore, take place within the context of predominantly cooperative arrangements. Plays for power or position among these modernized states occur in the non-zero-sum worlds of the IMF and NATO rather than in predominantly conflictual arenas.

The low policies, in short, have become central to international politics among the modernized states and involve the building up of international collective goods in defense and NATO, and in international wealth-and-welfare organizations such as GATT and the EEC. It is within the parameters set by the need for cooperation that interplays of power and position can occur. [...]

Two of the chief characteristics of foreign policies conducted under modernized conditions are, then, (1) their predominantly cooperative rather than conflictual nature; and (2) the change in goals from power and position to wealth and welfare – or, at least, the addition of these new goals to the more classical ones. Both factors are accompanied by the loss of autonomy of any society in international affairs.

Increased domestic demands and the allocation of resources

It is a paradox at the heart of foreign policies in all modernized societies that increased demands on their governments result in a short-term problem of resource allocation, with the result that predominantly external goals decrease in priority relative to predominantly domestic goals. At the same time, however, increased 'inward-looking' has been offset by the increased sensitivity of domestic conditions to international events as a result of international interdependence, and by absolute increases in international activities taken on by the citizens of all modernized societies.

One of the distinctive features of all modernized governments, democratic and authoritarian alike, is that they have assumed great multifunctionality. Both ideally and actually, they are not merely regulative agencies in a 'night-watchman' state, but are and are seen as creators and redistributors of wealth. Increasing demands on governments have helped to create the modern social-service state and themselves result from the increased politicization of citizens in modernized societies. A government is impaled upon the 'dilemma of rising demands and insufficient resources'[4] when its domestic demands are greater than its resources and when at the same time it must maintain even existing levels of commitments abroad. The demands may arise from the politicized poor who want a greater share in economic prosperity, the military for new weapons systems, the need for maintenance of public order in societies increasingly sensitive to labor and minority group disruption, etc. These are added to the 'rising cost and widening scope of activities required to keep mature urban societies viable'.[5] One inexorable result of these increased demands on governments is the curtailment of external commitments, or the decreased relative priority of external goals. Such curtailments add a dimension to the costs of independence. [...]

Changes in the processes of foreign policy-making

Like other processes of policy-making, those associated with foreign policy change under modernization. Cabinet-style decision-making gives way to administrative politics as the information that must be gathered for policy-making increases, as the number of states and functional areas that must be dealt with increases, and as personnel standards become professionalized. Despite the predictions made at the turn of the century by the ideologues of democracy, policy-making has not been 'democratized' so much as it has been 'bureaucratized'. At the same time, great losses of control from the top have occurred and have been well documented.

The major transformation brought about by changes in the policy-making process has been the decreased relevance of rationality models for understanding policy and the increased importance of the bureaucratic model. Policy-making in modern bureaucracies undermines the ability of a political leader to pursue rationally any explicit external goals. Rather, interest-group politics assume greater importance and foreign policy becomes more and more a reflection of what occurs in the bureaucracies upon which leadership depends for information and position papers.

Policy-making in modern bureaucracies, with regard to foreign as well as domestic affairs, involves both lateral bargaining among the members of various administrative units and vertical or hierarchical bargaining among members of various strata in a single organization. The single spokesman in foreign affairs, long prescribed as a necessity for security, is made impossible by the characteristics of modern bureaucracies. Plurality in the number of foreign policy voices accompanies the increased significance of routine, daily decision-making in low-policy areas that contrasts with the more unified and consistent nature of decision-making in crises and in high politics. With such increases in routine, control at the top becomes more difficult. The several aspects of control of routine can be summarized under two headings: the organizational problem and the problem of size.

Modern governments are organized predominantly along functional domestic lines into such departments as agriculture, labor, and education. The domestic–foreign distinction that seemed to fit the nineteenth-century model of governmental organization conflicts dramatically with the needs of even the predominantly domestic organizational structures of modernized governments. Here, the distinctive feature is that each domestic function has external dimensions: most of the predominantly domestic departments and ministries of modern governments have some kind of international bureau. The proliferation of these international bureaus severely undercuts the ability of one foreign ministry or department to control the external policies of its government, thus severely restricting the coordination of foreign policies. The problem is all the more serious in so far as the distinction between high policies and low policies in foreign affairs has become increasingly blurred.

One way this problem is dealt with is by the formation of committees that cross-cut several cabinet organizations, serving to coordinate both information and decision-making at several levels. Each American administration since World War II has tried to reorganize foreign policy decision-making to counter the disability, but no permanent decision-making structures have been devised. Other governments tackle the problem by forming *ad hoc* interministerial committees to meet specific problems.

In addition to decreased control as a result of 'domestic orientation' in modern governments, there is the added difficulty of coordinating a large bureaucracy dealing predominantly with foreign affairs. At the turn of the last century, one of the problems of control stemmed from the lack of coordination between foreign ministries and ministries of the armed forces. Thus, for example, French armed forces often freely occupied underdeveloped areas in Africa and Southeast Asia without the knowledge of the foreign minister. Today the problem of size presents no less formidable an information gap at the top of large bureaucracies. With more information available than ever, its channeling to the right person has become an organizational problem no foreign ministry has mastered.

Modernization, then – usually associated with the rationalization of political structures that foster increased control over the events in a society as well as over the environment in which men live – also creates certain disabilities that impede rational and efficient foreign policies. But modernization has also exacerbated another problem of control that has always been central to international politics – the control of events external to a state. This problem, which originates in the political organization of international society, is the one to which I now turn.

Modern foreign policies and problems of control

The problem of control in international affairs arises from the condition of international society, which, conceived as a collection of nominally sovereign political units, has no overarching structure of political authority. The difficulty of coordination and control of events external to a society, always the major problem of international stability, is compounded by the development of interdependencies among modernized societies, for interdependence erodes the autonomy of a government to act *both* externally and internally, though the juridical status of sovereign states has not been significantly altered.

With the development of high levels of interdependence, all kinds of catastrophes, from nuclear holocaust to inflation or depression, can also become worldwide once a chain of events is begun. These disasters could be logical consequences of benefits derived from international collective goods.

One reason why modern governments have lost control over their foreign relations is that there has been an increasing number of international interactions, especially among the populations of pluralistic societies, in nongovernmental contexts. This increase was one of the first changes modernization brought in the foreign policies of states. It first became noticeable at the turn of the century with the rise of the 'new imperialism' characterized by the rapidly increased mobility of people, of money, and of military equipment. It is associated today with the multinational corporation and with other new units of international activity that have varying degrees of autonomy abroad and whose external operations frequently act at cross-purposes with the foreign policy goals of their governments. They also contribute a large portion of any state's balance-of-payments accounts and therefore affect the monetary stability not only of a single state, but of the system of states in general. [...]

A second aspect of the problem of control stems from the decreasing number of instrumentalities relative to the number of goals associated with any government. An optimum policy situation is one where the number of instruments available for use exceeds the number of goals. In principle, an infinite number of policy mixes exist, in that one instrument can substitute for another and 'it will always be possible to find one among the infinity of solutions ... for which welfare, however defined, is a maximum'.[6] This is not only the most efficient situation, but it is also the fairest, for it allows any pressure to be 'distributed more evenly over the various social groups'.[7] When, however, the number of instruments is smaller than the number of goals, there is no clear solution on grounds of efficiency or fairness.

It is precisely this situation that occurs with the breakdown of the domestic–foreign distinction and with increases in international interdependence. As long as the two spheres remain more or less distinct, policies in either area can be implemented with different sets of instrumentalities. As soon as the separation is eroded, the spillover of effects from one sphere to the other results in the reduction of the number of usable instrumentalities.

This is true for two reasons. First, since policy instruments have recognizable effects both internally and externally, it is more and more frequently the case that any one instrument can be used for either domestic or external purposes. However, domestic wage increases can be used for the purpose of establishing higher general levels of living. At the same time, the propensity to consume imported goods increases directly with wage increases and depresses any balance-of-payments surplus – a situation that is worsened by the positive effect of wage increases on prices and the subsequent negative effect on exports.

Second, what is optimally desired is that objectives be consistent. 'If they are not consistent, no number of policy instruments will suffice to reach the objectives.'[8] As long as domestic and foreign affairs were separated, consistency was a problem only within each sphere. With interdependence, not only must domestic and foreign goals be compatible with each other, but so must the goals of a set of societies if welfare effects are to be spread optimally. Consistency then becomes more difficult because of the economic nature of the objectives and the diversity of political units in international society.

Together with increased international transactions associated with growing interdependence, there have also developed rising levels of transactions internal to modernized states as well as higher levels of national integration. It is often concluded that the increases in national cohesiveness that accompany modernization counteract international interdependence.[9] Actually the reverse is true.

There is a fairly simple relation between rising levels of transactions internal to one state and increased interdependence among states. As *internal* interdependencies increase and as governmental organizations are institutionalized, even if international transactions remain constant (and they do not) *international* interdependencies also increase. This is true because sensitivity to transnational activities increases the domestic implications of international transactions. For example, as the levels of interdependence within a state rise, the same order of trade has increased implications for domestic employment, fiscal, monetary, and welfare policies. It is precisely this element of interdependence that is fundamental and that Deutsch and other theorists have overlooked. [...]

CONCLUSIONS

The transformations in all three aspects of foreign policies – in their contents, the processes associated with policy formation, and the control of policy effects – offer the citizens of any modernized society opportunities for increased wealth and welfare that were unthinkable in any system with much lower levels of interdependence. They also increase the chances of instability for international society as a whole; for interdependence has increased far in advance of either the instruments capable of controlling it or of available knowledge of its effects. There are, however, two aspects of modernization and foreign policy that, in conclusion, must be highlighted.

First, the various changes discussed above pertain to all modernized societies and are affected very little by ideology or by particular sets of political institutions. To be sure, it may make some difference whether institutions are democratic or nondemocratic in particular instances. In the long run, however, the general influences that have transformed foreign policies are ubiquitous.

Second, these changes are likely to be dispersed throughout the international system far ahead of other aspects of modernity. They are, therefore, likely to characterize the foreign policies of some less modernized societies before these societies become relatively modernized – or even if they do not become modernized. The speed with which modernity spreads will, therefore, only increase the problems of control and will make more urgent the need for establishing new mechanisms of international order.

NOTES

1   Carl J. Friedrich, 'Intranational Politics and Foreign Policy in Developed (Western) Societies', in R. Barry Farrell (ed.), *Approaches to Comparative and International Politics* (Evanston, 1966), p. 97.
2   A balanced analysis of both schools of thought can be found in Pierre

Hassner, 'The Nation State in the Nuclear Age', *Survey*, LXVII (April 1968), pp. 3–27.

3   K. Knorr, *On the Uses of Military Power in the Nuclear Age* (Princeton, 1966), p. 22.

4   Harold and Margaret Sprout, 'The Dilemma of Rising Demands and Insufficient Resources', *World Politics*, XX (July 1968), pp. 660–93.

5   Ibid., p. 685.

6   Jan Tinbergen, *On the Theory of Economic Policy*, 2nd edn (Amsterdam, 1963), pp. 37–8.

7   Ibid., p. 41.

8   Richard N. Cooper, *The Economics of Interdependence: Economic Policy in the Atlantic Community* (New York, 1968), p. 155.

9   See the works of Karl W. Deutsch, including Deutsch *et al.*, *France, Germany and the Western Alliance: A Study of Elite Attitudes on European Integration and World Politics* (New York, 1967).

2.4 Organization and bureaucratic politics
I.M. Destler

Source: *Presidents, Bureaucrats and Foreign Policy* (Princeton University Press, Princeton, 1974), pp. 52–81.

Destler begins by identifying the main characteristics of the 'bureaucratic politics' school of analysis. He proceeds to a discussion of the possible pitfalls and developments in the approach and ends by considering the troubling implications for the content of foreign policy and the reform of the policy process implicit in the nature of bureaucratic politics.

Bureaucratic politics is the process by which people inside government bargain with one another on complex public policy questions. Its existence does not connote impropriety, though such may be present. Nor is it caused by political parties and elections, though both influence the process in important ways. Rather, bureaucratic politics arises from two inescapable conditions. One is that no single official possesses either the power, or the wisdom, or the time to decide all important executive branch policy issues himself. The second is that officials who have influence inevitably differ in how they would like these issues to be resolved. [...]

What specific insights does the bureaucratic politics view of government have to offer? How does it depict the actual workings of the foreign affairs bureaucracy? The basic concepts can be grouped under four general headings:

1. Power and perspective
2. Issues as a flow
3. Constraints, channels, and maneuvers
4. Foreign policy as bureaucratic political outcome

POWER AND PERSPECTIVE

Power is spread unevenly among many individuals in different governmental positions.

The 'diversity of values and goals and of alternative means and policies'[1]

Rational policy-making may be salutary as an ideal, and reasoned analysis may be able to improve policy-making at many points. But there is no way for reason alone to overcome the diversity of goals and means that are inevitable among participants in foreign policy-making. Goals are based on value preferences as well as rational analysis. And even differences as to means of achieving common goals cannot be resolved by reason. Our understanding of the likely consequences of particular policies is very poor, since they involve complex chains of human interaction with each step very hard to predict. [...]

Perspective: Men in positions

More than one sage has been credited with the maxim, 'Where you stand depends on where you sit'. While officials' views and actions are not predetermined by the positions they hold, they are greatly influenced by them. For each official has a separate job to do, whether it be President or Air Force Chief of Staff or Turkey desk officer in State. Each receives a different mix of information. Each is subject to a different mix of pressures. Each must maintain the loyalty of a different group of subordinates, the respect of a different group of peers, the confidence of a different boss. Thus each views a problem from his own particular 'perspective'.

Men's perspectives grow narrower the further down in the hierarchy they sit. Even on a matter as critical as the Cuban missile crisis, the Chief of Naval Operations' determination to run what he judged a militarily sound blockade and protect his ships against possible encounters with Russian submarines conflicted with the President's broader need to avoid provoking the Soviets and give them 'time to see, think, and blink'. And not only do men in positions tend to see issues in terms of their positions. They also tend to press for their resolution in the direction that will most strengthen their ability to do their particular jobs. [...]

Bargaining advantages: Who influences what how much?

Differences among men sharing power can only be resolved by bargaining. Thus officials strive to be *effective* in influencing their colleagues. But they are not equally successful, and they do not come to the battle equally armed. Nor does the fight necessarily go to the swiftest of tongue, the man with the best rational arguments. For persuasion requires not just logic but a hearing, and some are more listened to than others.

To influence particular issues bureaucrats need 'bargaining advantages', sources of influence which make others take them seriously. Allison lists these as 'drawn from formal authority and obligations, institutional backing, constituents, expertise, and status'. Hilsman cites as 'sources of power' within the executive branch 'the confidence of the President', 'position and title', 'representing a particular constituency', 'institutional backing', and 'statutory or designated authority and responsibility'.[2]

ISSUES AS A FLOW

The discussion thus far treats 'issues' as if each arose separately, and as though bargaining took place over the issue in its entirety. But officials usually consider issues not as whole but one piece at a time, with decisions on many 'pieces' adding up to 'policy' over time. Also, each piece must compete for their attention with pieces of many other issues. And issues tend to be broader than particular individuals' jurisdictions, so that lateral bargaining becomes a critical element.

Issues as bits and pieces

Issues generally arise not all at once or once and for all, but bit by bit. So while bureaucrats *may* be thinking in terms of the larger question, battles tend to be fought over how to handle today's problem. [...]

Issues as simultaneous games

'Players' involved in foreign policy-making, particularly top officials, have 'a full plate', a diet of diverse problems in the form of memos, orders for their signature, Presidential recommendations requested. This diet is so rich and varied that it is difficult for them even to taste all the problems set before them, let alone digest them. They are fighting on a number of issues simultaneously, so they must weigh in on one and quickly move on to the next. They must also consider each policy game not entirely on its own terms, but also for its relationship to other games. [...]

Issues as overflowing jurisdictions

In testifying before the Jackson Subcommittee, Robert Lovett complained that 'the idea seems to have got around that just because some decision may affect your activities, you automatically have a right to take part in making it'.[3] But looked at from the official's vantage point, this 'idea' is inescapable. [...]

The concept of foreign policy-making as bureaucratic politics does not *depend* on issues being interdepartmental. If they were not, bargaining would still take place, both up-and-down and laterally between offices within particular departments. But the interdepartmental character of practically all important issues complicates the game considerably by increasing the number of players and the range of perspectives involved. It reduces the number of issues where a decision can be worked out under the general authority of any one official short of the President. Conversely it increases the number which must be resolved by lateral bureaucratic compromises, or by 'escalation' to higher levels.

CONSTRAINTS, CHANNELS, AND MANEUVERS

Like any political system, the foreign affairs policy-making process is characterized by shared beliefs and allegiances, 'rules of the game' affecting who has a chance to influence what issue when, and a set of relatively standard maneuvers for influence.

Common commitments and perceptions

There is a widely shared conviction in the government that the United States should have a strong and effective foreign policy, and that positive actions should be taken to further this aim. Thus, as Halperin notes, 'Senior participants in the process ... by and large believe that they should, and do, favor support of policies which are in the national interest.'[4] Partly because of this belief, even those with narrower aims generally feel they can win only by framing their cases as plausible arguments for the broader national interest.

A related factor encouraging agreement is what Halperin calls 'widely shared values and images of the world'. These tend to determine which proposals will be taken seriously and which considered unreasonable. They may at times diverge rather far from reality. For example, a player suggesting the existence of anything but a solid Russia–China alliance at the time of the 1958 Quemoy crisis would have undercut his credibility and his ability to influence that issue, since he would be contradicting the conventional bureaucratic wisdom of the time.

Rules of the game structuring bureaucratic politics

There will always be, at any given time, a set of 'rules' about the channels through which particular types of issues move, the people entitled to be consulted or to 'clear' proposed documents, the individual or office having 'the action' or primary responsibility, etc. Some of these are informal understandings relying heavily on personal relationships. Some are more formal and result from the need for standard operating procedures to handle regular phenomena – rules for routing and answering cables, channeling budget and planning documents, signing off on foreign aid agreements, moving issues up for Presidential or Secretarial action. The influence of such formal procedures is both real and limited. The most critical issues tend to jump the bounds of regular channels, above all because of the involvement of top officials, who seek to handle things their own ways. But their ability to influence these issues effectively can be strongly affected by the involvement and leverage such procedures provide them and their underlings.

Maneuvers for influence

Officials seeking approval or disapproval of particular policy courses or actions will engage in maneuvers designed to make their viewpoints prevail. Not only will they seek to structure their proposals for maximum appeal to others whose agreement is needed or desired. They will also seek on occasion to change the composition of the relevant group of people, shutting some out because 'security' requires it, bringing others in by placing the issue in a broader context or raising it before a broader forum, redefining the issue in order to transfer the action to someone else, eliminate the need for certain concurrences, etc. [...]

FOREIGN POLICY AS BUREAUCRATIC POLITICAL OUTCOME

What results from this bureaucratic political system is, of course, foreign policy. But it is not necessarily 'policy' in the rational sense of embodying the decisions made and actions ordered by a controlling intelligence focusing primarily on our foreign policy problems. Instead it is the 'outcome' of the political process, the government actions resulting from all the arguments, the building of coalitions and countercoalitions, and the decisions by high officials and compromises among them. Often it may be a 'policy' that no participant fully favors, when 'different groups pulling in different directions yield a resultant distinct from what anyone intended'.[5] Any year's defense budget offers innumerable good examples. Often it is difficult to determine where and when in the system a particular policy direction was decided upon.

Moreover, policy is not usually the outcome of any particular battle, but the cumulation of outcomes of a number of battles fought over time. 'Rather than through grand decisions on grand alternatives', Hilsman has written, 'policy changes seem to come through a series of slight modifications of existing policy, with the new policy emerging slowly and haltingly by small and usually tentative steps, a process of trial and error in which policy zigs and zags, reverses itself, and then moves forward in a series of incremental steps.' 'Incrementalism', or step-by-step, trial-and-error policy-making, can be the most rational strategy when the impact of policy changes is hard to assess in advance. Lindblom has made this point with particular persuasiveness. But as it occurs in bureaucratic politics, incremental policy-making reflects more the internal dynamics of decision-making than any conscious design to maximize our ability to cope with an unruly world.[6]

TWO POSSIBLE PITFALLS OF THE BUREAUCRATIC POLITICS VIEW

Any generalizing set of concepts tends to bring certain phenomena to prominence, risking an exaggeration of their importance and a neglect of other factors. Thus, even if one accepts the foregoing description as a generally valid picture of 'the way things are' in foreign policy decision-making, one must guard against its possible pitfalls. Two are of particular importance to those concerned with foreign affairs organization. The first is the danger that concentrating on what happens within the executive branch may lead to neglect of the broader national politics of foreign policy-making. The second is the emphasis which analysts of bureaucratic politics have tended to give to certain types of bureaucratic motivation, and the danger that this might blind one to other types of behavior of considerable importance to organizational reformers. [...]

But concentrating on the bureaucracy can be misleading. For though career bureaucrats may deal largely with others within the government, Presidents and Cabinet members must operate in a wider arena. In particular, if our foreign policy goals and means cease to have broad general support in the larger society, the opportunities and channels for outside influence multiply. The President and his top officials must then become effective persuaders in this broader public arena or see important elements of policy slip from their grasp. Thus President Nixon, relatively successful in taming the foreign affairs bureaucracy on the major issues, has suffered far stronger Congressional challenges on national security matters than any predecessor since the pre-war Roosevelt.

Hilsman offers a useful compromise, one that allows concentration on the executive branch while taking broader influences into account. He describes the policy-making arena as a number of 'concentric rings', with the 'innermost circles' being entirely within the executive branch. It makes sense for a study of foreign affairs organization to concentrate on these 'innermost circles', analyzing organizational reforms and strategies heavily in terms of their impact on intra-executive branch decision-making. But it is important not to forget that the politics of the federal bureaucracy is, in the words of one authority, a 'subsystem of the American political system' as a whole.[7]

PROBLEMS OF INTEREST AND MOTIVATION

A more complicated problem for those applying the bureaucratic politics approach, however, is the question of the interests and motivations of individuals and their organizations.

Politics is often characterized as the interplay of individual and group interests. Yet it is not by accident that nowhere in our description of the fundamentals of bureaucratic politics is the question of individual interest directly discussed, except as it relates to players' perspectives and their needs for effectiveness. Due to the limits of rational analysis and the impact of particular perspectives, bureaucratic politics is a logical outgrowth of the nature of government and foreign policy even if the only interest of each official is to do his own job effectively. The bureaucratic politics view need not assume that officials are inordinately self-seeking, or committed only to the interests of their organizations. In fact, as noted by Schilling, Allison, and Hilsman, one considerable reason why battles are often so heated is that men have strong convictions about what the 'right policy' is.

When in the late 1950's, for example, intelligence officials leaked secret information foreshadowing an upcoming 'missile gap' to Democratic senators and sympathetic members of the press, it was not because they were disloyal, but because they were deeply convinced that the nation was in peril. They had tried and failed to convince the top levels of the Eisenhower administration of the validity of their projections, and they felt completely justified in taking matters into their own hands by going over the President's head to Congress, the press, and the public.[8]

But men do of course have more selfish interests as well. They may seek power for its own sake, or financial reward, or prestige, or personal advancement, or a larger role for their agency programs. Sometimes they pursue these goals unabashedly, recognizing them as self-interest. More often, probably, they grow to equate the importance of their function and the strength of their organization with the broader national interest and welfare. Admirals are generally sincere when they urge a stronger navy as vital to America's security. Foreign Service officers genuinely believe that the nation benefits when the great majority of Ambassadorships are filled from their ranks.

However, because analysts of bureaucratic politics are concerned primarily with explaining what influences foreign policy, they tend to portray officials who actively seek to affect that policy and strive to build up their bargaining advantages in order to accomplish this aim. Such officials are aggressive about getting involved in issues which relate to their responsibilities. They tend to see this relationship broadly, jumping into matters well beyond those where they have primary action responsibility.

But often men seek not to plunge aggressively into what others see as none of their business, but rather to draw lines separating their jurisdictions so as to minimize conflict. After all, classical economic theorists usually placed more value on competition than business practitioners. The latter often sought protection and security from the buffeting of market forces. Similarly, many officials seek not to expand the range of their jobs but to cut them down to manageable size. Secretary Rusk put the problem succinctly in 1963: 'There are those who think that the heart of a bureaucracy is a struggle for power. This is not the case at all. The heart of the bureaucratic problem is the inclination to avoid responsibility.'[9]

And in contrast to the 'serious bureaucrat' which bureaucratic politics descriptions tend to emphasize, there is that opposite stereotype – of the man who takes refuge in nit-picking rules, refuses to give a straight answer or make a clear decision, lives in a world rather narrowly bounded by his own particular agency and program, and reserves his greatest interest for the annual unveiling of the new government pay scale. His behavior might be described as a flight from bureaucratic politics.

There is, of course, no reason why the foreign affairs government cannot be thought of as a political system without assuming that all participants are equally power-oriented or politically motivated. We certainly think this way about our larger national political system, and our citizens show a wide variance in political interest and effectiveness. But to balance and deepen the basic picture developed so far, it is useful to highlight two important ways in which men tend to be more concerned with protecting the inner life and existence of their organizations than with building broader policy influence. One is the tendency of organizations to develop their own subcultures. The second is the tendency to give priority to a parochial piece of policy 'territory'.

ORGANIZATIONAL SUBCULTURES

Many men spend the major part of their working lives in one large government organization or career service. How they relate to those inside the organization may well become more important to both their psychic well-being and their personal advancement than how they relate to those outside. It is not surprising, then, that organizations develop their own informal subcultures, which – like the broader national culture within which they develop – both prescribe certain patterns of belief and behavior and penalize those who do not conform to them.

Probably the most important example of this phenomenon in the international affairs bureaucracy is the State Department's Foreign Service. In a notable effort to describe this subculture, Andrew Scott argues that most Foreign Service officers share an 'ideology' composed of various 'prevalent beliefs' which are 'perfectly plausible' but, like those in most ideologies, contain 'a mix of truths, half-truths, and errors'. A typical belief is that 'the really important aspects of the foreign affairs of the United States are the political ones – the traditional ones of negotiation, representation, and reporting'. One critically important aspect of this ideology, Scott holds, is the 'extent to which it encourages officers to become inward-looking and absorbed in the affairs of the Service'.[10] [...]

PAROCHIALISM AND JURISDICTIONS

Organizations, like individuals, have parochial perspectives and priorities. Anthony Downs has developed the concept of 'territoriality', suggesting that bureaucracies – like animals and nations – tend to 'stake out and defend territories surrounding their nests or "home bases"'. Certain parts of 'policy space' comprise a bureau's *heartland*, where it is sole determinant of policy; surrounding this will be the *interior fringe*, where the bureau's interest is primary but where other agencies have some influence. Outside of this is *no-man's land*, where no bureau dominates but many have influence.

Territorial boundaries are never absolutely clear; 'the inherent dynamism of human life' prevents jurisdictional lines from ever reaching an equilibrium. Because policy issues often cut across any possible allocation of jurisdictions, 'Every large organization is in partial conflict with every other social agent with which it deals.' But 'the basic nature of all such struggles is the same – each combatant needs to establish a large enough territory to guarantee his own survival'.[11]

The last quotation hints at a broader phenomenon. For, contrary to what certain elements of the bureaucratic politics view might lead one to assume, organizations tend to choose clear primary responsibility for a narrow policy area over the opportunities and dangers inherent in contesting for influence across a broader policy range. They will give primacy to fortifying the heartland. Members of the Joint Chiefs of Staff do not go out of their way to challenge the pet proposals of other services – rather, they trade support of these for reciprocal support of their own services' priorities. Foreign Service officers seldom make hard-nosed challenges of military tactics. They prefer to confine their involvement to the 'political' aspects, and hope the military will reciprocate by staying out of 'diplomacy'. [...]

IMPLICATIONS FOR FOREIGN POLICY-MAKING

The nature of the bureaucratic political process seems to contradict almost the very notion of our government even pretending to make coherent, purposive foreign policy. And further investigation does nothing to brighten the picture. In fact, when one draws on other analyses of organizational behavior, the problems become even more complex, and even less susceptible to clear-cut reform.

'Pluralists' describing the politics of domestic policy-making have sometimes gone beyond *description* to *prescription*, to asserting 'confidence in the capability of the political process to produce the right results'.[12] Such faith in political competition finds its parallel in Adam Smith's notion of the 'invisible hand', a guiding principle whereby the sum of economic actions taken by individuals for their own selfish purposes would lead to the best possible outcome for society as a whole. But is the outcome of the *internal* competition of bureaucratic politics the kind of policy that will be successful in dealing with a troubled *outside* world?

Huntington feels he can answer this question with 'qualified optimism'. He sees one major virtue as stability: 'the forces of pluralism correct and counterbalance the instabilities, enthusiasms, and irrationalities of the prevailing mood'. Hilsman carries such optimism a step further. 'In spite of the untidiness and turmoil of the politics of policy-making in Washington', he writes,

> such an open process of conflict and consensus-building, debate, assessment, and mutual adjustment and accommodation can be solidly effective in the assessment of broad policy alternatives if the conditions are right. The conditions are, first, that the subject is one on which the competing groups are knowledgeable. Second, both the participating constituencies within the government and the 'attentive publics' outside must be well informed. Third, all levels of government, those who will carry out the policy as well as those who decide it, must be responsive to the decision and persuaded by it. Under these conditions, the chances are good that the policy will be wise, that the effort and sacrifice required will be forthcoming, and that the work of carrying out the policy will go forward intelligently and energetically.[13]

But without denying that wise policy may emerge 'if the conditions are right', it seems doubtful that the results will always, or even usually, be so reassuring. The central danger is inherent in the notion of policy emerging from bureaucratic competition, responsive more to the internal dynamics of our decision-making process than to the external problems on which it is supposed to center. As Schilling has noted, the bureaucratic political process can produce 'no policy at all', stalemate; 'compromised policy', with the direction hardly evident; or 'unstable policy', where 'changes in the *ad hoc* groupings of elites point policy first in one and then in another direction'. It can result in 'contradictory policy', where different government organizations pursue conflicting courses; 'paper policy', officially promulgated without the support needed for effective implementation; or 'slow' policy, since competition and consensus-building take time.[14]

Moreover, just to influence policy, officials need to apply inordinate attention to internal conflict, thereby limiting the time they can focus on the overseas situation toward which policy is ostensibly directed. As Stanley Hoffmann has noted, 'There inevitably occurs a subtle (or not so subtle) shift from the specific foreign-policy issues to be resolved, to the positions, claims, and perspectives of the participants in the policy machine. The demands of the issue and the merits of alternative choices are subordinated to the demands of the machine and the needs to keep it going. Administrative politics replaces foreign policy.'[15]

The troubling logic of policy-making by bureaucratic politics is taken one step further by Halperin. He depicts bureaucrats who are so deeply engrossed in intra-governmental maneuvering that the actions which result are seldom clear signals to other countries. Foreign bureaucrats in turn receive and interpret these signals selectively since they are looking for evidence to support them in their own internal bureaucratic battles. Thus 'communications' between nations tend to become dialogues between the largely deaf and dumb. Similarly, Neustadt's analysis of the Suez and Skybolt crises in *Alliance Politics* emphasizes how American and British officials concentrating on their own intra-governmental games regularly misinterpreted the motives and constraints of their allied counterparts.

Furthermore, if bureaucratic politics causes officials to shift their focus from substantive policy issues to 'the positions, claims, and perspectives of the participants in the policy machine', organizational subcultures can cause a further shift, turning men away from the inter-agency bureaucratic competition and toward concern primarily with relationships within their own organizations. This can lead to strikingly inappropriate, unresponsive behavior in relation to those outside the organization.

RESISTANCE TO CHANGE

If the inward-looking nature of the bureaucratic political process seems its most dangerous fault, it is hardly its only one. A closely related problem is the bias against change. Superficially one might expect the opposite. Classical economists thought that competition would cause a steady surge of new ideas, from men seeking the rewards that would come from 'building a better mousetrap'. More recently economists have had doubts, noting that industries which most closely approximated the free enterprise model of many competitive firms (like housing construction) tend to be particularly backward in developing new techniques.

Bureaucratic politics seems to bias policy outcomes against change for not dissimilar reasons. A small businessman cannot afford to innovate because the rewards are uncertain and delayed and because he must survive in today's market. Similarly the bureaucrat seeks effectiveness in today's government, and this generally means moving with prevailing policy tides rather than challenging them. As Roger Fisher writes, a Washington official seeking a quick response to an overseas problem knows that 'if the cable can be worded so that it is simply an application of a prior decision or a prior statement by the President or another high official, the cable will be more difficult for others to object to, it can be cleared at a low level, and it can be dispatched more quickly'.[16]

More generally, the problem is what Schilling has called the 'gyroscopic' effect. Policies once adopted tend to become self-perpetuating because, in Henry Kissinger's words, 'An attempt to change course involves the prospect that the whole searing process of arriving at a decision will have to be repeated.' [...]

Resistance to change also arises from certain inherent problems of large organizations. One is the need for routines to structure an organization's response to particular events. To make possible coordinated and effective action by large numbers of people, organizations devise standard operating procedures or programs prescribing the roles of individuals and units in dealing with recurring events or predictable threats. Such 'routines' can range from the standard procedures for processing and funding of technical assistance requests to contingency plans to cope with a Soviet ground invasion of Western Europe. An organization can have only a limited number of such routines in its repertoire; these constitute the organization's coordinated action capabilities at any one time. They are also difficult and time-consuming to change. Those for dealing with crises are necessarily 'precooked', plans devised in advance for contingencies as defined by the organization. When an actual event comes, the organization can only respond to it by doing what it has already established procedures for doing. [...]

RESISTANCE TO CONTROL

In the end, all of these problems are part of the largest one of all. Running through both our criticism of traditional approaches and our discussion of bureaucratic politics is a common theme – the limits of high officials' control over what the foreign affairs government is doing. Some writers have suggested the problem is insoluble. Gordon Tullock, for example, argues that distortions in the flow of communications, information, and orders up and down the hierarchy lead after a certain point to 'bureaucratic free enterprise', with activities by bureaucrats on the firing line essentially unrelated to what bosses want. Others, like Downs, are more moderate, but still argue that 'no one can fully control the behavior of a large organization', and that 'the larger any organization becomes, the weaker is the control over its actions exercised by those at the top'.[17]

IMPLICATIONS FOR ORGANIZATIONAL REFORM

The implications of all this for those who seek to organize for purposive and coherent foreign policy are obvious and unfavorable. The system as it seems to operate directs men's attention more to intra-governmental matters than to the overseas situations policy must influence; clings to old policies because of the difficulty of changing them; and resists efforts to control it from the top. Though competition may sometimes have positive effects, there is no reason to believe that these will be the rule rather than the exception. And if bureaucratic politics turns men's energies inward from the substantive policy problem to the bureaucratic political one, organizational subcultures can narrow attention still further, encouraging a flight from inter-agency bureaucratic politics to an emphasis on intra-agency relationships.

The danger which the existing system poses for coherent and purposive foreign policy may explain the allure of the sorts of reform proposals which have been recurrent in the post-war period. One is tempted to urge that policy-making be 'rationalized', or authority be joined to responsibility. Yet politics and large organizations are not evils to be exorcized by the proper mix of admonition and formal restructuring, but basic, persistent 'facts of life'. The reformer faces a world, to borrow two of Neustadt's characterizations, of 'intractable substantive problems and immovable bureaucratic structures', of 'emergencies in policy with politics as usual'.[18] And he must extend to the entire government Neustadt's depiction of a President who feels the urgent need for wise policy but recognizes that our arrival at such policy is anything but automatic.

For if there is no reason to deny the perils of bureaucratic politics, no more can one ignore its pervasiveness. So the organizational reformer must begin by dealing with the government as it is, not as he

I.M. Destler

would like it to be. The bureaucratic political view is particularly valuable because it forces attention to leverage. If, for example, one proposes to increase policy coherence by establishing a new central official, it makes sense to ask first whether he can achieve the leverage, the 'bargaining advantages' to make his role effective. But one must ask whether the person being placed in such a position will be one with, in Rusk's words, 'the inclination to avoid responsibility'. For giving a man all of the bargaining advantages in the world is of little use if he will not use them. Interestingly, then, part of organizational reform inevitably involves not the banishment of 'politics' from decision-making, but rather an effort to ensure that officials upon whom one's strategy depends can play the game effectively.

NOTES

1 Roger Hilsman, 'The Foreign-Policy Consensus: An Interim Research Report', *Journal of Conflict Resolution* (December 1959), p. 365.
2 Graham T. Allison, 'Conceptual Models and the Cuban Missile Crisis', *American Political Science Review* (September 1969), p. 706; R. Hilsman, *To Move a Nation* (Doubleday, 1967), p. 7.
3 US Senate Committee on Government Operations, Subcommittee on National Policy Machinery, *Organizing for National Security*, vol. 1 (1961), p. 15.
4 Morton H. Halperin, 'The Decision to Deploy the ABM: Bureaucratic Politics in the Pentagon and White House in the Johnson Administration' (prepared for delivery at the 66th Annual Meeting of the American Political Science Association, Los Angeles, California, 8–12 September 1970), p. 8.
5 Allison, 'Conceptual Models', p. 707.
6 Hilsman, *To Move a Nation*, p. 5; C.E. Lindblom, *The Intelligence of Democracy* (Free Press, 1965), ch. 9.
7 Hilsman, *To Move a Nation*, pp. 541–3; Alan A. Altschuler, *The Politics of the Federal Bureaucracy* (Dodd, Mead and Company, 1968), p. v.
8 Hilsman, *To Move a Nation*, p. 10.
9 US Senate Committee on Government Operations, Subcommittee on National Security Staffing and Operations, *Administration of National Security*, Staff Reports and Hearings (1965), p. 403.
10 Andrew M. Scott, 'The Department of State: Formal Organization and Informal Culture', *International Studies Quarterly* (March 1969), pp. 2–5; 'Environmental Change and Organizational Adaptation: The Problem of the State Department', *International Studies Quarterly* (March 1970), p. 87.
11 Anthony Downs, *Inside Bureaucracy* (Little Brown and Company, 1967), pp. 212–16.
12 Allen Schick, 'Systems Politics and Systems Budgeting', *Public Administration Review* (March/April 1969), p. 142.
13 Samuel P. Huntington, *The Common Defense* (Columbia University

Press, 1961), p. 446; Hilsman, *To Move a Nation,* p. 549.
14 Warner R. Schilling, 'The Politics of National Defense: Fiscal 1950', in
    Warner R. Schilling, Paul F. Hammond and Glenn H. Snyder, *Strategy,
    Politics and Defense Budgets* (Columbia University Press, 1962), pp. 25,
    26, 218–22.
15 Stanley Hoffmann, *Gulliver's Troubles, or the Setting of American
    Foreign Policy* (McGraw-Hill, for the Council on Foreign Relations,
    1968), p. 177.
16 Roger Fisher, *International Conflict for Beginners* (Harper and Row,
    1969), p. 180.
17 Gordon Tullock, *The Politics of Bureaucracy* (Public Affairs Press,
    1965), pp. 167–70; Downs, *Inside Bureaucracy,* p. 262.
18 Richard E. Neustadt, 'Staffing the Presidency', in Altschuler, *Politics of
    the Bureaucracy,* p. 120; *Presidential Power* (Signet, 1960), p. 17.

2.5 'Foreign' policies of US publics

Chadwick F. Alger

Source: *International Studies Quarterly*, vol. 21, no. 2 (International Studies Association/Sage, 1977), pp. 277–93.

To help American citizens to understand the link between their lives and events and processes in the world outside, Alger suggests that it is necessary to break down the view of states as interacting billiard balls that has dominated scholarly writings and everyday thinking. He offers six stages for differentiating the nation-state which serve to extend the image of a plurality of interests from the arena of domestic policy into that of foreign policy. He ends by suggesting that this breaking up of the state opens up the path for international partici- pation by the individual.

AN UNDIFFERENTIATED NATION-STATE VIEW

A useful starting point for our consideration of successive stages of analytic differentiation of foreign policy processes is Figure 1. It portrays nations as a set of interacting 'billiard balls'. It presumes that relations between nation-states are largely determined by basic characteristics, such as resources, technology, and population. This image of the world implies that a nation-state has a hard shell that separates it from the rest of the world. This view is reinforced by political maps, and it facilitates the expectation that foreign policy is a single thing that ought to be controlled by one person or one group. But if people involved in a diversity of national and international activities are to be able to develop an efficacious participatory relationship with international processes, they require images of inter- national processes that link them to these processes.

Figure 1 Undifferentiated nation-state view of international relations

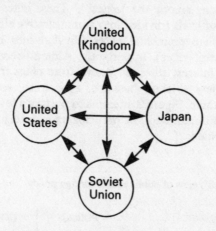

STAGES OF NATION-STATE DIFFERENTIATION

The internal society

Gabriel Almond, writing in 1950, provided a classic differentiation of the internal domain. His seminal work, *The American People and Foreign Policy*, did for foreign policy what Wilson's *Congressional Government* had done for the legislative process. Almond laid bare the difference between expectations based on democratic norms and the ways in which foreign policy is formulated in the United States:

> There are inherent limitations in modern society on the capacity of the public to understand the issues and grasp the significance of the most important problems of public policy. This is particularly the case with foreign policy where the issues are especially *complex* and *remote*. The function of the public in a democratic policy-making process is to set certain policy criteria in the form of widely held values and expectations. It evaluates the results of policies from the point of view of their conformity to these basic values and expectations. The policies themselves, however, are the products of leadership groups ('elites') who carry on the specific work of policy formulation and policy advocacy.[1] (emphasis added)

Almond observed that the 'general public' was only occasionally concerned about foreign affairs. More sustained interest comes from the 'attentive public' which 'is informed and interested in foreign policy problems, and which constitutes the audience for the foreign policy discussions among the "elites"'.[2] These elites consist of both governmental officials (divided into administrative elites and political elites) and nongovernmental elites (divided into communications elites and interest elites). Importantly, Almond recognizes that the foreign policy interest elites are drawn from elites from a variety of sectors of society – labor, business, agriculture, veterans, women, religion, and ethnic. Figure 2 attempts to portray a few critical aspects of Almond's differentiation of participants in foreign policy-making in the United States. [...]

Figure 2 Almond's view of public role in foreign policy

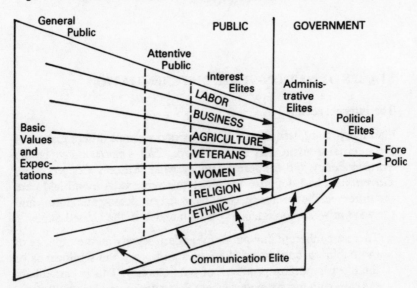

Note: This figure, based on Almond's discussion, was drawn by the author of this paper.

The national government

A second development in foreign policy analysis has been differentiation of the national governmental participants in international relations. Writing in 1959, Wolfers provided a graphic dissent from the custom of treating national governments as single actors:

Some democratic states have exhibited such pluralistic tendencies that they offer to the world a picture of near-anarchy. They seem to speak to the world with many and conflicting voices and to act as if one hand – agency or faction – does not know what the other hand is doing.... [In] some ... new states ... integration is so poor that other states must deal with parts, rather than with a fictitious whole, if diplomacy is to be effective.[3]

Evolving tendencies to consider national governments as pluralistic actors are represented by Deutsch's discussion of 'linkage groups',[4] Rosenau's delineation of 'issue areas',[5] and his work on 'linkage politics'.[6] While the analytic perspectives developed under these labels are not limited to governmental actors, it is this aspect of this work that is relevant at this point in our discussion. Figure 3 portrays the differentiation contributed by this perspective.

Figure 3 Linkage group or issue area view of intergovernmental relations

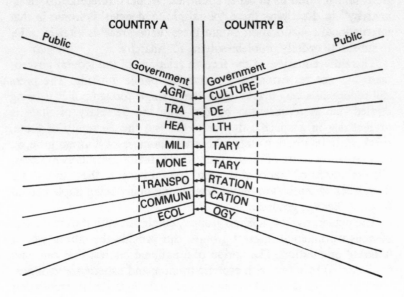

As changes in technology and communication have extended the boundaries of human enterprises, responsible officials in national governments increasingly find that problems like ecology and energy

can only be attacked in collaboration with counterparts in other countries. This was dramatized when the Nixon Administration's 'Project Independence' was followed shortly by an effort to set up an International Energy Agency in the context of OECD. Recent UN conferences and other related international collaboration on food, natural resources, population, and environment underline the development of 'linkage groups' in specific 'issue areas'. In many cases the contact among national 'linkage groups' is virtually continuous, such as in the context of the specialized agencies of the UN system. A total of some 200 permanent organizations link national governments in collaboration on fisheries, wheat, coffee, oil, tin, and the like.

A diversity of 'linkage groups' in the US government are simultaneously pursuing the interest of their group and that of their public clientele in the United States. These groups sometimes act at crosspurposes; the diversity of interests pursued by such groups belies the myth of *a* national interest. More correctly, a diversity of interests to be found within the boundaries of the United States are increasingly finding that they cannot effectively pursue their interests in isolation from similar interests in other countries. Wolfers' reference to 'nearanarchy'[7] in describing these 'pluralistic tendencies' is ironic in that international collaboration within these 'issue areas' is vital in order to substitute orderly problem-solving for anarchy.

This differentiation of the foreign relations of the federal government has not yet extensively permeated public thinking. The press still reports in a way that suggests that a single foreign policy is being carried out as represented by the issue the Secretary of State is dramatizing in a specific day or week. But the Secretary of State, particularly in a nation-state with a vast number of 'linkage groups', only perceives some of these groups and actually controls even fewer. His definitions of 'national interest' (plural because they, too, differ from week to week) are only a few among many being implemented by these 'linkage groups'.

The perspective of 'linkage groups', combined with differentiation of nongovernmental interest groups, can provide the citizen with a different orientation. The notion of a national interest that can only be discerned by a few with esoteric training and experience vanishes. Taking the mysticism out of foreign policy through the differentiation of 'issue areas' does not mean that the problems to be faced are simple. However, people who feel competent enough to become involved in domestic issues become more aware of ways to participate in their international dimension. This perspective also suggests that those who attempt to affect governmental policy on a significant domestic issue are likely not to be effective unless they are attentive to the international dimensions of these issues.

Impact of nongovernmental international relations on government foreign policies

The analytic differentiation of nongovernmental international relations provides an extended public with a critical analytic tool to facilitate their perception and interpretation of their own actual and potential links to international social and economic processes. 'Transnational relations' is a term which has come into use to refer to the international relations of nongovernmental organizations. Angell analyzes the role of migration, visiting of relatives and friends abroad, service in the Peace Corps, studying and research abroad, technical assistance missions, religious missions, business missions, and participation in international nongovernmental organizations.[8] Keohane and Nye include many of these and add foundations, revolutionary organizations, airlines, labor, space, and nuclear energy.[9]

Angell as well as Keohane and Nye are primarily concerned with the ways in which transnational relations have an impact on the policies of national governments, the third analytic distinction to be treated in this paper. Several mechanisms for this impact are discerned: changed attitudes of those who participate in transnational relations,[10] the development of transnational interest groups, and dependence of governments on services provided by transnational activities (e.g. travel and communications). Figure 4 illustrates the impact of transnational activity on national governments.

The transnational perspective challenges the widespread assumption that all roads to influence on international affairs lead directly to Washington! The domestic or foreign national government may be more effectively reached through an international nongovernmental organization. Furthermore, participation in these activities provides experience and socialization that would be very difficult to replicate through courses in schools or domestic activity alone.

Impact of governments on nongovernmental international relations

Keohane and Nye offer a fourth perspective that is the reverse of the third. National governments sometimes use transnational relations in order to increase their influence on other national governments and other societies. For example, in the mid-1960s the United States attempted to retard the development of France's nuclear capability by

Figure 4 Impact of transnational relations on government foreign policy

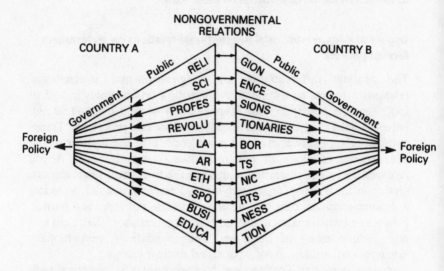

forbidding IBM-France to sell certain types of computers to the French government.[11] The CIA has infiltrated a variety of transnational activities (press, business). Because governmental funds are often provided for overseas private philanthropic activity (e.g. surplus food and equipment), the US government often has considerable influence on the distribution of these materials. A figure similar to Figure 4 could be drawn to illustrate the influence which flows from government A through transnational relations to affect the foreign policy of government B.

It is quite customary for private citizens involved in international activity to accede to the request of their national government for assistance and support – in the 'national interest'. Yet governmental collaboration has often engendered suspicion of nongovernmental international activity and diverted it from its own goals. As citizens involved in these activities become increasingly sensitized to the diversity of interests that are served by the foreign activities of governments, they may examine specific governmental activities more carefully before they participate.

Foreign policies of nongovernmental sectors

The fifth perspective does not view nongovernmental international activity as something that is either intended to affect governmental

Figure 5 Foreign policies of nongovernmental sectors

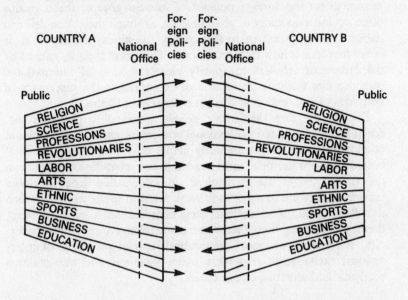

policy or to be used by it for its interests, but as activity that has its own goals. This kind of transnational activity has been most widely recognized in the activities of multinational corporations. Otherwise, it is given only slight attention in the transnational literature, and it is very difficult to enable most people to see this as a distinct foreign policy option. Keohane and Nye recognize the presence of 'autonomous or quasiautonomous *actors* in world politics',[12] with chapters on revolutionary movements, trade unions, multinational business enterprises, and the Roman Catholic Church. But their interest is primarily focused on the interplay between governmental and nongovernmental forces, although their volume includes descriptive material on how nongovernmental interests achieve goals through transnational activity without governmental involvement.

Figure 5 portrays the foreign policies of diverse sectors of the publics of two countries. Interest elites are largely responsible for defining these policies and implementing them in relations with counterparts from other countries. Governments are left out of this figure to signify that interest elites do develop and carry out foreign policies that are intended neither to fulfill governmental policy not to influence it. For example, much humanitarian activity of churches fulfills policy that is based on humanitarian aspects of church doctrine. The figure is not intended to suggest that governments cannot affect the foreign policies of interest groups; these groups often act independently of governments, although they often defer to national governments in foreign policy questions because of their belief that 'this is how things are done'. This belief is partly caused by the failure of scholars to specify clearly models of international relations that facilitate perception of exceptions to the supremacy of national governments over foreign policy (as in Figure 5).

Despite the fact that many people involved in philanthropic, scientific, religious, and professional activity frequently cross national boundaries, most are customarily active only within their national boundaries. For example, most academic and scientific associations in the United States are dependent on information from a global network if they are to make their work relevant to the world in which it will be used. Nevertheless, they organize on a national basis, thereby socializing their members into a relatively provincial fraternity. It becomes necessary to establish special programs of international exchange to resocialize a few members into transnational academic and scientific communities.

Implementation of foreign policies through international organizations

The sixth step in analytic differentiation of foreign policy analysis has been stimulated by increasing attention to the 200 international governmental organizations (IGOs) and 2,700 international non-governmental organizations (INGOs), reflecting virtually all the pursuits of humankind, from athletics to zoology. The public at large is only cognizant of a very few of the IGOs, such as the UN and NATO, and only a small number of INGOs, such as the Red Cross and the Olympics. Most members of national organizations have little knowledge, if any, about the international extensions of these associations, because relationships with international bodies are usually carried out by officials in the national office of these associations. Thus, the nation-state model tends to be replicated in nongovernmental international relations. Nongovernmental organizations (NGOs) within nations tend to have a 'national capital' with a 'foreign office' of specialists in the international relations of the association. Local, state, and regional leaders tend to defer to the national office on international issues. One reason that INGOs tend to mirror the nation-state system and thereby reinforce it is that strong national organizations are required if nongovernmental interests are to influence national governments. But it is also because of rote repetition of the nation-state model displayed by national governments.

As national governments have created an increasing number of IGOs to handle common problems, national nongovernmental organizations have followed suit. An increasing number of important issues are being debated in IGOs, such as recent UN conferences on food, population, environment, and the law of the sea, and national organizations in different countries are drawn into collaborative relationships to counter the influence of coalitions of national governments. Certain sectors of labor and of consumers are recognizing that transnational organizations may be required to compete with the transnational activities of business firms and banks.

Figure 6 portrays (for country A) the implementation of foreign policies by nongovernmental groups in one sector, education. Educational nongovernmental organizations from a number of countries come together (left side of figure) in INGOs, such as the International Association of Universities, the Council on International Educational Exchange, and the Association of Arab Universities, to achieve common goals. Educational sectors of national governments do likewise (right side of figure), in organizations such as UNESCO, the Southeast Asian Ministers of Education Organization, and the Central American Office of Education Planning. Efforts are made to influence the educational policies of IGOs in the direction of common policies developed in educational INGOs. Both INGOs and IGOs may also attempt to affect the educational policies of national governments and national nongovernmental organizations directly.

Figure 6 Implementation of foreign policies of nongovernmental sectors through international organizations

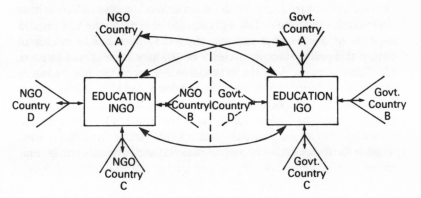

A critical value of analytic differentiation in foreign relations is the diversified strategy it suggests to the citizen interested in understanding and perhaps eventually having some control over the international social and economic processes that impinge on his everyday life. Explication of the various sectors of governmental foreign affairs helps him to pinpoint his efforts to affect governmental policies. But he may also think about participating directly in bilateral and multilateral foreign relations – both as a means for affecting the policies of his national government and other national governments and as a way to achieve international goals directly.

[Alger goes on to differentiate the state still further by looking at the link between cities in different countries and the role of individuals, organizations and sectors of the community within them. He urges an end to the myth of the division between local and international issues and offers a roadmap for the individual to participate in international affairs.]

As the citizen searches for the relevant unit for a specific problem, she might have a mental picture of options something like Figure 7. She can participate through international organizations, national organizations, state (or regional) organizations, and city organizations, or she may choose direct individual activity. With respect to any of the four territorial units, she may choose to (1) influence government directly, (2) work through a nongovernmental organization to influence government, or (3) work through a nongovernmental organization to have direct international impact. This roadmap offers the citizen 13 avenues for international participation.

International (11, 12, 13)   Those people who tax themselves 1 per cent of their annual income and send it directly to the UN Secretary General use route 13. They do this because of dissatisfaction that their country contributes less a percentage of GNP to the UN than 45 per cent of the member nations. Since they have not been able to change this policy through routes 9 or 10, they have shifted to route 13. Those who support the International League for the Rights of Man in its lobbying efforts for human rights at the United Nations are using route 12. People who work for the rights of political prisoners through Amnesty International often use route 11, attempting to influence policies of national governments (other than their own) through the direct action of an international nongovernmental organization.

Figure 7 Routes to international participation

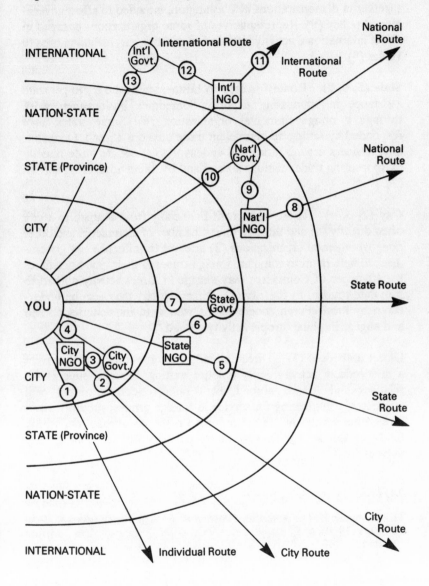

National (8, 9, 10) These are the routes most perceived and used by US citizens. Public activity against the Vietnam war used all of these routes. There were efforts to affect the national government directly (10) through letters and personal pleas to officials. A number of nongovernmental organizations, as well as individuals, joined together in demonstrations in Washington, intended to affect governmental policy (9). Representatives of some organizations engaged in direct international activity intended to end the war, including trips to Hanoi (8).

State (5, 6, 7)   Route 7 is used by businessmen who try to get state assistance in stimulating exports. Sometimes businessmen work through a nongovernmental organization (6). Some states have responded by setting up permanent trade missions abroad. Occasionally, business organizations will endeavor to stimulate trade directly by sponsoring trade missions abroad and by direct advertising abroad (7).

City (2, 3, 4)   Those who profit financially from tourism in a city often directly (4) and through their Chamber of Commerce and other nongovernmental organizations (3) attempt to influence city government to help them to stimulate foreign travel to their city. Sometimes the Chamber of Commerce may engage in direct activity abroad to stimulate tourism to the city (2). Direct activity may also be undertaken by local church congregations who send missionaries abroad and engage in philanthropic activity abroad.

Direct individual (1)   Direct individual international activity covers a multitude of activity, such as letter writing, financial support for relatives and friends abroad, ham radio operators, direct mail purchases, volunteering for service in foreign armies, subscription to foreign magazines and direct purchase of books abroad, depositing funds in foreign banks, and direct participation in revolutionary movements.

NOTES

1   G. Almond, *The American People and Foreign Policy* (Praeger, New York, 1950), p. 5.
2   Ibid., p. 138.
3   A. Wolfers, 'The Actors in International Politics', in W.T. Fox (ed.), *Theoretical Aspects of International Relations* (University of Notre Dame Press, Notre Dame, In., 1959), p. 102.
4   K. Deutsch, 'External Influences on the International Behaviour of States', in R.B. Farrell (ed.), *Approaches to Comparative and International Politics* (Northwestern University Press, Evanston, Ill., 1966), pp. 5–26.

5 J.N. Rosenau, 'Pre-theories and Theories of Foreign Policy', in R.B. Farrell (ed.), *Approaches to Comparative and International Politics* (Northwestern University Press, Evanston, Ill., 1966), pp. 167–208.
6 J.N. Rosenau (ed.), *Linkage Politics* (Free Press, New York, 1969).
7 Wolfers, 'The Actors in International Politics'.
8 R. Angell, *Peace on the March* (Van Nostrand, New York, 1969).
9 R.O. Keohane and J.S. Nye (eds), 'Transnational Relations and World Politics', *International Organization*, 25 (Summer 1971), entire issue.
10 Angell, *Peace on the March.*
11 Keohane and Nye, 'Transnational Relations', p. 341.
12 Ibid.

2.6 Transnational organizations in world politics

Samuel P. Huntington

Source: *World Politics*, vol. XXV (Princeton University Press, Princeton, April 1973), pp. 333–68.

Huntington's aim is to analyze the roots and extent of the 'transnational organizational revolution' in world politics. He begins by assessing the political and other origins of transnational organizations – especially in terms of their links to American political dominance. He goes on to analyze the connections between transnational bodies and national societies, and particularly their requirements for access to those societies. Here, he poses a contrast with intergovernmental bodies, which typically require accord between states as a basis for their operations.

THE TRANSNATIONAL ORGANIZATIONAL REVOLUTION

Anaconda	J. Walter Thompson	Ford Foundation
Intelsat	Air France	Catholic Church
Chase Manhattan	Strategic Air Command	CIA
AID	Unilever	World Bank

These twelve organizations appear to have little in common. They are public and private, national and international, profit-making and charitable, religious and secular, civil and military, and, depending on one's perspective, benign and nefarious. Yet they do share three characteristics. First, each is a relatively large, hierarchically organized, centrally directed bureaucracy. Second, each performs a set of relatively limited, specialized, and, in some sense, technical functions: gathering intelligence, investing money, transmitting messages, promoting sales, producing copper, delivering bombs, saving souls. Third, each organization performs its functions across one or more international boundaries and, insofar as is possible, in relative disregard of those boundaries. They are, in short, *transnational organizations*, and the activities in which they engage are *trans-*

national operations. Such organizations have existed before in history. Armies and navies, churches and joint stock companies, as well as other types of organizations have been involved in transnational operations in the past. During the twenty-five years after World War II, however, transnational organizations: (a) proliferated in number far beyond anything remotely existing in the past; (b) individually grew in size far beyond anything existing in the past; (c) performed functions which they never performed in the past; and (d) operated on a truly global scale such as was never possible in the past. The increase in the number, size, scope, and variety of transnational organizations after World War II makes it possible, useful, and sensible to speak of a *transnational organizational revolution* in world politics. The purpose of this essay is to analyze, in a preliminary way, the sources, nature, and dynamics of this revolution, and to speculate on its implications for politics at the national and international levels. [...]

The terms 'international', 'multinational', and 'transnational' have been variously used to refer to the control of an organization, the composition of its staff, and the scope of its operations. Terminological confusion is further compounded because one word, 'national', serves as the opposite of each of these three terms. To minimize ambiguity, at least on these pages, and to maintain some critical distinctions, each of these terms will in this essay be used to refer to only one of these organizational dimensions. An organization is 'transnational' rather than 'national' if it carries on significantly centrally-directed operations in the territory of two or more nation-states. Similarly, an organization will be called 'international' rather than 'national' only if the control of the organization is explicitly shared among representatives of two or more nationalities. And an organization is 'multinational' rather than 'national' only if people from two or more nationalities participate significantly in its operations. [...]

THE SIGNIFICANCE OF TRANSNATIONALISM

Nationalism, internationalism, and transnationalism have all been major factors on the contemporary world scene. At the end of World War II, observers of world politics expected nationalism to be a major force, and their expectations were not disappointed. The decline of Europe encouraged the blossoming forth of nationalist movements in Asia and Africa, and by the early 1960s colonialism in the classic familiar forms was virtually finished and scores of new nation-states had been formally recognized. The end of colonialism, however, did not mean the end of nationalism, in the sense of the behavioral and attitudinal manifestations by a people of their presumed ethnic or racial identity, nor the end of the political disruption of the newly independent nation-states. Colonialism led peoples of various ethnic or racial identities to suppress their antagonisms in order to win independence. The achievement of independence raised the question of *whose* independence had been achieved, and led to a re-awakening and, in some cases, a totally new awakening of communal antagonisms. Nationalism increasingly has meant 'subnationalism', and has thus become identified with political fragmentation. Nationalism has remained a force in world politics, but a force which promises almost as much disruption in a world of independent states as it did in a world of colonial empires.

At the close of World War II, internationalism was also expected to be a wave of the future, and the United Nations was created to embody that hope and to make it reality. While nationalism has remained strong but its impact has changed, internationalism, in contrast, has failed to gain the role and significance which it was expected to achieve. The great hopes for international organizations – that is, organizations whose activities involve the active cooperation of distinct national (private or public) delegations – have not been realized. In one form or another, internationalism involves agreement among nation-states. Interests have to be shared or to be traded for an international organization to work. This requirement puts an inherent limit on internationalism. The United Nations and other international organizations have remained relatively weak because they are inherently the arenas for national actors; the extent to which they can become independent actors themselves is dependent on agreement among national actors.

An international organization requires the identification and creation of a common interest among national groups. This common interest may be easy to identify, such as the exchange of mail. Or it may be the product of extensive and time-consuming negotiation among national units. A transnational organization, on the other hand, has its own interest which inheres in the organization and its functions, which may or may not be closely related to the interests of national groups. Nations participate in international organizations; transnational organizations operate within nations. International organizations are designed to facilitate the achievement of a common interest among many national units. Transnational organizations are designed to facilitate the pursuit of a single interest within many national units. The international organization requires *accord* among nations; the transnational organization requires *access* to nations. These two needs, accord and access, neatly summarize the differences between the two phenomena. The restraints on an international organization are largely internal, stemming from the need to produce consensus among its members. The restraints on a transnational organization are largely external, stemming from its need to gain operating authority in different sovereign states. International organizations embody the principle of nationality; transnational organizations try to ignore it. In this sense the emergence of transnational organizations on the world scene involves a pattern of cross-cutting cleavages and associations overlaying those associated with the nation-state.

The emergence of transnational organizations on such a large scale was, in large part, unanticipated. Internationalism was supposed to furnish the threads tying the world together. In actuality, however, every international organization at some point finds itself limited by the very principle which gives it being. Much of the disappointment with the UN and its various agencies stems precisely from the failure to recognize this fact. While national representatives and delegations engage in endless debate at UN conferences and councils, however, the agents of the transnational organizations are busily deployed across the continents spinning the webs that link the world together. The contrast between the two forms of organization can be seen in the difference between the great bulk of UN bodies which are basically international in character and thus dependent for action on agreement among national delegations, and one organization that is formally international in control and related to the UN but in practice quite autonomous, which operates successfully in a transnational manner. Perhaps significantly, that organization, the World Bank, is headquartered in Washington, not in New York.

A similar contrast exists between private transnational organizations and international non-governmental organizations (or INGOs). Like transnational organizations, INGOs multiplied rapidly in numbers and functions in the decades after World War II. Of the INGOs in existence in 1966, 50 per cent were founded after 1950 and 25 per cent were founded in 1960 or later. During these same years, however, the average size of the INGOs did not increase and, if anything, decreased. In 1964 the mean INGO budget was $629,000 and the mean INGO staff encompassed nine people. INGOs simply did not have the resources, scope, or influence of nationally controlled, transnational, non-governmental organizations such as the Ford Foundation, IBM, or Exxon.

Transnational organizations thus may, in theory, be nationally or internationally, privately or governmentally controlled. The need to reach agreement among national units, however, restricts the purposes and activities of international bodies. Free of this internal constraint, nationally controlled organizations are much better able to formulate purposes, to mobilize resources, and to pursue their objectives across international boundaries. [...]

A distinctive characteristic of the transnational organization is its broader-than-national perspective with respect to the pursuit of highly specialized objectives through a central optimizing strategy across national boundaries. The 'essence' of a transnational corporation, as Behrman has argued, 'is that it is attempting to treat the various national markets as though they were one – to the extent permitted by governments'.[1] In similar fashion, a transnational military organization treats the problems of defense of different national territories as if they were part of a single whole. For its specialized purpose, its arena assumes continental or global proportions and it thinks in continental or global terms. [...]

THE AMERICAN SOURCES OF TRANSNATIONALISM

The principal sources of the transnational organizational revolution are to be found in American society and in the global expansion of the United States during the two decades after World War II. This does not mean that transnational organizations and operations are only created by Americans. It does mean that the proliferation of transnational operations in recent years was initially and predominantly an American phenomenon. Transnational organizations in large part developed out of American national organizations (governmental or non-governmental) or out of international organizations in which Americans played the leading roles. Transnationalism is one of the more important legacies for world politics of two decades of American expansion into world politics.

Two preconditions, technological and political, exist for the development of transnationalism. For an organization to operate on a global or semi-global basis, it must have means of communication and transportation. Otherwise it will be only a crossnational organization, a federation of local satrapies each of which is more responsive to its local leadership than to centralized direction. There has to be the technological and organizational capability to operate across vast distances and in differing cultures. The transnational corporation rests on the fact that 'technology and corporate organization in all of the advanced countries have now reached levels of capability that permit focus on markets and production across, and indeed without reference to, national boundaries'.[2] Jet aircraft and communications satellites are to the transnational organizations of today what the iron horse and telephone were to the 'trans-state' organizations of the United States in the 1880s. These technological capabilities to make 'illusions of distance', in Albert Wohlstetter's phrase, were in large part developed within the United States and have been pre-eminently employed by the United States.

An organization can normally (there are notable exceptions) employ its technological capability to operate in a society only if it has the permission of the government of that society. Political access, consequently, has to go hand in hand with technical capability to make transnationalism a reality. Throughout the two decades after World War II, the power of the United States Government in world politics, and its interests in developing a system of alliances with other governments against the Soviet Union, China, and communism, produced the underlying political condition which made the rise of transnationalism possible. Western Europe, Latin America, East Asia, and much of South Asia, the Middle East, and Africa fell within what was euphemistically referred to as 'the Free World', and what was in fact a security zone. The governments of countries within this zone found it in their interest: (a) to accept an explicit or implicit guarantee by Washington of the independence of their country and, in some cases, of the authority of the government; and (b) to permit access to their territory by a variety of US governmental and non-governmental organizations pursuing goals which those organizations considered important. Communist governments, of course, by and large did not permit such access, although at times they were incapable of stopping it (for instance, U-2 flights over the Soviet Union in the 1950s). Other governments (Burma, the UAR, Syria) terminated such access or permitted it only on a very restricted basis. The great bulk of the countries of Europe and the Third World, however, found the advantages of transnational access to outweigh the costs of attempting to stop it. [...]

Transnationalism is the American mode of expansion. It has meant 'freedom to operate' rather than 'power to control'. US expansion has been pluralistic expansion in which a variety of organizations, governmental and non-governmental, have attempted to pursue the objectives important to them within the territory of other societies. In some respects, the US surge outward was almost as pluralistic as the outward surge of Western Europe in the sixteenth and seventeenth

218 *Samuel P. Huntington*

centuries. One could then speak of Western expansion but not of *the* Western empire because there were Spanish, Dutch, Portuguese, French, and English empires. Similarly, one can properly speak now of American expansion but not of *the* American empire, because there are so many of them. 'The *Pax Americana*', as I.F. Stone put it, 'is the "internationalism" of Standard Oil, Chase Manhattan, and the Pentagon.'[3] And, one must add, of much else besides. [...]

American expansion has thus involved the generation and spread of transnational organizations pursuing a variety of specific goals in a multiplicity of territories. Economic aid missions, military bases, and corporate investments are only the most obvious and tangible symbols of US-based transnationalism. This type of pluralistic, segmented expansion also led groups in other societies to create parallel and often competing transnational structures. The principal legacy of American expansion about the world is a network of transnational institutions knitting the world together in ways that never existed in the past. The question for the future is whether and how the contraction of the world brought about by the expansion of the American role will survive the contraction of that role. Once the political conditions which gave it birth disappear, how much transnationalism will remain?

[Huntington goes on to discuss transnational organizations in terms of the patterns of authority they demonstrate. The first element in such patterns is the source of control; the second is the degree of centralization or decentralization in the organizational structure; and the third is the variation in nationality of the personnel in transnational organizations. At this point, Huntington turns to the links between transnational organizations and national politics.]

TRANSNATIONAL ORGANIZATIONS IN NATIONAL POLITICS

In most instances, a transnational organization can conduct its operations only with the approval of the government claiming sovereignty over the territory in which it wishes to operate. Consequently, the transnational organization and the national government have to reach an *access agreement* defining the conditions under which the operations of the former will be permitted on the territory of the latter. The contents of this agreement will reflect the relative bargaining strengths of the two parties. In some instances, the transnational organization may have a clear upper hand and be able to secure access on very favorable terms. It may, for instance, in classic imperial form, be able to threaten sanctions by the national government of its home territory if it is not given access on the terms which it desires. More generally, the terms of the access agreement will reflect: (a) the benefits which each side perceives for itself in the conclusion of an arrangement; (b) the inherent strength of each side in terms of economic resources, coercive power, leadership skill, and organizational coherence; and (c) the alternatives open to each side to secure what it wishes through arrangements with another organization or another government.

Apart from the instances where the transnational organization can bring coercive pressure to bear on the national government, the latter will presumably agree to the operations taking place on its territory only if those operations themselves serve the purposes of the national government or are compatible with those purposes, or if the transnational organization has paid a price to the government to make those operations acceptable. In either case, the local national government receives benefits by trading upon its control of access to the national territory. As transnational organizations become larger and more numerous, the demands for access to the territory of nation-states will also multiply. The value of that access, consequently, will also go up. The national governments who control access will thus be strengthened. In this sense, the growth of transnational operations does not challenge the nation-state but reinforces it. It increases the demands for the resource which the nation-state alone controls: territorial access. Within the nation-state, those groups which dominate the national government are similarly able to use the increased value of their control over access to the national territory to strengthen their own position *vis-à-vis* other groups in their society.

The price that a transnational organization has to pay for access to national territory will thus, in part, depend on the extent to which the government controlling that territory perceives those operations as contributing to its purposes. If the operations clearly serve the government's purposes, it may offer considerable inducements to the transnational organization to locate its operations there. This might be the case, for instance, with a factory which not only provided local jobs but also either met an urgent local need for its product or earned needed foreign exchange by the export of its product. It would also be the case with military installations which contributed to local defense. In other instances, however, the installations of the transnational organization may contribute very little to the purposes of the local government. This is presumably more likely to be the case the more global the scope of the overall operations of the transnational organization and the more tightly integrated the conduct of those operations. In these cases, the transnational organization may have to pay a heavy price to conduct its operations on a particular piece of territory. [...]

One of the curious phenomena of post-World War II international politics was, indeed, the striking contrast which often existed between the awesome and overwhelming military, logistical, material, technological, and economic presence of US-based transnational organizations in a society, which at times seemed likely to suffocate the local society, and the degree of political influence which the US Government exercised on the government of that society. The former often seemed out of all proportion to the latter. American organizations easily penetrated the local society; the local government easily, blandly, and, to Americans, infuriatingly, resisted the advice and demands of the US Government. The American presence may have been overwhelming; American influence almost always fell far short of that.

The reasons for this gap lie, of course, in the motives for the presence of the US-based transnational organizations and in the nature of their operations. The American organizations were often present in the country not to serve the needs of that country as defined by its rulers and elite, but to serve their own interests which, however, might well be rationalized in terms of the interests of the local country. The Americans were there in the way in which they were there because they were convinced that it was important *for them* for them to be there, not because the local government thought that it was important *for it* for them to be there. [...]

The political costs of maintaining a presence thus often exceeded the local benefits generated by that presence. In addition, however, to the extent that the goals of the US-based transnational organizations reflected only the general interests of the organizations and were not specific to the society in which the operation occurred, the transnational organizations themselves had no interest in the local political system so long as it did not obstruct their ability to operate. US-based transnational organizations indeed often went to extreme lengths to deny that their local operations had any effect on local politics. Far from wishing to exercise political influence in the local society, their goal was to be as far removed from local politics as possible. The transnational religious activities of the Catholic Church, it has been argued, are facilitated by the separation of state and church in a country.[4] The transnational economic and military activities of US-based transnational organizations are similarly facilitated if these operations can be separated from local politics. From the viewpoint of the transnational organization, the ideal situation would be one in which the local political system and the transnational operation had nothing to do with each other. The typical American attitude would be: 'Let us operate our air base; mine copper; provide technical advice to the engineering school – all without involvement with local politics.' The aim of the Americans would not be to control the local government, but to avoid it.

The operations of transnational organizations thus usually do not have political motivations in the sense of being designed to affect the balance of power within the local society. They do, however, often have political consequences that actually affect that balance. Insofar as the transnational organizations have to come to terms with the dominant groups in the local political system in order to secure access to a country, their operations will tend to reinforce, or at least not injure, the position of those groups. The immediate general impact of transnational operations on a society is thus likely to be a con-servative one. The longer-run general impact, however, may be quite different. The transnational organization typically brings into the local society new activities which could not be performed as well by local organizations. Insofar as the transnational organization is itself based in an economically more developed society than the one in which it is conducting its operations, it tends to be a major trans-mission belt for new styles of life, new ideas, new technology, and new social and cultural values that challenge the traditional culture of the local society. In addition, of course, while the immediate impact of transnational operations generally reinforces the powers that be, it may also redistribute power among those powers. The transnational organization brings new resources – equipment, technology, capital, personnel – into the society. Quite apart from whatever purposes it may have, the way in which those resources enter the society, and their location in that society, will benefit some specific groups at the expense of others. Investments by transnational corporations stimulate growth in some industries and regions but not in others. Economic and military assistance programs strengthen economic planning agencies and military services as against other bureaucratic and political groups.

Access agreements between governmentally controlled transna-tional organizations and national governments obviously appear in the traditional form of intergovernmental agreements. In substance, however, they often differ little from the agreements negotiated between a privately controlled transnational organization and a national government. The weight of the controlling government presumably plays a significantly greater role, however, in the negotiation of the former than of the latter. Officials on both sides may see the intergovernmental access agreement as an integral part of their overall political and diplomatic relations. With respect to private organizations, however, pressure from the home government generally does not, except in unusual cases such as the Middle East in the 1920s, play a significant role in securing initial access. The home government is much more likely to enter the picture if the host government attempts to terminate access or to change the conditions of access. In the past, this could and, at times, did produce US military or paramilitary intervention (as in Guatemala in 1954) to maintain the access of US-controlled transnational corporations and agencies. More frequently, actions by governments denying or curtailing transnational operations are met by diplomatic protests and economic sanctions by the home government. With some exceptions (of which Vietnam is the most notable), the bulk of US Government interventions – military, economic, and political – in the domestic politics of Third-World states after World War II have been relatively discrete, *ad hoc* efforts to maintain or to restore previously existing access conditions for US-based transnational organizations rather than efforts to achieve more comprehensive purposes. [...]

TRANSNATIONAL ORGANIZATION VS. THE NATION-STATE?

The rise of transnational organizations after World War II was a product of American expansion on the one hand and technological development on the other. For a quarter of a century these two trends reinforced each other. Now, however, the American impetus to involvement in the world is waning. The American will to lead, to promote economic and cultural interaction and integration, to maintain militarily the outer boundaries of a world-wide system and to foster politically free access within that system has declined markedly. In the immediate future, US Government-based transnational organizations are likely to decline in importance compared to privately controlled organizations; US-controlled transnational organizations will decline in relative significance compared to those controlled by other nations and by international bodies. The question remains, however, how these changes in the relationships among nation-states will affect the overall role of transnational organizations.

The pre-eminence of one nation-state in large portions of the world favors the emergence of transnational organizations under the sponsorship and control of that nation-state. This is peculiarly the case when that state has a highly pluralistic and open political and institutional tradition that is conducive to the generation of transnational bodies. World politics is now moving in the direction of a bipolar military balance between the superpowers, a multipolar diplomatic and economic balance among the great powers, and increasing discrepancies in power tending toward regional hegemonies among the less developed states. This structure of world politics could be far less conducive to the emergence and operation of transnational organizations than one in which one center predominated. Clearly it favors a dispersion of control over transnational organizations. It may also favor a slowdown in their numerical growth and some restriction in the geographical scope of their activities.

While the political preconditions for transnationalism have changed significantly, the technological dynamic has continued without slowdown. 'The extraordinary improvements in international communication and transportation seem destined to continue, accompanied by more Intelsats, Concordes, IBM 370s, and all the other modern instruments for shrinking time and space. The relative decline in the costs of communication and transportation is likely to increase the advantages of large-scale producing units and to increase the size of manageable enterprises.'[5] Business corporations, aid agencies, military services, foundations, churches, public service organizations, all will have an increasing capacity to operate on a global scale and, presumably, increasing incentives to capitalize on the opportunities which this capacity gives them. Functional bureaucracies will feel ever more cramped by national boundaries and will devise means to escape beyond the boundaries within which they were born and to penetrate the boundaries within which they can prosper. Existing transnational organizations will find it in their interest to continue to integrate their activities and to tighten the organizational bonds which cut across national borders.

Politics and technology thus seem to be at odds. On the one hand, in an atmosphere of American political withdrawal and balance-of-power diplomacy, national governments may feel increasingly confident in confronting transnational organizations. A nationalist backlash could be in the making, producing new restrictions on the autonomy and scope of transnational organizations, and in some cases ousting transnational organizations from the national territory and bringing their local assets under full national control. Given this scenario, the transnational organization could be seen as a transient phenomenon unable to outlast the political conditions responsible for its emergence. Transnational operations could fragment and disappear in the face of a rise in nationalist autarky.

Some observers, on the other hand, have seen the rise of the transnational organization, particularly the 'multinational' business corporation, as challenging the future of the nation-state. As one leading American banker put it, 'the political boundaries of nation-states are too narrow and constricted to define the scope and sweep of modern business'. We have, consequently, seen the rise of 'the new globalists', the 'advance men' of 'economic one-worldism' who see 'the entire world as a market', and we may be evolving into a period in which 'businessmen often wear the robes of diplomats' and 'are more influential than statesmen in many quarters of the globe'.[6] The transnational corporation, George Ball has said, 'is a modern concept evolved to meet the requirements of the modern age' while the nation-state 'is still rooted in archaic concepts unsympathetic to the needs of our complex world'.[7] In similar terms, Arthur Barber has argued that the transnational corporation 'is acting and planning in terms that are far in advance of the political concepts of the nation-state'. Just as the Renaissance ended feudalism and the dominant role of the Church, so this twentieth-century renaissance is 'bringing an end to middle-class society and the dominance of the nation-state'.[8]

These predictions of the death of the nation-state are premature. They overlook the ability of human beings and human institutions to respond to challenges and to adapt themselves to changed environments. They seem to be based on a zero-sum assumption about power and sovereignty: that a growth in the power of transnational organizations must be accompanied by a decrease in the power of nation-states. This, however, need not be the case. Indeed, as we have argued, an increase in the number, functions, and scope of transnational organizations will increase the demand for access to national territories and hence also increase the value of the one resource almost exclusively under the control of national governments. The current situation is, in this respect, quite different from that which prevailed with respect to state governments and national corporations within the United States in the nineteenth century. There, the Supreme Court held that except in rare circumstances, state governments could not deny or restrict access to their territory by businesses based in other states. The interstate commerce clause left such regulatory power to Congress. In the absence of any comparable global political authority able to limit the exclusionary powers of national governments, transnational organizations must come to terms with those governments.

By and large, private transnational corporations have recognized this fact and have attempted to deal with national governments in a conciliatory manner. The proponents of the transnational corporation also recognize this fact when they argue that the imposition of local restrictions and controls on the operation of the transnational corporation will 'necessarily impede the fulfillment of the world corporation's full potential as the best means yet devised for using world resources according to the criterion of profit, which is an objective standard of efficiency'. To avoid this situation, they advocate creating by treaty an International Companies Law which could 'place limitations ... on the restrictions that a nation-state might be permitted to impose on companies established under its sanction'.[9] The probability of national governments arriving at an international agreement to limit their own authority, however, would appear to be fairly remote at the present time. In the absence of any such mutual voluntary abnegation of power, the national governments will retain their control over access.

National governments capitalize on that control by granting access on conditions satisfactory to them. A government may, of course, use its control over access foolishly or corruptly. If, however, it uses it wisely, granting access to private, governmental, and international transnational organizations in such a way as to further its own objectives, it is far from surrendering its sovereignty. It is, instead, capitalizing on its control over one resource in order to strengthen itself through the addition of other resources. The widespread penetration of its society by transnational organizations will, obviously, have significant effects on that society. But that does not necessarily mean an impairment of the sovereignty of the national government. [...]

The end of the European colonial empires was followed by the creation of a large number of new nation-states often lacking established institutions, consensus on the bases of legitimacy, and sizeable, technically well-trained, and politically skilled elites, as well as any inherited sense of national unity and identity. Many such countries in Africa and some in Latin America and Asia have been labeled 'non-viable'. Yet at the same time, many such countries are also in the grip of fissiparous tendencies that threaten to break up the existing fragile nation-state into even smaller units. While functional imperatives seem to be making transnational organizations bigger and bigger, cultural and communal imperatives seem to be encouraging political units to become smaller and smaller. 'Tribalism' in politics contrasts with 'transnationalism' in economics. Yet these contrasting patterns of development are also, in some measure, reinforcing. The nation-states of today which are labeled 'unviable' and those still smaller entities which may emerge in the future could well be made viable by the operations of transnational organizations that link activities within one state to those in other states. The sovereignty of the government may, in this sense, be limited, but the sovereignty of the people may be made more real by the fact that the 'sovereign' unit of government is smaller, closer, easier to participate in, and much easier to identify with.

With respect to the coexistence of the nation-state and the transnational organization, the case can, indeed, be made that at the present time the existence of one not only implies but requires the existence of the other. These two entities serve different purposes and meet different needs. They are often in conflict, but the conflict is rooted in differences rather than similarities in function. Two states may conflict because they wish to exercise sovereignty over the same piece of territory; two corporations may conflict because they sell similar goods in the same market; two parties may conflict because they attempt to win the same votes. In all these cases the competitive entities are similar in function, structure, and purpose. The competing entities are essentially duplicates of each other. Such *duplicative conflict* is often zero sum in character and involves, potentially at least, the survival of one or both parties to the conflict. *Complementary conflict*, in contrast, involves entities performing essentially different functions; the competition stems from this dissimilarity of function. In these instances, the existence of the parties is not usually at stake. Each has some interest in the survival of the other as an inherent component of a system of which they are both part. Within that system, each also has a role to play which inevitably brings it into conflict with the other type of institution, playing a different role. This conflict is incidental to each institution's performance of its respective functions, and the conflict between the institutions is limited by their difference in functions. In a sense, the conflicts are almost jurisdictional in nature, an inevitable friction in the working of the system. [...]

The conflict between national governments and transnational organizations is clearly complementary rather than duplicative. It is conflict not between likes but between unlikes, each of which has its own primary set of functions to perform. It is, consequently, conflict which, like labor–management conflict, involves the structuring of relations and the distribution of benefits to entities which need each other even as they conflict with each other. The balance of influence may shift back and forth from one to the other, but neither can displace the other.

In fact, the balance between a transnational organization and a national government often does appear to move through three phases. In the first phase, the initiative lies with the transnational organization which often secures access to the territory controlled by the government on very favorable terms. In the second phase, the government asserts control over the local operations, perhaps even displacing the transnational authority completely. In the third phase, the transnational organization returns to the scene and a new equilibrium is worked out between the two entities. [...]

The novelty and, indeed, the revolutionary character of the transnational organization stem in large part from the fact that it has emerged apart from the existing structure of international relations. It is an outgrowth of the nation-state, but it is founded on a principle entirely different from nationality. In economic history, the impetus for change came from neither feudal lord nor feudal peasant but rather from a new urban class of merchants and entrepreneurs who developed alongside but outside the feudal social structure. And, as Marx recognized, this was the revolutionary class. Similarly, today the revolutionary organizations in world politics are not the national or international organizations which have been part of the nation-state system, but rather the transnational organizations which have developed alongside but outside that system. Just as the bourgeoisie represented a principle of production foreign to the feudal system, so does the transnational organization represent a principle of organization foreign to the nation-state system. In Marx's terms, the capitalist forces of production outran the feudal relations of production. Today, man's capacities for organization are outrunning the nation-state system. Internationalism is a dead end. Only organizations that are disinterested in sovereignty can transcend it. For the immediate future a central focus of world politics will be on the coexistence of and interaction between transnational organizations and the nation-state.

NOTES

1   Jack N. Behrman, *Some Patterns in the Rise of the Multinational Enterprise*, Research Paper no. 18 (Graduate School of Business Administration, University of North Carolina. Chapel Hill, NC, 1969), p. 61.

2   Sidney E. Rolfe, 'The International Corporation in Perspective', in Sidney E. Rolfe and Walter E. Damm (eds), *The Multinational Corporation in the World Economy* (New York, 1970), p. 12.

3   *I.F. Stone's Bi-Weekly*, XVIII (13 July 1970), p. 1.

4   Ivan Vallier, 'The Roman Catholic Church: A Transnational Actor', in Robert O. Keohane and Joseph S. Nye, Jr (eds), *Transnational Relations in World Politics* (Cambridge, Mass., 1972), pp. 137–8.

5   Raymond Vernon, *Sovereignty at Bay* (New York, 1971), pp. 251–2.

6   William I. Spencer (President, First National City Corporation), 'The New Globalists' (Address before American Chamber of Commerce, Frankfurt, Germany, 6 September 1972).

7   George W. Ball, 'Cosmocorp: The Importance of Being Stateless', *Atlantic Community Quarterly*, VI (Summer 1968), p. 165.

8   Arthur Barber, 'Emerging New Power: The World Corporation', *War/Peace Report*, VIII (October 1968), p. 7.

9   George W. Ball, 'Making World Corporations Into World Citizens', *War/Peace Report*, VIII (October 1968), p. 10.

2.7 Transgovernmental relations and international organizations

Robert O. Keohane and Joseph S. Nye

Source: *World Politics*, vol. XXVII, no. 1 (Princeton University Press, Princeton, 1974), pp. 39–62.

Keohane and Nye set out to contest the 'realist' claim that international organizations are no more than instruments of state policy. They suggest that such institutions can influence the activities of civil servants, who try to co-ordinate policy with their counterparts in other countries or seek their support for domestic policy initiatives.

'Realist' analyses of world politics have generally assumed that states are the only significant actors; that they act as units; and that their military security objectives dominate their other goals. On the basis of these assumptions it is easy to conclude that international organizations – defined as intergovernmental organizations – are merely instruments of governments, and therefore unimportant in their own right. Compared with the hopes and dreams of world federalists, the Realist position reflects reality: international organizations in the contemporary world are not powerful independent actors, and relatively universal organizations such as the United Nations find it extraordinarily difficult to reach agreement on significant issues. It is therefore not surprising that students of world politics have paid relatively slight attention to these entities, particularly after hopes for a major United Nations peacekeeping role were dashed in the early 1960s.

The Realist model on which the above conclusions about international organizations are based is now being called into question. Faced with a growing complexity of actors and issues, a number of analysts have begun to pay more attention to transnational relations. In this article we will contend that if critiques of Realist models of world politics are taken seriously, they not only call into question state-centric conceptions of 'the international system', but also throw doubt upon prevailing notions about international organizations. If one relaxes the Realist assumptions, one can visualize more significant roles for international organizations in world politics.

In an important recent contribution to the literature on transnational relations, Samuel P. Huntington argues explicitly that international organizations are relatively insignificant in contemporary world politics:

... internationalism involves agreement among nation-states.

... every international organization at some point finds itself limited by the very principle which gives it being.

The international organization requires *accord* among nations; the transnational organization requires *access* to nations.... International organizations embody the principle of nationality; transnational organizations try to ignore it.

While national representatives and delegations engage in endless debate at UN conferences and councils, however, the agents of the transnational organizations are busily deployed across the continents, spinning the webs that link the world together.

Internationalism is a dead end.[1]

Like Huntington, we begin with the proposition that transnational relations are increasingly significant in world politics. But we reach very different conclusions about the roles of international organizations.

Before making this argument systematically in the remainder of this paper, we must briefly deal with the issue of how transnational relations should be defined. Huntington defines 'transnational organizations' as organizations sharing three characteristics: they are large bureaucracies; they perform specialized functions; and they do so across international boundaries. He explicitly includes governmental entities, such as the United States Agency for International Development (AID) or the Central Intelligence Agency (CIA) and intergovernmental organizations such as the World Bank, along with nongovernmental entities such as multinational enterprises, the Ford Foundation, and the Roman Catholic Church. Although this definition has the virtue of pointing out similarities between governmental and nongovernmental bureaucracies operating across national boundaries, it obscures the differences. Some of Huntington's observations are clearly meant to apply only to nongovernmental organizations. He argues, for instance, that 'The operations of transnational organizations ... usually do not have political motivations in the sense of being designed to affect the balance of power within the local society.'[2] But this hardly applies to the Agency for International Development or the Central Intelligence Agency, both of which he designates as 'transnational'. He contends, on the basis of literature about multinational enterprises, that personnel arrangements of transnational organizations move toward dispersed nationality patterns, in which country subdivisions are primarily managed by local personnel; yet no evidence is presented that this is true for AID or the CIA, much less for the Strategic Air Command – another 'transnational' organization by Huntington's definition. Furthermore, the trends over time seem to diverge, and when Huntington discusses these trends, he finds himself distinguishing between 'US Government-controlled transnational organizations' and private groups.[3]

The anomalies into which Huntington is led convince us that for most purposes it is useful to retain the governmental–nongovernmental distinction, thus facilitating the task of examining both the differences between patterns of governmental and nongovernmental activity and the effects of each on the other. Only if one were to use organization theory in a sustained way to explain behavior of large bureaucracies that operate across international boundaries would it seem wise to adopt Huntington's definition.

The argument leads us also to reconsider some of our own past usage. In this article we will restrict the term 'transnational' to nongovernmental actors, and the term 'transgovernmental' to refer to sub-units of governments on those occasions when they act relatively autonomously from higher authority in international politics. In other words, 'transnational' applies when we relax the assumption that states are the only actors, and 'transgovernmental' applies when we relax the assumption that states act as units.

Our choice of definition is not a matter of semantics but is related directly to the argument of this paper. Transnational activity makes societies more sensitive to one another, which may lead governments to increase their efforts to control this nongovernmental behavior. Such efforts, if pursued by more than one government, make governmental policies sensitive to one another: since one government may deliberately or inadvertently thwart the other's purposes, governments must design their own policies with the policies of others in mind. The result of this may well be attempts at policy co-ordination, which will increase direct bureaucratic contacts among governmental sub-units, and which may, particularly in a multilateral context, create opportunities for international organizations to play significant roles in world politics. [...]

TRANSGOVERNMENTAL RELATIONS

During the last century, governments have become increasingly involved in attempting to regulate the economic and social lives of the societies they govern. As a result, they have become more sensitive to external disturbances that may affect developments within their own societies. For instance, integration of money markets internationally, in the context of governmental responsibility for national economies, has made government policy sensitive both to changes in interest rates by other governments and central banks, and to movements of funds by nongovernmental speculators. These sensitivities are heightened further by the expanding decision domains of transnational organizations such as multinational business firms and banks, reinforced by decreases in the cost of transnational communications.

As the agenda broadens, bureaucracies find that to cope effectively at acceptable cost with many of the problems that arise, they must deal with each other directly rather than indirectly through foreign offices. [...] There have always been such contacts. What seems to be new is the order of magnitude of transgovernmental relations, as bureaucracies become more complex and communications and travel costs decrease.

We define transgovernmental relations as sets of direct interactions among sub-units of different governments that are not controlled or closely guided by the policies of the cabinets or chief executives of those governments. Thus we take the policies of top leaders as our benchmarks of 'official government policy'. Lack of control of sub-unit behavior by top leadership is obviously a matter of degree, and in practice by no means free of ambiguity. The policy of the central executive is often unclear, particularly on details, and policy means different things at different organizational levels. 'One man's policy is another man's tactics.'[4] As one observer put it, 'Central policy is always waffled; actors latch on to the waffled parts and form coalitions to shift policy at their level.'[5] Nonetheless, to treat all actors as equal and to ignore the existence of a political hierarchy charged with 'course-setting' and maintaining some hierarchy of goals is to misrepresent both constitutional and political reality. It is precisely because this central policy task has become more difficult in the face of greater complexity that both the opportunities and the importance of transgovernmental interactions may be expected to have increased.

It is quite conceivable that executives entrusted with responsibility for central foreign policy, such as presidents and prime ministers, will themselves attempt to collaborate with one another in ways that conflict with the behavior of their respective bureaucracies. Yet we will regard only the relatively autonomous activities of the lower-level bureaucracies, as opposed to those of top leadership, as being transgovernmental. Otherwise, we would find ourselves in the anomalous position of regarding a head-of-state meeting, at which new initiatives that deviate from established policy are taken, as an example of 'transgovernmental politics' when indeed it is almost the paradigm case for the state-centric model whose inadequacies we are criticizing. The point of our terminology is to focus attention on bureaucratic contacts that take place below the apex of the organizational hierarchy – rather than merely to apply a new label to behavior that is easily subsumed by traditional models.

In view of our interest in the opportunities that transgovernmental relations may create for international organizations, we will concentrate in this essay on *cooperative* behavior among governmental sub-units. It should be recognized, however, that conflict is not excluded from transgovernmental relations any more than from other aspects of world politics. [...]

We will distinguish two major types of essentially cooperative transgovernmental behavior. Transgovernmental *policy coordination* refers to activity designed to facilitate smooth implementation or adjustment of policy, in the absence of detailed higher policy directives. Another process, *transgovernmental coalition building*, takes place when sub-units build coalitions with like-minded agencies from other governments against elements of their own administrative structures. At that point, the unity of the state as a foreign policy actor breaks down. Although transgovernmental policy coordination and transgovernmental coalition building are analytically distinct processes, they merge into one another at the margin. While bearing in mind that the distinction is in some cases an artificial convenience, we will look at the two processes in turn.

Transgovernmental policy coordination

The most basic and diffuse form of transgovernmental policy coordination is simply informal communication among working-level officials of different bureaucracies. Such communication does not necessarily contradict the conventional conceptualization of states as coherent coalitions *vis-à-vis* the outside world, although it may have side effects that influence policy. Face-to-face communications often convey more information (intended or unintended) than indirect communications, and this additional information can affect policy expectations and preferences. It is well known that international organizations frequently provide suitable contexts for such transgovernmental communication. As one official said of INTERPOL, 'What's really important here are the meetings on a social level – the official agenda is only for show.'

Where patterns of policy coordination are regularized, it becomes misleading to think of governments as closed decision-making units. It has been argued, for example, that in the 1960s Canadian officials in Washington were 'often able to inject their views into the decision-making process at various stages, almost as if they were American, and to actually participate, particularly in the economic sector, in the formulation of American policy'.[6] In the Skybolt affair of 1962, British complacency about American planning, before cancellation was announced, was reinforced by 'a steady stream of reassurances [that] flowed back and forth between the Air Forces. The USAF saw a staunch ally in Her Majesty's Government, and *vice versa.*'[7]

From regularized coordination over a period of time, changes in attitudes may result. When the same officials meet recurrently, they sometimes develop a sense of collegiality, which may be reinforced by their membership in a common profession, such as economics, physics, or meteorology. Individual officials may even define their roles partly in relation to their transnational reference group rather than in purely national terms. [...]

Regularized patterns of policy coordination can therefore create attitudes and relationships that will at least marginally change policy or affect its implementation. This has been evident particularly in relations among close allies or associates, for instance between the United States and Canada or among countries of the British Commonwealth. Even in relations among countries that are politically more distant from one another, policy coordination between bureaucracies with similar interests may occasionally take place. According to press reports, at any rate, United States and Soviet space officials who were engaged in technical talks on space cooperation in 1971 went considerably further than the National Security Council had authorized at that time.

Patterns of regularized policy coordination have a significance that is not limited to the examples we have cited. As such practices become widespread, transgovernmental elite networks are created, linking officials in various governments to one another by ties of common interest, professional orientation, and personal friendship. Even where attitudes are not fundamentally affected and no major deviations from central policy positions occur, the existence of a sense of collegiality may permit the development of flexible bargaining behavior in which concessions need not be requited issue by issue or during each period. [...]

Transgovernmental coalition building

Transgovernmental policy coordination shades over into transgovernmental coalition building when sub-units of different governments (and/or intergovernmental institutions) jointly use resources to influence governmental decisions. To improve their chances of success, governmental sub-units attempt to bring actors from other governments into their own decision-making processes as allies. When such coalitions are successful, the outcomes are different than they would be if each coalition partner were limited to his own nationality. The politics of such situations are more subtle and the rules less clear than in the classical coalition theorists' cases of electoral coalitions where resources are directly transferable into influence through a set of generally accepted rules, or national bureaucratic coalitions in which players hold formal positions that legitimize their rights to participate.

Transgovernmental coalitions may be employed by sub-units of powerful states such as the United States as means by which to penetrate weaker governments. US aid agencies in the 1950s and 1960s frequently played a large role in writing requests for aid from the US on behalf of potential recipients, and on occasion even served a liaison function among several ministries of a foreign government. [...]

Transgovernmental coalitions, however, can also help agencies of other governments penetrate the US bureaucracy. In 1961, when the US Weather Bureau disagreed with the State Department's position at the United Nations on the control of the World Weather Watch, the Director of the US Weather Bureau telephoned his Canadian counterpart and they discussed the common interests of their respective weather bureaus. The position of the two weather bureaus became the official Canadian position, which led in turn to defeat of the State Department's proposals. In the late 1960s, a US Defense Department official, worried that delay in returning Okinawa to Japanese control might harm United States–Japanese relations, worked out with a Japanese counterpart how to phrase Japanese messages to ensure that they would enter the right channels and trigger the desired response in the US bureaucracy. In 1968, an Air Force general, to whom the responsibility for negotiating with Spain about military bases had been delegated, conferred secretly with his Spanish counterparts without informing civilian officials of the progress of his negotiations, and agreed to a negotiating paper that proved to be unacceptable to the Department of State. As this last case indicates, transgovernmental coalitions are not always successful: the agreement reached, which would have been favorable to the Spanish Government, was disowned by the United States, and a negative reaction against Spain took place in the Senate.

It is obviously a necessary condition for explicit transgovernmental coalitions that sub-units of government have broad and intensive contacts with one another. In some sense, a degree of transgovernmental policy coordination is probably a precondition for such explicit transnational coalitions. A second set of necessary conditions has to do with conflict of interest among sub-units and the degree of central control by top executive leaders. For a transgovernmental coalition to take place, a sub-unit of one government must perceive a greater common interest with another government, or sub-units of another government, than with at least one pertinent agency in its own country; and central executive control must be loose enough to permit this perception to be translated into direct contacts with the foreign governments or agencies in question. Figure 1 illustrates four types of political situations based on these two dimensions.

Sub-units in a governmental system of Type 1 are most likely to seek, or be amenable to, transgovernmental coalitions. High conflict of interest among sub-units of the government suggests that there may be sub-units of other governments with which advantageous coalitions can be made; low executive power indicates that the central officials' ability to deter such coalitions is relatively small. In the other three types, by contrast, the conventional assumption of unitary actors is more likely to be valid for external affairs, although for different reasons. In Type 2 conflict is contained by a strong executive; sub-units may perceive potentially advantageous transgovernmental coalitions, but they do not dare attempt to consummate them directly. In Type 3, low conflict of interest among domestic governmental sub-units ensures that the option of national coalition generally seems more attractive than the transgovernmental alternative, even in the absence of strong central control. Type 4, of course, exemplifies the traditional situation: national coalition reinforced by effective hierarchy.

Relatively frequent contacts among governmental sub-units, looseness of governmental hierarchies (low executive control), and relatively high conflict of interest within governments are all necessary

Figure 1 Conflict of interest and executive power in foreign policy: four types

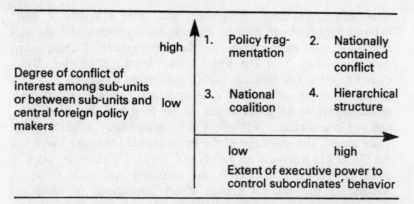

conditions for the development of explicit transgovernmental co-alitions. But they are not in themselves sufficient. In the first place, for coalitions to be feasible, actors with common interests must be able to combine their resources effectively. That means that political resources (such as funds, prestige, information, and consent – where required, for instance, by the rules of an international organization) of actors outside a government must be valuable to at least some actors within it. This requires a political context that is relatively open and free of xenophobia, since in a xenophobic society foreign resources are heavily devalued, or regarded negatively, by virtue of their origin. Even in democratic societies, the borderline between legitimate transgovernmental behavior and treason may be unclear.

The need for resources that can be aggregated suggests that transgovernmental behavior may be particularly important in issue areas in which functionally defined international organizations operate. The procedures of the organization itself, for reaching agreement among its members, ensure that the resources of one actor – at least its votes – may be useful to another; insofar as the organization has a specialized, functional orientation, the activities of national representatives may not be closely supervised by top leaders or their agents. More generally, the greater the natural sensitivity of governmental policies and the wider the acceptance of joint decision making on issues that cross national lines, the greater the legitimacy of transgovernmental bargaining is likely to be. An international organization, by symbolizing governments' beliefs in the need for joint decision making, tends to strengthen the legitimacy of this activity.

INTERNATIONAL ORGANIZATIONS AND POTENTIAL COALITIONS

Recurrent international conferences and other activities of international organizations help to increase transgovernmental contacts and thus create opportunities for the development of transgovernmental coalitions. [...] The organizations' definitions of which issues cluster together and which should be considered separately may help to determine the nature of interdepartmental committees and other arrangements within governments. In the long run, therefore, international organizations will affect how government officials define 'issue areas'. The existence of the International Monetary Fund and the General Agreement on Tariffs and Trade, for example, helps to focus governmental activity in the monetary and trade fields, in contrast to the area of private direct investment, in which no comparable international organization exists.

The fact that international organizations bring officials together should alert us to their effect in activating *potential* coalitions in world politics. Many sub-units of governments, which do not as a matter of course come into contact with each other, may have common or complementary interests. Indeed, we may speak of some potential coalitions as *de facto* 'tacit coalitions' if the independent actions of one member seem to serve the interests of others and vice versa. One of the important but seldom-noted roles of international organizations in world politics is to provide the arena for sub-units of governments to turn potential or tacit coalitions into explicit coalitions characterized by direct communication among the partners. In this particular bit of political alchemy, the organization provides physical proximity, an agenda of issues on which interaction is to take place, and an aura of legitimacy. Informal discussions occur naturally in meetings of international organizations, and it is difficult, given the milieu, for other sub-units of one's own government to object to these contacts.

Even without an active secretariat, therefore, international organizations are of considerable relevance in many issue areas of world politics because they help to transform potential or tacit coalitions into explicit ones. When issues are linked or dealt with in institutional arenas with broad mandates, heterogeneous coalitions can be formed. Narrow institutional mandates discriminate against such coalitions. Thus, by defining the issues to be considered together, and by excluding others, international organizations may significantly affect political processes and outcomes in world politics, quite apart from active lobbying by their secretariats.

The second important role for international organizations, however, is the active one. Most intergovernmental organizations have secretariats, and like all bureaucracies they have their own interests and goals that are defined through an interplay of staff and clientele. International secretariats can be viewed both as catalysts and as potential members of coalitions; their distinctive resources tend to be information and an aura of international legitimacy. [...]

Examples of alliances between parts of secretariats and governments are not hard to find. Many organizations have divisions that are regarded as fiefdoms of particular governments. In a number of cases, lower-level officials of a secretariat have lobbied with governments in efforts to thwart the declared policy of their secretaries-general. Representatives of UN specialized agencies in developing countries often strengthen old-line ministries against their rivals in central planning offices. Chilean conservatives have used IMF missions to bolster their political positions. With reference to the World Health Organization (WHO), Harold Jacobson argues that 'many government representatives to WHO almost can be viewed as the director-general's agents or lobbyists within country sub-systems'.[8] In some cases, international organizations initiate the formation of transgovernmental coalitions; in others, they or their own sub-units are recruited to the coalitions by sub-units of governments.

It must be recognized, however, that this activist, coalition-building role of international organizations is usually closely circumscribed. By no means is it a sure recipe for success. Yet the alternatives of passivity or of frontally challenging traditional notions of national sovereignty are usually less attractive. Secretariat officials often find the only feasible alternative to be to help governments, or sectors of governments, to perceive problems differently and to use their own resources in innovative ways. [...]

Coalition building shades down into transgovernmental policy coordination in this example, as is frequently the case. On a long-term and somewhat diffuse basis, the communications that take place as a result of policy coordination and conferences may be as important as the coalitions that form on particular issues. As we have seen earlier, international organizations facilitate face-to-face meetings among officials in 'domestic' agencies of different governments who would have little to do with each other in traditional interstate politics. Strategically-minded secretariats of international organizations could very well plan meetings with a view toward this transgovernmental communications function. Recurrent interactions can change officials' perceptions of their activities and interests. As Bauer, Pool, and Dexter have pointed out in their discussion of the United States politics of foreign trade, concentrating only on pressures of various interests for decisions leads to an overly mechanistic view of a continuous process and neglects the important role of communications in slowly changing perceptions of 'self-interest'.[9]

Conditions for the involvement of international organizations

To the extent that transgovernmental relations are common in a given issue area, under what conditions should we expect international organizations, in the sense of intergovernmental organizations, to be involved in them? One set of cases is obvious: where the international organization itself has created the network of elites. Thus, both the International Labor Organization (ILO) and the World Health Organization (WHO), as described by Cox and Jacobson, are characterized by extensive 'participant subsystems' that link national trade unions, employers, and government officials to the ILO secretariat, and health-care professionals to WHO's bureaucracy.[10]

More generally, however, we would expect international organizations to become involved in transgovernmental politics on issues requiring some central point or agency for coordination. This implies that international organizations are likely to be most extensively involved on complex, multilateral issues in which major actors perceive a need for information and for communication with other actors, in addition to the traditional functions, as listed by Skolnikoff, of '1) provision of services, 2) norm creation and allocation, 3) rule observance and settlement of disputes, and 4) operation'.[11] Insofar as patterns of politics follow the transgovernmental mode, increasing the number of actors will tend to create greater demands for communication with other actors (often of different types), as well as for information about both technical and political conditions. International secretariats staffed with knowledgeable individuals, even without traditional sources of power, have the opportunity to place themselves at the center of crucial communications networks, and thereby acquire influence as brokers, facilitators, and suggestors of new approaches. They will continue to be dependent on governments for funds and legal powers; but the relevant agencies of governments may be dependent on them for information and for the policy coordination, by a legitimate system-wide actor, which is required to achieve their own objectives.

NOTES

1 Samuel P. Huntington, 'Transnational Organizations in World Politics', *World Politics*, XXV (April 1973), pp. 333–68; quotations from pp. 338, 339 and 368 respectively. (See article 2.6 in this section.)
2 Ibid., p. 358.
3 Ibid., pp. 348–9.
4 Raymond Bauer, 'The Study of Policy Formation', in Raymond Bauer and Kenneth Gergen (eds), *The Study of Policy Formation* (New York, 1968), p. 2.
5 M.S. Hochmuth, Comments at Transnational Relations Study Group Seminar, Center for International Affairs, Harvard University, 8 February 1972.
6 Dale Thompson, Testimony before Standing Committee on External Affairs and National Defense, House of Commons (Canada), *Minutes of Proceedings and Evidence*, 28 April 1970.
7 Richard E. Neustadt, *Alliance Politics* (New York, 1970), p. 37.
8 Harold K. Jacobson, 'WHO: Medicine, Regionalism, and Managed Politics', in Robert W. Cox and Harold K. Jacobson (eds), *The Anatomy of Influence: Decision Making in International Organisation* (New Haven, 1973), p. 214.
9 Raymond Bauer, Ithiel de Sola Pool and Lewis Dexter, *American Business and Foreign Policy* (New York, 1963), ch. 35, especially pp. 472–5.
10 Jacobson, 'WHO', pp. 194–205 and Robert W. Cox, 'ILO: Limited Monarchy', in Cox and Jacobson (eds), *The Anatomy of Influence*, pp. 114–27.
11 Eugene B. Skolnikoff, 'Science and Technology: The Implications for International Institutions', *International Organization*, XXV (Autumn 1971), p. 772.

2.8 International organizations and their roles

Charles Pentland

Source: J. Rosenau, K.W. Thompson and G. Boyd (eds), *World Politics* (Free Press, New York, 1976), pp. 631–56.

Pentland argues that international organizations can play three different, though not mutually exclusive, roles in world politics. First, they can be used by states as instruments of foreign policy in accordance with the traditional state-centric view; second, they can serve to modify states' behavior; and third, they can achieve a measure of autonomy and operate as actors in their own right.

INTERNATIONAL ORGANIZATIONS AS INSTRUMENTS OF POLICY

As instruments for the collective pursuit of foreign policy goals, international organizations are subject to evaluation by member states in terms of their utility. From national capitals the whole field of international organizations is likely to be perceived as an array of more or less useful pieces of machinery through which to enhance national policy aims. This instrumental outlook means that, as with other modalities of foreign policy, the national policymaker weighs the costs and benefits (insofar as they can be estimated) of participating in an international organization or attempting to mobilize it for specific purposes. Such utilitarian calculations are made both by small states pursuing policy goals through coalitions and by major powers which may by themselves be able decisively to influence the organization's performance.

Clearly states vary greatly in their ability to mobilize and manage international organizations for the pursuit of their foreign policy goals, and organizations in turn vary in the degree to which they can be so used. Major powers can often determine if organizations will be active at all in areas of interest to them. In regional organizations especially, a hegemonic state can usually be assured of sufficient small power backing to permit it to manage the organization toward acceptable decisions. Its calculations will tend to center less on the probability of creating a winning coalition around itself (this being assumed) than on the relative virtues of multilateral and unilateral action. For smaller powers, largely incapable of effective unilateral action and much less sure of their ability to create winning coalitions to control the multilateral setting, the calculations have to be more subtle and complex.

Important for both great and small powers are the power disparities embodied in the organization and the degree to which any working consensus created among the members is likely to be compatible with their particular interests. A good measure of the power relationship is the 'presence' of the state in the organization, reflected in its contribution of finances and personnel, its demands for action, and its level of participation in decision making. The degree of compatibility between the working consensus of the organization and the state's interests can be seen in the responsiveness of the organization's policy decisions and executive actions to the state's original demands.

[Pentland proceeds to discuss this view in the context of global and regional organizations and concludes as follows.]

[...] it is comparatively rarely that international organizations serve directly as controlled, effective instruments of one state's foreign policy. In these rare cases the dominant state's support for, and demands on, the organization will far outstrip those of any other member; it will have ready-made majorities of its clientele to determine the outcome of all decisions it considers important; and the actions of the organization will amount to putting a multilateral gloss on a unilateral interest. The cold war alliances, the UN on rare occasions such as the Korean action, and the OAS are about the only international organizations which fit this pattern to any notable extent. It is worth adding that smaller members of a hegemonic organization may find this situation the most rational in terms of their own policy goals. The theory of 'collective goods' suggests that the small can in fact 'exploit' the large, since the marginal cost of producing the good (such as security or wealth) shared by all members of the organization is lowest for the hegemonic state. Collective goods 'may be provided to an almost "optimal" degree in a group in which one member is very much larger than all the other members'.[1] The cost–benefit calculus, then, does not necessarily indicate that collaboration on an egalitarian basis is always the best for a small state seeking to maximize foreign policy goals. Sometimes, to use international organizations as foreign policy instruments may be, in effect, to 'use' the hegemonic state. At other times, it may mean establishing a dominant coalition which controls decisions and allocates the proceeds among its members.

But generally, to speak of international organizations as instruments of state policy is to stress the element of 'free' intergovernmental collaboration towards shared or convergent objectives. In an increasingly interdependent world, unilateralism is impossible because 'more and more goods are becoming collective at the international level'.[2] The calculus of utility for most states, therefore, is concerned neither with the pros and cons of collaboration *per se* nor with the probabilities of successfully manipulating any organization. Rather it is concerned with ongoing judgments about the responsiveness of various organizations in providing the state with an acceptable share of the collective goods produced, and about the optimum amount of resources to commit to their common production. These calculations are rarely all that visible or precise, but the occasional surfacing of debates over the American contribution to the UN budget or over what constitutes a 'just return' from the European Community should remind us of their continuing importance for the functioning of international organizations.

INTERNATIONAL ORGANIZATIONS AS SYSTEMIC MODIFIERS OF STATE BEHAVIOR

Since 'instruments' are supposed to be neutral and to lack any life or direction but that imparted by their users, the thrust of the first perspective on international organizations is to minimize their status as independent entities in the international system. Viewed as restraints on the behavior of states, however, international organizations begin to take on a life of their own as part of the landscape of the international system. From this perspective international organizations are not seen as actors in their own right, equivalent to and interacting with states; rather they are institutional channels, obstacles, and aids collectively created by states which modify the traditionally *laissez-faire* character of their relationships.

As such, international organizations become an institutional manifestation of the general set of restraints placed on states by the international system. Their effectiveness as modifiers of state behavior will depend to a great extent on the general structural pattern of this system. Four aspects of this structural pattern are commonly singled out as important in this respect: (1) the degree of polarization, (2) the power and status hierarchies, (3) the linkage of central system and regional subsystems, and (4) the degree of transnational interdependence. The question facing international organizations is the extent to which they must be adapted to these structural patterns in order effectively to influence state behavior. If they do not adapt at all to structural change, they risk becoming peripheral to states' interests. If, on the other hand, they mirror the structural patterns too accurately, they may be incapable of muting any conflicts which run along those structural lines. The UN's Economic Commission for Europe illustrates this dilemma well. At the height of the cold war, the Commission (concerned with fostering East–West economic cooperation) had little relevance for either side. Had it, however, adapted its decision-making structure and policies to reflect Europe's bipolar structure, it might have forsaken what little integrative influence it had, as well as the opportunity of becoming the economic vehicle for détente.

What mix of structural patterns in the international system is most likely to enhance the restraining role of international organizations? Ideally, first of all, polarization into rigid alliance systems should be at a minimum. Tight bipolarity, in which every state is bound to one bloc or the other, is the least congenial setting for global international organizations, although it may give rise to hegemonic or regional institutions within each bloc as means of control or internal conflict resolution. Between the blocs, however, accommodation and inter-action tend to be limited to the leaders, whose bilateral dealings give little role to a global organization. Multipolarity, on the other hand, increases states' freedom of maneuver and the variety of their interactions, while the absence of clientelistic bloc structures means they must pursue collective goods through wider collaboration.

Second, the influence of international organizations is likely to be greater to the extent that power, wealth, and status are distributed evenly among the states. If there are huge disparities between one state and all the rest, international organizations are likely to be instruments of hegemonic control, restraining all states but the superpower. If there are several large states which are in basic agreement about the international order, as in the European Concert, the organization becomes an instrument of oligarchic control. Only a relatively egalitarian system permits a true collective system of restraint to operate, since the capabilities of potential violators are less likely to outweigh those of the rest of the community of states.

Concerning the optimum relationship between global system and regional subsystem, different arguments are defensible. One, which stresses 'islands of peace' and 'division of labor', suggests that discontinuities between the two levels actually aid international organizations. Conflicts can be localized within regional organizations and dealt with by the states most directly concerned. The other argument stresses the 'indivisibility of peace' and points to the superior resources of the global organizations, as well as the dangers of balkanization. In this view the intensification of regional inter-actions among states is liable to paralyze global organizations.

The development of transnational interdependence, finally, is usually held to be a vital underpinning for international organizations. Steadily growing flows of goods, services, money, people, and ideas between countries represent that fabric which stands to be damaged or destroyed should the states' collective system of self-control fail. We might expect, then, that organizations which follow particularly intense patterns of interdependence would draw the greatest degree of commitment and compliance from their member states. This commitment and compliance would probably be a product not so much of legal or coercive restraints as of a process of socialization occurring among political, economic, and administrative elites as they interacted with each other in a multilateral context. International organizations, in short, can restrain states by means of internalized norms as well as the more evident external pressures.

[Pentland then investigates the relevance of these four factors in the context of empirical examples before coming to the third and final role.]

INTERNATIONAL ORGANIZATIONS AS ACTORS

Viewed as restraints on the behavior of states, international organiz-ations begin to take on independent life. But it is a limited sort of independence: the organizations are created and sustained by the states in a collective act of self-limitation or self-enhancement, and there is certainly no expectation that they will come to coexist with, or even supersede, their creators as the dominant actors in the inter-national system. In the postwar period, however, it has become apparent that some international organizations promise (or threaten, depending on one's perspective) to do just this. At present their numbers are fewer than some would claim, but their implications are far-reaching for the future of international politics.

Becoming an actor means, essentially, to achieve some degree of autonomy and some capacity to influence other actors. Autonomy is the product of what Schmitter calls 'organizational development', or a 'process whereby an initially dependent system, created by a set of actors representing different and relatively independent nation-states, acquires the capabilities of a self-maintaining and self-steering system, one whose course cannot be predicted solely from knowledge of its environment'.[3] A capacity to influence other actors (or, indeed, to resist influences from other actors) is based on resources – expert information, finances, decision-making capacity, popular support or legitimacy, enforcement capabilities, and diplomatic skills – which accrue independently to the organization. To analyze international organizations in these terms is not necessarily to assume the inevitability or desirability of their challenging the supremacy of the nation-state, or indeed even to assume that such organizational development necessarily occurs at the expense of the national autonomy. It is simply to recognize that some international organizations are more highly developed than others and that their impact on the international system is thus rather more forceful. An important task of the theory of international organization is to determine why this is so.

Focusing on organization development does require one conceptual clarification. Although international organizations are essentially associations of states, it is not the aggregation of states as such which we normally describe as 'developing'. It is, rather, some emergent property which, even in a minimally endowed organization, represents something greater than the sum of the members. That property is best, although by no means exclusively, represented in the institutions of the organization, especially the administrative arm, or secretariat.

[The discussion then considers the varying levels of autonomy enjoyed by the UN Secretariat and the EEC Commission.]

CONCLUSIONS

International organizations are of interest to the statesman and the theorist of world politics because of the variety of roles they play in the international system and the widely differing interpretations which can be attached to those roles. First, international organizations are used by states, individually or collectively, as instruments of foreign policy. Second, they act, by their very presence in the system, to modify states' behavior. Third, they sometimes achieve a degree of autonomy and influence as political actors in their own right. The fact that most international organizations are perceived or expected – from a variety of perspectives – to play two or possibly all three of these roles simultaneously underlines that the roles are not mutually exclusive and in fact may at times be mutually reinforcing.

Observers of, or participants in, international organizations may have divergent expectations as to their future development. Accordingly, they may apply different standards in measuring an organization's success or failure. But on such organizations' contribution to the complexity of the international system there is little disagreement. If international organizations alleviate some problems for states, they also create new ones. And if, for the theorist, they do not yet seriously challenge the traditional state-centered model of the international system, they do complicate and compromise it somewhat.

The instrumentalist perspective, being predominantly the view from the national capital, is perhaps easiest reconciled with the classic model. The actions and development of international organizations simply reflect national interest, whether pursued by a hegemonic power or compromised within a more egalitarian multilateral setting. Success is thus judged in terms of utility for the pursuit of national objectives. Viewed as modifiers of state behavior, second, international organizations may still be compatible with the state-centered model, since that model has always acknowledged the constraints placed on states by their existence in the ordered but competitive context of the international system. Minimally, international organizations can be seen simply as the institutional embodiment of this kind of constraint. Clearly, however, they have now developed well beyond that point. The scale of the security problem, as well as that of a wide range of economic, social, and technical problems, has begun to outstrip the capacities of all national governments. Organizations based on the consequent intergovernmental and transnational interdependencies are of a different order entirely from those which represented the constraints of the classic *laissez-faire* state system. Concerning international organizations as actors, finally, expectations are greatest, criteria of success most severe, and the classic state-centered model under the most stress. International organizations are expected to exploit and build upon the interdependence of states to develop their own autonomy and influence in the international system. At the very least, nation-states will have to coexist with new regional and functional actors. And very possibly these actors will gain power and legitimacy at their expense. In such an event, the classic model would begin to look hopelessly outmoded. [...]

NOTES

1 B.M. Russett and J.D. Sullivan, 'Collective Goods and International Organization', *International Organization*, 25 (Autumn 1971), p. 853.
2 Ibid., p. 849.
3 P.C. Schmitter, 'The "Organizational Development" of International Organizations', *International Organization*, 25 (Autumn 1971), p. 918.

2.9 Of blind men, elephants and international integration

Donald J. Puchala

Source: *Journal of Common Market Studies*, vol. 10, no. 3 (Blackwell, 1972), pp. 267–84.

After denying that contemporary international integration is federalism, nationalism at the international level, functionalism or power politics, Puchala suggests it can be best thought of in terms of a Concordance System characterized by a complex set of actors, a distinctive process of institutionalized bargaining and an atmosphere dominated by pragmatism and mutual responsiveness.

[Puchala tells the tale of the blind men who tried to find out what an elephant looked like by touching it. He compares the differing conclusions they reached to the scholarly attempts to theorize about international integration: in both cases concentration on parts of the 'beast' produces erroneous conclusions about what it is like as a whole. He begins his own analysis by claiming that integration is something peculiar to the post-World War II era and then examines and rejects in turn the conventional models used to describe and explain it.]

(1) Contemporary international integration is not federalism

At least it is not classical federalism. Thus far, the patterns of political-economic interaction in different regions of the world – Western Europe, Central America, East Africa, Eastern Europe – which have attracted the attentions of students of international integration, have not by and large resembled patterns suggested by the federalist model. For example, no new central governments have been established to assume functions traditionally allotted to federal governments. Not even in Western Europe are new central authorities representing groups of states in international relations. On the occasions when the Commission speaks for the Six internationally, as in the case of the Kennedy Round negotiations or with regard to association agreements, its positions symbolize multi-lateral diplomatic compromises among six governments much more than they represent the policies of any central or 'federal' government. In addition, even when the Commission intermittently speaks for the 'Six' each member-state continues to speak for itself in world councils and capitals. Then, too, let us not forget that all international integration arrangements currently in existence, including the Western European system, are functionally limited mostly to economic concerns, and therefore poorly approximate the functionally diffuse systems implicit in the federalist model.

In fairness, it is true that analysts using federalist models as guides to inquiry have looked upon contemporary international integration as 'emergent' rather than 'mature' federalism.[1] Nevertheless, the point is that they have been preoccupied (if not obsessed) with questions about the degree of central authority present, the degree of state sovereignty relinquished, and the parcelling of prerogative, power and jurisdiction among national and international authorities. Moreover, these same analysts have tended to equate 'progress' or 'success' in international integration with movement toward central government.

Such analysis is of course legitimate. But it has not been very productive. Most obviously it has not turned up very much federalism in contemporary international integration. But more importantly, conceptualizing and conducting inquiry in terms of the federalist model has tended to blind analysts to a number of interesting questions. Most broadly, is it really true that no progress toward international integration in various parts of the world has been made simply because little movement in the direction of regional central government has been registered? More provocatively perhaps, to what extent does participation in an international integration arrangement actually enhance rather than undermine national sovereignty? Relatedly, to what extent does an international integration arrangement preserve rather than supersede an international state system? Clearly, the analyst in the federalist mode is not prompted to ask these latter sorts of questions. Is he missing something of significance?

(2) Neither is international integration actually 'nationalism' at the regional level

So ingrained has the nationalism model become in Western political thinking and analysis, that we find it difficult to conceive of a non-national international actor, or a political system uncomplemented by an underlying community of people or peoples. Naturally, then, when talk of and movement toward regional unity in different parts of the world attracted the attentions of scholars, a good many assumed that movement toward international integration had to be progress toward the social and cultural assimilation of nationalities. [...] But though we were guided by validated and operational theories of nationalism, and despite the fact that we wielded the most sophisticated methodological tools of modern social science, our researches turned up few 'Europeans', even fewer 'Central Americans' and 'East Africans' and no 'East Europeans' at all.[2] This lacking evidence of progress toward the social and cultural assimilation of nationalities led some analysts to conclude that contemporary international integration was more myth than reality – no nationalism, therefore no integration![3] Others, however, cherished evidence drawn from youth studies and concluded that regional nationalism, at least in Western Europe, was present after all, and that the heyday of European community would arrive as the current younger generation gained maturity and as its members acquired positions of influence and responsibility.[4] Still others, convinced that assimilation simply had to be a component of contemporary international integration, worded and reworded survey questions until 'regional nationality' did at last emerge in poll results, irrespective of whether it existed in respondents' attitudes.

Credit goes to the nationalism analysts for recognizing that contemporary international integration requires a particular kind of attitudinal environment. However, the environment they seek has failed to materialize. Problems in using the nationalism model as a guide to analyzing contemporary international integration are similar to those involved in using the federalism model. First, testing the model against reality in Western Europe, in Central America and elsewhere produces negative results. Regional nationalism, as noted, turns out not to be a component of international integration. Second, as with the federalist case, asking the analytical questions suggested by the nationalism model, deters thinking about a range of interesting alternative questions. For example, the analyst guided by the nationalism model is directed toward asking questions about people-to-people interactions and transactions, about similarities and differences in peoples' life styles, value systems and cultural norms, and especially about their attitudes toward one another and attendant perceptions of 'we-ness'. But are these really the appropriate questions to ask about the attitudinal environments supportive of inter-governmental cooperation and international institutionalization?

Does it really matter what peoples think about one another? Or rather, does it perhaps matter more what these people think about international cooperation and about supranational decision-making? The point here is that while the analyst guided by the nationalism model has been primarily concerned with links and bonds among peoples, he has by and large ignored links and bonds between peoples and their governments and between peoples and international organizations and processes. Is he missing something of significance?

(3) Nor is contemporary international integration functionalism in the Mitrany tradition

Functionalist analysts have achieved greater descriptive accuracy than others grappling with contemporary international integration.[5] Part of this accuracy, of course, must be accounted for by the fact that architects of international integration in Western Europe and elsewhere were directly influenced by functionalist thinking and therefore constructed their systems from functionalist blueprints. Still, let us give credit where credit is due. Functionalist analysts have accurately located the origins of international cooperation in realms of functional interdependence; they have pinpointed the significance of sector approaches; they have grasped the importance of non-governmental transnational actors.

Yet, very little in contemporary international integration has actually 'worked' the way the functionalist design said that it would. Most revealingly, national governments have remained conspicuous and pivotal in internationally integrating systems, quite in contrast to the functionalist model which shunts these to the periphery of action. Leadership, initiative and prerogative have by and large remained with national governments. They have not gravitated to technocrats, bureaucrats and non-governmental actors. Moreover, national governments participating in international integration schemes have proven far more interested in 'welfare' pursuits and far more restrained in 'power' pursuits than functionalist theorizing would have led us to believe. Equally significant, functional task-areas in international economics, communications, science and technology, which the functionalist model stipulates immune from international politics, have in fact turned out to be the central issue-areas in the lively international politics of international integration. There are simply no non-political issues in relations among states!

Most important, the functionalist model misses the essence of the growth and expansion of international regimes during international integration. So concerned are functionalist analysts with sector-to-sector task expansion, that many have failed first to recognize that this sectoral 'spillover' is but one possible variety of expansion or growth during international integration. It is also, incidentally, the variety of growth that is least in evidence in existing cases. But, at least two other varieties can be monitored. First, there is expansion in the volume of internationally coordinative activities within given functional sectors. In addition, and much more important, there is possible expansion in the *political system* brought into being when functional sectors are integrated internationally. Such systemic expansion is evidenced by the entrance of increasing numbers of actors and interests into international program planning and policy making.

Second, neither have functionalist analysts been fully cognizant of the fact that sector-to-sector task expansion, spillover or its variants index integrative progress only if one assumes that 'functional federation' or multi-sector merger is the end product of international integration. Here again, we are evaluating the present in terms of a hypothetical future which may never come about. If multi-sector merger is not the end product of international integration, if integration does not really go very far beyond the nation-state, then other varieties of systemic growth which reflect activity and complexity rather than extension might be the more telling indicators of healthy and productive international integration.

In sum, the functionalist analyst too has been partially strait-jacketed by his framework for thinking about international integration. He asked how men may achieve international cooperation by circumventing politics among nations. But, he has not asked how international cooperation is in fact achieved during international integration in the very course of international politics. Then, he has asked how functional integration spreads or spills over in the direction of federal government. But, in light of what has actually come to pass in Western Europe, might it not have been more productive to ask how a program of transnational sectoral merger fits into and becomes an integral part of a broader pattern of intra-regional international relations? That is, what if the termination state for international integration in fact resembles Western Europe, *circa* 1970? Why do some sectors get merged and others do not? More significantly, what kind of international politics results in a system where some functional sectors are transnationally merged and others are not? Impressionistically speaking, it would seem that this 'broader pattern of intraregional international relations', this complex of merged and unmerged sectors and the aggregation of associated governing authorities of one type or another begins to approximate what we are really talking about when we speak of contemporary international integration. Does the functionalist analyst really recognize this? Is he missing something if he does not?

(4) Nor, finally, is contemporary international integration simply power politics

The school of analysts who have looked upon and thought about international integration within the framework of 'Realist' or *Macht Politik* models have fallen short of understanding what the phenomenon is or involves. To these analysts, international integration is a process of mutual exploitation wherein governments attempt to mobilize and accumulate the resources of neighboring states in the interest of enhancing their own power.[6] Power is to be enhanced so that traditional ends of politics among nations may be accomplished – i.e. international autonomy, military security, diplomatic influence and heightened prestige. In Realist thinking, international organizations created in the course of international integration are but instruments to be used by national governments pursuing self-interests. They are made at the convergent whims of these governments, and flounder or fossilize as their usefulness as instruments of foreign policy comes into question. Over all, the Realist analyst argues that what we are observing 'out there' and calling international integration are really international marriages of convenience, comfortable for all partners as long as self-interests are satisfied, but destined for divorce the moment any partner's interests are seriously frustrated. Hence, international integration drives not toward federalism or nationalism or functionalism, but toward disintegration. It never gets beyond the nation-state.

The wisdom of the Realist model is that it conceives of international integration as a pattern of international relations and not as something above, beyond or aside from politics among nations. But the shortcoming in the model is that it conceives of international integration as *traditional international relations* played by traditional actors, using traditional means in pursuit of traditional ends. So convinced is the political Realist that 'there is nothing new under the sun' in international relations that he never seriously asks whether international actors other than national governments may independently influence the allocation of international rewards. Nor does he ask whether actors committed to international integration may be pursuing any other than the traditional inventory of international goals – autonomy, military security, influence and prestige. Do these really remain important goals in contemporary international relations? Nor, finally, does the Realist ask how actors committed to integration agreements in fact define their self-interests. Could it be that actors engaged in international integration actually come to consider it in their own self-interest to see that their partners accomplish their goals? In sum, by assuming that international politics remains the 'same old game' and that international integration is but a part of it, the Realist analyst is not prompted to ask what is new in contemporary international relations. Is he missing something of significance?

TOWARD A NEW CONCEPTUALIZATION

If there has been a central theme running through my review of analytical models, it is that our conventional frameworks have clouded more than they have illumined our understanding of contemporary international integration. No model describes the integration phenomenon with complete accuracy because all the models present images of what integration could be or should be rather than what it is here and now. Furthermore, attempts to juxtapose or combine the conventional frameworks for analytical purposes by and large yield no more than artificial, untidy results. Clearly, to surmount the conceptual confusion we must set aside the old models, and, beginning from the assumption that international integration could very well be something new that we have never before witnessed in international relations, we must create a new, more appropriate, more productive analytical framework. I contend that this new model must reflect and raise questions about what international integration *is* in Western Europe, Central America, East Africa, etc., *at present.* We must, in other words, stop testing the present in terms of progress toward or regression from hypothetical futures since we really have no way of knowing where or how contemporary international integration is going to end up. The remainder of this essay is a very preliminary step in the direction of a new conceptualization of contemporary international integration.

Is it really an 'elephant' after all?

Complexity of structure

I will hypothesize, though I cannot argue the case as convincingly as I would like to at this moment, that *contemporary international integration can best be thought of as a set of processes that produce and sustain a Concordance System at the international level.* 'Concordance', according to dictionaries I have consulted, means 'agreement' or 'harmony', and 'concord', its root, refers to 'peaceful relations among nations'. A 'Concordance System' by my definition is an international system wherein actors find it possible consistently to harmonize their interests, compromise their differences and reap mutual rewards from their interactions. I selected the term 'Concordance System' primarily because I found it necessary to have a name for what I believe I see coming into being 'out there' in the empirical world. But what we call this product of international integration is not very important; how we describe it is centrally important.

What does a Concordance System look like? First, states or nation-states are among the major component units of the system, and national governments remain central actors in it. While it can and will be argued that contemporary international integration does in fact go 'beyond the nation-state' both organizationally and operationally, it nonetheless does not go very far beyond. It certainly does not drive the state into oblivion, economic, political or otherwise. Neither does it relegate the national government to obscurity. Whatever may be the indeterminate future of present-day regional common markets, harmonization agreements and other varieties of integrative ventures here subsumed under the label 'Concordance System' these are presently clusters of cooperatively interacting states. For all we know now, 'international integration' may never be more than this. Therefore, what we are really talking about when we speak of contemporary international integration are neither federations, nor nationalities, nor functional latticeworks, but *international state systems* of a rather interesting kind.

Hopefully having made the point that national governments remain important actors in Concordance Systems, it now must be said that one of the most interesting features of these systems is that national governments are not the only important actors. In fact, the most complex Concordance Systems may include actors in four organizational arenas – the subnational, the national, the transnational and the supranational. In contrast to familiar federal systems, there is no prevailing or established hierarchy or superordination–subordination relationship among the different kinds of actors in the system. Instead, each of the actors remains quasi-autonomous (more or less so depending upon issues in question), all are interdependent, and all interact in pursuit of consensus that yields mutual rewards. [...]

Novelty in process

Aside from complexity of structure, a number of other distinctive features characterize the Concordance System. Some of these have to do with the nature of interaction processes within the system. First, the Concordance System tends to be a highly institutionalized system wherein actors channel the bulk of their transactions in all issue-areas through organizational networks according to routinized procedures. That is, the process of international interaction within the Concordance System is much more bureaucratic than it is diplomatic. 'Bureaucratic' as I use it here is not meant belittlingly. Quite to the contrary, just as efficient bureaucracy tends to reflect advanced civilization, 'bureaucratic international relations' reflects ordered, standardized, planned, efficient problem-solving in relations among nations. In the Concordance System conflict is effectively regulated and cooperation is facilitated via institutionalized, constitutional, precedential or otherwise standardized, patterned procedures which all actors commit themselves to use and respect. In a way, we can say that the Concordance System characteristic of contemporary international integration is the farthest thing removed from the traditional anarchy of international politics, but which is yet not a state, nation-state or federation. Let it be noted, however, that a Concordance System need not be institutionally centralized. Transactions are channeled through institutions, to be sure, but the Concordance System may include any number of functionally specific organizations and any number of standardized procedures, while it includes nothing even vaguely resembling an overarching central government. In this way, again, the Concordance System remains essentially an international system.

By looking at processes within the Concordance System somewhat more abstractly, we are able to note two further distinctive features of the system. First, political conflict is an integral part of the international interaction pattern. It occurs both within and between all action arenas. But, quite in contrast to the modalities of traditional international relations, and accordingly baffling to analysts of the Realist school, more conflict within the Concordance System follows from divergent views about 'ways to cooperate' rather than from fundamental incompatibilities in the interests of the various actors. That is, common, convergent, or at least compatible ends among actors are prerequisites for the emergence of a Concordance System; if these are not present no Concordance System will develop. What actors within the system tend to disagree about most often are the kinds of procedures they will commit themselves to as they bureaucratize their international relations. Therefore, in observing Concordance Systems we should expect to find conflict, we should expect this to be initiated over questions of establishing new harmonizing procedures, and we should expect it to be terminated in agreements on new procedures acceptable to all actors. In this sense, conflict may well be functional to the Concordance System. But to be sure, incompatibilities in actors' basic interests and questions about ultimate ends and goals do intermittently crop up within Concordance Systems, as they certainly did during Charles de Gaulle's challenges to the EEC system in Western Europe. When such questions do emerge and are openly contested, they become dysfunctional to the continuation of the Concordance System and could lead to its deterioration.

Second, *bargaining among actors* toward the achievement of convergent or collective ends is the predominant style of interaction within the Concordance System. This bargaining, with exchanged concessions and ultimate compromises, tends to characterize interactions within and between all action arenas. As such, coercion and confrontation are both alien to the Concordance System, are considered illegitimate by actors and occur infrequently. In the vocabulary of the Theory of Games, primitive confrontation politics and resultant constant-sum gamesmanship are alien to Concordance Systems. Much more typical is the variable-sum game pattern which rewards all actors for their cooperative behavior and penalizes them for competitive behavior. Moreover, the game as played in the Concordance System is a 'full information' game where players readily learn of rewards from cooperation and penalties from competition by communicating openly with one another. In short, there is no premium on secrecy and deception in the politics of the Concordance System as there often tends to be in more traditional diplomacy. Of course, none of this is to say that lapses into confrontation politics, attempts at punishment and retaliation, and zero-sum gamesmanship are completely extinguished in Concordance Systems. Again, however, to the extent that these vestiges of traditional international politics enter into interaction patterns of the Concordance System, the system itself comes into jeopardy.

Some attributes of atmosphere

The Concordance System survives and thrives in a distinctive attitudinal environment. Four features of this psychological setting are especially notable.

First, pragmatism is the prevailing political doctrine of the Concordance System. If the term pragmatism sounds overly formal, call it 'down-to-earthism'. What it means is that international social, economic and political problems are looked upon by actors involved first as real, second as soluble and third as approachable by whatever means seem most promising of rapid, efficient solution. Pragmatism does not cherish any cosmic first principles, such as those that found socialism, nationalism, communism or liberalism, nor does it project utopian visions. It rather equips its adherents to pour themselves into problem-solving without anxiety about doctrinal purity. Lerner and Gordon admirably capture the pragmatic atmosphere of the present-day Western European Concordance System: 'The collapse of traditional ideologies has made the European elites into pragmatists. They have tried to face the new realities of their postwar situation in ways that work.... They can now work more effectively with each other on problems of common interest even when they do not share a common ideology that tells them how to talk about these problems.... This is what we call, 'the new pragmatism'.[7]

Second, and perhaps relatedly, the Concordance System is supported by perceptions of international interdependence, or, if not this, then at least by perceptions of national inadequacy. Again, after Lerner and Gordon, and with respect to Western European elite thinking: 'Indeed, there has been a convergent consensus in Europe over the last decade (1955–1965) that national options are not viable and that transnational choices are the only realistic alternatives.'[8] One of the first steps toward a Concordance System, perhaps, is the emergence of the realization on the part of governments and peoples that they need one another in vital ways. But, let it be noted that such perceptions of national inadequacy and international interdependence as are found among elites (and masses also) within Concordance Systems are not negations of the nation-state, nor are they reflections of a new cosmopolitanism. They are rather recognitions of modern economic and technological forces that transverse national frontiers, recognitions that states can no longer relieve internal pressures by external imperialism, and indeed affirmations that nation-states can be preserved as distinct entities only through the international pooling of resources to confront problems that challenge their separate existence.

Third, and again probably relatedly, the 'atmosphere' within the Concordance System, especially in councils where common programs are formulated and decided upon, is one of high mutual sensitivity and responsiveness. To begin with, actors within the system tend to possess a good deal more information about one another and about one another's goals, objectives, preferences and needs than is common in more traditional diplomacy where emphasis is upon one's own needs and upon ways to fulfill these regardless of what the other fellow may want. But even more important, actors within the Concordance System feel some compulsion to see to it that their partners' needs as well as their own are fulfilled in decisions made and programs executed. All of this may sound rather strange to the student of traditional international relations. Nevertheless, it is precisely this atmosphere of shared compulsion to find mutually rewarding outcomes, this felt and shared legitimacy in concession-making, and this reciprocal sensitivity to needs that markedly distinguishes between the new international politics of the Concordance System and the traditional politics of the Machiavellian world.

Fourth, and finally, the Concordance System includes people, or, better stated, peoples. These are the mass populations of the nation-states within the system. What is distinctive about these peoples is that they accord legitimacy to the structures and processes of the system. For one thing, they accept the subnational–national–transnational–supranational political environment that surrounds them, and they defer to the outcomes of the bargaining processes in the multi-arena system. Put more simply, the mass populations of the Concordance System see the system itself as legitimate, and its decisional outputs as authoritative. They comply accordingly. Again, this is a far cry from traditional international relations in the age of integral nationalism! In addition, let it be underlined that mass populations within the Concordance System need not be assimilated into a supranationality. In fact, they may not even like one another very much. They do, however, recognize, accept and bow to the necessities of international cooperation in an age of interdependence, and they support international integration accordingly.

262   *Donald J. Puchala*

NOTES

1 William Diebold, 'The Relevance of Federalism to Western European Economic Integration', In Arthur W. Macmahon (ed.), *Federalism: Mature and Emergent* (Doubleday, Garden City, NY, 1955), pp. 433–57.
2 K.W. Deutsch *et al.*, *France, Germany and the Western Alliance, A Study of Elite Attitudes on European Integration and World Politics* (Scribner, New York, 1967), pp. 252–64.
3 Ibid., pp. 298–300.
4 R. Inglehart, 'An End to European Integration?', *American Political Science Review*, 61 (March 1967), pp. 91–105.
5 In this regard see, especially, R. Inglehart and E. Haas, 'International Integration: The European Process and the Universal', *International Organization*, 15: 3 (Summer 1961), pp. 366–92.
6 The Realist model is most elegantly set forth in Raymond Aron, *Peace and War: A Theory of International Relations*, translated by Richard Howard and Annette Baker Fox (Doubleday, Garden City, NY, 1966), pp. 21–196.
7 Daniel Lerner and Morton Gordon, *Euratlantica. Changing Perspectives of the European Elites* (MIT Press, Cambridge, Mass., 1969), p. 242.
8 Ibid., p. 241.

2.10 The world polity and the nation-state system

Seyom Brown

Source: *International Journal*, vol. xxxix, no. 3 (Canadian Institute of International Affairs, 1984), pp. 509–28.

Brown argues that the world polity goes beyond the nation-state system, although nation-states remain a major sub-system in world politics. Traditionally, the nation-state system has performed several important functions: the provision of public order, the regulation of commerce, the enhancement of social justice, the control of access to and exploitation of natural resources, and the maintenance of cultural diversity. These activities have also provided the basis for world order based on the nation-state system, but increasingly this seems an inadequate foundation. Brown goes on in this extract to argue that the world polity is evolving into a polyarchy, with a variety of actors and processes for ensuring order.

THE NATION-STATE SYSTEM AS AN INADEQUATE SUBSYSTEM OF THE WORLD POLITY

The nation-state system has indeed proven to be a remarkably durable human invention – dating, in the eyes of many historians, back to the Treaty of Westphalia (1648) which ended the wars of religion – and there is no prospect of its total collapse so long as the great powers avoid stumbling into World War III. However, day by day the evidence grows that neither the separate nation-states nor the system of relations between them can adequately perform the standard tasks of governance. A manifestation of this inadequacy is the proliferation of transnational and subnational organizations and movements – representing diverse religious, ethnic, geographic, economic, and professional groups and interests – which are allocating resources and values and managing conflict (often unsuccessfully) within and among themselves, and as often as not bypassing the institutions of the central national government. Increasingly, the span of political authority and legal control of the nation-states are revealed to be incongruent with the intense clusters of interaction between peoples. 'Nations,' as it were, do not match states; economies have become disjoined from polities; those who profoundly affect one another's lives are often not politically or legally accountable to each other.

Deficiencies as a world order system

The ability of the nation-state system to maintain world public order and to preserve the sovereign independence of its members, large and small, has depended upon credible alliance commitments designed to redress imbalances of military power which might tempt aggressor nations. The viability of this equilibrating mechanism of the system has been cast into severe doubt by the development of weapons that have made all states – even the superpowers – unconditionally vulnerable to virtually total destruction.

It is now widely recognized, even though rarely admitted explicitly by alliance statesmen, that no country can count on any of its alliance partners joining it in a hot war against an enemy armed with a substantial nuclear arsenal. China learned this cruel lesson during its confrontations with the United States in the 1950s over the islands in the Formosa Strait; drawing the logical implication from Khrushchev's failure to issue meaningful and timely counterdeterrent threats, Mao Zedong decided to develop a nuclear arsenal of his own. North Vietnam learned a similar lesson during the decade of United States military intervention in the Indochina conflict, when both the Soviet Union and China loudly proclaimed they would not stand idly by if the United States went to war against their smaller ally, but in fact did precisely that. The Soviet Union has yet to engage in direct military action against a United States ally; but anticipating that someday the event may occur, potential victims do not have great confidence that the United States will put valour ahead of prudence at the 'moment of truth'.

President Charles de Gaulle spoke the unspeakable in the late 1950s, warning that if the French did not develop their own nuclear deterrent force there might come an awful day when France and the rest of Western Europe would be incinerated by a Soviet nuclear attack and Eastern Europe would be in turn incinerated by a United States blow, while the two superpowers refrained from directly attacking each other. De Gaulle's nightmare was simply an evocative political expression of what had become axiomatic to professional strategists: that the more stable the United States–Soviet balance of terror, the more flimsy were United States guarantees of protection.

The actions of China and France gave the superpowers nightmares of their own. Most countries would attempt to gain nuclear weapons, and as more did the chances of someone starting a world-destroying nuclear holocaust would multiply.

The self-equilibrating forces of the nation-state system seemed to come into play as Moscow and Washington combined to prevent the spread of nuclear weapons. Under the Non-Proliferation Treaty of 1968, jointly drafted by the Soviet Union, the United States, and the United Kingdom, the two superpowers and other signatories possessing nuclear weapons pledged to refrain from transferring a nuclear weapons capability to non-nuclear states, while the nuclear have-not signatories agreed not to develop or to receive nuclear weapons. In return for their self-denial, the nuclear have-not signatories were assured in the treaty of special 'security guarantee' actions (which remained largely unspecified) by the superpowers in the event of a have-not state being threatened by a nuclear-armed state.

But France and China refused to sign the treaty, branding it a device designed by the United States and the Soviet Union to preserve their strategic duopoly. A number of middle-ranking countries – among them Brazil, India, the Republic of South Africa, and Israel – also refused to sign what they claimed was a discriminatory effort to legitimize a 'class' system in international society: one group of countries belonging to the nuclear club and another, presumably the less responsible countries, expected to place their trust in the nuclear club to manage the global balance of power.

By 1984 over a third of the world's countries had either not signed or not ratified the Non-Proliferation Treaty. By 1990 most of these countries will have the technical capability to develop nuclear weapons. Many already have the capability. When any one of these countries crosses the threshold between being simply nuclear-capable and actually deploying nuclear weapons, contagion is likely to set in. Once the process of proliferation is under way, it would be unrealistic to assume that Japan would be willing to maintain its non-nuclear status. Nor would other states aspiring to be major powers – Brazil, Argentina, Indonesia, Vietnam, Nigeria – deny themselves what was becoming an ordinary attribute of military prowess. The proliferation of nuclear weapons throughout the international system will exacerbate fear and suspicion between allies as well as adversaries and provide more opportunities for leakage of dangerous nuclear materials and even fully assembled weapons to terrorist groups.

Thus the nuclear age, which at its dawning seemed as if it might bring a more integrated nation-state system, has only intensified the structural contradictions in the system – figuratively and literally increasing the likelihood of its eventual atomization.

The socially integrating impact of the nuclear age appears to be taking place *outside the system*, so to speak. The fear of a species-destroying holocaust has been perhaps the greatest stimulant in history to the emergent countercultures of *anti*-nationalism and pacifism, which are profoundly antithetical to the cultural and political norms of the nation-state system. The anti-nuclear movements in Western Europe, Japan, the United States, Canada, and even (in their suppressed form) in Eastern Europe are linked not only in their opposition to The Bomb but also in their animosity toward the inherited state system itself. The anti-nationalism is often amorphous and somewhat deceptive in its inchoateness, for it is frequently combined with vigorous opposition to one's country becoming the lackey of one of the superpowers, and as such can appear to be an expression of nationalism. But the nationalism usually goes only so far as opposition to oppressive dependence on an external power; it does not extend to a worship of the national flag and other symbols of patriotism – my country right or wrong. Quite the contrary.

Deficiencies as a regulator of the transnational economy

The ability of the nation-state system to ensure that public safety, orderly commerce, social justice, and cultural integrity are sustained within the territorial confines of particular countries is undermined when national policies for regulating the national market can be ignored or overwhelmed by buyers and sellers unaccountable to the political and legal institutions of the nation. In a system of sovereign nation-states, a country heavily involved in the transnational economy, such that the health of its national economy is substantially dependent upon foreign imports or exports or investments, has by that fact placed its polity at the mercy of foreigners. Thus, in the nation-state system there is an inherent contradiction between the most basic formal legal structure and the political economic realities where international commerce is flourishing. Something has to give way: either national sovereignty or international commerce. Because of the high material incentives in the contemporary world for all countries to indulge heavily in international commerce, the basic long-term trend is toward a global transnational economy, despite fitful 'protectionist' attempts in many countries to insulate the domestic economy from disruptive external developments. But the polity is not organized on a transnational basis.

The incapacity of national governments and the governments of local subdivisions of nation-states to regulate the transnational economy does not bode well for the effectiveness of social policies designed to transfer resources and other benefits from the more successful competitive members of society to those handicapped in some way for competition in the market. If corporations are able to relocate production facilities to avoid paying high wages and benefits to their labour forces and to avoid high taxes, or if they can avoid local taxes by transnational relocations of financial assets within the corporation, then, in many countries, the fruits of decades of domestic political struggle to legislate 'progressive' redistribution of income will be left to wither.

Developing countries anxious to attract foreign investment and manufacturing subsidiaries – despite standard Third World rhetoric against the multinational corporation – are competing with each other to assure international corporate managers that there will be few onerous restrictions on their activities and that they will not have to hand over a large part of the subsidiary's earnings to the host-country government. This is one of the reasons why many poor countries have postponed for so long the 'social overhead' programmes (especially in the field of public health) which would help their most impoverished elements. General 'infrastructure' projects, such as the construction of road, water, and waste disposal systems, usually of indirect but substantial benefit to the poorest segments of society, are also likely to be given secondary priority or to be postponed in favour of specialized infrastructure projects desired by the corporate sectors. The social service state will have to come after economic development, and the development process itself may well enlarge pre-existing social inequities.

This loss of social regulatory power by domestic polities as the economy becomes more and more transnational cannot be compensated for by giving regulatory power to transnational polities without some fundamental alterations in the structural base of the nation-state system. Short of such worldwide political reform, the expansion of economic transnationalism constitutes a general and basic disenfranchisement of national populations. The loss of national sovereignty, without other major changes in the world polity, means the loss of popular sovereignty, and the return of socio-economic power to unaccountable oligarchical élites. In such a polity, the ability of citizens to compel those with power to respect basic human rights would also be reduced.

A more subtle effect of the overbearing influence of the transnational economy on society is its erosion of diverse cultural forms. The global market tends to be a great homogenizer, to the disappointment of those who search for exotic items in the shops of other countries. Cultural uniqueness is often economically inefficient, and its preservation therefore requires intervention in the name of the community's non-economic values. The preservation of cultural diversity has been one of the main contributions of the nation-state system to world society; for it has been only through the ability of national governments to give legal protection to such non-economic values and, indeed, sometimes to become the major instrument of their expression and propagation that special cultures have been able to resist bombardment and pulverization by the globally dominant culture of modern industrial society. Thus the increasingly inadequate reach of national governments into the functioning of the transnational economy, involving as it often does a loss of control over what comes into the domestic market, is depriving world society of perhaps its only existing effective means of husbanding the pluralism that has hitherto stimulated mankind's proudest accomplishments in the realms of philosophy, literature, fine arts, science, and even technological-economic development.

Insufficient ability to protect the natural environment

As knowledge has grown about the inter-relatedness of the global environment and the extent to which perturbances to an ecosystem in one political jurisdiction can often affect ecosystems to which it is linked in other jurisdictions (even in remote places), the potentially harmful consequences of the poor match between the political-legal structure of world society and the natural structure of the physical environment have become more evident. The progress of technology has worsened the damaging implications of this incongruence. Humans have learned to produce large-scale and severe alterations of the environment affecting the health of ecosystems that traverse national lines and are sometimes global in scope. Yet in most regions of the globe there are no legal mechanisms which the nationals of an affected country can invoke to compel actors engaging in disturbing actions in another country's jurisdiction, or even in such 'commons' as the high seas or outer space, to consult with them or to be held in any way internationally accountable for the damage inflicted on commonly used resources.

PROGNOSIS: ANARCHY OR POLYARCHY?

A situation of anarchy prevails where individuals or groups are accountable to no one but themselves for what they do to others. In the world polity, under the nation-state system, while there might at times and places have seemed to be virtual anarchy between the states, the states themselves (or at least a goodly number of them) have been able to maintain relatively effective systems of governance within their borders. Nevertheless, the conditions necessary to avoid anarchy even within the nation-states are being undermined by new material and social forces which neither the separate national governments nor the nation-state *system* seem able to contain.

First, given today's military technologies, war, if it does break out between certain nation-states, can rapidly (almost instantaneously) become total war – leaving a heap of smouldering radioactive rubble where civilizations once held sway. In areas that have been part of the nuclear battlefield, there will in all likelihood be a complete breakdown of human capacities for large-scale community organization, with recovery measured in decades, if indeed recovery still has meaning at all.

Secondly, because of the growing interdependence of states and the swiftness with which resources and other assets can be transferred in and out of national jurisdictions by transnational corporate enterprises and financial networks, national polities have been losing a good part of their capacity for self-government. The most powerful economic actors and agencies (including both private and state-run enterprises) can affect the lives of large numbers of the world's population, while remaining substantially impervious to controls legislated by popular parliaments and not legally accountable to any agencies representing the interests of the communities they affect.

Thirdly, technological developments have given nation-states an increasing ability to disrupt the conditions of life within each other's jurisdictions through environmental actions which are transmitted through nature's vast web of interlinked ecosystems. The conventional instruments of statecraft – diplomacy, treaties whose enforcement depends upon the action of national agencies, international forums with no authoritative legislative competence and no supranational capacity to administer resolutions – appear inadequate to the task of subordinating environment-damaging technologies to the civil needs of the world polity or even to the purposes of domestic polities.

A drift toward anarchy is certainly plausible; but such a prognosis overlooks the organizational inventiveness of the human animal. Where national governments have been losing their grip, provincial or local governments have been moving in to take up the slack, often negotiating trade and investment arrangements with similar subunits of government in other countries. Where public organizations have faltered in providing essential social amenities to inhabitants of national or local commonwealths, non-governmental associations of self-help (often catering to members of particular religious or ethnic groups) have stepped into the void. Moreover, unregulated markets are hardly anarchic; the régime of supply and demand, where it holds sway, creates its own incentives for public order, stability of contract and monetary relationships, and even a certain amount of justice.

Not anarchy but *polyarchy* is the more appropriate concept for describing and understanding the emergent patterns in the world polity.

In a polyarchic system there is no dominant structure for managing co-operation and conflict. Nation-states, subnational groups, trans-national special interests and communities, all compete for the support and loyalty of individuals, and in this shifting context of power relationships, conflicts often need to be resolved through ad hoc bargaining. The role of the nation-state in the global polyarchic system varies in different localities and regions. Paradoxically, where national societies are the weakest in relation to alternative forms of human association, they are also likely to be the most assertive in maintaining the traditional prerogatives of the nation-state. Those countries whose socio-economic systems are most vulnerable to the actions of more powerful countries, multinational corporations, or other transnational forces tend to be the most rigid defenders of national sovereignty and unfettered domestic jurisdiction. They also tend to exhibit the least tolerance for sub-national or transnational political, religious, and ethnic movements. It is hardly surprising that the most determined strongholds of nation-statism are found among the new nations of the Third World and the communist countries. In the highly industrialized countries, the opportunities for building transnational associations and for travel are conducive to cosmo-politan attitudes among both corporate and political élites, while the more 'protectionist' elements of the society are often branded as reactionary.

Polyarchy can, of course, degenerate into anarchy, for the reasons I have indicated. Moreover, it can produce its own patterns of polarized alienation and discontent, as the less mobile, less cosmo-politan segments of local and global societies feel disenfranchised, as it were, in the face of the ability of the affluent élites to make the world run without being substantially accountable to popular parliaments and assemblies. However, the 'statesmen' of the polyarchic system also have the opportunity to anticipate or respond in an enlightened way to such disenfranchisement – whether real or simply felt – on the part of less cosmopolitan groups. They can seek to transform the fragmented polyarchic pattern into worldwide and regional communities in which the complex interdependencies are matched by political and legal processes and institutions, making people accountable to one another to the extent that they affect each other's lives.

The model for such a world system is the modern, ethnically diverse greater metropolitan area, such as New York or Los Angeles. These megalopolises comprise numerous municipal and special-purpose jurisdictions, many of which overlap, but they lack a strong central government for the whole metropolitan area. The polyarchic 'global city' could exhibit an analogous structure. Public services – physical safety, education, cultural activities, public utilities – could be largely provided within locally demarcated political units (some of them still the smaller nation-states of the traditional international system); but where a high degree of co-ordination is required across national boundaries – air travel and telecommunications, and the use of the oceans, great river systems, the atmosphere, and outer space – multinational or transnational institutions, with memberships and spans of control congruent with the interdependent relationships, could be accorded the responsibility for co-ordination, rule making, and even rule enforcement.

The nation-states surely have a crucial role to play in the polyarchic world as far ahead as we can see. But it is time that we start to view them as only one element of the world polity rather than its essence.

Part III
The politics of dominance and dependence

INTRODUCTION

The articles in this section draw on a radical perspective which is critical of the prevailing structure of the international arena. Dominance and dependence are evaluative as well as descriptive terms and they are designed to draw attention to the mechanisms which advocates of this perspective see as perpetuating inequality within the world community. The roots of this perspective can be traced back to Marx who believed that it is possible to develop a scientific understanding of the exploitation which takes place in capitalist systems and to identify the forces of change which can transform such systems and bring an end to exploitation. But Marx is now seen to have taken insufficient account of the international system in his theory. This dimension, however, was later embraced by Lenin whose theory of imperialism explained how the acquisition of colonies was related to the development of capitalism. Lenin also tried to show that conflict among the imperialist states was an inevitable feature of capitalism but this view was contested by Kautsky who identified the potential for 'ultra-imperialism' with capitalists cooperating in order to ensure the continuation of a system from which they all benefited. Major disagreements about essential features of this perspective persist among contemporary theorists. It is also worth noting that not everyone working within this perspective can be identified as a Marxist.

The first two items in this section are concerned with imperialism. O'Connor (3.1) argues that Lenin, writing in an era of colonialism, failed to appreciate the need to distinguish between colonialism and imperialism. In the aftermath of decolonization, the importance of this distinction is much more apparent and O'Connor, after examining a Marxist and a non-Marxist view of nineteenth-century colonialism, goes on to present a Marxist view of the contemporary world which links imperialism to the domination of the capitalist world economy by the United States. Galtung (3.2) provides a more abstract theory of imperialism in the modern world. It takes account of class conflict and inequality both within and between states. Galtung's model shows how the ruling class of an imperial state can use the ruling class of a penetrated state as a bridgehead in the process of establishing imperialism. Class conflict – a central feature of classical Marxism – is thereby related to the explanation of imperialism.

Wallerstein (3.3) offers a broader framework for thinking about dominance and dependency in the international system. He argues that in the course of world history there have been two types of world systems: first, world empires, where the structure of the centralized political system coincides with the structure of the centralized economic system and, second, world economies where the integrated structure of the world economy is contrasted with the fragmented political structure provided by a system of independent states. Both types of system are characterized by inequality but the remarkable fact about the contemporary world economy is that it can be traced back to the sixteenth century. Wallerstein attributes the survival of the system to the existence of semi-peripheral states which have acted as a cushion between the exploiting centre states and the exploited periphery.

Gereffi (3.4) accepts Wallerstein's general framework but draws attention to the impressive growth of interdependence in the contemporary international arena. At first sight, the creation of mutually dependent relationships would seem to negate the ideas of dominance and inequality in the system. But Gereffi stresses that the structure of dependence is asymmetrical so that, for example, while Mexico is highly dependent on the United States, the United States is only marginally dependent on Mexico. The asymmetry serves further to concentrate power at the centre of the system.

Marxists have also begun to pay very close attention to transnationalism which, like interdependence, is a central feature of the second perspective. Transnationalism, however, is now seen in a very different light and is considered to be a factor which reinforces global inequality. Sunkel and Fuenzalida (3.5) identify the existence of a transnational community with a distinctive culture which embraces a small segment of the population living at the centre and periphery of the world economy. This community is shown to be benefiting from the process of transnationalization at the expense of the rest of the world community.

The process of transnationalization has been enormously assisted since the end of the Second World War by the development of technology which has transformed information into one of the most important commodities in the modern world. Technology, according to Locksley (3.6), has made it possible to monitor what is going on around the globe and to coordinate this information on an instantaneous basis. But this capacity is only available to the transnational elite. Locksley explores how information technology has been developed and used and he argues that the major effect has been to promote the interests of international capital. According to Sunkel and Fuenzalida (3.5), however, there is a growing potential for polarization and conflict between institutions representing the transnational interests of international capital and the nation-states where they are physically located. The same point is made by Hymer (3.7) in his examination of the multinational corporation, which is widely depicted as the major agent of transnationalization. By using information technology, multinational corporations have been able to impose increasing centralization on the world economy. But Hymer argues that this process will be threatened in the Third World if there is a failure to ensure that sufficient benefits trickle down to the national communities. Without these benefits, the multinational corporations will come to rely increasingly on repression. According to Luckham (3.8), however, the state apparatus in many Third World states has already been militarized and operates on the basis of repression. These regimes, therefore, often inadvertently, provide an environment which allows international capital to pursue its interests in an unrestrained fashion.

The final two items in this section both present something of a challenge to the established orientation of the perspective. Brewer (3.9) argues that Marxist analysis has in recent years tended to become somewhat myopic because of its preoccupation with the growing gap between the centre and the periphery of the world economy. In his review of some of the recent literature on this relationship, he reasserts the significance of the state in the modern world and raises questions about the continued hegemony of the United States (a point also made by Wallerstein). But Brewer also draws attention to the controversial thesis (at least for some Marxists) that the dynamics of capitalism require peripheral countries to be developed. Brewer is thus sceptical of the claim that capitalism is preventing the development of the Third World. He suggests that classical Marxism supports this conclusion. Finally, Block (3.10) reassesses Marxist theories of the state. He questions the traditional view, drawn upon by Wallerstein, for example, that the ruling class in a capitalist state has the capacity to maintain and shape the international system in ways which will promote the interests of international capital. Block suggests that there is a division of labour between capitalists who are simply concerned about the need to accumulate profits and state managers who adhere to a broader perspective and who recognize the need to develop long-term strategies to sustain the international system even at the expense of undermining the capacity to make short-term profits.

Despite the disagreements, all the authors in this section are critical of the prevailing world order which they believe perpetuates inequality. They are also committed to the view that the existing structures will have to be eradicated before inequality can be eliminated. There is little optimism, however, that such a transformation is likely to be brought about in the near future.

3.1 The meaning of economic imperialism

James O'Connor

Source: R.I. Rhodes (ed.), *Imperialism and Underdevelopment: a Reader* (Monthly Review Press, New York, 1970), pp. 101–50.

O'Connor identifies three general doctrines of imperialism: the first disassociates capitalism from imperialism and explains the European expansion which began in the 1880s in political terms; the second examines that same expansionism but interprets it in terms of the needs of monopoly capitalism; and the third concentrates on contemporary world capitalism and identifies a neo-imperialism which does not require the territorial control of traditional colonialism.

IMPERIALISM: A POLITICAL PHENOMENON

The first doctrine disassociates capitalism from imperialism. For Joseph Schumpeter, the leading exponent of this view, imperialism is 'a heritage of the autocratic state ... the outcome of precapitalist forces which the autocratic state has reorganized ... [and] would never have been evolved by the "inner logic" of capitalism itself'.[1] The 'inner logic' of capitalism consists of nothing more or less than free trade and 'where free trade prevails *no* class has an interest in forcible expansion as such ... citizens and goods of every nation can move in foreign countries as freely as though those countries were politically their own'. Only the 'export monopolist interests' – in particular, monopolies in the metropolitan countries which dump surplus commodities abroad behind high tariff walls – profit from imperialism. Schumpeter was confident that these interests would not survive capitalism's 'inner logic'. His confidence was, of course, misplaced; as we will see, the national and regional economic policies of the advanced capitalist countries today rightly merit Joan Robinson's label – the New Mercantilism. The reason is not hard to find: Schumpeter selected one characteristic of capitalism, 'rationality', which he considered central, to the exclusion of other features.

The vast majority of bourgeois economists in the past and present adopt a position similar to Schumpeter's, even though few today would share his optimism in connection with the revival of free trade. The generally accepted 'comparative advantage' theory of Ricardo and Mill holds that all parties in international commodity trade under competitive conditions and benefit in accordance with the strength of the demand for their respective commodities. Nationalist economic policy and monopoly restricted free trade and inhibited the growth of income and economic well-being, but these barriers have been lowered by the breakup of the European empires. The trademark of this doctrine is that exploitative economic relations between the advanced and backward capitalist countries cannot survive in a world of politically independent countries. According to this line of thinking, the real problems of world capitalism today spring from the misplaced faith of the ex-colonies that nationalist economic policies which have created new and higher barriers to international invest- ment and trade can put the backward countries on the path of self- sustained economic growth.

Schumpeter and other bourgeois writers uncritically disassociate capitalism from imperialism for three reasons: first, because their criteria for distinguishing and identifying imperial and colonial relationships are ordinarily political and not economic (for example, Hans Kohn has developed the most sophisticated typology of imperialism, which he understands in terms of the distribution of political power[2]); second, because they do not consider capitalism as such to be an exploitative system; third, because imperialism histori- cally has contained certain features identified with the theme of expansionism which have not been uniquely associated with any given economic and social system. Thus bourgeois writers have concluded not only that imperialism predates capitalism, but also that imperial- ism is essentially an anachronistic system.

[O'Connor then considers how both in pre-capitalist and capitalist societies and in mercantile and industrial capitalist societies economic expansionism has assumed very different forms, before returning to the second general doctrine.]

[In relation to this doctrine] Lenin's ideas have dominated the field. Yet Lenin owed much to John A. Hobson's *Imperialism*, published in 1902, a book which is frequently (and legitimately) read as the precursor of Lenin's study. Thus we will begin by sketching out the main ideas of Hobson and Lenin, later subjecting them to analysis on the basis of theoretical and historical studies published in recent years.

Hobson and Lenin wrote about imperialism during the heyday of colonialism (1885–1914), which naturally enough appeared to be *the* most significant economic-political phenomenon of the time. By making colonialism their focal point, however, both men equated imperialism and colonialism and thus failed to understand the significance of the 'imperialism of free trade' – an expression coined to describe British economic expansion from the 1840s to the 1880s. Moreover, they barely acknowledged United States expansion and could not anticipate future modes of imperialist controls which have proved to be even more effective than formal colonial rule.

The distinctive feature of Hobson's theory is his conception of colonialism as the reflection of the unfulfilled promise of liberal democracy. As Hobson saw it, inequalities in the distribution of wealth and income in Britain dampened the consumption power of the British working classes, which in turn made it unprofitable for capitalists to utilize fully their industrial capacity. Unable to find profitable investment outlets at home, British capitalists subsequently sought them abroad in the economically underexploited continents. Britain therefore acquired colonies as a dumping ground for surplus capital. The end of imperialist conquest and de-colonization would come about only when the British working classes acquired more economic and political power through trade unionism and parliamentary representation, which would set the stage for a thoroughgoing redistribution of income and hence the development of a home economy in which the volume of consumption corresponded more closely to the volume of production.

Hobson supported his thesis not only by his faith in the promise of liberal democracy, but also by reference to changes in Britain's trade and investments. He tried to show that the expansion of empire during the last two decades of the nineteenth century, when most of the world not already independent or under European rule was carved up among the European powers, resulted in a *decline* in British trade with her colonies in relation to trade with noncolonies. He also underlined the obvious fact that the new colonies in Africa and Asia failed to attract British settlers in significant numbers. Through a process of elimination Hobson thus hit on what he considered to be the crucial element in British imperialism – foreign investments. He linked the vast overflow of capital from Britain during this period – British overseas investments rose from 785 million pounds in 1871 to 3,500 million pounds in 1911 and annual net foreign investments were frequently greater than gross domestic fixed investments – with the frantic struggle by the European powers for colonies, and inferred that the former caused the latter. The political struggles between the major European powers were thus dissolved into struggles for profitable investment outlets, and the explorers, missionaries, traders, and soldiers of the period were seen as the puppets of London's financial magnates.

Lenin agreed with Hobson that the prime cause of capital exports was the vast increase in the supply of capital in the metropolitan countries, especially Britain, and played down the role of the demand for capital in the underdeveloped regions. He also, like Hobson, causally linked foreign investments with the acquisition of colonies. The distinctive element in Lenin's theory related to the *cause* of the surplus of capital.

Lenin understood that imperialism is a *stage* of capitalist development, and not merely one possible set of foreign policy options among many. In particular, imperialism is the monopoly capitalist stage, and exhibits five basic features:

(1) The concentration of production and capital, developed so highly that it creates monopolies which play a decisive role in economic life.
(2) The fusion of banking capital with industrial capital and the creation, on the basis of this financial capital, of a financial oligarchy.
(3) The export of capital, which has become extremely important, as distinguished from the export of commodities.
(4) The formation of the international capitalist monopolies which share out the world among themselves.
(5) The territorial division of the whole earth completed by the great capitalist powers.[3]

The key element is the formation of local and international monopolies behind high tariff barriers in the metropolitan countries. Monopolistic organization develops 'precisely out of free competition' in essentially four ways. First, the concentration (growth in absolute size) of capital leads to the centralization (growth in relative size) of capital. Second, monopoly capital extends and strengthens itself by the seizure of key raw materials. Third, financial capital, or the investment banks, 'impose an infinite number of financial ties of dependence upon all the economic and political institutions of contemporary capitalist society', including nonfinancial capital. Fourth, 'monopoly has grown out of colonial policy. To the numerous "old" motives of colonial policy, the capitalist financier has added the struggle for the sources of raw materials, for the exportation of capital, for "spheres of influence", i.e., for spheres of good business, concessions, monopolist profits, and so on; in fine, for economic territory in general.' In short, the new colonialism opposes itself to the older colonial policy of the 'free grabbing' of territories.

The cause of the surplus of capital and capital exportation, and of monopolistic industry, is the tendency of the rate of profit to fall. Two underlying forces drive down the rate of profit in the metropolitan country. First, the rise of trade unions and social democracy, together with the exhaustion of opportunities to recruit labour from the countryside at the going real wage, rule out possibilities for increasing significantly the rate of exploitation. Second, labor saving innovations increase the organic composition of capital. Monopoly is thus in part formed in order to protect profit margins. At the same time, economies of large-scale production (internal expansion) and mergers during periods of economic crises (external expansion) strengthen pre-existing tendencies toward monopolistic organization.

Meanwhile, in the economically underexploited regions of the world, capital yields a substantially higher rate of return. For one thing, the composition of capital is lower; for another, labor is plentiful in supply and cheap; and, finally, colonial rule establishes the preconditions for monopolistic privileges. Rich in minerals and raw materials required by the development of metals, automotive, and other heavy industries in the metropolitan powers, the underexploited regions naturally attract large amounts of capital. Consequently, foreign investment counteracts the tendency for the rate of profit to fall in the metropolitan economy. On the one hand, high profit margins in the colonies pull up the average return on capital; on the other hand, the retardation of capital accumulation in the home economy recreates the reserve army of the unemployed, raises the rate of exploitation, and, finally, increases the rate of profit.

Pushing this thesis one step forward, the precondition for a truly 'favorable' investment climate is indirect or direct control of internal politics in the backward regions. Economic penetration therefore leads to the establishment of spheres of influence, protectorates, and annexation. Strachey suggests that the backward regions assumed a dependency status (the last step before outright control) in relation to the metropolitan powers chiefly because the former were in debt to the latter. What was significant about the shift from consumer goods to capital goods in world trade was that the colony-to-be needed long-term credits or loans to pay for the capital goods, and that, finally, the relationship between the backward country and the metropolitan country became one of debtor and creditor. And from this it was but a small step to dependence and domination.

Whatever the exact sequence of events which led to colonialism, Lenin's economic definition of colonialism (and imperialism) is monopolistically regulated trade and/or investment abroad at higher rates of profit than those obtaining in the metropolitan country. 'As soon as political control arrives as handmaid to investment', Dobb writes, 'the opportunity for monopolistic and preferential practices exists'. The essential ingredient of colonialism therefore is 'privileged investment: namely, investment in projects which carry with them some differential advantage, preference, or actual monopoly, in the form of concession-rights or some grant of privileged status'.[4]

[O'Connor then raises three objections to these theories: that Lenin exaggerated the break in continuity generated by the events of the 1880s; that both Hobson and Lenin were wrong in supposing that vast amounts of capital flowed into the new colonies; and that formal political control was not necessary in order to maintain Britain's economic interests.]

NEO-IMPERIALISM: CONTROL WITHOUT COLONIALISM

A brief sketch cannot even begin to resolve the many theoretical and historical questions which run through the two major contending doctrines of nineteenth-century imperialism. It is clear, however, that two features of imperialism are not in dispute. The first concerns the general description of economic organization and economic policy. As we have seen, Dobb considers the essential ingredients of imperialism to be 'privileged investment ... investment in projects which carry with them some differential advantage'. This feature must be placed in a wider frame of reference, as in Paul Sweezy's description of imperialism as 'severe rivalry [between advanced capitalist countries] in the world market leading alternatively to cutthroat competition and international monopoly combines'.[5] Schumpeter's view of imperialism is very similar. Cutthroat competition and international monopoly combines are seen as 'protective tariffs, cartels, monopoly prices, forced exports (dumping), an aggressive economic policy, and aggressive foreign policy generally'.[6] A second general area of agreement (generally implicit in the writings of both Marxists and non-Marxists) is that modern imperialism, whatever its causes, depends on colonial rule as the main form of economic and political control of the economically backward region and that political independence would significantly reduce, or eliminate entirely, exploitative imperialist relations.

Opposed to these doctrines is what may be called the neo-Leninist, or modern Marxist theory of imperialism. The increasing economic domination exercised by the United States in the world capitalist economy and the failure of the ex-colonies to embark on sustained economic and social development have caused older Marxist economists to rework original doctrines and have given rise to a new theory of neo-colonialism. Many of its outlines are still indistinct, but there is broad agreement that a sharp distinction should be made between colonialism and imperialism, while the original Leninist identity between monopoly capitalism and imperialism should be retained. In this view, monopoly capitalism remains an aggressively expansionist political-economic system, but colonialism is seen as merely one *form* of imperialist domination, and frequently an ineffective one at that.

The phrase 'neo-colonialism' was first used in the early 1950s. Anti-colonial leaders in Asia and Africa focus on the element of control – in the words of Sukarno, 'economic control, intellectual control, and actual physical control by a small but alien community, within a nation'.[7] To cite a specific illustration of economic neo-colonialism, Nkrumah denounced as 'neo-colonialism' the economic association of France's African colonies with the European Common Market. An example in which the political element was in the fore was France's claim to the right to suppress the revolt against the puppet ruler of Gabon in February 1964 in order to defend French economic interests in that country. A comprehensive summary of the chief manifestations of neo-colonialism was made at the Third All-African People's Conference held in Cairo in 1961:

> This Conference considers that neo-colonialism, which is the survival of the colonial system in spite of formal recognition of political independence in emerging countries, which become the victims of an indirect and subtle form of domination by political, economic, social, military, or technical [forces], is the greatest threat to African countries that have newly won their independence or those approaching this status....
>
> This Conference denounces the following manifestations of neo-colonialism in Africa:
>
> (a) Puppet governments represented by stooges, and based on some chiefs, reactionary elements, antipopular politicians, big bourgeois compradors, or corrupted civil or military functionaries.
>
> (b) Regrouping of states, before or after independence, by an

imperial power in federation or communities linked to that imperial power.

(c) Balkanization as a deliberate political fragmentation of states by creation of artificial entities, such as, for example, the case of Katanga, Mauritania, Buganda, etc.

(d) The economic entrenchment of the colonial power before independence and the continuity of economic dependence after formal recognition of national sovereignty.

(e) Integration into colonial economic blocs which maintain the underdeveloped character of African economy.

(f) Economic infiltration by a foreign power after independence, through capital investments, loans, and monetary aids or technical experts, of unequal concessions, particularly those extending for long periods.

(g) Direct monetary dependence, as in those emergent independent states whose finances remain in the hands of and directly controlled by colonial powers.

(h) Military bases sometimes introduced as scientific research stations or training schools, introduced either before independence or as a condition for independence.[8]

This description supports two broad generalizations. First, modern imperialism requires the active participation of the state in international economic relationships; imperialist nations cannot singly or collectively implement a neo-colonialist policy – via agencies such as the European Common Market, for example – without state capitalism. Secondly, neo-colonialist policy is first and foremost designed to prevent the newly independent countries from consolidating their political independence and thus to keep them economically dependent and securely in the world capitalist system. In the pure case of neo-colonialism, the allocation of economic resources, investment effort, legal and ideological structures, and other features of the old society remain unchanged – with the single exception of the substitution of 'internal colonialism' for formal colonialism, that is, the transfer of power to the domestic ruling classes by their former colonial masters. Independence has thus been achieved on conditions which are irrelevant to the basic needs of the society, and represents a part denial of real sovereignty, and a part continuation of disunity within the society. The most important branch of the theory of neo-colonialism is therefore the theory of economic imperialism.

The definition of economic imperialism which we employ is the economic domination of one region or country over another –

specifically, the formal or informal control over local economic resources in a manner advantageous to the metropolitan power, and at the expense of the local economy. Economic control assumes different forms and is exercised in a number of ways. The main form of economic domination has always been control by the advanced capitalist countries over the liquid and real economic resources of economically backward areas. The main liquid resources are foreign exchange and public and private savings, and real resources consist of agricultural, mineral, transportation, communication, manufacturing and commercial facilities and other assets. The most characteristic modes of domination today can be illuminated by way of contrast with examples drawn from the colonial period.

Examples of control over foreign exchange assets are numerous. In the colonial era the metropolitan powers established currency boards to issue and redeem local circulating medium against sterling and other metropolitan currencies. In its purest form, the currency board system required 100 per cent backing of sterling for local currency. The East African Currency Board, for example, was established in 1919, staffed by British civil servants appointed by the Colonial Office, and at one time exercised financial domination over Ethiopia, British and Italian Somaliland, and Aden, as well as the East African countries. The Board did not have the authority to expand or contract local credit, and therefore expenditures on local projects which required imported materials or machinery were limited to current export earnings, less outlays for essential consumer goods, debt service, and other fixed expenses. Measures to expand exports were thus necessary preconditions of local initiatives toward economic progress. In this way, British imperialism indirectly controlled the allocation of real resources.

This mode of control still survives in modified form in the Commonwealth Caribbean economies and elsewhere. The Jamaican central bank, for example, has limited power to influence the domestic money supply, but sterling and local currency are automatically convertible in unlimited amounts at fixed rates of exchange. The local government is thus prohibited from financing investment projects by inflation, or forced savings; nor are exchange controls and related financial instruments of national economic policy permitted. The structure and organization of the commercial banking system aggravates the situation. Local banks are branches of foreign-owned banks whose headquarters are located in the overseas financial centers and are more responsive to economic and monetary changes abroad than in the local economy; specifically, local banks have contracted credit at times when foreign exchange assets have been accumulating. This combination of monetary and financial dependence has caused artificial shortages of funds and prevented the Jamaican government from allocating local financial resources in a rational manner.

A more characteristic form of control over foreign exchange today is private direct investment. In the nineteenth and early twentieth centuries, backward countries were often able to attract portfolio investments and local governments and capitalists were thus able to exercise some control over the use of foreign exchange made available by long-term foreign investment. Today direct investment constitutes the great mass of long-term capital exported on private account by the metropolitan countries. Foreign exchange receipts typically take the form of branch plants and other facilities of the multinational corporations – facilities which are difficult or impossible to integrate into the structure of the local economy. What is more, satellite countries which depend on direct investment ordinarily provide free currency convertibility and hence foreign-owned enterprises which produce for local markets have privileged access to foreign exchange earned in other sectors of the economy.

Another feature of economic domination is the control of local savings, which assumes two forms. First, economic rule means that local government revenues, or *public* savings, are mortgaged to loans received from the metropolitan powers. An extreme example is Liberia – a country with an open door policy with regard to foreign capital – which in 1963 expended 94 per cent of its annual revenues to repay foreign loans. In the nineteenth century, persuasion, coercion, and outright conquest often insured that tariffs and other taxes were turned over to foreign bondholders. In the absence of direct colonial rule, however, foreign lending was frequently a precarious undertaking. Latin American countries, for example, had an uneven history of bond payments. Foreign loans today are secured in more peaceful and more effective ways. The international capital market is highly centralized and dominated by the agencies of the main imperialist powers – the International Bank for Reconstruction and Development, the International Monetary Fund, and other financial institutions. No longer is it possible for borrowing countries to play one lending country off against another, or to default on their obligations or unilaterally scale down their debt without shutting the door on future loans.

[...] Secondly, *private* savings are mobilized by foreign corporations and governments in order to advance the interests of foreign capital. Foreign companies float local bond issues, raise equity capital, and generally attempt to monopolize available liquid resources in order to extend their field of operations and maximize profits. World Bank affiliates finance local development banks which scour the country for small and medium-size savings to funnel into local and foreign enterprise. The United States government acquires a significant portion of the money supply of India and other countries through its policy of selling surplus foodstuffs for local currencies which it makes available to United States corporations. In these and other ways foreign interests today exercise control of local private savings.

A final feature of economic domination is the control of mineral, agricultural, manufacturing, and other real assets, and the organization and management of trade by foreign corporations. In Africa, for example, French bulk-buying companies in the ex-colonies monopolize the purchase and sale of coffee, peanuts, palm-oil products, and other commodities produced by small and medium-sized growers. In Mexico, one foreign corporation organizes the great part of cotton production and exportation. Frequently control of commerce necessitates financial domination. The United States, for example, has penetrated Mexico's financial structure with the aim of restricting Mexican–Latin American trade in order to insure control of Latin American markets for itself. Control of iron, copper, tin, oil, bauxite, and other mineral resources is in the hands of a handful of giant corporations. In some countries, foreign interests dominate the commanding heights of the economy – transportation, power, communication, and the leading manufacturing industries. These examples should suffice to show that foreign control of real, as well as of liquid, assets extends into all branches of local economies and penetrates every economically backward region in the world capitalist system.

[Later in the article O'Connor seeks to identify the characteristics of an imperialist foreign policy in the changed circumstances of the modern world.]

MODERN IMPERIALISM'S FOREIGN POLICY

Whether or not private capital responds to the incentives held out by national governments and international agencies depends on a host of factors, chief among which are the investment 'climate' in the satellite economies and the character of other state political-economic policies. Suffice it for now to note some of the major differences between imperialist foreign policy in the nineteenth and mid-twentieth centuries.

First, and most obvious, modern imperialism attempts to substitute informal for formal modes of political control of countries in the backwash of world capitalism. The methods of establishing political control are varied. The use of old economic and political ties is practised whenever possible; these include the relationships formed within the British Commonwealth and the French Community, closed currency zones, preferential trading systems, military alliances, and political-military pacts. Economic, political and cultural missions, labor union delegations, joint military training programs, military grants, bribes to local ruling classes in the form of economic 'aid', substitute for direct colonial rule. Only when indirect policies fail are the older instruments of coercion and force brought into play, and the principle of continuity in change applies. An excellent example is the US-instigated and supported counter-revolution in Guatemala in 1954, the accomplishments of which the State Department listed under four headings:

1. The conclusion of an agreement with a United Fruit Company subsidiary providing for the return of property expropriated by the Arbenz Government.
2. The repeal of the law affecting remittances and taxation of earnings from foreign capital.
3. The signing of an Investment Guarantee Agreement with the United States.
4. The promulgation of a new and more favorable petroleum law.

Within Guatemala, the Armas regime in the post-1954 period was maintained in office via contracts with United Fruit, Bond and Share, and other monopolies.

Secondly, contemporary imperialist states enjoy relatively more financial, and hence political, autonomy. In the nineteenth century, imperialist countries regarded themselves as dependent on the private capital market for raising funds for discretionary state expenditures and were compelled to pursue economic and fiscal policies designed to make it possible for their colonies to meet their private debt service. The dominant state capitalist countries today are financially independent and can follow a more flexible policy toward their satellites. The reason is that both the potential and actual economic surplus are comparatively large. The potential surplus is large because the normal tendency of monopoly capitalist economies is stagnation and unemployment of labor and capital, attributable to a deficiency of aggregate demand. State expenditures – including military expenditures and foreign loans and grants – normally increase not only aggregate demand but also real income and output, and hence the tax base. A rise in expenditures thus increases revenues, even if tax rates remain unchanged. State expenditures are partly self-financing and virtually costless in terms of the real resources utilized. The actual economic surplus constitutes a relatively large portion of national product because of technological and productivity advances. For these reasons, taxes (and state expenditures) make up a large share of national product with few serious adverse effects on economic incentives, and thus on total production itself.

The significance of the financial independence of the contemporary imperialist state for foreign policy lies in its ability to export capital – or absorb the surplus overseas – without a *quid pro quo*. The Marshall Plan, the extensive program of military aid and grants, and the low-cost loans extended to backward countries by AID are the main examples of this mode of surplus absorption. The surplus absorption capacity of satellite countries which are closely tied to the United States' political-military bloc is for practical purposes unlimited. Two factors, however, circumscribe state grants without a *quid pro quo*. First, low-cost state loans and grants-in-aid, or capital exports which are not extended on normal commercial principles, compete 'unfairly' with private loans and are resisted by private capitalist interests in the metropolitan economy. Second, metropolitan governments are unable to discipline their satellites effectively unless there are economic strings attached to international loans. Moreover, state bilateral and multilateral loans financed in private capital markets in the advanced countries must earn a return sufficient to cover the cost of borrowing and administration. Opportunities for capital exports extended on commercial principles are limited by the availability of profitable investment projects.

Nineteenth- and mid-twentieth-century imperialism depart in a third important respect. In the nineteenth century there were few important antagonisms between Great Britain's role as the leading national capitalist power on the one hand, and as the dominant imperialist power on the other. Policies designed to expand Britain's home economy extended capitalist modes of production and organization to the three underexploited continents, directly and indirectly strengthening the growing British imperial system. For this reason, foreign policy ordinarily served private foreign investors and other private interests oriented to overseas activity. Only occasionally – as in the case of Disraeli's decision to purchase Suez Canal shares in 1875 – was foreign investment employed as a 'weapon' of British foreign policy. Even less frequently did Britain promote private foreign investments with the purpose of aiding global foreign policy objectives.

By way of contrast, the national and international ambitions of the United States in the mid-twentieth century are continually in conflict. In the context of the limited absorption capacity of the backward capitalist world and international competition from other advanced capitalist economies and the socialist countries, the United States is compelled to employ a wide range of policies to expand trade and investment. To further national ends, a 'partnership' between 'public lending institutions' and 'private lenders' – with the former 'leading the way' for the latter – has been formed. Underlining the role of the state in the service of the multinational corporations, in 1962 Secretary of State Rusk described the newer government policies which extend beyond state loan programs; investment guarantee programs in forty-six backward capitalist countries which cover currency inconvertibility, expropriation, war, revolution, and insurrection; instructions to local embassies to support business interests by making 'necessary representations to the host governments'; the creation of a new Special Assistant for International Business in the State Department in order to insure that private business interests receive 'prompt representation' in the government. Especially in the case of disguised public loans or special forms of private loans (see above), the commitment of the United States government to national capitalist interests inhibits state policies which seek to strengthen the industrial bourgeoisie and ruling classes in other advanced countries and the national bourgeoisie in the backward nations. Perhaps this is the most important limit on capital exports on public account.

As the leading international power, the United States is under constant and growing pressure to strengthen world capitalism as a system, including each of its specific parts. Policies which aim to recruit new members for local comprador groups, stimulate the development of capitalist agriculture and the middle farmers, reinforce the dominance of local financial and commercial classes, and reinvigorate local manufacturing activities – these general policies pose a potential or real threat to the interests of United States' national capital. Alliance for Progress funds destined for the middle sectors of Latin American agriculture, Export–Import Bank loans to foreign commercialists, loans and grants to foreign governments dominated by the urban bourgeoisie, loans and subsidies to the Indian iron and steel industry, Mexican industry and agriculture, and other branches of production in countries which are slowly industrializing – these and other stopgap and long-range measures help to keep the backward countries in the imperialist camp in the short run, but directly or indirectly create local capitalist interests which may demand their independence from United States' capital in the long run.

United States' private capital increasingly requires the aid of the state, and the state enlists more and more private and public capital in its crusade to maintain world capitalism intact. Specific and general capitalist interests serve each other, finally merging into one phenomenon, a certain oneness emerges between them. This must have, finally, its institutional reflection. The multinational corporation has become the instrument for the creation and consolidation of an international ruling class, the only hope for reconciling the antagonisms between national and international interests.

NOTES

1   Joseph Schumpeter, *Imperialism and Social Classes* (1919; reprinted Augustus Kelly, New York, 1951), pp. 98, 128.
2   Hans Kohn, 'Reflections on Colonialism', in Robert Strausz-Hupé and Harry W. Hazard (eds), *The Idea of Colonialism* (London, 1958).
3   V.I. Lenin, *Imperialism: The Highest Stage of Capitalism* (New York, 1926), pp. 71–6.
4   Maurice Dobb, *Political Economy and Capitalism* (London, 1937), pp. 239, 234.
5   Paul M. Sweezy, *The Theory of Capitalist Development* (1942; reprinted, Monthly Review Press, New York, 1964).
6   Schumpeter, *Imperialism and Social Classes*, p. 110.
7   Kenneth J. Twitchett, 'Colonialism: An Attempt at Understanding Imperial, Colonial and Neo-Colonial Relationships', *Political Studies*, 13: 3 (October 1965).
8   'Neo-Colonialism', *Voice of Africa*, 1: 4 (April 1961), p. 4.

3.2 A structural theory of imperialism

Johan Galtung

Source: *Journal of Peace Research*, vol. 13, no. 2 (1971), pp. 81–94.

Galtung develops a theory of imperialism to account for inequality within and between nations and the resistance of this inequality to change. He distinguishes between Centre and Periphery countries and argues that those in power in the former have a community of interest with those in power in the latter. The result is a relationship which operates at the expense of the majority of the people in Peripheral countries, but which is largely in the interest of the majority of the people in Centre countries.

INTRODUCTION

This theory takes as its point of departure two of the most glaring facts about this world: the tremendous inequality, within and between nations, in almost all aspects of human living conditions, including the power to decide over those living conditions; *and* the resistance of this inequality to change. The world consists of Center and Periphery nations; and each nation, in turn, has its centers and periphery. Hence, our concern is with the mechanism underlying this discrepancy.

[Galtung goes on to discuss this discrepancy in terms of imperialism.]

Briefly stated, imperialism is a system that splits up collectivities and relates some of the parts to each other in relations of *harmony of interest*, and other parts in relations of *disharmony of interest*, or *conflict of interest*.

DEFINING 'CONFLICT OF INTEREST'

'Conflict of interest' is a special case of conflict in general, defined as a situation where parties are pursuing incompatible goals. In our special case, these goals are stipulated by an outsider as the 'true' interests of the parties, disregarding wholly or completely what the parties themselves say explicitly are the values they pursue. One reason for this is the rejection of the dogma of unlimited rationality: actors do *not* necessarily know, or they are unable to express, what their interest is. Another, more important, reason is that rationality is unevenly distributed, that some may dominate the minds of others, and that this may lead to 'false consciousness'. Thus, learning to suppress one's own true interests may be a major part of socialization in general and education in particular.

Let us refer to this true interest as LC, *living condition.* It may perhaps be measured by using such indicators as income, standard of living in the usual materialistic sense – but notions of *quality of life* would certainly also enter, not to mention notions of *autonomy.* But the precise content of LC is less important for our purpose than the definition of conflict of interest:

> There is *conflict,* or *disharmony of interest,* if the two parties are coupled together in such a way that the LC *gap* between them is *increasing.*
>
> There is *no conflict,* or *harmony of interest,* if the two parties are coupled together in such a way that the LC *gap* between them is *decreasing down to zero.*

[...] It is clear that the concept of interest used here is based on an ideology, or a *value premise of equality.* An interaction relation and interaction structure set up such that inequality is the result is seen as a coupling not in the interest of the weaker party. This is a value premise like so many other value premises in social science explorations, such as 'direct violence is bad', 'economic growth is good', 'conflict should be resolved', etc. As in all other types of social science, the goal should not be an 'objective' social science freed from all such value premises, but a more honest social science where the value premises are made explicit.

DEFINING 'IMPERIALISM'

We shall now define imperialism by using the building blocks presented in the preceding two sections. In our two-nation world, imperialism can be defined as one way in which the Center nation has power over the Periphery nation, so as to bring about a condition of disharmony of interest between them. Concretely, *imperialism* is a relation between a Center and a Periphery nation so that

(1) there is *harmony of interest* between the *center in the Center* nation and the *center in the Periphery* nation,
(2) there is more *disharmony of interest* within the Periphery nation than within the Center nations,
(3) there is *disharmony of interest* between the *periphery in the Center* nation and the *periphery in the Periphery* nation.

Diagrammatically it looks something like Figure 1. This complex definition, borrowing largely from Lenin, needs spelling out. The basic idea is, as mentioned, that the center in the Center nation has a bridgehead in the Periphery nation, and a well-chosen one: the center in the Periphery nation. This is established such that the Periphery center is tied to the Center center with the best possible tie: the tie of harmony of interest. They are linked so that they go up together and down, even under, together.

Figure 1 The structure of imperialism

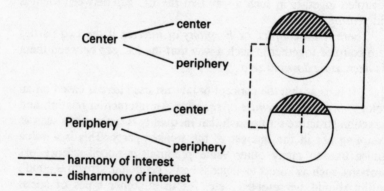

Center — center
       — periphery

Periphery — center
         — periphery

————— harmony of interest
- - - - - disharmony of interest

Inside the two nations there is disharmony of interest. They are both in one way or another vertical societies with LC gaps – otherwise there is no possibility of locating a center and a periphery. Moreover, the gap is not decreasing, but is at best constant. But the basic idea, absolutely fundamental for the whole theory to be developed, is that *there is more disharmony in the Periphery nation than in the Center nation.* At the simplest static level of description this means there is more inequality in the Periphery than in the Center. At the more complex level we might talk in terms of the gap opening more quickly in the Periphery than in the Center, where it might even remain constant. Through welfare state activities, redistribution takes place and disharmony is reduced for at least some LC dimensions, including income, but usually excluding power.

If we now would capture in a few sentences what imperialism is about, we might perhaps say something like this:

In the Periphery nation, the center grows more than the periphery, due partly to how interaction between center and periphery is organized. Without necessarily thinking of economic interaction, the center is more enriched than the periphery. However, for part of this enrichment, the center in the Periphery only serves as a transmission belt (e.g. as commercial firms, trading companies) for value (e.g. raw materials) forwarded to the Center nation. This value enters the Center in the center, with some of it drizzling down to the periphery in the Center. Importantly, there is less disharmony of interest in the Center than in the Periphery, so that *the total arrangement is largely in the interest of the periphery in the Center.* Within the Center the two parties may be opposed to each other. But in the total game, the periphery see themselves more as the partners of the center in the Center than as the partners of the periphery in the Periphery – and this is the essential trick of the game. Alliance formation between the two peripheries is avoided, while the Center nation becomes more and the Periphery nation less cohesive – and hence less able to develop long-term strategies. [...]

THE MECHANISMS OF IMPERIALISM

The two basic mechanisms of imperialism both concern the *relation* between the parties concerned, particularly between the nations. The first mechanism concerns the *interaction relation* itself, the second how these relations are put together in a larger interaction structure:

(1) the principle of *vertical interaction relation*
(2) the principle of *feudal interaction structure.*

The basic point about interaction is, of course, that people and nations have different values that complement each other, and then engage in exchange. Some nations produce oil, other nations produce tractors, and they then carry out an exchange according to the principles of comparative advantages. Imagine that our two-nation system has a prehistory of no interaction at all, and then starts with this type of interaction. Obviously both will be changed by it, and more particularly: a gap between them is likely to open and widen if the interaction is cumulatively asymmetric in terms of what the two parties get out of it.

To study whether the interaction is symmetric or asymmetric, on equal or unequal terms, *two* factors arising from the interaction have to be examined:

(1) *the value-exchange between the actors – inter*-actor effects
(2) *the effects inside the actors – intra*-actor effects.

In *economic* relations the first is most commonly analyzed, not only by liberal but also by Marxist economists. The inter-actor flow can be observed as flows of goods and services in either direction, and can literally be measured at the main points of entry: the customs houses and the national banks. The flow both ways can then be compared in various ways. Most important is the comparison in terms of *who benefits most*, and for this purpose intra-actor effects also have to be taken into consideration. [...]

It is certainly meaningful and important to talk in terms of unequal exchange or asymmetric interaction, but not quite unproblematic what its precise meaning should be. For that reason, it may be helpful to think in terms of three stages or types of exploitation, partly reflecting historical *processes* in chronological order, and partly reflecting types of *thinking* about exploitation.

In the first stage of exploitation, A simply engages in looting and takes away the raw materials without offering anything in return. If he steals out of pure nature there is no human interaction involved, but we assume that he forces 'natives' to work for him and do the extraction work. It is like the slave-owner who lives on the work produced by slaves – which is quantitatively not too different from the landowner who has land-workers working for him five out of seven days a week.

In the second stage, A starts offering something 'in return'. Oil, pitch, land, etc. is 'bought' for a couple of beads – it is no longer simply taken away without asking any questions about ownership. The price paid is ridiculous. However, as power relations in the international systems change, perhaps mainly by bringing the power level of the weaker party up from zero to some low positive value, A has to contribute more: for instance, pay more for the oil. The question is now whether there is a cut-off point after which the exchange becomes equal, and what the criterion for that cut-off point would be. Absence of subjective dissatisfaction – B says that he is now content? Objective market values or the number of man-hours that have gone into the production on either side?

There are difficulties with all these conceptions. But instead of elaborating on this, we shall rather direct our attention to the shared failure of all these attempts to look at *intra*-actor effects. Does the interaction have enriching or impoverishing effects *inside* the actor, or does it just lead to a stand-still? This type of question leads us to the third stage of exploitation, where there may be some balance in the flow between the actors, but great differences in the effect the interaction has within them.

As an example let us use nations exchanging oil for tractors. The basic point is that this involves different levels of processing, where we define 'processing' as an activity imposing Culture on Nature. In the case of crude oil the product is (almost) pure Nature; in the case of tractors it would be wrong to say that it is a case of pure Culture, pure *form* (like mathematics, music). A transistor radio, an integrated circuit, these would be better examples because Nature has been brought down to a minimum. The tractor is still too much iron and rubber to be a pure case.

The major point now is the *gap in processing level* between oil and tractors and the differential effect this gap will have on the two nations. In one nation the oil deposit may be at the water-front, and all that is needed is a derrick and some simple mooring facilities to pump the oil straight into a ship – e.g. a Norwegian tanker – that can bring the oil to the country where it will provide energy to run, among other things, the tractor factories. In the other nation the effects may be extremely far-reaching due to the complexity of the product and the connectedness of the society. [...]

If the first mechanism, the *vertical interaction relation*, is the major factor behind inequality, then the second mechanism, the *feudal interaction structure*, is the factor that maintains and reinforces this inequality by protecting it. There are four rules defining this particular interaction structure:

(1) interaction between Center and Periphery is *vertical*;
(2) interaction between Periphery and Periphery is *missing*;
(3) multilateral interaction involving all three is *missing*;
(4) interaction with the outside world is *monopolized* by the Center with two implications:
   (a) Periphery interaction with other Center nations is *missing*
   (b) Center as well as Periphery interaction with Periphery nations belonging to other Center nations is *missing.*

This relation can be depicted as in Figure 2. As indicated in the figure the number of Periphery nations attached to any given Center nation can, of course, vary. In this figure we have also depicted the rule 'if you stay off my satellites, I will stay off yours'.

Figure 2 A feudal Center–Periphery structure

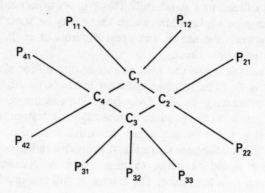

Some important *economic* consequences of this structure should be spelled out.

First and most obvious: the *concentration on trade partners*. A Periphery nation should, as a result of these two mechanisms, have most of its trade with 'its' Center nation. In other words, empirically we would expect high levels of *import concentration* as well as *export concentration* in the Periphery, as opposed to the Center, which is more free to extend its trade relations in almost any direction – except in the pure case, with the Periphery of other Center nations.

Second, and not so obvious, is the *commodity concentration*: the tendency for Periphery nations to have only one or very few primary products to export. This would be a trivial matter if it could be explained entirely in terms of geography, if e.g. oil countries were systematically poor as to ore, ore countries poor as to bananas and coffee, etc. But this can hardly be assumed to be the general case: Nature does not distribute its riches that way. There is a historical rather than a geographical explanation to this. A territory may have been exploited for the raw materials most easily available and/or most needed in the Center, and this, in turn, leads to a certain social structure, to communication lines to the deposits, to trade structures, to the emergence of certain center groups (often based on ownership of that particular raw materials), and so on. To start exploiting a new kind of raw material in the same territory might upset carefully designed local balances; hence, it might be easier to have a fresh start for that new raw material in virgin territory with no bridgehead already prepared for imperialist exploits. In order to substantiate this hypothesis we would have to demonstrate that there are particularly underutilized and systematically underexplored deposits precisely in countries where one type of raw materials has already been exploited.

The combined effect of these two consequences is a *dependency* of the Periphery on the Center. Since the Periphery usually has a much smaller GNP, the trade between them is a much higher percentage of the GNP for the Periphery, and with both partner and commodity concentration, the Periphery becomes particularly vulnerable to fluctuations in demands and prices. At the same time the center in the Periphery depends on the Center for its supply of consumer goods. Import substitution industries will usually lead to consumer goods that look homespun and unchic, particularly if there is planned obsolescence in the production of these goods in the Center, plus a demand for equality between the two centers maintained by demonstration effects and frequent visits to the Center.

However, the most important consequence is political and has to do with the systematic utilization of feudal interaction structures as a way of protecting the Center against the Periphery. The feudal interaction structure is in social science language nothing but an expression of the old political maxim *divide et impera*, divide and rule, as a strategy used systematically by the Center relative to the Periphery nations. How could – for example – a small foggy island in the North Sea rule over one quarter of the world? By isolating the Periphery parts from each other, by having them geographically at sufficient distance from each other to impede any real alliance formation, by having separate deals with them so as to tie them to the Center in particularistic ways, by reducing multilateralism to a minimum with all kinds of graded membership, *and* by having the Mother country assume the role of window to the world.

However, this point can be much more clearly seen if we combine the two mechanisms and extend what has been said so far for relations between Center and Periphery *nations* to relations between center and periphery *groups* within nations. Under an imperialist structure the two mechanisms are used not only between nations but also within nations, but less so in the Center nation than in the Periphery nation. In other words, there is vertical division of labor within as well as between nations. And these two levels of organization are intimately linked to each other (as A.G. Frank always has emphasized) in the sense that the center in the Periphery interaction structure is also that group with which the Center nation has its harmony of interest, the group used as a bridgehead.

Thus, the combined operation of the two mechanisms at the two levels builds into the structure a subtle grid of protection measures against the major potential source of 'trouble', the periphery in the Periphery. [...]

Obviously, the more perfectly the mechanisms of imperialism within and between nations are put to work, the less overt machinery of oppression is needed and the smaller can the center groups be, relative to the total population involved. *Only imperfect, amateurish imperialism needs weapons; professional imperialism is based on structural rather than direct violence.*

THE TYPES OF IMPERIALISM

We shall now make this more concrete by distinguishing between five types of imperialism depending on the *type* of exchange between Center and Periphery nations:

(1) *economic*
(2) *political*
(3) *military*
(4) *communication*
(5) *cultural.*

The order of presentation is rather random: we have no theory that one is more basic than the others, or precedes the others. Rather, this is like a Pentagon or a Soviet Star: imperialism can start from any corner. They should all be examined regarding the extent to which they generate interaction patterns that utilize the two *mechanisms* of imperialism so as to fulfill the three *criteria* of imperialism, or at least the first of them.

The most basic of the two mechanisms is *vertical* interaction, which in its modern form is conceived of as interaction across a gap in processing level. In other words, what is exchanged between the two nations is not only not the same things (which would have been stupid) but things of a quite different kind, the difference being in terms of where the most complex and stimulating operations take place. One tentative list, expanding what has been said in the previous section about economic interaction, might look like Table 1. [...]

The vertical nature of this type of *economic* interaction has been spelled out in detail above since we have used that type of imperialism to exemplify definition and mechanisms. Let us look more at the other types of vertical interaction.

The *political* one is clear: the concept of a 'mother' country, the

Table 1 The five types of imperialism

Type	Center nation provides:	Periphery nation provides:
Economic	processing, means of production	raw materials, markets
Political	decisions, models	obedience, imitators
Military	protection, means of destruction	discipline, traditional hardware
Communication	news, means of communication	events, passengers, goods
Cultural	teaching, means of creation – autonomy	learning, validation – dependence

Center nation, is also an indication of how the decision-making center is dislocated, away from the nation itself and towards the Center nation. These decisions may then affect economic, military, communication, and cultural patterns. Important here is the division of labor involved: some nations produce decisions, others supply obedience. The decisions may be made upon application, as in 'bilateral technical assistance', or in consultation – or they may simply emerge by virtue of the model–imitator distinction. Nothing serves that distinction quite so well as unilinear concepts of 'development' and 'modernization', according to which Center nations possess some superior kind of structure for others to imitate (as long as the Center's central position is not seriously challenged), and which gives a special aura of legitimacy to any idea emanating from the Center. Thus, structures and decisions developed in the 'motherland of liberalism' or in the 'fatherland of socialism' serve as models by virtue of their place of origin, not by virtue of their substance.

The *military* implications or parallels are also rather obvious. It cannot be emphasized enough that the economic division of labor is also one which ensures that the Center nations economically speaking also become the Center nations in a military sense: only they have the industrial capacity to develop the technological hardware – and also are often the only ones with the social structure compatible with a modern army. He who produces tractors can easily produce tanks, but he who delivers oil cannot defend himself by throwing it in the face of the aggressors. He has to depend on the tank-producer, either for protection or for acquisition (on terms dictated by the Center).

And just as there is a division of labor with the Center nation producing manufactured goods on the basis of raw materials extracted in the Periphery nation, there is also a division of labor with the *Center nations processing the obedience provided by the Periphery nations into decisions that can be implemented.* Moreover, there is also a division of labor with the Center providing the protection (and often also the officers or at least the instructors in 'counter-insurgency') and the Periphery the discipline and the soldiers needed – not to mention the apprentices of 'military advisors' from the Center.

As to the fourth type, *communication* imperialism, the emphasis in the analysis is usually turned toward the second mechanism of imperialism: the feudal interaction structure. That this largely holds for most world communication and transportation patterns has been amply demonstrated. But perhaps more important is the vertical nature of the division of labor in the field of communication/transportation. It is trivial that a high level of industrial capacity is necessary to develop the latest in transportation and communication technology. The preceding generation of *means of communication/transportation* can always be sold, sometimes secondhand, to the Periphery as part of the general vertical trade/aid structure, alongside the *means of production* (economic sector), the *means of destruction* (military sector), and the *means of creation* (cultural sector). The Center's planes and ships are faster, more direct, look more reliable, attract more passengers, more goods. And when the Periphery finally catches up, the Center will already for a long time have dominated the field of communication satellites.

One special version of this principle is a combination of cultural and communication exchange: *news communication.* We all know that the major agencies are in the hands of the Center countries, relying on Center-dominated, feudal networks of communication. What is not so well analyzed is how Center news takes up a much larger proportion of Periphery news media than vice versa, just as trade with the Center is a larger proportion of Periphery total trade than vice versa. In other words, the pattern of partner concentration as something found more in the Periphery than in the Center is very pronounced. The Periphery nations do not write or read much about each other, especially not across bloc borders, and they read more about 'their' Center than about other Centers – because the press is written and read by the center in the Periphery, who want to know more about that most 'relevant' part of the world – for them.

Another aspect of vertical division of labor in the news business should also be pointed out. Just as the Periphery produces raw material that the Center turns into processed goods, *the Periphery also produces events that the Center turns into news.* This is done by training journalists to see events with Center eyes, and by setting up a chain of communication that filters and processes events so that they fit the general pattern.

The latter concept brings us straight into *cultural* imperialism, a subtype of which is scientific imperialism. The division of labor between teachers and learners is clear: it is not the division of labor as such (found in most situations of transmission of knowledge) that constitutes imperialism, but the location of the teachers, and of the learners, in a broader setting. If the Center always provides the teachers and the definition of that worthy of being taught (from the gospels of Christianity to the gospels of Technology), and the Periphery always provides the learners, then there is a pattern which smacks of imperialism. The satellite nation in the Periphery will also know that nothing flatters the Center quite so much as being encouraged to teach, and being seen as a model, and that the Periphery can get much in return from a humble, culture-seeking strategy (just as it will get little but aggression if it starts teaching the Center anything – like Czechoslovakia, who started lecturing the Soviet Union on socialism). For in accepting cultural transmission the Periphery also, implicitly, validates for the Center the culture developed in the center, whether that center is intra- or international. This serves to reinforce the Center as a center, for it will then continue to develop culture along with transmitting it, thus creating lasting demand for the latest innovations. Theories, like cars and fashions, have their life-cycle, and whether the obsolescence is planned or not there will always be a time-lag in a structure with a pronounced difference between center and periphery. Thus, the tram workers in Rio de Janeiro may carry banners supporting Auguste Comte one hundred years after the center of the Center forgot who he was....

In science we find a particular version of vertical division of labor, very similar to economic division of labor: the pattern of scientific teams from the Center who go to Periphery nations to collect data (raw material) in the form of deposits, sediments, flora, fauna, archeological findings, attitudes, behavioral patterns, and so on for data processing, data analysis and theory formation (processing, in general) in the Center universities (factories), so as to be able to send the finished product, a journal, a book (manufactured goods) back for consumption in the center of the Periphery – after first having created a demand for it through demonstration effect, training in the Center country, and some degree of low level participation in the data collection team. This parallel is not a joke, it is a *structure*. If in addition the precise nature of the research is to provide the Center with information that can be used economically, politically, or militarily to maintain an imperialist structure, the cultural imperialism becomes even more clear. And if to this we add the *brain drain* (and body drain) whereby 'raw' brains (students) and 'raw' bodies (unskilled workers) are moved from the Periphery to the Center and 'processed' (trained) with ample benefits to the Center, the picture becomes complete.

3.3 The rise and future demise of the world capitalist system: concepts for comparative analysis

Immanuel Wallerstein

Source: *Comparative Studies in Society and History*, vol. 16, no. 4 (1974), pp. 387–415.

Wallerstein examines the functions of states within the capitalist world-economy. He identifies three structural positions – core, peripheral and semi-peripheral – the last of which is essential to the smooth running of the world-economy since it acts as a bridge between core and periphery and a channel for development. He goes on to review historical evidence for this pattern and to project it into the future.

The structural differences of core and periphery are not comprehensible unless we realize that there is a third structural position: that of the semi-periphery. This is not the result merely of establishing arbitrary cutting-points on a continuum of characteristics. Our logic is not merely inductive, sensing the presence of a third category from a comparison of indicator curves. It is also deductive. The semi-periphery is needed to make a capitalist world-economy run smoothly. Both kinds of world-system, the world-empire with a redistributive economy and the world-economy with a capitalist market economy, involve markedly unequal distribution of rewards. Thus, logically, there is immediately posed the question of how it is possible politically for such a system to persist. Why do not the majority who are exploited simply overwhelm the minority who draw disproportionate benefits? The most rapid glance at the historic record shows that these world-systems have been faced rather rarely by fundamental system-wide insurrection. While internal discontent has been eternal, it has usually taken quite long before the accumulation of the erosion of power has led to the decline of a world-system, and as often as not, an external force has been a major factor in this decline.

There have been three major mechanisms that have enabled world-systems to retain relative political stability (not in terms of the particular groups who will play the leading roles in the system, but in terms of systemic survival itself). One obviously is the concentration of military strength in the hands of the dominant forces. The modalities of this obviously vary with the technology, and there are to be sure political prerequisites for such a concentration, but nonetheless sheer force is no doubt a central consideration.

A second mechanism is the pervasiveness of an ideological commitment to the system as a whole. I do not mean what has often been termed the 'legitimation' of a system, because that term has been used to imply that the lower strata of a system feel some affinity with or loyalty towards the rulers, and I doubt that this has ever been a significant factor in the survival of world-systems. I mean rather the degree to which the staff or cadres of the system (and I leave this term deliberately vague) feel that their own well-being is wrapped up in the survival of the system as such and the competence of its leaders. It is this staff which not only propagates the myths; it is they who believe them.

But neither force nor the ideological commitment of the staff would suffice were it not for the division of the majority into a larger lower stratum and a smaller middle stratum. Both the revolutionary call for polarization as a strategy of change and the liberal economium to consensus as the basis of the liberal polity reflect this proposition. The import is far wider than its use in the analysis of contemporary political problems suggests. It is the normal condition of either kind of world-system to have a three-layered structure. When and if this ceases to be the case, the world-system disintegrates.

In a world-empire, the middle stratum is in fact accorded the role of maintaining the marginally-desirable long-distance luxury trade, while the upper stratum concentrates its resources on controlling the military machinery which can collect the tribute, the crucial mode of redistributing surplus. By providing, however, for an access to a limited portion of the surplus to urbanized elements who alone, in pre-modern societies, could contribute political cohesiveness to isolated clusters of primary producers, the upper stratum effectively buys off the potential leadership of coordinated revolt. And by denying access to political rights for this commercial–urban middle stratum, it makes them constantly vulnerable to confiscatory measures whenever their economic profits become sufficiently swollen so that they might begin to create for themselves military strength.

In a world-economy, such 'cultural' stratification is not so simple, because the absence of a single political system means the concentration of economic roles vertically rather than horizontally throughout the system. The solution then is to have three *kinds* of states, with pressures for cultural homogenization within each of them – thus, besides the upper stratum of core states and the lower stratum of peripheral states, there is a middle stratum of semi-peripheral ones.

The semi-periphery is then assigned as it were a specific economic role, but the reason is less economic than political. That is to say, one might make a good case that the world-economy as an economy would function every bit as well without a semi-periphery. But it would be far less *politically* stable, for it would mean a polarized world-system. The existence of the third category means precisely that the upper stratum is not faced with the *unified* opposition of all the others because the *middle* stratum is both exploited and exploiter. It follows that the specific economic role is not all that important, and has thus changed through the various historical stages of the modern world-system. We shall discuss these changes shortly.

Where then does class analysis fit in all of this? And what in such a formulation are nations, nationalities, peoples, ethnic groups? First of all, without arguing the point now, I would contend that all these latter terms denote variants of a single phenomenon which I will term 'ethno-nations'.

Both classes and ethnic groups, or status groups, or ethno-nations are phenomena of world-economies and much of the enormous confusion that has surrounded the concrete analysis of their functioning can be attributed quite simply to the fact that they have been analyzed as though they existed within the nation-states of this world-economy, instead of within the world-economy as a whole. This has been a Procrustean bed indeed.

The range of economic activities being far wider in the core than in the periphery, the range of syndical interest groups is far wider there. Thus, it has been widely observed that there does not exist in many parts of the world today a proletariat of the kind which exists in, say, Europe or North America. But this is a confusing way to state the observation. Industrial activity being disproportionately concentrated in certain parts of the world-economy, industrial wage-workers are to be found principally in certain geographic regions. Their interests as a syndical group are determined by their collective relationship to the world-economy. Their ability to influence the political functioning of this world-economy is shaped by the fact that they command larger percentages of the population in one sovereign entity than another. The form their organizations take has, in large part, been governed too by these political boundaries. The same might be said about industrial capitalists. Class analysis is perfectly capable of accounting for the political position of, let us say, French skilled workers if we look at their structural position and interests in the world-economy. Similarly with ethno-nations. The meaning of ethnic consciousness in a core area is considerably different from that of ethnic consciousness in a peripheral area precisely because of the different class position such ethnic groups have in the world-economy.

Political struggles of ethno-nations or segments of classes within national boundaries of course are the daily bread and butter of local politics. But their significance or consequences can only be fruitfully analyzed if one spells out the implications of their organizational activity or political demands for the functioning of the world-economy. This also incidentally makes possible more rational assessments of these politics in terms of some set of evaluative criteria such as 'left' and 'right'.

The functioning then of a capitalist world-economy requires that groups pursue their economic interests within a single world-market while seeking to distort this market for their benefit by organizing to exert influence on states, some of which are far more powerful than others but none of which controls the world-market in its entirety. Of course, we shall find on closer inspection that there are periods where one state is relatively quite powerful and other periods where power is more diffuse and contested, permitting weaker states broader ranges of action. We can talk then of the relative tightness or looseness of the world-system as an important variable and seek to analyze why this dimension tends to be cyclical in nature, as it seems to have been for several hundred years.

We are now in a position to look at the historical evolution of this capitalist world-economy itself and analyze the degree to which it is fruitful to talk of distinct stages in its evolution as a system. The emergence of the European world-economy in the 'long' sixteenth century (1450–1640) was made possible by an historical conjuncture: on those long-term trends which were the culmination of what has been sometimes described as the 'crisis of feudalism' was super-imposed a more immediate cyclical crisis plus climatic changes, all of which created a dilemma that could only be resolved by a geographic expansion of the division of labor. Furthermore, the balance of inter-system forces was such as to make this realizable. Thus a geographic expansion did take place in conjunction with a demographic expansion and an upward price rise.

The remarkable thing was not that a European world-economy was thereby created, but that it survived the Hapsburg attempt to transform it into a world-empire, an attempt seriously pursued by Charles V. The Spanish attempt to absorb the whole failed because the rapid economic–demographic–technological burst forward of the preceding century made the whole enterprise too expensive for the imperial base to sustain, especially given many structural insufficiencies in Castilian economic development. Spain could afford neither the bureaucracy nor the army that was necessary to the enterprise, and in the event went bankrupt, as did the French monarchs making a similar, albeit even less plausible, attempt.

Once the Hapsburg dream of world-empire was over – and in 1557 it was over forever – the capitalist world-economy was an established system that became almost impossible to unbalance. It quickly reached an equilibrium point in its relations with other world-systems: the Ottoman and Russian world-empires, the Indian Ocean proto-world-economy. Each of the states or potential states within the European world-economy was quickly in the race to bureaucratize, to raise a standing army, to homogenize its culture, to diversify its economic activities. By 1640, those in northwest Europe had succeeded in establishing themselves as the core states; Spain and the northern Italian city-states declined into being semi-peripheral; northeastern Europe and Iberian America had become the periphery. At this point, those in semi-peripheral status had reached it by virtue of decline from a former more pre-eminent status.

It was the system-wide recession of 1650–1730 that consolidated the European world-economy and opened stage two of the modern world-economy. For the recession forced retrenchment, and the decline in relative surplus allowed room for only one core state to survive. The mode of struggle was mercantilism, which was a device of partial insulation and withdrawal from the world-market of *large* areas themselves hierarchically constructed – that is, empires within the world-economy (which is quite different from world-empires). In this struggle England first ousted the Netherlands from its commercial primacy and then resisted successfully France's attempt to catch up. As England began to speed up the process of industrialization after 1760, there was one last attempt of those capitalist forces located in France to break the imminent British hegemony. This attempt was expressed first in the French Revolution's replacement of the cadres of the regime and then in Napoleon's continental blockade. But it failed.

Stage three of the capitalist world-economy begins then, a stage of industrial rather than of agricultural capitalism. Henceforth, industrial production is no longer a minor aspect of the world market but comprises an ever large percentage of world gross production – and even more important, of world gross surplus. This involves a whole series of consequences for the world-system.

First of all, it led to the further geographic expansion of the European world-economy to include now the whole of the globe. This was in part the result of its technological feasibility both in terms of improved military firepower and improved shipping facilities which made regular trade sufficiently inexpensive to be viable. But, in addition, industrial production *required* access to raw materials of a nature and in a quantity such that the needs could not be supplied within the former boundaries. At first, however, the search for new markets was not a primary consideration in the geographic expansion since the new markets were more readily available within the old boundaries, as we shall see.

The geographic expansion of the European world-economy meant the elimination of other world-systems as well as the absorption of the remaining mini-systems. The most important world-system up to then outside of the European world-economy, Russia, entered in semi-peripheral status, the consequence of the strength of its state-machinery (including its army) and the degree of industrialization already achieved in the eighteenth century. The independences in the Latin American countries did nothing to change their peripheral status. They merely eliminated the last vestiges of Spain's semi-peripheral role and ended pockets of non-involvement in the world-economy in the interior of Latin America. Asia and Africa were absorbed into the periphery in the nineteenth century, although Japan, because of the combination of the strength of its state-machinery, the poverty of its resource base (which led to a certain disinterest on the part of world capitalist forces), and its geographic remoteness from the core areas, was able quickly to graduate into semi-peripheral status.

The absorption of Africa as part of the periphery meant the end of slavery world-wide for two reasons. First of all, the manpower that was used as slaves was now needed for cash-crop production in Africa itself, whereas in the eighteenth century Europeans had sought to *discourage* just such cash-crop production. In the second place, once Africa was part of the periphery and not the external arena, slavery was no longer economic. To understand this, we must appreciate the economics of slavery. Slaves receiving the lowest conceivable reward for their labor are the least productive form of labor and have the shortest life span, both because of undernourishment and maltreatment and because of lowered psychic resistance to death. Furthermore, if recruited from areas surrounding their work-place the escape rate is too high. Hence, there must be a high transport cost for a product of low productivity. This makes economic sense only if the purchase price is virtually nil. In capitalist market trade, purchase always has a real cost. It is only in long-distance trade, the exchange of preciosities, that the purchase price can be in the social system of the purchaser virtually nil. Such was the slave trade. Slaves were bought at low immediate cost (the production cost of the items actually exchanged) and none of the usual invisible costs. That is to say, the fact that removing a man from West Africa lowered the productive potential of the region was of *zero* cost to the European world-economy since these areas were not part of the division of labor. Of course, had the slave trade totally denuded Africa of all possibilities of furnishing further slaves, then a real cost to Europe would have commenced. But that point was never historically reached. Once, however, Africa was part of the periphery, then the real cost of a slave in terms of the production of surplus in the world-economy went up to such a point that it became far more economical to use wage-labor, even on sugar or cotton plantations, which is precisely what transpired in the nineteenth-century Carib-bean and other slave-labor regions.

The creation of vast new areas as the periphery of the expanded world-economy made possible a shift in the role of some other areas. Specifically, both the United States and Germany (as it came into being) combined formerly peripheral and semi-peripheral regions. The manufacturing sector in each was able to gain political ascen-dancy, as the peripheral subregions became less economically crucial to the world-economy. Mercantilism now became the major tool of semi-peripheral countries seeking to become core countries, thus still performing a function analogous to that of the mercantilist drives of the late seventeenth and eighteenth centuries in England and France. To be sure, the struggle of semi-peripheral countries to 'industrialize' varied in the degree to which it succeeded in the period before the First World War: all the way in the United States, only partially in Germany, not at all in Russia.

The internal structure of core states also changed fundamentally under industrial capitalism. For a core area, industrialism involved divesting itself of substantially all agricultural activities (except that in the twentieth century further mechanization was to create a new form of working the land that was so highly mechanized as to warrant the appellation industrial). Thus whereas, in the period 1700–40, England not only was Europe's leading industrial exporter but was also Europe's leading agricultural exporter – this was at a high point in the economy-wide recession – by 1900, less than 10 per cent of England's population were engaged in agricultural pursuits.

At first under industrial capitalism, the core exchanged manufactured products against the periphery's agricultural products – hence, Britain from 1815 to 1873 as the 'workshop of the world'. Even to those semi-peripheral countries that had some manufacture (France, Germany, Belgium, the US), Britain in this period supplied about half their needs in manufactured goods. As, however, the mercantilist practices of this latter group both cut Britain off from outlets and even created competition for Britain in sales to peripheral areas, a competition which led to the late nineteenth-century 'scramble for Africa', the world division of labor was reallocated to ensure a new special role for the core: less the provision of the manufactures, more the provision of the machines to make the manufactures as well as the provision of infra-structure (especially, in this period, railroads).

The rise of manufacturing created for the first time under capitalism a large-scale urban proletariat. And in consequence for the first time there arose what Michels has called the 'anti-capitalist mass spirit',[1] which was translated into concrete organizational forms (trade-unions, socialist parties). This development intruded a new factor as threatening to the stability of states and of the capitalist forces now so securely in control of them as the earlier centrifugal thrusts of regional anti-capitalist landed elements had been in the seventeenth century.

At the same time that the bourgeoisies of the core countries were faced by this threat to the internal stability of their state structures, they were simultaneously faced with the economic crisis of the latter third of the nineteenth century resulting from the more rapid increase of agricultural production (and indeed of light manufactures) than the expansion of a potential market for these goods. Some of the surplus would have to be redistributed to someone to allow these goods to be bought and the economic machinery to return to smooth operation. By expanding the purchasing power of the industrial proletariat of the core countries, the world-economy was unburdened simultaneously of two problems: the bottleneck of demand, and the unsettling 'class conflict' of the core states – hence, the social liberalism of welfare-state ideology that arose just at that point in time.

The First World War was, as men of the time observed, the end of an era; and the Russian Revolution of October 1917 the beginning of a new one – our stage four. This stage was to be sure a stage of revolutionary turmoil but it also was, in a seeming paradox, the stage of the *consolidation* of the industrial capitalist world-economy. The Russian Revolution was essentially that of a semi-peripheral country whose internal balance of forces had been such that as of the late nineteenth century it began on a decline towards a peripheral status. This was the result of the marked penetration of foreign capital into the industrial sector which was on its way to eliminating all indigenous capitalist forces, the resistance to the mechanization of the agricultural sector, the decline of relative military power (as evidenced by the defeat by the Japanese in 1905). The Revolution brought to power a group of state-managers who reversed each one of these trends by using the classic technique of mercantilist semi-withdrawal from the world-economy. In the process of doing this, the now USSR mobilized considerable popular support, especially in the urban sector. At the end of the Second World War, Russia was reinstated as a very strong member of the semi-periphery and could begin to seek full core status.

Meanwhile, the decline of Britain which dates from 1873 was confirmed and its hegemonic role was assumed by the United States. While the US thus rose, Germany fell further behind as a result of its military defeat. Various German attempts in the 1920s to find new industrial outlets in the Middle East and South America were unsuccessful in the face of the US thrust combined with Britain's continuing relative strength. Germany's thrust of desperation to recoup lost ground took the noxious and unsuccessful form of Nazism.

It was the Second World War that enabled the United States for a brief period (1945–65) to attain the same level of primacy as Britain had in the first part of the nineteenth century. United States growth in this period was spectacular and created a great need for expanded market outlets. The Cold War closure denied not only the USSR but Eastern Europe to US exports. And the Chinese Revolution meant that this region, which had been destined for much exploitative activity, was also cut off. Three alternative areas were available and each was pursued with assiduity. First, Western Europe had to be rapidly 'reconstructed', and it was the Marshall Plan which thus allowed this area to play a primary role in the expansion of world productivity. Secondly, Latin America became the reserve of US investment from which now Britain and Germany were completely cut off. Thirdly, Southern Asia, the Middle East and Africa had to be decolonized. On the one hand, this was necessary in order to reduce the share of the surplus taken by the Western European intermediaries, as Canning covertly supported the Latin American revolutionaries against Spain in the 1820s. But also, these countries had to be decolonized in order to mobilize productive potential in a way that had never been achieved in the colonial era. Colonial rule after all had been an *inferior* mode of relationship of core and periphery, one occasioned by the strenuous late-nineteenth-century conflict among industrial states but one no longer desirable from the point of view of the new hegemonic power.

But a world capitalist economy does not permit true imperium. Charles V could not succeed in his dream of world-empire. The Pax Britannica stimulated its own demise. So too did the Pax Americana. In each case, the cost of *political* imperium was too high economically, and in a capitalist system, over the middle run when profits decline, new *political* formulae are sought. In this case the costs mounted along several fronts. The efforts of the USSR to further its own industrialization, protect a privileged market area (Eastern Europe), and force entry into other market areas led to an immense spiralling of military expenditure, which on the Soviet side promised long-run returns, whereas for the US it was merely a question of running very fast to stand still. The economic resurgence of Western Europe, made necessary both to provide markets for US sales and investments and to counter the USSR military thrust, meant over time that the Western European state structures collectively became as strong as that of the US, which led in the late 1960s to the 'dollar and gold crisis' and the retreat of Nixon from the free-trade stance which is the definitive mark of the self-confident leader in a capitalist market system. When the cumulated Third World pressures, most notably Vietnam, were added on, a restructuring of the world division of labor was inevitable, involving probably in the 1970s a quadripartite division of the larger part of the world surplus by the US, the European Common Market, Japan, and the USSR.

Such a decline in US state hegemony has actually *increased* the freedom of action of capitalist enterprises, the larger of which have now taken the form of multinational corporations which are able to maneuver against state bureaucracies whenever the national politicians become too responsive to internal worker pressures. Whether some effective links can be established between multinational corporations, presently limited to operating in certain areas, and the USSR remains to be seen, but it is by no means impossible.

This brings us to the seemingly esoteric debate between Liu Shao-Chi and Mao Tse-Tung as to whether China was, as Liu argued, a socialist state, or whether, as Mao argued, socialism was a *process* involving continued and continual class struggle. No doubt to those to whom the terminology is foreign the discussion seems abstrusely theological. The issue, however, is real. If the Russian Revolution emerged as a reaction to the threatened further decline of Russia's structural position in the world-economy, and if fifty years later one can talk of the USSR as entering the status of a core power in a *capitalist* world-economy, what then is the meaning of the various so-called socialist revolutions that have occurred in a third of the world's surface? First let us notice that it has been neither Thailand nor Liberia nor Paraguay that has had a 'socialist revolution' but Russia, China and Cuba. That is to say, these revolutions have occurred in countries that, in terms of their internal economic structures in the pre-revolutionary period, had a certain minimum strength in terms of skilled personnel, some manufacturing, and other factors which made it plausible that, within the framework of a capitalist world-economy, such a country could alter its role in the world division of labor within a reasonable period (say 30–50 years) by the use of the technique of mercantilist semi-withdrawal. (This may not be all that plausible for Cuba, but we shall see.) Of course, other countries in the geographic regions and military orbit of these revolutionary forces had changes of regime without in any way having these characteristics (for example, Mongolia or Albania). It is also to be noted that many of the countries where similar forces are strong or where considerable counterforce is required to keep them from emerging also share this status of minimum strength. I think of Chile or Brazil or Egypt – or indeed Italy.

Are we not seeing the emergence of a political structure for *semi-peripheral* nations adapted to stage four of the capitalist world-system? The fact that all enterprises are nationalized in these countries does not make the participation of these enterprises in the world-economy one that does not conform to the mode of operation of a capitalist market-system: seeking increased efficiency of production in order to realize a maximum price on sales, thus achieving a more favorable allocation of the surplus of the world-economy. If tomorrow US Steel became a worker's collective in which all employees without exception received an identical share of the profits and all stockholders were expropriated without compensation, would US Steel thereby cease to be a capitalist enterprise operating in a capitalist world-economy?

What then have been the consequences for the world-system of the emergence of many states in which there is no private ownership of the basic means of production? To some extent, this has meant an internal reallocation of consumption. It has certainly undermined the ideological justifications in world capitalism, both by showing the political vulnerability of capitalist entrepreneurs and by demonstrating that private ownership is irrelevant to the rapid expansion of industrial productivity. But to the extent that it has raised the ability of the new semi-peripheral areas to enjoy a larger share of the world surplus, it has once again depolarized the world, recreating the triad of strata that has been a fundamental element in the survival of the world-system.

Finally, in the peripheral areas of the world-economy, both the continued economic expansion of the core (even though the core is seeing some reallocation of surplus internal to it) and the new strength of the semi-periphery have led to a further weakening of the political and hence economic position of the peripheral areas. The pundits note that 'the gap is getting wider', but thus far no one has succeeded in doing much about it, and it is not clear that there are very many in whose interests it would be to do so. Far from a strengthening of state authority, in many parts of the world we are witnessing the same kind of deterioration Poland knew in the sixteenth century, a deterioration of which the frequency of military coups is only one of many signposts. And all of this leads us to conclude that stage four has been the stage of the *consolidation* of the capitalist world-economy.

Consolidation, however, does not mean the absence of contradictions and does not mean the likelihood of long-term survival. We thus come to projections about the future, which has always been man's great game, his true *hybris*, the most convincing argument for the dogma of original sin. Having read Dante, I will therefore be brief.

There are two fundamental contradictions, it seems to me, involved in the workings of the capitalist world-system. In the first place, there is the contradiction to which the nineteenth-century Marxian corpus pointed, which I would phrase as follows: whereas in the short-run the maximization of profit requires maximizing the withdrawal of surplus from immediate consumption of the majority, in the long-run the continued production of surplus requires a mass demand which can only be created by redistributing the surplus withdrawn. Since these two considerations move in opposite directions (a 'contradiction'), the system has constant crises which in the long-run both weaken it and make the game for those with privilege less worth playing.

The second fundamental contradiction, to which Mao's concept of socialism as process points, is the following: whenever the tenants of privilege seek to co-opt an oppositional movement by including them in a minor share of the privilege, they may no doubt eliminate opponents in the short-run; but they also up the ante for the next oppositional movement created in the next crisis of the world-economy. Thus the cost of 'co-option' rises ever higher and the advantages of co-option seem ever less worthwhile.

There are today no socialist systems in the world-economy any more than there are feudal systems because there is only *one* world-system. It is a world-economy and it is by definition capitalist in form. Socialism involves the creation of a new kind of *world*-system, neither a redistributive world-empire nor a capitalist world-economy but a socialist world-government. I don't see this projection as being in the least utopian but I also don't feel its institution is imminent. It will be the outcome of a long struggle in forms that may be familiar and perhaps in very new forms, that will take place in *all* the areas of the world-economy (Mao's continual 'class struggle'). Governments may be in the hands of persons, groups or movements sympathetic to this transformation but *states* as such are neither progressive nor reactionary. It is movements and forces that deserve such evaluative judgments.

NOTE

1   Robert Michels. 'The Origins of the Anti-Capitalist Mass Spirit', in *Man in Contemporary Society* (Columbia University Press, New York, 1955), vol. 1, pp. 740–65.

3.4 Power and dependency in an interdependent world: a guide to understanding the contemporary global crisis

Gary Gereffi

Source: *International Journal of Comparative Sociology*, vol. 25, nos 1–2 (1984), pp. 509–28.

Gereffi argues that with the growing internationalization of capital since the Second World War states have become increasingly interdependent. But levels of dependency are not symmetrical and power is still concentrated at the centre of the world economy. He illustrates the argument by looking at the problem of Third World debt, showing that the source of the problem and its solution lie in the developed world.

[Gereffi discusses initially how rapid economic growth after the Second World War internationalized the world economy, making all states increasingly interdependent. The developed states, however, have become stronger in the process while the underdeveloped states have become weaker. As a result of this growing asymmetry, in times of economic crisis, almost inevitably, adjustments are made in the world economy to suit the developed states. Gereffi goes on to examine the effects of these crises from the perspective of the underdeveloped countries.]

THIRD WORLD DEPENDENCY AND THE WORLD RECESSION

The increased internationalization of the center countries has made them more interdependent on one another and indeed more sensitive to fluctuations in the world economy generally. The great advantage of the center countries, however, is that they have the capital, technology, and markets needed for their development process to be relatively self-sustaining. This is not true of most of the third world. The development of peripheral nations usually requires critical external complements. The more extensive this external reliance – on imported goods, foreign direct investment, foreign loans, export markets for commodities or manufactured items, etc. – the more dependent the country is. To better appreciate the degree of asymmetry involved in first world–third world relations, it is worthwhile to look more closely at the United States' ties with Latin America, and especially Mexico. [...]

Mexico is in many ways a symbol of the asymmetry of first world–third world relations and of the third world's vulnerability to the world recession. Despite attempts to diversify its trade and investment ties, Mexico remains overwhelmingly dependent on the United States. Three-quarters of its exports and over two-thirds of its imports were carried out with the United States in 1980. While Mexico is the United States' third most important trading partner (after Canada and Japan), the situation looks quite different from north of the border. The United States received 5 per cent of its imports from Mexico and sent 6 per cent of its exports there in 1980. What is a huge proportion of Mexico's trade is thus a small share of US trade. Furthermore, Mexico regularly runs a trade deficit with the United States which stood at $1.6 billion in 1979. One of the obvious political implications of this asymmetry is that US domestic economic decisions will affect Mexico much more than Mexico's decisions affect the United States.

Mexico's trade imbalances are compounded by other forms of dependency. Approximately three-quarters of the FDI [Foreign Direct Investment] in Mexico is by US-based firms. (Mexico absorbs about 3 per cent of all US direct investment abroad.) US TNCs [transnational corporations] in Mexico tend to be among the largest firms and they are in the fastest growing industries, such as chemicals, rubber, machinery, metal fabrication, transportation equipment, and food processing. The potential power of TNCs to set guiding policy is increased by the fact that most of these industries are oligopolies in which the conduct of a few big sellers largely determines industry performance. Mexico's reliance on its neighbor to the north also is evident in a different sort of economic activity: tourism. Mexico ranked fourth worldwide in tourist income in 1979 ($1.4 billion) and it has the largest tourist industry in Latin America. In 1980 tourism was expected to net $1.6 billion, or 38 per cent of Mexico's balance of payments and 6 per cent of its GNP. Since 85 per cent of Mexico's tourist arrivals come from the United States, continued prosperity in this sector is heavily dependent on the condition of the US economy.

Undocumented workers are one of the most sensitive problems

dividing the United States and Mexico. With high levels of un-employment and underemployment (estimated at nearly 70 per cent in rural areas) and with demographic patterns projecting a significant labor surplus situation well into the next century, Mexico views the continuing flow of undocumented workers northward as an important safety valve that helps assure its social and political stability. The incentive for these workers is predominantly economic, due to huge real-wage differentials between the United States and Mexico that for many low-skill occupations range between 8:1 and 13:1. These differentials have widened even more with the recent devaluation of the Mexican peso. Given the losses already suffered by US workers due to the recession in their own country, the mounting pressures on the American side to restrict the flow of undocumented Mexican workers into the United States are taken very seriously indeed by the Mexican government. They further call into question what is already a very uncertain economic forecast for Mexico in the coming years.

The most explosive issue facing Mexico and other third world nations today, however, is 'the debt bomb'. Over slightly more than a decade the external debt owed by governments and state enterprises in developing countries to foreign creditors has skyrocketed tenfold, from $64 billion in 1970 to about $600 billion in 1982. The external debt burden, while a common phenomenon throughout the third world, is particularly acute in Latin America which owes around $300 billion or one-half of all developing country external public debt. The amounts owed by the largest third world borrowers in 1983 are staggering: Brazil, $90 billion; Mexico, $83 billion; Argentina, $40 billion; Venezuela, $32 billion; Poland, $24 billion; Chile, $21 billion; Nigeria, $15 billion; and Peru, $12 billion. This transfer of external financial resources has been described as 'the most rapid, most concentrated, most massive flow of investment capital to the Third World in history'.[1]

With the unprecedented expansion of third world external public debt came a significant change in its composition: more and more loans were acquired from private sources, particularly commercial banks active on the Eurocurrency market. In Latin America and elsewhere, the proportion owed to private rather than official creditors rose from less than one-half in 1970 to approximately two-thirds in 1980. This new mix produced a more onerous debt structure for two reasons: it shortened the average maturities of the external public debt and its cost depended on floating rather than fixed interest rates (i.e. interest rates adjusted about every six months to reflect changes in market rates). At a more general level, this privatization of financial flows allowed private banking institutions to displace TNCs and official aid as the most important source of foreign capital available to third world countries. In the 1960s official aid accounted for 50 per cent, foreign direct investment by TNCs for 30 per cent, and bank loans and bonds for only 10 per cent of the total flow of external financial resources to Latin America; by the end of the 1970s, banks and bondholders were responsible for 65 per cent of this flow, FDI was just over 15 per cent, and official aid stood at only 12 per cent.

The debt burden grew after the quadrupling of oil prices in 1973, when private banks experienced a sudden increase in loanable funds as the Arab oil revenues (petrodollars) flooded bank coffers. This excess liquidity created pressure on the banks to expand their loan portfolios. With commodity prices generally up at the time, third world nations appeared an attractive place in which to stash the petrodollars, a process called recycling. Most developing countries jumped at this opportunity because they faced mounting deficits from their oil import bills. The crunch for heavy borrowers came as the global recession began to spread. The slump in the center countries hurt third world economic performance in various ways: commodity prices fell, the terms of trade became more adverse, export markets were eroded, and interest rates rose (a rise in part triggered by the growing budget deficits in the United States). Pretty soon, developing nations were forced to borrow more and more just to meet repayment schedules of old loans. By 1982, many of these countries were in a situation where virtually their entire export revenues were insufficient to service their external public debt (see Table 1). And the banks, who could not afford to have these countries default, have been forced to continue lending. The claims of the nine largest US banks on Mexico, Brazil, and Argentina alone equaled 112 per cent of the banks' capital in mid-1982. It is a debt trap from which both sides are finding it difficult to escape.

A lasting solution must go to the heart of the third world debt problem: countries are trying to finance long-term development projects by short-term liabilities. But from what quarter can we expect change to come? It is unlikely that the major third world debtors will voluntarily reduce their borrowing because total export revenues are already inadequate in some cases to service the existing external debt and further cutbacks would force the curtailment of almost all imports and domestic subsidies for essential goods and development programs – a politically unpopular (if not fatal) course of action. The large banks also are reluctant to voluntarily reduce

Table 1 Estimated external debt service payments, 1982 (per cent of exports of goods and services)

Country	Total	Interest	Principal[a]
Argentina	179	44	135
Mexico	129	37	92
Ecuador	122	30	92
Brazil	122	45	77
Chile	116	40	76
Venezuela	95	14	81
Colombia	94	25	69
Philippines	91	18	74
Peru	90	21	69
Turkey	68	13	55
Korea	53	11	43
Thailand	48	10	38
Egypt	48	7	41
Yugoslavia	46	14	32
Algeria	39	12	27
Indonesia	27	8	19
Taiwan	21	5	16
Nigeria	20	7	13
Malaysia	17	5	12

[a] All debts due within the year, including amortization of medium- and long-term debt plus short-term debt outstanding at the beginning of the year.

Source: Morgan Guaranty Trust Company, 'World Financial Markets', October 1982, p. 5.

their lending to a sustainable rate because they are vulnerable to the threat of default if they force third world nations to borrow less.

The key actor in managing the international debt crisis is the International Monetary Fund (IMF), which at the behest of the United States is adopting an ever more assertive role. Traditionally, the IMF imposed austerity programs on countries that required emergency loans or needed to reschedule their external debt in order to avoid default. For the first time, however, the IMF is now applying conditionality to lending banks as well as to borrowing countries. The IMF loan package for Mexico in 1982, for example, was not approved until the banks had agreed to provide $5 billion; this pattern was repeated in rescue packages assembled by the IMF for Argentina, Brazil, and Yugoslavia.

The commercial banks, which historically have resisted attempts to intervene in their global operations by their governments and by international agencies, are hailing a new era of cooperation with officialdom. This is not surprising when one realizes that, in effect, the IMF is acting as enforcer of the banks' loan contracts. Continued access to IMF funds is contingent on the debtor's regular payments on its commercial interest. Both the US Federal Reserve system and the IMF have allowed the banks a free hand in setting the terms for new bank loans and rescheduling. The banks have seized this opportunity to sharply increase the interest margin charged on rescheduled loans and to tack on additional hefty fees which will cost Mexico, to take a well known case, about $800 million over the base interest rate in 1983. From the banks' perspective, loans to troubled borrowers like Mexico and Brazil are at present among the most lucrative assets on their books. There also appears to be an implicit US government guarantee for these new loans to uncreditworthy borrowers, although neither banks nor government officials will admit this openly.

The danger for the future is that banks are assuming a larger and larger role in the financing of foreign governments, and eventually the line between the foreign policy interests of the United States (and other center countries) and the commercial interests of private banks will be blurred to the point of nonexistence. Because private bankers are virtual newcomers to the politics of collecting debts from third world nations, they have pressured Washington and the IMF to come to their assistance. This worked to Chase Manhattan's good fortune in the case of Iran, for example, where billions of dollars in Iranian loans were wiped off its books after the US government decided to freeze the post-Shah regime's assets in the United States and permit banks to seize those deposits to pay off their Iranian loans. Government officials, on the other hand, will find it tempting to turn to banks as instruments of foreign policy when faced with the prospect of a friendly nation going bankrupt. The third world liquidity crisis of the 1980s has altered, then, not only the way in which banks and governments deal with international debt problems, but more importantly how they deal with each other.

CONCLUSIONS

The growing internationalization of the center countries since 1970 and the decline in the relative economic importance of the United States have contributed to the emergence of a more interdependent world. This interdependence, however, is still fundamentally asymmetrical. The contemporary global crisis may have been aggravated by the policies and problems of the third world nations, but it was not caused or dominated by them. The inflation, unemployment, and economic stagnation that have characterized the international recession are a product of long-run structural trends in the world economy and of macroeconomic and even domestic (e.g. federal budgetary) decisions emanating from the center countries. It is instructive and maybe ironic that the world's two most populous nations, China and India, have up to now escaped serious slowdowns in growth because their economies are more self-sufficient than most others and therefore less vulnerable to events in the industrialized world.

The solution to the global crisis will not come from a dismantling of the international economy or a generalized movement toward greater autarky, however. Paradoxically, perhaps, the returns to most third world countries would probably be improved by a more genuinely *open* international system. The success of the most rapidly growing of the developing nations (the so-called semiperiphery), for example, has been predicated on open access to core country markets, especially for their manufactured exports; substantial imports of intermediate and capital goods from the center countries have been an important element of their growth strategies as well. The effects of the world recession are beginning to alter this pattern. The acute financial crises that have erupted like brush fires across the third world recently have led a number of governments to devalue their currencies and cut imports. Some center countries, who claim that imports of manufactures from the third world have contributed to their economic declines, are consciously moving in the direction of discriminatory policies that aim to co-opt or tame a handful of the most advanced developing nations. This approach will not yield the intended result of a more productive and dynamic manufacturing sector in the centers, although it is easy to see why organized labor prefers the minimal but predictable gains to be had from protectionism. Industrial policy in the developed countries would be more effective if it promoted positive structural adjustments that would help absorb the workers displaced from traditional manufacturing jobs. This means recognizing and adapting to changes in the industrial capacity and export potential of third world nations.

NOTE

1   Jeff Frieden, 'Third World Indebted Industrialization: International Finance and State Capitalism in Mexico, Brazil, Algeria and South Korea', *International Organization,* 35: 3 (Summer 1981), pp. 407–31, p. 407.

3.5 Transnationalism and its national consequences

Osvaldo Sunkel and Edmundo F. Fuenzalida

Source: Jose J. Villamil (ed.), *Transnational Capitalism and National Development: New Perspectives on Dependence* (Harvester Press, Brighton, 1979), pp. 67–93.

Sunkel and Fuenzalida argue that the development of capitalism at the centre and periphery of the world economy has been profoundly affected by a process of transnationalization which has created a transnational community with a distinctive culture. They point to potential sources of conflict between national and transnational communities and the attempts being made to reassert the national community.

THE MAIN COMPONENTS OF TRANSNATIONAL CAPITALISM

(a) The transnational institutions

The dominant institution of the global system is the transnational corporation (TNC); dominant because it is the focus of crucial decision-making with respect to what to produce, by whom, how, for whom, and where in the world market. Dominant also because, as a group, they are highly influential institutions with respect to national and global society, politics and culture.

But the TNCs are by no means the only important institutions in the global system. They may have more visibility because of their enormous economic and political power and influence, the conflicts and confrontations with states in which they have been involved, and the huge amount of resources that they devote to promote their image, but there is a whole network of other institutions that support the operations of the TNCs. Some of them are intergovernmental institutions, such as the IMF, the World Bank or the OECD in the economic sphere, or NATO and the Rio Pact in the military sphere, with as high a visibility as the one enjoyed by the TNCs. Others, public and private, operate at the national or subnational level and

325

have less obvious links to the global system but in fact operate as parts of it. Those engaged in foreign aid, export promotion and finance activities, both civilian and military, fall in this category.

Particular importance should be given to those educational institutions that prepare the staff of the transnational institutions, usually outstanding universities and polytechnics in the richer countries and their 'subsidiaries' in the Third World. These institutions share with the magazines, newspapers of worldwide circulation, news agencies, multinational advertising companies and television networks, the task of elaborating and diffusing the vision of the world that promotes the interests of the TNCs.

Finally, there are the transnational journals and the informal networks of scientists and professionals, with their periodical and highly publicized meetings and conferences which provide not only basic information but also the human inventory from which specialized staff is recruited.

(b) The transnational community

The global system is operated by a stratum of society that appropriates most of the surplus produced by it. Their position in the productive structure ranges from that of owners of the means of production and the top managerial and financial positions, through the higher professional, technical and bureaucratic ones, both in private and public institutions.

The basis of their hegemony is the specialized knowledge they possess, and their indispensability in the process of creation and application of that knowledge to the production of new goods and services and to the process of innovation and production differentiation that is the main reason for the superiority of the TNCs.

As stated above, the activities of the TNCs are supported by the scientific and technological progress generated by the institutions of higher learning, as well as by the highly skilled personnel trained by them. The transnational community, therefore, has its base not only in the TNCs, and in all the economic sectors in which these operate (industry, agriculture, mining, transportation, construction, marketing, information, mass media, banking and finance, tourism, entertainment, etc.), but also in the other transnational institutions. On the basis of their specialized knowledge, professional organization and social prestige, these elites have a measure of control over these institutions, and the power to capture part of the economic surplus, which allows them to sustain relatively high standards of living.

(c) The transnational culture

The stratum of society that we have called the transnational community is made up of people that belong to different nations, but who have similar values, beliefs, ideas (and a *lingua franca* – English), as well as remarkably similar patterns of behaviour as regards career patterns, family structures, housing, dress, consumption patterns and cultural orientations in general. The transnational community, then, shares what could be considered a transnational culture. As any other culture, this transnational culture has two main components: specialized and common culture.

The first emerges out of the specialized scientific–technological activities carried out by the members of the transnational community – and is a necessary input for the expansion of industrial capitalism. This segment of the culture is permeated by the specialized knowledge possessed by its carriers, the one that has allowed them to become members of the transnational community in the first place. Since this knowledge is based on the progress attained by the systematic application of the so-called 'scientific method' to every aspect of reality, the transnationals' approach to the world and to themselves is heavily influenced by a belief in the effectiveness of 'problem solving' through rational analysis and the application of 'the scientific method'.

The second component of transnational culture is common culture. Transnational capitalism has affected habits, ideas, beliefs, values and behaviour in matters such as family life, housing, consumption patterns, and other aspects of everyday life. One of the most important effects has probably been on consumption patterns, as the cultural feature of the dynamics of oligopoly capitalism has been the creation of a homogeneous market for consumption goods and services on the worldwide scale. The transnational community is the best and most complete and coherent expression of these new consumption patterns, but they spread over wider sectors of the population as a consequence of the demonstration effect and the active and extensive use of the mass media. The consequence on the lower income classes is a partial adoption of these new consumption patterns and the distortion of the existing ones. This refers not only to the better known examples related to consumer durables, but to basic food, as when bread substitutes for maize or manioc.

(d) The spatial organization of transnational capitalism

The recent technological revolutions in transportation and communications have drastically reduced the costs of distance and time. The application of electronic innovations to production processes has allowed further disaggregation of the labour process into distinct and simple tasks. Production processes can therefore be separated into specific stages, and these distributed all over the world on the basis of locational advantages such as cheap and disciplined labour, access to markets, government subsidies, access to strategic resources or inputs and the absence of environmental regulations. In other terms, the geographical decentralization of production facilities within and among countries can proceed much further than ever before, taking advantage of locational factors, while at the same time maintaining centralized control over planning, finance, manpower, marketing, production and innovation.

Distinct types of spatial configurations tend to take place as a consequence: on the one hand, a functional separation of managerial, scientific and technological, and production activities, into downtown business districts, areas of concentration of academic establishments and peripheral industrial areas. On the one hand, a hierarchical decentralization between world headquarters in central countries, located in cities such as New York, London, Paris, Frankfurt and Tokyo; regional headquarters located in the cities of the more transnationalized countries of the various regions of the Third World, such as Mexico City, Sao Paulo, Nairobi and Singapore; and national headquarters, usually in the capitals of less important or strategic countries. The scope for independent policy, planning and decision making becomes more restricted when moving from world to national or local levels, and some functions disappear altogether. Innovative scientific and technological activities, for instance, will take place almost entirely at world level, as will overall strategic planning, and financial and manpower management. This obviously implies increasing rigidity and declining autonomy as one moves towards the local production unit, and this is a source of friction and conflict with the national/local environment.

At all levels, the transnational institutions have to establish contacts and relationships with national and/or local governments, business firms, and the labour market, both for professional, technical and bureaucratic personnel as well as for skilled and unskilled labour. In time this process brings about the development of national and local counterpart institutions and communities, increasingly integrated into the transnational institutions and communities. These communities will tend to concentrate in suburban residential areas, which will reproduce the urban structure, housing and life styles of the transnational communities of the central countries. Local middle and higher income segments of the population will seek to extend these life styles to themselves, as a means of incorporation into the consumption patterns of the transnational sector.

Although the members of the transnational community that live in the central countries have much in common with those living in the peripheral ones, there is a division of labour between the two, and important differences between them. As regards the first aspect, high level personnel of the transnational corporations will remain in the central countries, as the functions of devising global strategy and planning are retained there; so will most of the personnel dealing with innovation, both in science and technology as well as in production and marketing. At the local level the highest functions will be those of administering and implementing global strategies.

As a consequence of these spatial patterns, national and local resources will be allocated preferentially to expanding the 'modern' sectors of towns and cities, while older quarters decay and slum areas proliferate, accentuating the characteristic heterogeneity of contemporary cities: modern residential, business, government, industrial and even working class areas intermingled with older and decaying residential, business, government, working class and industrial areas, all of it surrounded by growing slum areas.

In synthesis, the transnational institutions and communities are spatially scattered around the world in an archipelago of nuclei of 'modernity', linked among themselves through a number of centralized hierarchical structures that define dominant and dependent nuclei. These nuclei interact with national and local societies, parts of which have become more or less integrated into the transnational nuclei, while the rest is indirectly related or affected through the labour market, the exchange of goods and services, the socialization agencies of education and the mass media and the reallocation of resources brought about by transnational influences.

Since the size, importance and type of transnational nuclei varies from country to country, as do the socio-cultural and geo-political characteristics of national and local societies, each country will present the same generic similarity of the interaction between a new and expanding transnational nucleus and a pre-existing society, but will also show great differences according to the nature of the society in which this interaction takes place. Comparative studies of these different types of situations seem therefore crucial for a better understanding of the transnationalization process under different sets of national characteristics.

(e) The transnational system and the nation state

The transnational system has developed an economic infrastructure of TNCs and related institutions, it has a population which constitutes the transnational communities, these communities share a common culture, and all of these elements are established in certain territories. But while these elements are components of the transnational system, they also happen to be under the jurisdiction of national states. In other words, the transnational system overlaps with a system of nation states. As a consequence there may be a coincidence with the objectives and procedures of the state and its socio-political base, but there are also bound to be conflicting situations when the aims and procedures of each system are different.

From the point of view of its global rationality, a TNC may want its subsidiary in a given country to produce a certain product for the local market, employing its own technology, imported inputs and capital goods, buying out or displacing local competitors, keeping full control of its capital, management and organization procedures, using its own public and labour relations practices and remitting the maximum amount of profits to headquarters. The national government may want to strengthen national capitalists, have the subsidiary produce for export, buy inputs locally, have nationals share in ownership, management and technological know-how, adapt to local organization, accounting and labour relation practices, minimize its remittances abroad, maximize reinvestment locally and pay taxes on profits. This is, of course, the traditional conflict over the conditions for foreign private investment, and it deals essentially with the sharing of the additional income generated by the subsidiaries.

A much more fundamental question is that related to the whole strategy of development, heavily influenced by the local transnational nucleus, seeking to reproduce the living standards, patterns of consumption and culture that characterize transnational nuclei elsewhere. The main instrument through which this aim can be achieved is the state, and access, control and influence over it becomes crucial. This was achieved in recent decades as a consequence of the expansion and transformation of the functions of the state brought about by the internal and external pressures for economic and social development. The new activities of the state were heavily promoted by international technical assistance, which introduced new approaches and methods in public administration and planning. A new and enlarged government bureaucracy emerged, both civilian and military, whose function was to modernize and rationalize the state in its promotion of economic and social development, as well as in its capacity to deal with internal conflicts and subversion. These new social sectors share to a very large extent the values, principles and methods of the transnational community, and have a direct interest in the transnationalization process. Through its global and local influence, as well as its strategic internal presence within the state itself, the transnational community acquired significant influence over the process of resource allocation and policy making, quite out of proportion to its actual economic or political power. In their attempt to reproduce locally the methods and life styles of the developed countries, they have contributed significantly to a massive allocation of resources for the satisfaction of these 'needs', with extremely positive effects for the standards of living of a minority of the population, including themselves, and very negative consequences for the majority of the population.

Conventional development theory has argued that this conflict does not exist, at least in the longer term, because the expansion of the 'modern' (transnational) nucleus will increase the total product, and this will in turn bring about a 'spill over' that will improve the lot of the majority of the population in due time, as occurred in the now developed countries. Our argument, on the contrary, is that contemporary transnational capitalist growth has produced cumulative and increasing polarization, which in turn has affected relations between the nation state and transnational capitalism.

The conflicts between the nation state and transnational capitalism were overshadowed to some extent by the formidable expansion of transnational capitalism until the early 1970s. This expansion created the impression of a coincidence of interests between both. But the crisis and recession of recent years is pointing in the direction of increasing conflicts between national interests and transnational capitalism.

Indeed, one of the increasingly serious problems that the nation state has had to confront since 1973 is the decline in economic growth rates, the tendencies to increasing external and fiscal imbalance, the consequent increased indebtedness and inflationary pressures, the continuous increase in unemployment, underemployment and poverty and the increasingly limited room for manoeuvre in its redistribution policies. This is particularly serious in the case of the so-called developing countries, but is also becoming a matter of concern in the developed countries, as TNCs increasingly invest abroad, establishing productive facilities for serving local markets or for re-export to the developed countries. Employment opportunities are thereby doubly threatened and political pressure is increasing for protectionist policies to be adopted.

This is one example of the contradictions between the expansion of the transnational system and its requirement of political stability, both in developed as well as in underdeveloped countries. In developed countries, where average levels of living are very high, and inequality is less acute, stabilization and 'incomes' policies have so far been able to deal with short-term economic disequilibria. There are nevertheless very serious long-term structural problems as regards access to natural resources, the environment, growing structural unemployment and others which are not unrelated to the expansion and characteristics of transnational capitalism.

In underdeveloped countries, where the level of average income is low, inequality is severe, and poverty widespread, growing economic disequilibria and political tensions can only be contained by means of force. The spread of authoritarian and military regimes in the countries of the Third World in recent years is undoubtedly related to these tendencies.

Differences arise also because transnational elites in underdeveloped countries find themselves in a much more exposed and segregated position with respect to the rest of their society and because they have to perform the functions of articulating their country to the global system while preserving the integrity of their nation state. They tend to be more closely linked to the state and more explicitly political.

The objective pressures for adopting protectionist and nationalistic policies in developed and underdeveloped countries have been mounting, but the actual possibilities of disengaging to a greater extent internal processes from international phenomena have simultaneously become much more severely restricted. The transnational system has not only developed strong structural links across national frontiers, both economic, social, cultural, and political, but a set of international organizations and institutions, such as the OECD, the IMF and the World Bank among others have been established, a semblance of a global state, with the aim of maintaining the transnational system and dealing with any threats to its functioning. Therefore, socio-political 'adjustments' tend to take place internally rather than internationally.

THE PROCESS OF TRANSNATIONALIZATION OF THE GLOBAL SYSTEM

Techno-industrial capitalism, in its contemporary form as a global transnational system, is the product of a long historical process. [...] The following main historical stages can be identified: a formative period of capitalism as a worldwide commercial system, from the last third of the fifteenth century to the last third of the eighteenth century; the emergence of the first historical instances of industrial capitalism and modern nation states, during the last third of the eighteenth century and the first third of the nineteenth century; internal consolidation and external imperial expansion of the first industrial capitalist states, from about 1825 to the 1870s; industrial capitalism as a global trading, financial and investment system, in its international–imperial organization phase, between 1870 and 1914; crisis of international–imperial capitalism, the emergence of a socialist alternative and attempts at reorganization of industrial capitalism as a response to it, between 1914 and 1945; techno-industrial capitalism as a global system in its transnational organization phase, as a response to the previous crisis period and the internal consolidation and external expansion of the socialist alternative, from about 1945 to the present.

The process of reorganization of the capitalist system after the long period of crisis from 1914 to 1945 evolved out of different national situations. The countries that had been liberated from German occupation by the USSR, or that had undergone a socialist revolution made up the socialist block under the leadership of the Soviet Union. The industrialized countries of Western Europe, whether defeated (Germany, Italy) or victorious (France, UK, Holland, Belgium), were severely weakened by the war effort and confronted very serious internal political problems, with strong left wing parties of a reformist or revolutionary character. Japan's situation in Asia was similar to that of the former Western European countries. In the colonies of the industrialized countries of Western Europe and Japan in Africa, Asia and Latin America the nationalist struggle for independence became more intense, taking advantage of the crisis of the metropolitan powers and the presence of the socialist countries. The independent non-industrialized states on these continents, mostly those in Latin America, had embarked on protectionist policies of import substitution industrialization during the crisis and war years and were pressing for international acceptance and support for their policies.

The USA emerged as the single most powerful economic, political and military power from the period of crisis and war, and as the new centre of the capitalist system. In 1948, it launched a massive economic, diplomatic, military and ideological offensive in order to contain the expanding socialist block and the threat of left wing parties in many capitalist countries both in the Centre and in the Periphery. A global network of international treaties of mutual defence between the US and countries on the borders of the socialist world was built up and US military bases maintained or established in their territories.

The reconstruction of the economies of the industrialized countries of Western Europe and of Japan was promoted through a massive transfer of financial resources and technology (Marshall Plan) and the creation of the OECD and the EEC. Further industrialization and modernization of the independent states, especially in Latin America was also supported at a later stage through technical aid, financial cooperation and promotion of private foreign investment. Finally, a network of international, economic, financial and technical assistance organizations was created, aimed at reconstructing the international system that had broken down during the period of crisis, at dismantling the protectionist structures and policies that all countries had adopted during that period, and at promoting the reincorporation of underdeveloped countries into that system, once the reconstruction and revival of European capitalism was well underway.

These processes, and certain fundamental characteristics of the economy and society of the USA, constitute the immediate origin of the emerging transnational system. The westward territorial expansion of the American economy and society took place in sparsely populated areas, at the expense of relatively primitive indigenous societies, and largely over the North American subcontinent, a vast contiguous territory richly endowed with natural resources. The continental dimension of the country and its vast internal market, as well as the relative scarcity of labour, favoured the development of capital intensive technology, mass production and very large oligopolistic business organizations, with wide geographical coverage. Science, technology and business had become closely associated in the development of mass production. Moreover, as a consequence of the Great Depression and World War II, which brought about government intervention in the economy and a great war effort, a symbiosis of government, large corporations and science and technology took place.

This dynamic core of the American economy and society, which had remained relatively 'isolationist' until the Second World War – with the exception of the Caribbean and Central America – penetrated throughout the world during the war, and remained and expanded afterwards, in the 1950s and 1960s during the period of the Cold War. This was instrumental in the worldwide expansion of American techno-industrial capitalism. It was also fundamental in the reconstruction and development of a similar 'style' of capitalist development in the former European and Japanese capitalist centres, where similar dynamic oligopolistic cores were formed or reconstructed, as well as in the underdeveloped countries, where expanding 'modern' sectors emerged.

Although the immediate origin of transnational capitalism is the oligopolistic corporate sector of the American economy, and the techno-scientific establishment of American society, as well as parts of its government apparatus, its American 'national' character has been gradually eroded as similar dynamic cores of business, science and technology and government have emerged in the revitalized industrial centres of Europe and Japan, and as their subsidiaries expand and penetrate the underdeveloped countries and even, to a more limited but growing extent, the socialist countries. The original American drive to reorganize capitalism has therefore been transformed, becoming a transnational drive, which is in turn penetrating and affecting American society itself, as well as others.

MECHANISMS OF INCORPORATION OF UNDERDEVELOPED COUNTRIES INTO THE GLOBAL SYSTEM

Since this paper is mainly concerned with the process of capitalist development in the countries of the Third World, we will limit our discussion to the effects of transnationalization on these countries. As these effects are greatly influenced by the way in which the transnationalization process manifests itself in each particular case, we will first examine briefly the various means through which national societies interact with the global system: (a) foreign investment in the primary export sectors, tourism and/or in the manufacturing sector, usually by establishing subsidiaries of transnational corporations; with two main variations in the case of manufacturing: production for the internal market or for export, usually to the more advanced industrial societies; (b) systematic use of the mass media (newspapers, radio, television) to create a demand for new consumption goods and services, employing advanced techniques of advertising; in most cases this implies the creation or expansion and modernization of a national system of communications; (c) foreign public loans and technical assistance to rationalize, modernize and expand the state apparatus, with particular emphasis on economic and social infrastructure and military institutions; in recent years there has been increasing access to a new and rapidly expanding private international financial market; (d) scholarship programmes, both civilian and military, to train local personnel in the educational institutions of the core countries in the different branches of science and engineering and in the new disciplines of management, planning, national accounting, information processing, mass media, marketing, and 'national security'; (e) reform of the educational institutions in order to educate locally human resources able to replace foreign technicians; (f) generalization of the criteria, priorities and methods of the transnational style to all areas of social life, from economic activities to health, education, housing.

These various mechanisms have been in evidence in the different underdeveloped countries since the early 1950s. They did not all commence simultaneously, and they were promoted by different social and professional groups, economic interests and government departments, both from the underdeveloped as well as from the industrial countries. But even if they were not intended to operate simultaneously and coherently, it soon became apparent that they constituted a new kind of process of technological innovation in its widest sense, a whole package of mutually reinforcing innovations in production, consumption, organization, behaviour and values, both in the private and public sectors – in short, a new culture. During the international phase of industrial capitalism the mechanism of incorporation into the global system was primary-product exports and the main technological innovation was the railway. Furthermore, the social groups affected were highly restricted. As a consequence 'modernization' was an 'enclave' phenomenon. Transnational modernization, with its emphasis on developing a mass consumption market, its reliance on the mass media, on large-scale, capital-intensive and technologically sophisticated local production units, on planned government and international action and on the local reproduction of the 'model' offered by the industrial countries, has had much more far reaching aggregate effects, both intended as well as unintended.

EFFECTS OF TRANSNATIONALIZATION ON UNDERDEVELOPED SOCIETIES

In general, these effects are threefold. The first one is the emergence of a dependent nucleus of the global system in the underdeveloped society, with its own institutions, culture and community, that differentiates itself sharply from the rest of the society, and that controls to a large extent the machinery of an increasingly repressive state.

The institutions that become integrated into this nucleus include the subsidiaries of the TNCs in the different sectors of the economy; the larger local firms that use advanced technology, both private and public; the specialized government agencies that deal with the planning and implementation of ambitious development projects and with the overall planning of 'areas' such as health, education, the cities, transportation and communication; the higher educational institutions, especially those that are involved in scientific research; the international organizations; the armed forces.

The aggregate of these institutions provides jobs, income and goods and services for a segment of the local population, that therefore may share similar patterns of behaviour with the inhabitants of the dominant nucleus of the global system in the developed countries. Among the patterns of behaviour that are particularly striking are the residential areas of the capital cities of underdeveloped countries that reproduce the layout and architectural styles of similar residential areas in the dominant nucleus and that tend to be physically separated from the rest of the city.

The second effect is the creation of a mass of unemployed or underemployed people that, having very precarious and unstable sources of income, are forced to survive in conditions of extreme poverty, whereas at the same time they are stimulated to aspire to the level of living enjoyed by the people in the dependent nucleus of the global system. This state of affairs is the direct consequence of the destruction, displacement and/or stagnation of the traditional socio-economic institutions that offered them jobs, income and goods and services – however poor and primitive – by the more efficient ones brought in by the global system; the incapacity of the new capital-intensive activities to absorb the demographic increase of the work force and the un- and underemployment generated by transnationalization; the intense effort of the mass media to replace traditional goods and services by the products of the new economic activities that results in a change of the pattern of consumption in society; and the acceleration of the growth of the poorer population and of the labour force as a consequence of innovations, modernization and extension of the health services, which have reduced the mortality rates of the poor but not their birth rates.

As the process of transnationalization is basically urban, this mass of marginalized people concentrate in certain areas around the big cities, and mainly in the capital, where the aspired goods and services are on display, in dramatic contrast to the limited employment opportunities. There, they are physically segregated from the other segments of their own society. The glaring contrast between their own lot in life and that of their fellow countrymen that have found a place in the new system, and the objective scarcity of 'legitimate' ways to obtain the desired goods and services, leads them to react in various ways, both individually and collectively. The actions of the deprived bring in turn the reaction of the privileged, who turn to the state for protection. Since they, as a whole, control the state, its force is used against these masses, contributing to its authoritarian character.

As we have already indicated, the transnationalization and polarization effects described above have a third effect: the accentuation of the authoritarian and repressive character of the state as the hegemonic social groups become increasingly threatened. But there are also other types of responses that attempt to deal with the causal forces rather than with its consequences. These are attempts at severing the links of the society with the global system and at reorganizing it internally in a less polarized way, both in terms of social action and in social thinking. These attempts are a second order effect of the two aforementioned ones and range from the rediscovery and reformulation of the values, symbols and art, to the founding of political movements that have as their main goal the disengagement of the society or of parts of it, from the global system.

One can then perceive three dimensions to the process of transnationalization: transnational integration, national disintegration and attempts at reintegration. [...]

3.6 Information technology and capitalist development

Gareth Locksley

Source: *Capitalist and Class*, 27 (1986), pp. 81–105.

Advances in technology, Locksley argues, have turned information into a valuable asset and a new source of power, comparable to land and capital, which could in principle be used to improve the lives of everyone. In practice, developments in information technology (IT) are dominated by the military and multinational corporations. These organizations have shaped IT to promote centralization and surveillance and global relations are being restructured so as to develop the interests of international capital. Locksley concludes, however, by suggesting that this trend could be reversed and IT could be used to satisfy social needs.

INTRODUCTION

Information technology (IT) can be viewed as a collection of machines – computers, telephone exchanges, word processors, work stations of various description, robots, satellites, automatic cash dispensers, cable TV etc. Software is used to activate and operate these machines without human intervention or manage a user through the steps of an activity. Broadly there are two sets of machines that make up IT – computers and telecommunications. They share features of a common technology associated with digital electronics. The distinction between computers and telecommunications equipment has blurred so that their progress is described as convergent, a theme that recurs here. But there is much more to IT than machines. There is no activity that IT does not touch – in home, office, factory, culturally, politically, economically. IT has been boosted into Western societies as the vehicle for greater political participation, more leisure, greater equality between sexes and classes, more freedom, more choice. IT's potential for these developments is real but IT as implied can produce the opposite outcomes of more inequality, less freedom, less choice, greater centralisation of power and more intense and controlled work.

IT is a capitalist machine in capitalism. The IT environment (machine, software, institutions) reflects the structure of that society, underpinned by the dominance of men, the dominance of North over South, and, most fundamentally, by the logic of production for profit. Though IT is a new means of production, the combination of several new technologies, it is not revolutionary in the context of capitalism, merely a development of machines. It also opens up new areas for capitalist production through new products and services. Through cable TV and personal computer link-ups IT is extending capitalism into the home by the further commercialisation of culture.

IT is a stage in the progression of capitalist development specific to prevailing conditions. The current crisis of capitalism remains that of realising profits, of labour resistance, of bursts of intense competition between capitals. There is also an organisational crisis centred on the need to control globally dispersed units of economic activity and to reaffirm control over the work process. Corporations that successfully apply IT gain a competitive advantage that through the logic of the market forces others to follow. So there are two IT-related messages: for the public 'IT is good for you, it will transform your life'; for capital 'automate or die'. The market issues the second message and the logic of capital the first. IT nevertheless needs to be legitimised if it is to be introduced smoothly, so it is boosted by myth creation.

IT involves the movement of electronic signals from place to place, frequently across borders. Consequently, the doctrine of the supremacy of the free flow of goods, services, *and* information is central to IT in use. It is the same doctrine that underlies the rise of de-regulation, supply side economics, privatisation, the renewed action on the European Community's 'internal market', the end of exchange controls.

When the steam engine was introduced and spread, it brought about new means of production and communication. It allowed an extension of the capitalist system into new regions of the world and areas of economic activity. IT is a new ingredient in the giant recipe of capitalism – one that will transform very many of the individual courses, bring forth new ones, or delete old ones. But the essential flavour of the meal is the same. [...]

The military imperative

The perceived needs of the military have been a major force in the development of IT. Computers were developed to solve problems related to encryption, decoding and missile trajectory. Microelectronic technologies owe their genesis to the space race: US rockets were smaller than Soviet rockets, they could not carry sufficient computer hardware onboard because they were unable to match the pay-load of Soviet Russia's. Miniaturisation provided the solution and gave us the 'chip'. Operationally, military commanders are faced with multiple information sources which must be processed rapidly and whose complexity computers could manage. Whole defence systems like the North American Air Defense Command (NORAD) are now run on computers which receive, process, monitor and initiate actions on large volumes of data flows.

The military has also taken a keen interest in telecommunications because of its requirement to control dispersed units and receive information from them and to gather 'intelligence'. Telecommunications technologies have been developed to intercept and eavesdrop on 'enemy' communications. The major interest in space follows from the need for surveillance. Britain's GCHQ is part of the vast Signals Intelligence (SIGNIT) network that forms a global web from Australia's Pine Gap to Fort George G. Meade near Washington. The US National Security Agency (NSA), described as 'the largest single espionage factory the free world (has) ever known or could ever imagine' has a room containing eleven acres of computers and boasts the most sophisticated telecommunications system in the world. Because the military's computers need to communicate, say between battle tank commander, Field Commander and upwards, there has been a drive for convergence between computers and telecommunications. As long as computers are separate from communications their range of applications is limited.

Convergence is an imperative of the military. With the budget to back its needs the distinction between computers and telecommunications rapidly disappeared.

IT and the internationalisation of capital

In one important respect multinational corporations and the military share a common objective: the control of dispersed units. There has been an accelerating trend to the internationalisation of production, distribution and exchange. Raw materials and commodities have long been traded on international markets and a major feature of the post-war era has been the internationalisation of industrial and financial capital. For instance, in the UK only 18 per cent of exports in 1981 were not accounted for by MNCs. The decision of these MNCs determines an international flow of sub-assemblies, components and final products and causes associated activities in the service and financial sectors.

Direct foreign investment by MNCs has produced a response from financial capital which has followed the path of internationalisation in the same way as industrial capital. [For example, in] January 1985 the daily turnover on New York's foreign exchange market was ten times the daily total of imports and exports for the USA. These figures suggest the sheer volume of flows of information related to finance capital far exceeds those related to industrial capital. They also indicate the imperative for information handling in a dispersed and highly uncertain financial environment. Without telecommunications and computer technologies these activities could not take place at the same rate. They now facilitate the 24-hour global stock and financial markets.

The process of globalisation raised severe difficulties for those organisations involved because they wanted to control and co-ordinate every unit of their organisation whilst keeping the environment under surveillance. To perform the functions of production, distribution and exchange, information has to be collected, stored, retrieved, manipulated, up-dated and communicated. It is clear that these organisations searched for a technological solution to their problem and found it – like the military – in IT. Competition and the profit imperative of globalised capital explain the demand for and development of IT. [...]

Profit and de-socialisation

[Locksley then discusses in more detail how the production of the hardware and software for IT has become an important source of profit in the capitalist economy. The profit motive is also seen to be the major impetus behind the trend to de-socialize or privatize the world's major telecommunication systems. According to Locksley, once these systems are in private hands then they begin to serve the interests of the most profitable sectors of the market rather than satisfying social needs. He goes on to suggest that these developments have also facilitated the task of turning information into a commodity.]

INFORMATION AS COMMODITY AND RESOURCE

Very frequently information is held in common ownership. Often organisations are obliged to publish information. Successive Companies Acts and legislation have determined that various legal entities are required to provide information at no charge. Parliaments provide records of their proceedings, government departments and agencies similarly issue information to the public. In many ways information has existed outside general commodity production, accumulated in public libraries.

Information is a resource input to all economic activity. Sometimes it is the direct product of economic activity, at other times the by-product. Information has a clear use value in business which yields future income streams. Consequently organisations invest in the resource of information in the expectation of related rewards.

In a similar manner information is decisive in determining the life chances and opportunities of individuals and households. Of course a system of common ownership does not guarantee equality of access but the development of 'library' systems can be seen as an egalitarian move. Certainly the system of common ownership that has developed is far less exclusive than the system of access dominated by the ecclesiastical power structure of an earlier period. Clearly common ownership of information is a pre-requisite for egalitarian societies. This common ownership feature of information is also strongly associated with the concept of the welfare state and benefits systems. A benefits programme cannot exist without public information about targets, eligibility, point of contact, etc., and a central feature of the welfare system is the dissemination of information through public education.

The information economy is based on information as a commodity. This refers not just to the high profile information providers like Reuters but to a wide range of activities. These include Pay TV, Cable TV and Direct Broadcast by Satellite (DBS) where information and entertainment are treated as commodities for the household. The same applies to many of the new interactive services available through the phone/home computer/TV link-up. These are the new technologies enabling a greater commercialisation of culture where culture is not only a commodity but reinforces the conditions of general commodity production. Information technology has made concrete the concept of the global village and the global shopping centre. It provides for the marketing, design, production and replacement of the 'world' car, soft drink, computer, and establishes the necessary conditions for private consumption.

Our routine activities create information. When this is captured and amassed it can be transformed into a commodity. Personalised 'junk mail' is one example of this form of commodity information. Details about the interests, income, composition, debts, purchases, travel, reading, etc., of households and groups are regularly collected and traded as commodities. What was once 'ours' is now in the hands of someone else. The essence of a commodity is private ownership for it is through this relationship that it achieves exchange value. The information economy will increasingly transform the common ownership of information into one of exclusivity through private ownership so that information as a commodity can generate private income.

Information can convert something that is useless into a resource. IT through satellites can gather information that performs this transformation. Satellites observe large areas at once including those areas that are inaccessible by any other means. Remote sensing technology can distinguish between crops, indicate the health of crops, identify the likely presence of minerals and water, measure the depths of coastal water, track the movement of fish, warn of flooding, predict the weather and provide maps and charts. Clearly this form of IT can transform the wealth-creating process especially for poor, less developed countries. In the US, such earth resources satellites, called Landsat, developed and owned by the Federal government, gather very large quantities of information that can convert what appears useless into a resource. Landsat is in the process of being sold to private commercial interests so that the exchange value of its information can be realised. (Apparently there are plans to sell off US weather satellites.)

In history certain key resources have held such a position that whichever group controlled the resource dominated all other groups. Land and capital have fallen into this category. Increasingly because of technological developments information meets the criterion for special status resource because it is a key resource within the economic activity of large corporations and because of the alchemy it performs on apparently useless material. At the same time information is a commodity requiring a system of private ownership that expropriates. An extreme example of dispossession is found in 'artificial' intelligence and robots where the skills of labour are captured within IT products.

The enhanced dual nature of information facilitated by information technology derives from the specific needs and actions of the military and the giant corporations. Multinational corporations and the military machine require up-to-the-minute information management. For them it is necessary to establish and maintain control over their operations (work) and conflict in order to sustain their positions. When a Bank of America executive observed that the value of information was approaching the value of money he was recognising that information was joining the elite of resources. For many corporations and agencies, information is more scarce than capital and in this new status, information is also assuming the political status associated with capital. At the same time information as a commodity is growing rapidly in importance as something that is traded and as a factor that reinforces capitalism. Information technology is the instrument that allows the resource and commodity of information to be developed and gain ascendancy. The current phase of capitalist development is one characterised by the elevation of information and its associated technology into the first division of key resources and commodities. Information is a new form of capital. As such the controllers of information, usually the controllers of capital, will dominate the political economy. [...]

GLOBAL RESTRUCTURING OF IT

[Locksley goes on to argue that the IT industry is now dominated by two firms: International Business Machines (IBM) and the American Telephone and Telegraph Company (AT&T). The position of these two firms is seen to be comparable to that of Ford and General Motors in an earlier stage of capitalist development. Locksley indicates that these two firms will determine the direction which IT takes.]

IT AND THE LESS DEVELOPED COUNTRIES (LDCS)

LDCs are clearly not a homogeneous group. Here a simple distinction is made between the poorest countries and the Newly Industrialised Countries (NICs). There is no doubt that the poor countries will not be participating in the production side of IT. However, the technical flexibility of IT offers the prospect of greater decentralisation and a wider access and distribution of information. This resource could provide a significant push towards development in the poor countries. Earth resource satellites, agricultural data banks, educational and health services through IT could help to improve and sustain some development. However, the likely outcomes in practice are greater disparity and centralisation. The key to exploitation of IT is communications facilities. When these are widely available the prospects for information transfers to the poor countries will be enhanced. Table 1 illustrates the distribution of telephone densities in the world.

Table 1 Telephones per 100 inhabitants

World	19.1
Industrialised countries	44.5
Developing countries	2.8
Africa	0.8
Asia and Pacific	2.0
Latin American and Caribbean	5.5

The disparities between regions strongly correlate with each region's ability to participate in the information society (as users of information) and the information economy (as workers). But the telephone density figures mask deeper issues. Within developing countries the telephone facilities that exist are highly concentrated in a few main centres, where the telephone density is typically 10 times that in the rest of the country (compared to 1.5 times in industrial countries). There is usually no service to provincial towns and frequently 70 per cent of a country's population has no access to a telephone, while the quality of international telecommunications links is very good. The available systems have been designed for the use of capital, financial and industrial, integrating the major centres of the poor and developing country to loci in the North and centralising the global decision-making process. Another facet of communications hidden behind the figures is the inefficiencies within these countries created by their lack of communications and the huge rate of return that investment in telecommunications would produce. The average economic rate of return on telecommunications investment is potentially about 30 per cent as calculated by the World Bank.

Consequently, the telecommunications system that prevails in poor countries, designed for the use of multinational capital, strengthens the centre–periphery relationship and retards the prospects for growth in those countries because it sustains inefficiencies and cripples domestic development. At the same time the form of these telecommunications structures precludes the type of information transfer that is technically feasible.

'Electronic colonialism'

There are some message transfers, largely one-way and mostly radio and TV programmes with associated advertising. McPhail has termed this transfer 'electronic colonialism'.[1] The concern is with the content of the message and the commercialisation of culture whereby the ideology of the North is beamed by satellite or other means to every village. A recent film on West Pacific Islanders who held sharks to be their ancestors forcibly demonstrated the impact of the digital gunboats. A single TV in a village pushing out regular commercials for a well-known soft drink and other products had transformed the local economy. Children began to demand processed food, mothers engaged in the cash economy to satisfy their children; the men sold their sacred shark fins to raise cash and traditional structures collapsed.

But there is an even more pernicious aspect to electronic colonialism. This concerns the effect on both the self-image of poor countries generated by Northern news and information providers like Associated Press, Reuters and Agence France Press and the received behavioural modes of journalism inherited from past colonial powers. The former stigmatises poor countries as earthquakes, disasters and human zoos. The journalistic style of Western media factories is centred on opposition, the extraordinary, drama which are technically only suited to multi-media interactive systems. 'Yet these attitudes ... are anathema to governments desperately seeking consensus by highlighting the importance of "doing something small but useful every day". These governments (of poor countries) want the media to emphasise the stolid yet "heroic" consistency of a society "in the making".'[2] Poor countries have severely criticised the doctrine of the free flow of information made so much easier through developments in IT and are campaigning for a New World Information Order. As yet IT only stretches the gap between the North and the poor countries. If anything IT is further undermining their position rather than providing any advancement.

The impact on NIC industrial strategy

Many of the newly industrialised countries (NICs) have participated in the developments in IT though they experience the same electronic colonialism as poor countries. Mostly they have provided multi-national capital with low cost assembly lines for labour-intensive operations. Hong Kong, Malaysia, Singapore, Taiwan, South Korea and Indonesia host US, Japanese and European corporations from the electronics/IT sector. Usually young female workers are employed, in conditions far below those of their home counterparts, at low pay and with no possibility of trade union representation. The foreign earnings of these countries have become closely linked with the decisions of the multinationals operating in the sector. For instance, in 1981 semiconductor microcomponents exports earned the Philippines around $636 million, 11 per cent of all exports. Semiconductors have surpassed the performance of sugar, coconut oil and copper, traditionally the country's top foreign exchange earners.

However, the position of some NICs is weakened by technological developments in IT that affect not only IT sub-assemblies and hardware but their entire industrialisation programmes. As micro-electronic technology has progressed, fewer and fewer components are required on any printed circuit board. These are the labour-intensive off-shore assembly tasks performed in NICs. At the same time greater emphasis is given to quality control and testing (and control over the labour process). Automation of testing and com-ponent mounting is undermining the attractions of off-shore assembly for IT corporations so a gradual process of withdrawal to the 'mainland' is underway. Moreover, the advent of cheap forms of automation simultaneously eats into the 'comparative advantage' of developing countries in all the labour-intensive assembly-type oper-ations that they host. For example, in garments manufacture auto-matic micro-processor controlled cutting machinery, which can minimise wastage and change patterns on command, can be inte-grated into automated sewing machines similarly designed and controlled. These developments weaken the attraction of cheap labour especially when capital allowances and subsidies are available at 'home'.

The advent of IT can therefore undermine development programmes in NICs where their attraction to MNCs are superseded by new IT production technologies. In some of the NICs, however, indigenous capital has made some headway, competing in both their (often protected) domestic markets, as well as the international market. This has been especially so in South Korea, which has relied little on foreign MNCs, even in IT-related sectors of the industry. In others like Singapore, which remains highly dependent on MNCs, some advance is being made in attracting foreign capital by upgrading to more capital-intensive production, emphasising skill and scientific content. Taken as a whole, the success of the NICs depends upon access to venture capital and technology and their ability to compete in less labour-intensive, higher-skill product markets, not to mention their ability to sell products in an increasingly protectionist world market.

CONCLUSION

The major impact of IT is to bring about a re-structuring of global relations. It is most apparent in the process of accumulation in the IT sectors accelerating the centralisation of capital in media, information, hardware and distribution interests. There is an evolving system of power relations based on information. The controllers of information are fostering the ideology of the free flow of information and the tenet that the market provides the best solution to the distribution and creation of information and culture. These controllers of information are gaining ascendancy though they are normally the controllers of capital. Their actions are influencing the distribution of income globally and are generating a new class system centred on stocks, flows and contributions to information.

Accompanying the process of accumulation is an evolving distribution of decision-making and jobs. The information economy is related to the distribution of computers which manage information. Data can be transferred at low cost and high speed between computers via satellite links. This development encourages the use of large capacity main-frame computers – the type that are IBM's stock in trade. Small computers feed into larger models. It is no accident that IBM operates the Satellite Business System to perform this function because it sustains the demand for its models. Consequently only a limited number of large main-frames on a limited number of sites are technically required. The outcome is a centralised decision-making structure restricted to a small number of locations. The distribution of the stock of large computers and their manufacture is heavily skewed to the North and, overwhelmingly, the US jobs are associated with this distribution in decision-making, operations, maintenance, development, etc. Consequently, the outcome is to reinforce the centre–periphery relationship of decision-making and skilled jobs.

Another feature of IT in this phase of capitalist development is the necessity for private ownership of information. The information society is still a class society with information entering generalised commodity production.

Systems could have been devised that provided greater equality of access to information (including technology). But the essence of capitalism is exclusion. In an age where it is possible to provide super abundant information there will be (globally) a large class of information-poor, who in turn will be politically and economically weak because they have no access to the abundance of information. At the same time the accelerating commercialisation of culture and the new IT-related delivery systems reinforce the values of capitalism.

IT is essential to the development of the capitalist system but these technologies could radically change the nature of the system. IT offers the potential for many Utopian and socialist aspirations. The quantity of necessary labour required for any given level of output can be dramatically reduced with the application of IT. But these prospects are severely constrained by political notions of waged work and leisure plus a general tendency to workerism within those parties based on workers. IT should cause a thorough overhaul of political thinking on income distribution, education, leisure, waged work, retirement, informed by a genuine position on equality. A progressive strategy for IT would emphasise the widest possible access to the technology and the communications networks. The Technology Shops in the Netherlands and the Greater London Council's Technology Networks are examples of bringing information technology into the community. These enable people to learn what the technology is capable of doing and allowing them, with expert assistance, to design equipment and application to suit their own needs. This local approach to IT can help to foster community-controlled projects but cannot circumvent centrally imposed technology environments.

The same sort of approach can be applied to local communications networks providing access to relevant data bases, community programming for TV and radio or electronic mail and consumer information. There is enough space on the new cable networks for these services.

The local state has an important part to play in progressive strategies for IT but sooner or later multinational capital must be confronted. The best opportunities lie with defending public control over the communications networks – both telecommunications and broadcasting. Active intervention would allow for a socially determined allocation of resources between networks and for control over the content and range of 'messages'. This is to confront multinational capital directly because of its role as the emerging allocator of resources in these areas, and by challenging the ideology of the free flow of information through markets. This means to move to a New World Information Order to encompass the needs of the South. Clearly the immediate task is to start in the North with the local state and to challenge at every opportunity the falsehood that our information needs are best served through the market. Such strategies should have an international dimension by opening up local state facilities to poor countries – through training, access to data bases and technology.

The alternative is more of the same – capitalist IT. IT really offers the prospects for a liberated, leisured, egalitarian society. But IT remains a capitalist machine and is used to sustain capitalism. The classic confrontation between progressive forces and multinational capital characterises the current position. The costs of the products are falling. Demonstrations of the progressive prospects can be set up, effective and viable projects can be mounted. These can form the nucleus of a campaign to apply IT to social need and Utopian ideals.

NOTES

1 T. McPhail, *Electronic Colonialism* (Sage, 1980).
2 B. Murphy, *The World Wired Up* (Comedia, 1983), p. 101.

3.7 The multinational corporation and the law of uneven development

Stephen Hymer

Source: J.N. Bhagwati (ed.), *Economics and World Order* (Collier-Macmillan, London, 1972), pp. 113–40.

Hymer describes the process by which multinational corporations contribute to the development of an international hierarchy and thus restrict the possibilities for national development in peripheral areas. He then examines the possibilities for the continued viability of a global economy based on MNCs, given the problems created by the exclusion of many areas from the benefits of their activities, the need to maintain a modernized 'centre' to the world economy, and the rather ambivalent role of state authorities.

[Hymer begins the article by outlining the historical evolution of the multinational corporation and then turns to the implications for the future of the pattern of industrial organization implicit in that evolution.]

UNEVEN DEVELOPMENT

Suppose giant multinational corporations (say 300 from the US and 200 from Europe and Japan) succeed in establishing themselves as the dominant form of international enterprise and come to control a significant share of industry (especially modern industry) in each country. The world economy will resemble more and more the United States economy, where each of the large corporations tends to spread over the entire continent, and to penetrate almost every nook and cranny. What would be the effect of a world industrial organization of this type on international specialization, exchange and income distribution? The purpose of this section is to analyse the spatial dimension of the corporate hierarchy.

A useful starting point is Chandler and Redlich's scheme for analysing the evolution of corporate structure. They distinguish 'three levels of business administration, three horizons, three levels of task, and three levels of decision making ... and three levels of policies'.[1] Level III, the lowest level, is concerned with managing the day-to-day operations of the enterprise, that is with keeping it going within the established framework. Level II, which first made its appearance with the separation of head office from field office, is responsible for coordinating the managers at Level III. The functions of Level I – top management – are goal-determination and planning. This level sets the framework in which the lower levels operate. In the Marshallian firm, all three levels are embodied in the single entrepreneur or undertaker. In the national corporation, a partial differentiation is made in which the top two levels are separated from the bottom one. In the multidivisional corporation, the differentiation is far more complete. Level I is completely split off from Level II and concentrated in a general office whose specific function is to plan strategy rather than tactics.

The development of business enterprise can therefore be viewed as a process of centralizing and perfecting the process of capital accumulation. The Marshallian entrepreneur was a jack-of-all-trades. In the modern multidivisional corporation, a powerful general office consciously plans and organizes the growth of corporate capital. It is here that the key men who actually allocate the corporation's available resources (rather than act within the means allocated to them, as is true for the managers at lower levels) are located. Their power comes from their ultimate control over *men* and *money* and although one should not overestimate the ability to control a far-flung empire, neither should one underestimate it. [...]

What is the relationship between the structure of the microcosm and the structure of the macrocosm? The application of location theory to the Chandler–Redlich scheme suggests a *correspondence principle* relating centralization of control within the corporation to centralization of control within the international economy.

Location theory suggests that Level III activities would spread themselves over the globe according to the pull of manpower, markets, and raw materials. The multinational corporation, because of its power to command capital and technology and its ability to rationalize their use on a global scale, will probably spread production more evenly over the world's surface than is now the case. Thus, in the first instance, it may well be a force for diffusing industrialization to the less developed countries and creating new centres of production. (We postpone for a moment a discussion of the fact that location depends upon transportation, which in turn depends upon the government which in turn is influenced by the structure of business enterprise.)

Level II activities, because of their need for white-collar workers, communications systems, and information, tend to concentrate in large cities. Since their demands are similar, corporations from different industries tend to place their coordinating offices in the same city, and Level II activities are consequently far more geographically concentrated than Level III activities.

Level I activities, the general offices, tend to be even more concentrated than Level II activities, for they must be located close to the capital market, the media, and the government. Nearly every major corporation in the United States, for example, must have its general office (or a large proportion of its high-level personnel) in or near the city of New York, because of the need for face-to-face contact at higher levels of decision making.

Applying this scheme to the world economy, one would expect to find the highest offices of the multinational corporations concentrated in the world's major cities – New York, London, Paris, Bonn, Tokyo. These, along with Moscow and perhaps Peking, will be the major centres of high-level strategic planning. Lesser cities throughout the world will deal with the day-to-day operations of specific local problems. These in turn will be arranged in a hierarchical fashion: the larger and more important ones will contain regional corporate headquarters, while the smaller ones will be confined to lower-level activities. Since business is usually the core of the city, geographical specialization will come to reflect the hierarchy of corporate decision making, and the occupational distribution of labour in a city or region will depend upon its function in the international economic system. The 'best' and most highly paid administrators, doctors, lawyers, scientists, educators, government officials, actors, servants and hair-dressers, will tend to concentrate in or near the major centres.

The structure of income and consumption will tend to parallel the structure of status and authority. The citizens of capital cities will have the best jobs – allocating men and money at the highest level and planning growth and development – and will receive the highest rates of remuneration. (Executives' salaries tend to be a function of the wage bill of people under them. The larger the empire of the multinational corporation, the greater the earnings of top executives, to a large extent independent of their performance. Thus, growth in the hinterland subsidiaries implies growth in the income of capital cities, but not vice versa.)

The citizens of capital cities will also be the first to innovate new products in the cycle which is known in the marketing literature as trickle-down or two-stage marketing. A new product is usually first introduced to a select group of people who have 'discretionary' income and are willing to experiment in their consumption patterns. Once it is accepted by this group, it spreads, or trickles down to other groups via the demonstration effect. In this process, the rich and the powerful get more votes than everyone else; first, because they have more money to spend, second, because they have more ability to experiment, and third, because they have high status and are likely to be copied. This special group may have something approaching a choice in consumption patterns; the rest have only the choice between conforming or being isolated.

The trickle-down system also has the advantage – from the centre's point of view – of reinforcing patterns of authority and control. According to Fallers,[2] it helps keep workers on the treadmill by creating an illusion of upward mobility even though relative status remains unchanged. In each period subordinates achieve (in part) the consumption standards of their superiors in a previous period and are thus torn in two directions: if they look backward and compare their standards of living through time, things seem to be getting better; if they look upward they see that their relative position has not changed. They receive a consolation prize, as it were, which may serve to keep them going by softening the reality that in a competitive system, few succeed and many fail. It is little wonder, then, that those at the top stress growth rather than equality as the welfare criterion for human relations.

In the international economy trickle-down marketing takes the form of an international demonstration effect spreading outward from the metropolis to the hinterland. Multinational corporations help speed up this process, often the key motive for direct investment, through their control of marketing channels and communications media.

The development of a new product is a fixed cost; once the expenditure needed for invention or innovation has been made, it is forever a bygone. The actual cost of production is thus typically well below selling price and the limit on output is not rising costs but falling demand due to saturated markets. The marginal profit on new foreign markets is thus high, and corporations have a strong interest in maintaining a system which spreads their products widely. Thus, the interest of multinational corporations in underdeveloped countries is larger than the size of the market would suggest.

It must be stressed that the dependency relationship between major and minor cities should not be attributed to technology. The new technology, because it increases interaction, implies greater interdependence but not necessarily a hierarchical structure. Communications linkages could be arranged in the form of a grid in which each point was directly connected to many other points, permitting lateral as well as vertical communication. This system would be polycentric since messages from one point to another would go directly rather than through the centre; each point would become a centre on its own; and the distinction between centre and periphery would disappear.

Such a grid is made *more* feasible by aeronautical and electronic revolutions which greatly reduce costs of communications. It is not technology which creates inequality; rather, it is *organization* that imposes a ritual judicial asymmetry on the use of intrinsically symmetrical means of communications and arbitrarily creates unequal capacities to initiate and terminate exchange, to store and retrieve information, and to determine the extent of the exchange and terms of the discussion. Just as colonial powers in the past linked each point in the hinterland to the metropolis and inhibited lateral communications, preventing the growth of independent centres of decision making and creativity, multinational corporations (backed by state powers) centralize control by imposing a hierarchical system.

This suggests the possibility of an alternative system of organization in the form of national planning. Multinational corporations are private institutions which organize one or a few industries across many countries. Their polar opposite (the antimultinational corporation, perhaps) is a public institution which organizes many industries across one region. This would permit the centralization of capital, i.e. the coordination of many enterprises by one decision-making centre, but would substitute regionalization for internationalization. The span of control would be confined to the boundaries of a single polity and society and not spread over many countries. The advantage of national planning is its ability to remove the wastes of oligopolistic anarchy, i.e. meaningless product differentiation and an imbalance between different industries within a geographical area. It concentrates *all* levels of decision making in one locale and thus provides each region with a full complement of skills and occupations. This opens up new horizons for local development by making possible the social and political control of economic decision making. Multinational corporations, in contrast, weaken political control because they span many countries and can escape national regulation.

A few examples might help to illustrate how multinational corporations reduce options for development. Consider an underdeveloped country wishing to invest heavily in education in order to increase its stock of human capital and raise standards of living. In a market system it would be able to find gainful employment for its citizens within its *national boundaries* by specializing in education-intensive activities and selling its surplus production to foreigners. In the multinational corporate system, however, the demand for high-level education in low-ranking areas is limited, and a country does not become a world centre simply by having a better educational system. An outward shift in the supply of educated people in a country, therefore, will not create its own demand but will create an excess supply and lead to emigration. Even then, the employment opportunities for citizens of low-ranking countries are restricted by discriminatory practices in the centre. It is well known that ethnic homogeneity increases as one goes up the corporate hierarchy; the lower levels contain a wide variety of nationalities, the higher levels become successively purer and purer. In part this stems from the skill differences of different nationalities, but more important is the fact that the higher up one goes in the decision-making process, the more important mutual understanding and ease of communications become; a common background becomes all-important.

A similar type of specialization by nationality can be expected within the multinational corporation hierarchy. Multinational corporations are torn in two directions. On the one hand, they must adapt to local circumstances in each country. This calls for decentralized decision making. On the other hand, they must coordinate their activities in various parts of the world and stimulate the flow of ideas from one part of their empire to another. This calls for centralized control. They must, therefore, develop an organizational structure to balance the need for coordination with the need for adaptation to a patch-work quilt of languages, laws and customs. One solution to this problem is a division of labour based on nationality. Day-to-day management in each country is left to the nationals of that country who, because they are intimately familiar with local conditions and practices, are able to deal with local problems and local government. These nationals remain rooted in one spot, while above them is a layer of people who move around from country to country, as bees among flowers, transmitting information from one subsidiary to another and from the lower levels to the general office at the apex of the corporate structure. In the nature of things, these people (reticulators) for the most part will be citizens of the country of the parent corporation (and will be drawn from a small, culturally homogeneous group within the advanced world), since they will need to have the confidence of their superiors and to be able to move easily in the higher management circles. Latin Americans, Asians and Africans will at best be able to aspire to a management position in the intermediate coordinating centres at the continental level. Very few will be able to get much higher than this, for the closer one gets to the top, the more important is 'a common cultural heritage'.

Another way in which the multinational corporations inhibit economic development in the hinterland is through their effect on tax capacity. An important government instrument for promoting growth is expenditure on infrastructure and support services. By providing transportation and communications, education and health, a government can create a productive labour force and increase the growth potential of its economy. The extent to which it can afford to finance these intermediate outlays depends upon its tax revenue.

However, a government's ability to tax multinational corporations is limited by the ability of these corporations to manipulate transfer prices and to move their productive facilities to another country. This means that they will only be attracted to countries where superior infrastructure offsets higher taxes. The government of an under-developed country will find it difficult to extract a surplus (revenue from the multinational corporations, less cost of services provided to them) from multinational corporations to use for long-run development programmes and for stimulating growth in other industries. In contrast, governments of the advanced countries, where the home office and financial centre of the multinational corporation are located, can tax the profits of the corporation as a whole as well as the high incomes of its management. Government in the metropolis can, therefore, capture some of the surplus generated by the multinational corporations and use it to further improve their infrastructure and growth.

In other words, the relationship between multinational corporations and underdeveloped countries will be somewhat like the relationship between the national corporations in the United States and state and municipal governments. These lower-level governments tend always to be short of funds compared to the federal government which can tax a corporation as a whole. Their competition to attract corporate investment eats up their surplus, and they find it difficult to finance extensive investments in human and physical capital even where such investment would be productive. This has a crucial effect on the pattern of government expenditure. For example, suppose taxes were first paid to state government and then passed on to the federal government. What chance is there that these lower-level legislatures would approve the phenomenal expenditure on space research that now goes on? A similar discrepancy can be expected in the international economy with overspending and waste by metropolitan governments and a shortage of public funds in the less advanced countries.

The tendency of the multinational corporations to erode the power of the nation state works in a variety of ways, in addition to its effect on taxation powers. In general, most governmental policy instruments (monetary policy, fiscal policy, wage policy, etc.) diminish in effectiveness the more open the economy and the greater the extent of foreign investments. This tendency applies to political instruments as well as economic, for the multinational corporation is a medium by which laws, politics, foreign policy and culture of one country intrude into another. This acts to reduce the sovereignty of all nation states, but again the relationship is asymmetrical, for the flow tends to be from the parent to the subsidiary, not vice versa. The United States can apply its anti-trust laws to foreign subsidiaries to stop them from 'trading with the enemy' even though such trade is not against the laws of the country in which the branch plant is located. However, it would be illegal for an underdeveloped country which disagreed with American foreign policy to hold a US firm hostage for acts of the parent. This is because legal rights are defined in terms of property-ownership, and the various subsidiaries of a multinational corporation are not 'partners in a multinational endeavour' but the property of the general office.

In conclusion, it seems that a regime of multinational corporations would offer underdeveloped countries neither national independence nor equality. It would tend instead to inhibit the attainment of these goals. It would turn the underdeveloped countries into branch-plant countries, not only with reference to their economic functions but throughout the whole gamut of social, political and cultural roles. The subsidiaries of multinational corporations are typically amongst the largest corporations in the country of operations, and their top executives play an influential role in the political, social and cultural life of the host country. Yet these people, whatever their title, occupy at best a medium position in the corporate structure and are restricted in authority and horizons to a lower level of decision making. The governments with whom they deal tend to take on the same middle management outlook, since this is the only range of information and ideas to which they are exposed. In this sense, one can hardly expect such a country to bring forth the creative imagination needed to apply science and technology to the problems of degrading poverty. [...]

THE POLITICAL ECONOMY OF THE MULTINATIONAL CORPORATION

The viability of the multinational corporate system depends upon the degree to which people will tolerate the unevenness it creates. It is well to remember that the 'New Imperialism' which began after 1870 in a spirit of Capitalism Triumphant, soon became seriously troubled and after 1914 was characterized by war, depression, breakdown of the international economic system and war again, rather than Free Trade, Pax Britannica and Material Improvement.

A major, if not the major, reason was Great Britain's inability to cope with the byproducts of its own rapid accumulation of capital; i.e. a class-conscious labour force at home; a middle class in the hinterland; and rival centres of capital on the Continent and in America. Britain's policy tended to be atavistic and defensive rather than progressive, more concerned with warding off new threats than creating new areas of expansion. Ironically, Edwardian England revived the paraphernalia of the landed aristocracy it had just destroyed. Instead of embarking on a 'big push' to develop the vast hinterland of the Empire, colonial administrators often adopted policies to slow down rates of growth and arrest the development of either a native capitalist class or a native proletariat which could overthrow them.

As time went on, the centre had to devote an increasing share of government activity to military and other unproductive expenditures; they had to rely on alliances with an inefficient class of landlords, officials and soldiers in the hinterland to maintain stability at the cost of development. A great part of the surplus extracted from the population was thus wasted locally.

The new Mercantilism (as the Multinational Corporate System of special alliances and privileges, aid and tariff concessions is sometimes called) faces similar problems of internal and external division. The centre is troubled: excluded groups revolt and even some of the affluent are dissatisfied with the roles. (The much talked about 'generation gap' may indicate the failure of the system to reproduce itself.) Nationalistic rivalry between major capitalist countries (especially the challenge of Japan and Germany) remains an important divisive factor, while the economic challenge from the socialist bloc may prove to be of the utmost significance in the next thirty years. Russia has its own form of large-scale economic organizations, also in command of modern technology, and its own conception of how the world should develop. So does China to an increasing degree. Finally, there is the threat presented by the middle classes and the excluded groups of the underdeveloped countries.

The national middle classes in the underdeveloped countries came to power when the centre weakened but could not, through their policy of import substitution manufacturing, establish a viable basis for sustained growth. They now face a foreign exchange crisis and an unemployment (or population) crisis – the first indicating their inability to function in the international economy, and the second indicating their alienation from the people they are supposed to lead. In the immediate future, these national middle classes will gain a new lease on life as they take advantage of the spaces created by the rivalry between American and non-American oligopolists striving to establish global market positions. The native capitalists will again become the champions of national independence as they bargain with multinational corporations. But the conflict at this level is more apparent than real, for in the end the fervent nationalism of the middle class asks only for promotion within the corporate structure and not for a break with that structure. In the last analysis their power derives from the metropolis and they cannot easily afford to challenge the international system. They do not command the loyalty of their own population and cannot really compete with the large, powerful, aggregate capitals from the centre. They are prisoners of the taste patterns and consumption standards set at the centre, and depend on outsiders for technical advice, capital and, when necessary, for military support of their position.

The main threat comes from the excluded groups. It is not unusual in underdeveloped countries for the top 5 per cent to obtain between 30 and 40 per cent of the total national income, and for the top one-third to obtain anywhere from 60 to 70 per cent. At most, one-third of the population can be said to benefit in some sense from the dualistic growth that characterizes development in the hinterland. The remaining two-thirds, who together get only one-third of the income, are outsiders, not because they do not contribute to the economy, but because they do not share in the benefits. They provide a source of cheap labour which helps keep exports to the developed world at a low price and which has financed the urban-biased growth of recent years. Because their wages are low, they spend a moderate amount of time in menial services and are sometimes referred to as underemployed as if to imply they were not needed. In fact, it is difficult to see how the system of most underdeveloped countries could survive without cheap labour since removing it (e.g. diverting it to public works projects as is done in socialist countries) would raise consumption costs to capitalists and professional elites. Economic development under the multinational corporation does not offer much promise for this large segment of society and their antagonism continuously threatens the system.

The survival of the multinational corporate system depends on how fast it can grow and how much trickles down. Plans now being formulated in government offices, corporate headquarters and international organizations sometimes suggest that a growth rate of about 6 per cent per year in national income (3 per cent *per capita*) is needed. (Such a target is, of course, far below what would be possible if a serious effort were made to solve basic problems of health, education and clothing.) To what extent is it possible?

The multinational corporation must solve four critical problems for the underdeveloped countries, if it is to foster the continued growth and survival of a 'modern' sector. First, it must break the foreign-exchange constraint and provide the underdeveloped countries with imported goods for capital formation and modernization. Second, it must finance an expanded programme of government expenditure to train labour and provide support services for urbanization and industrialization. Third, it must solve the urban food problem created by growth. Finally, it must keep the excluded two-thirds of the population under control.

The solution now being suggested for the first is to restructure the world economy allowing the periphery to export certain manufactured goods to the centre. Part of this programme involves regional common markets to rationalize the existing structure of industry. These plans typically do not involve the rationalization and restructuring of the entire economy of the underdeveloped countries but mainly serve the small manufacturing sector which caters to higher-income groups and which, therefore, faces a very limited market in any particular country. The solution suggested for the second problem is an expanded aid programme and a reformed government bureaucracy (perhaps along the lines of the Alliance for Progress). The solution for the third is agribusiness and the green revolution, a programme with only limited benefits to the rural poor. Finally, the solution offered for the fourth problem is population control, either through family planning or counter-insurgency.

It is doubtful whether the centre has sufficient political stability to finance and organize the programme outlined above. It is not clear, for example, that the West has the technology to rationalize manufacturing abroad or modernize agriculture, or the willingness to open up marketing channels for the underdeveloped world. Nor is it evident that the centre has the political power to embark on a large aid programme or to readjust its own structure of production and allow for the importation of manufactured goods from the periphery. It is difficult to imagine labour accepting such a re-allocation (a new repeal of the Corn Laws as it were), and it is equally hard to see how the advanced countries could create a system of planning to make these extra hardships unnecessary.

The present crisis may well be more profound than most of us imagine, and the West may find it impossible to restructure the international economy on a workable basis. One could easily argue that the age of the multinational corporation is at its end rather than at its beginning. For all we know, books on the global partnership may be the epitaph of the American attempt to take over the old international economy, and not the herald of a new era of international cooperation.

CONCLUSION

The multinational corporation, because of its great power to plan economic activity, represents an important step forward over previous methods of organizing international exchange. It demonstrates the social nature of production on a global scale. As it eliminates the anarchy of international markets and brings about a more extensive and productive international division of labour, it releases great sources of latent energy.

However, as it crosses international boundaries, it pulls and tears at the social and political fabric and erodes the cohesiveness of national states. Whether one likes this or not, it is probably a tendency that cannot be stopped.

Through its propensity to nestle everywhere, settle everywhere, and establish connections everywhere, the multinational corporation destroys the possibility of national seclusion and self-sufficiency and creates a universal interdependence. But the multinational corporation is still a private institution with a partial outlook and represents only an imperfect solution to the problem of international cooperation. It creates hierarchy rather than equality, and it spreads its benefits unequally.

In proportion to its success, it creates tensions and difficulties. It will lead other institutions, particularly labour organizations and government, to take an international outlook and thus unwittingly create an environment less favourable to its own survival. It will demonstrate the possibilities of material progress at a faster rate than it can realize them, and will create a world-wide demand for change that it cannot satisfy.

The next round may be marked by great crises due to the conflict between national planning by governments and international planning by corporations. For example, if each country loses its power over fiscal and monetary policy due to the growth of multinational corporations (as some observers believe Canada has), how will aggregate demand be stabilized? Will it be possible to construct super-states? Or does multinationalism do away with Keynesian problems? Similarly, will it be possible to fulfil a host of other government functions at the supranational level in the near future? During the past twenty-five years many political problems were put aside as the West recovered from the depression and the war. By the late 1960s the bloom of this long upswing had begun to fade. In the 1970s, power conflicts are likely to come to the fore.

Whether underdeveloped countries will use the opportunities arising from this crisis to build viable local decision-making institutions is difficult to predict. The national middle class failed when it had the opportunity and instead merely reproduced internally the economic dualism of the international economy as it squeezed agriculture to finance urban industry. What is needed is a complete change of direction. The starting point must be the needs of the bottom two-thirds, and not the demands of the top third. The primary goal of such a strategy would be to provide minimum standards of health, education, food and clothing to the entire population, removing the most obvious forms of human suffering. This requires a system which can mobilize the entire population and which can search the local environment for information, resources and needs. It must be able to absorb modern technology, but it cannot be mesmerized by the form it takes in the advanced countries; it must go to the roots. This is not the path the upper one-third chooses when it has control.

The wealth of a nation, wrote Adam Smith two hundred years ago, is determined by 'first, the skill, dexterity and judgement with which labour is generally applied; and, secondly by the proportion between the number of those who are employed in useful labour, and that of those who are not so employed'.[3] Capitalist enterprise has come a long way from this day, but it has never been able to bring more than a small fraction of the world's population into useful or highly productive employment. The latest stage reveals once more the power of social cooperation and division of labour which so fascinated Adam Smith in his description of pin-manufacturing. It also shows the shortcomings of concentrating this power in private hands.

NOTES

1   A.D. Chandler and F. Redlich, 'Recent Developments in American Business Administration and their Conceptualization', *Business History Review* (Spring 1961).
2   L.A. Fallers, 'A Note on the Trickle Effect', in P. Bliss (ed.), *Marketing and the Behavioral Sciences* (Allyn and Bacon, 1963).
3   A. Smith, *The Wealth of Nations* (The Modern Library, New York, 1937 edn).

3.8 Militarism: force, class and international conflict

Robin Luckham

Source: M. Kaldor and A. Eide, *The World Military Order* (Macmillan, London, 1979), pp. 243–55.

Luckham analyses the role of the military in developing societies in terms of its relationship to the requirements of international capital and dependent capitalist development. He compares the different 'class projects' undertaken by the military in specific circumstances, and assesses their relationship to external intervention and internal contradictions.

There is no more eloquent testimony to the internationalism of the relations of domination than the uniformity of certain characteristics of professional armies: the hierarchy of ranks, the exclusiveness of the military brotherhood, the emphasis on rituals and emblems of rank, the codes of honour, the class distinctions between officers and other ranks. Part of this can be accounted for by the fact that a small number of models – basically British, French, German and American – have been consciously transplanted in the third world. But where other transplants like the ill-fated 'Westminster model' of parliamentary democracy did not take root, military organisations flourished. Organised force is essential for the reproduction of modern nation-states, voting is not.

Nevertheless armies are seldom monolithic institutions on which members of ruling classes can always rely. The use of military force to repress opponents of the regime or to settle struggles for political power often moves the conflict into the armed forces themselves, accentuating their internal contradictions and precipitating coups, mutinies and power struggles.

The majority of the countries of Africa, Asia, the Middle East and Latin America are under military rule. Still more of them have experienced military intervention or periods of military rule at some point or other during the past 30 years. And if one adopts broader criteria there are scarcely any where organised military force has *not* been used to keep in office or to change the regime or ruling class during the past three decades. Against this background most of the things social scientists have to say seem exceedingly banal. Much of the existing literature takes as its starting point the problem of assuring 'civilian control' over the military establishment: which can be looked at over a whole continuum of military participation in politics, ranging from gentlemanly bargaining over strategy or appropriations, outright blackmail of the regime, participation in the re-shuffling of ruling élites right through to direct military control of all the major political institutions of a society.

The absence of civilian control is only a 'problem', however, when contrasted with an idealised view of the relationship between soldiers and governments in the advanced bourgeois democracies. It is not an especially useful way of looking at the political institutions of Africa, Asia, the Middle East and Latin America, where military partici-pation rather than civilian control might be viewed as the 'normal' state of affairs. Nor does the idea of a continuum from civilian to military take us very far. To be sure, the difference between a military establishment which intervenes as a 'moderating power' to resolve conflicts between civilian factions as in Brazil before 1964 and one which attempts permanently to substitute itself for parts of the state superstructure, to become the State as it were, as in the same country after 1967, is important. Yet to view this as just a change from less to more military participation in political life is superficial, for the military's formal participation in politics is less important than the question of how far the state superstructure is or is not held together by organised coercion. To what extent do those who control that superstructure rely on repressive rather than ideological mechanisms to establish their hegemony?

The distinction between civilian and military regimes may well be less important than the similarities in the way they govern. Take a country like the Philippines where, under a civilian regime, civil liberties have been curtailed, the media browbeaten, trade unions deprived of the right to strike, opponents of the regime repressed. There is intensive surveillance by the police and military intelligence networks, internal warfare is waged against dissident Moslem minority groups, the military is frequently consulted about major government decisions, martial law is in operation and political offences are tried before military rather than civilian tribunals.

[...] Coups and military regimes are, to be sure, the prevailing trend in the third world, and this is hardly surprising. For when organised coercion is the main basis of state power, coups are to be expected merely because more 'democratic' methods of transferring power between different factions of the ruling classes cease to operate. But struggles to gain or to remain in power can also be waged by assassination, mob violence, surveillance and terror by the secret police, bribery and the skilful dispensation of political patronage. Frequent coups *may* betoken instability in the framework of the state – but not necessarily more so than votes of no confidence, reshufflings of cabinets and frequent elections in bourgeois democracies. Like the latter they speed the circulation of élites and the realignment of factions of the ruling classes more often than they bring about fundamental change in the organisation of state power and its allocation between (rather than within) social classes.

In Karl Marx's classic analysis of Bonapartism it was recognised that in periods of acute crisis or of historical transition between modes of production members of the ruling class would often be prepared to accept authoritarian government by a state machine over which it had relatively little direct control: the bourgeoisie would sometimes sacrifice its own class rule in order to secure the political stability on which the smooth functioning of a capitalist economy and its own class interests depend.[1]

Bonapartism, however, is not a magical category into which the analysis of the military can be hammered. The historical circumstances of the present-day third world bring together a different combination of elements from that which prevailed in nineteenth-century France. The crisis of hegemony suffered by ruling classes is permanent and endemic rather than temporary and exceptional. Uneven development superimposes all the contradictions between centre and periphery, capitalist and pre-capitalist social formations, class and tribe, region, religion and nation: and makes it all the more difficult for any single ruling class or fraction thereof to establish its ideological claims to rule.

Add to this the effects of a colonial situation in which an alien ruling class had to rely on state repression to secure its domination. And a process of decolonisation from which there emerged a disjuncture between the national ruling class on the one hand and the economically dominant class with its commanding heights in the boardrooms of international firms on the other. This gives the crisis of hegemony a peculiar neocolonial twist. For it has retarded the formation of homegrown bourgeoisies and made it more difficult for the latter to function as effective ruling classes able through their policies to exert control over the national economy. But at the same time it creates a problem for the representatives of international capital who have to find ways of influencing policy and the political structure in peripheral countries, despite their inability to act directly as a faction of the ruling class.

On the face of it the military seems to meet the political requirements of international capital under these troubled circumstances almost better than any other institution. A powerful, relatively autonomous state-apparatus – buttressed by military coercion – provides a framework of stability and predictability within which it is relatively easy for multinational capital to operate. Further, the fact that the military usually depends for its weapons purchases on international purchasing power earned in the world market and appropriated through the state tends to cement the alliance with international capital. In the same measure that external penetration weakens the class structure, it increases – through arms supplies, military assistance, and political support – the military establishment's size, claims on productive resources and autonomy relative to other fractions of the ruling class.

Yet to postulate in these general terms that the military appears to fit the political requirements of international capital – stability and a solution to the problems created by international capital's inability to act directly as a ruling class – does not mean that in any given country it will in fact carry out these functions; or do so in a uniform way from one country to another. To begin with, the military and military regimes are hardly ever in a simple sense the political servants of international capital or of great power governments. It would be quite grotesque to label Colonel Gadaffy of Libya, Lt. Colonel Mengistu of Ethiopia, the members of the Peruvian junta or indeed General Idi Amin as the agents of imperialism. Even the most reactionary Latin American regimes have a degree of autonomy: witness for example the edifying spectacle of the governments of Argentina, Brazil, Chile, El Salvador and Uruguay threatening to turn elsewhere for arms and military assistance if President Carter continues to cut back aid to countries with a record of violation of human rights.

Indeed, the military's *own* institutional and material interests lie in the direction of a strong nation-state with control over the surpluses generated in the national economy. This determines the *class project* carried out by the military in two main ways. First, through the compact established between the state and international capital in which the military has a direct interest as a state institution and an indirect interest through its linkages with the international arms economy. Second, through the role of organised force in resolving – or rather in repressing the symptoms of – the crises generated under

Table 1 Variations in military's class projects in dependent capitalist countries

Structure of economy	Nature of state project	Nature of crises	Nature of military project
1. *Petty capitalist commodity production* Agricultural and natural resource based commodities produced for export and/or local sale by indigenous producers under petty capitalist or pre-capitalist relations of production. Example: most countries of sub-Saharan Africa, Bangladesh.	1. Minimum conditions of law and order. 2. Mediation between petty producers and world market, either (i) via foreign merchant capital, or (ii) directly via state marketing monopolies. 3. Extraction of surplus from export–import trade and conversion into (i) increases in size, power and military spending of state apparatus or (ii) industrialisation programmes.	1. Political crises brought on by reinvigoration of pre-capitalist formations and loyalties (tribe, religion, languages, region, etc.) in response to competition for state power, jobs, economic resources and benefits. 2. Instability induced by fluctuations in commodity prices in world market, undermining regimes and their long-term economic plans.	1. (a) Holding fragile nation-state together and/or (b) using state machinery to establish hegemony of the particular tribal, religious, linguistic or regional groups who happen to control the military hierarchy. 2. Intervention to secure changes of regime in response to externally induced economic and political crises. 3. Reinforcement (through arms purchases) of pressure to earn foreign exchange in world market or to save it by engaging in import-substituting industrialisation.

2. Enclave commodity production

Agricultural commodities produced or natural resources extracted on large scale (a) by international capital or (b) by state capital incorporated in circuits of international capital through export of commodities and imports of technology.

Examples: most oil-producing (OPEC) countries and copper-producing (CIPEC) countries.

1. Minimum conditions of law and order.
2. Mediation between capital and labour in enclave enterprises, ensuring stability and quiescence of labour, in the last resort by physical repression.
3. Either (a) state is directly co-opted by foreign capital and serves its interests (e.g. Gabon, Central American banana republics) or (b) state expropriates foreign capital. The latter reorganises itself and appropriates its share of mineral rents by sales of technology, management agreements, military sales, etc.
4. (Where state not mouthpiece of foreign capital) promotion of natural resource ideologies: maximisation of mineral rents and of state's share therein; conversion of these surpluses into expansion of state apparatus and/or industrialisation.

1. Conflicts between central regions/groups/towns sharing the benefits of economic activity and employment created by enclave and peripheral regions/groups/rural areas.
2. Conflicts between capital and labour in enclave.
3. (a) Instability induced by fluctuations in commodity prices in world market, undermining regimes and their long-term plans, precipitating conflict between states and foreign capitalists *except* (b) when associations of producers (especially OPEC) exercise monopoly control in world market, minimising direct effect of externally induced crises on state machinery.

1. Establishment of physical control by centre over peripheral regions.
2. Intervention in conflicts between foreign or state capital and labour.
3. (a) Direct physical repression on behalf of foreign capital, particularly in times of economic and political crisis (e.g. Chile) or (b) intervention against foreign capital on behalf of nationalist projects to assure state control over natural resources (or support for such interventions by other groups or governments).
4. Reinforcement (through arms purchases) of pressures to maximise natural resource rents and to participate in international arms economy.

Table 1 continued

Structure of economy	Nature of state project	Nature of crises	Nature of military project
3. *Import-substituting industrialisation* Development of industrial base through either (a) foreign investment or (b) state investment or both, replacing goods previously imported. Examples: Brazil, Mexico, Argentina, Philippines and (combined with 2, above) Indonesia, Iran, Venezuela, Chile and Nigeria.	1. Maintenance of political stability to assure smooth process of industrialisation and to prevent flight of foreign capital. 2. Mediation between capital and labour; repression of latter to subsidise investment by the former. 3. State promotion of industrialisation, bringing about symbiosis of state, local and international capital. Variations in extent of penetration by international capital, in the mechanisms (e.g. direct investment versus sales of technology) by which it is achieved and in extent of state control over the process.	1. Conflicts between industrial/urban centres and rural/agricultural peripheries, intensified to extent that the latter subsidise process of industrialisation. 2. Conflicts between capital and labour in industrial sector, intensified to extent that profits and investment subsidised by low wages. 3. Marginalisation, creation of 'reserve army of unemployed' by industrialisation/urbanisation processes. 4. Crises created by exhaustion of process of import-substitution. Cycle of foreign exchange shortages, inflation, unrest, repression, military spending and more shortages, inflation, etc.	1. Establishment of physical control by centre over periphery. Repression of peasant movements, rural guerrillas, etc. 2. Intervention in conflict between foreign or state capital and labour, usually to repress the latter on behalf of the former, but not always (e.g. the Peronist alliance between the military and unions in Argentina). 3. Establishment of physical 'security' in restive urban areas. Repression of crime, squatters, demonstrations, urban guerrillas, etc. 4. Reinforcement (through arms purchases and sometimes arms manufacture) of import-substitution and of the crises induced by it.

| 4. *Export-promoting industrialisation*

Examples: South Korea, Taiwan, Singapore and (combined with 3, above) Philippines. | As above except foreign capital (a) more footloose because not tied to domestic resources or markets (b) tends to an even greater extent to be vertically integrated production and markets in central countries. For these reasons (a) political stability (and organised physical repression) are even more vital, and (b) the bargaining power of the state is weaker relative to that of international capital. | As above except (a) low wages often essential to attract foreign capital and hence greater repression of labour force, (b) vulnerability to crises in international markets for manufactures rather than to constraints of narrowness of domestic market. | As above, except military involved to an even greater extent in establishment of physical security (particularly in urban centres), repression and counter-revolution. |

different conditions of dependent capitalist development.

Accordingly, in Table 1 an attempt is made to show how different patterns of incorporation in the world economy shape the varying class projects of the military establishment. The first two patterns set forth in the table arise in economies which are based on the production of raw materials for the world market, though it makes a considerable difference whether these are produced (like many agricultural commodities) by numerous indigenous petty producers; or are extracted (like most minerals) through large investments of foreign capital. The third and fourth patterns are determined by the nature of a country's process of industralisation – whether by import-substitution or by the export of cheap manufactures produced by low-cost labour.

Armies and military regimes are seldom *directly* subservient to foreign capital. Even in countries whose economies are based on primary products extracted and sold abroad by foreign corporations, they often take up natural resource ideologies, and favour state expropriation of foreign capital to the extent this can be achieved (as by the oil producers) without serious damage to the economy's international earning power. In industrialising countries the same factors incline the military towards state investment and regulation of the economy. Such regulation need not interfere with the compact established with international capital and may indeed create a new, more organic symbiosis between the state and multinational corporations. Even when the major means of production are no longer in foreign hands militarism and state capitalism together may still reinforce the integration of the national economy and its class structure in the circuits of the international economy: because foreign exchange still has to be earned to pay for armaments, technology and the expansion of the state and military bureaucracy.

Few countries fit fair and square into any one of the categories in the table. Indeed, the military often plays a critical role in the transition from one pattern to another. The crisis which led first to the rise to power of the Allende regime in Chile and then to its overthrow by the soldiers in 1973 was, for example, brought on by the exhaustion of the process of import-substitution and the international forces set in motion by the government's expropriation of the foreign copper monopolies. In response to these external forces the military government has adopted economic policies – economic liberalisation, sale of state enterprises, the curtailment of import-substitution, withdrawal from the Andean Pact – which virtually amount to a reassertion of its traditional position in the international division of labour as a raw material producer.

Further, it is not necessary to assume that the class project the military finally takes up is necessarily agreed in advance or even understood by the officer corps, still less their men, nor that it will be stable. Periods of crisis bring major shifts in the way the military interposes itself in class conflict, which are usually accompanied by violent internal struggles. The social origins of the soldiers who win such struggles, their civilian allies and their original intentions will have some influence on the class project the military undertakes, but may be distorted by the circumstances with which they have to cope once they take power. Examples are not difficult to find: the Nigerian army intervened to establish national unity in 1966 but broke up into tribal and regional factions six months later; the Chilean military seized power with the active support of the national bourgeoisie in order to halt what was perceived as a process of national disintegration, and ended up restoring the dominance of foreign monopoly capital; the soldiers who took power in Brazil in 1964 quickly dropped their programme of economic and political liberalisation in favour of state-sponsored industrialisation under an authoritarian regime.

Although the crises of dependent capitalist development provoke military repression, this repression does not necessarily establish political order. Sometimes the military's weapons have simply turned conflict into more bloody conflict: witness, for example, the effects of military violence in Uruguay, in Bangladesh just before its war of liberation from Pakistan or indeed in Northern Ireland. Or the military itself has become deeply divided – as in Nigeria and the Lebanon before and during their respective civil wars – and thus unable to stand above the conflict. Nevertheless the fact that military force settles things in the last resort is critical, particularly in societies in permanent crisis, where the last resort is always close at hand.

Nor can one automatically assume that the military will intervene in these crises as the compliant ally of the dominant classes. Its internal fissures, as we have already seen, may create radical as well as reactionary tendencies both in the officer corps and among ordinary soldiers. On a number of occasions the military establishment has sided with the periphery against the centre – as in some African states where the recruitment base of the army has traditionally been in the less developed parts of the country – or with labour in its struggles with capital – as in the alliance between sections of the army and organised labour in Peronist Argentina in the 1940s.

Yet although particular factions of the military élite may intervene on behalf of peripheral or excluded classes and groups in times of crisis, the military establishment *as a whole* has a vested interest in what military ideologists call 'national security' and what its opponents call state and class domination. The natural response of professional soldiers is to suppress class struggle when it appears because it divides the nation, undermines the international economic standing of the economy – causing flights of foreign capital – and imposes certain real costs – casualties, disruption of routine, threats to its structure and its monopoly of organised force – upon the military establishment itself.

Let us turn, therefore, to the interrelation between the international system and armed force. This can be analysed at a number of levels. In the first place a world in which conflict is endemic and force governs the relations between nation-states enhances the influence of military organisations. More than 30 years ago Harold Lasswell suggested that growing international conflict would increasingly turn the world powers into 'garrison states' in which the influence of military managers of violence would predominate:[2] though he omitted to say that this conflict can sometimes itself be the consequence of the influence of these military managers in whose interests it is to exaggerate threats to security.

International insecurity contributes equally to military influence at the periphery. The armed forces are large and influential in most countries at the edge of the Cold War, like Greece, Turkey, Iran, Thailand and South Korea; and also in countries at the nodes of regional conflict as in the Middle East and the Horn of Africa. Military coups have frequently swept aside civilian governments which have failed (in the soldiers' view) to provide adequately for their country's security: for example the overthrow of the Egyptian monarchy by the Free Officers after humiliating defeats suffered at the hands of Israel; or the 1969 coup in Somalia which swept aside a civilian government which had pursued the broader conflict with Ethiopia with less enthusiasm than the soldiers desired. Soldiers are also quick to react to the international aspects of internal struggles. For example, the contagion effects between military coups, such as those which swept through west and central Africa in 1965–6. Or the spread of military garrison states in Latin America in the 1960s and 1970s; responding on the one hand to the establishment of socialism in Cuba and the spread of revolutionary movements across national boundaries; and on the other to the transnationalisation of American counter-insurgency training and doctrine.

As with military intervention in the internal politics of a country, so too there is a whole continuum of external intervention: from diplomatic pressure, economic aid and military assistance programmes; various forms of blackmail such as threats to withdraw economic and military assistance; covert subversion and the destabilisation of regimes in the style of the CIA or KGB; reassurance of recognition and support to coup-makers if successful; actual material support for a coup, or alternatively support in putting one down; military assistance and advice in counter-revolutionary operations; taking direct part in such operations (the US in the early stages of the Vietnam conflict); direct participation in a revolutionary war (the Chinese in Korea or the Cubans in Angola); through to actual invasion by troops in the intervening power (the US in the Dominican Republic and in Vietnam, or France and Britain in the Suez crisis).

Yet one cannot measure the effect of external pressures on the military, the class structure or the political system as a whole solely by the level to which overt foreign interference has *actually* been pushed. In some countries, like Chile, intervention may have taken place precisely because the contradictions are sharper than elsewhere and the hegemony of imperialist powers less secure. In others the class structure and internal political forces may be self-sustaining and direct intervention unnecessary. The arms trade and discreet military assistance programmes are often all that is required to keep the professional military establishment in operation and the stability of the political system within tolerable limits. And in others again, like Iran, Indonesia and Zaire, external penetration may be massive but multi-faceted, so that to take one aspect alone such as support for a coup, covert CIA activities, foreign aid and investment, military assistance, or diplomatic pressure, may give an incomplete picture of foreign influence because all are important together.

Conversely, however, direct intervention has sometimes created more contradictions than those it represses. The Suez crisis, the American intervention in Vietnam and the South African invasion of Angola are perhaps the most glaring examples, but there are several others. Failure to examine abortive as well as successful interventions might lead one to underestimate the *limits* imperialism faces, the contradictions it creates for itself and the strength of the forces opposed to it on the periphery. These limits arise at a number of different levels.

First, the strength and disposition of anti-imperialist forces themselves; in Vietnam for example, the military effectiveness of the liberation armies and the presence of the Russian nuclear deterrent to discourage escalation of the conflict by the Americans; in Angola the extremely prompt and effective assistance provided by the Cubans and Russians and the reluctance of the USA to risk a diplomatic showdown in Africa by openly intervening.

Second, differences among the major Western powers, as during the Suez crisis, when the disapproval of the Americans and their refusal to support British borrowing from the IMF to halt the run on the pound caused by the crisis, brought the Anglo-French invasion of Egypt to a grinding halt.

Third, the internal contradictions by which imperialist powers are sometimes weakened: the bitter opposition to the Suez invasion by the Labour party; or the economic burden of arms spending by the US government in Vietnam and the gathering strength of the anti-war movement. There are strong pressures impelling the major capitalist powers to intervene in their interests at the periphery. But it would be a mistake to regard them as monolithic and to underestimate the constraints according to which they operate.

Intervention, furthermore, is not exclusive to capitalist powers but has also been an integral part of the struggle against them. External support has been a crucial element in most contemporary revolutions: Russian support (however grudging) for the Chinese revolution; Russian and Chinese assistance in Vietnam; Arab and communist bloc help to the Algerians in their war of national liberation from France; the assistance of the Russians and Chinese and of neighbouring African countries to the armed struggle in Guinea-Bissau, Angola and Mozambique.

Nevertheless such assistance is not without its own contradictions. External aid cannot overcome unfavourable objective conditions; witness, for example, the failure of Che Guevara to bring revolution to Bolivia. It all too easily triggers off nationalist responses and accusations of 'social imperialism' against the donor: visible already, for instance, in the ambivalence of the Angolans about the continued presence in their country of their Cuban and Russian liberators. Recipients of socialist assistance – however worthy according to revolutionary criteria – are vulnerable to changes in the interests of the donors. The revolutions in Laos and Cambodia were delayed because the Vietnamese gave and withdrew assistance in accordance with the progress of their own struggle. Socialist rivalries – for example Chinese support for the FNLA and Cuban and Soviet for the MPLA in Angola – have sometimes helped to create divisions in liberation movements.

In a very real sense the intervention of socialist countries is also limited and shaped by the constraints of balance-of-power politics. In several Latin American countries the Moscow-controlled communist parties have been ambivalent towards armed struggle: fluctuating between support for insurrection and for more 'legitimate' activity in accord with the turns and swings of international politics. The support of socialist countries for the revolutions in former Portuguese Africa was covert and limited in quantity until the international political conjuncture became favourable to larger-scale involvement after the invasion of Angola by South Africa.

Despite the expansion of capital on a world scale there is little semblance of an international superstructure, comparable to the national state. There are instead only *partial* international super-structures: some based on region (the EEC, ASEAN, etc); some constituting military alliances between states (NATO, the Warsaw Pact and the moribund SEATO and CENTO); and some with specialised functions (the UN agencies, IMF, World Bank, etc). These do relatively little to bind the world system together. Indeed military alliances and regional pacts on the whole deepen the main fractures between blocs. Rather than superstructure it might be more apposite to talk of a 'superstruggle': but for the integrating mechanisms both of the international economy, which incorporates enterprises and states alike in the circuit of capital, and of balance-of-power politics which (at least for the time being) prevents the war of all against all.

Although most statesmen and military leaders subscribe to the concept of a balance of power – and thus make it take on the character of self-fulfilling prophecy – it is thoroughly ambiguous. The nature of the nuclear means of mass destruction on which the balance between the central world powers is based is such that balances computed merely in terms of the numbers of missiles, aircraft and nuclear warheads available to each side make little sense. Further, the very ability to participate depends on a very advanced technology and industrial base. The balance thus expresses the competing interests of the ruling classes of advanced industrial countries and the clientage of those of the third world.

Furthermore, a balance between societies with diverse modes of production is by no means a balance of equivalents. For its equilibrium is constantly disturbed by the contradictory pressures of capitalist and of socialist expansion towards the periphery. Such an international system does not even succeed in providing a political basis for the orderly expansion of capital on an international level; the tools of international economic management having proved woefully inadequate to deal with the current international economic crisis. Balance-of-power politics provides only temporary and largely inadequate solutions to the international pressures which beset the third world. Typically, it is devoted to stabilising the *existing* situation without getting to grips with the substantive issues, the very real contradictions which underlie conflicts such as the Middle East crisis or the wars of national liberation in Southern Africa.

The very severity of the present international crisis in some ways, however, provides favourable opportunities for the modification or destruction of existing relations of international domination: a nuclear stalemate in which great powers can be played off against each other; internal dissent within the large capitalist powers which makes it more difficult for their governments to pursue expansionist foreign policies; economic crisis which fuels this discontent inside capitalist countries, and, further, makes it difficult for them to finance external military ventures or to subsidise arms sales in order to gain political influence. The same crisis is also bringing things to a head in the periphery, concentrating economic grievances and mobilising popular forces (but also increasing the repression by dominant classes).

To the extent that attempts to stabilise the existing pattern of international arrangements merely buy time, in which lines of conflict harden and the international production and diffusion of destructive weapons continues, they might actually increase the ultimate danger. Weapons and military organisations – the means of force – are in the international domain, in that their deployment and/or use is a matter of common danger and common social concern for all mankind. Yet they are still appropriated and controlled by national ruling classes which use or threaten to use them to reproduce their national power and international interests. This makes social control over their use and conditions of lasting peace almost impossible to bring about without major transformation in the structures of international production, power and force. But the risks of the struggle to bring about such transformation impose heavy responsibilities on those who undertake it.

NOTES

1   Karl Marx, 'The Eighteenth Brumaire of Louis Bonaparte', in Karl Marx and Frederick Engels, *Selected Works* (Foreign Languages Publishing House, Moscow, 1958), vol. 1, pp. 243–344.
2   Harold Lasswell, 'The Garrison State', *American Journal of Sociology*, XLVI (January 1941).

3.9 Central and peripheral capital
Anthony Brewer

Source: *Marxist Theories of Imperialism: A Critical Survey* (Routledge and Kegan Paul, London, 1980), pp. 274–94.

Brewer challenges the prevailing Marxist view that capitalism necessarily accentuates established patterns of inequality. Since the Second World War, he argues, American hegemony has been replaced by a number of imperialist centres and capitalist development has taken place in several Third World states. He starts, therefore, by reassessing the multinational corporation which he sees as the dominant contemporary capitalist enterprise.

CENTRAL CAPITAL: UNITY OR RIVALRY?

Multi-national corporations, by definition, operate in several nation states. Other capitalist firms may be involved in the world economy through production for export, use of imported materials or components, through the use of technology on licence from abroad or through the export of technology, and so on. Commercial and financial capital is also internationalised. None of this means that capital exists that does not have a nationality, a definite base in a particular capitalist nation state. The idea that multi-national firms are somehow above the petty conflicts of nation states is an ideological fiction designed to defuse nationalist opposition to foreign capital.

Virtually all multi-nationals have in fact a very clear national base; not only does the parent company have a legal domicile (the use of tax havens may make legal registration misleading), but the company has originated within a particular country, and in almost all cases its top management is recruited there and the largest part of its capital and production is still located in its home country. The few exceptions consist of firms based in very small countries (e.g. Nestlé of Switzerland) and the two Anglo-Dutch giants (Shell and Unilever), which have a dual nationality.

Capital and the nation state have grown up together. The *analytical* primacy, in Marxist theory, of the economic over the political does not imply a *historical* order, nor does it imply that the division of the world into distinct nation states and the determination of their boundaries can be explained at the economic level. At the beginnings of capitalism, and for a long time after, the productive activities of industrial capital were locally based while the markets it served were as often local or international as national. It would be a mistake to think of an integrated national economy or national 'social formation' coming into existence and then conjuring up a state to suit its needs. Rather, the existence of a state (and the extension of its boundaries to the point where the resistance of other nation states limited further expansion) created and delimited national interests, national markets and so on. Each capital looked to its 'own' state for support against other capitals forming in other nation states and, through the common need for state support, formed an alliance with other regional capitals within the same nation. The need for compromise between different sectional interests within the capitalist class, and the need to contain conflict with other classes, has created a dense network of political and ideological links which is what constitutes a 'nation'.

As capital extends outside national boundaries, it must, of course, create links with other states as well, at least to the extent that it needs conditions that can only be provided by state action (a legal framework, a monetary system, infrastructure, etc.). Murray (1971) has discussed these questions, and drawn the general conclusion that internationalisation weakens the nation state *vis-à-vis* private capital, a conclusion contested by Warren (1971) and (briefly but cogently) by Rowthorn (1971). Rowthorn argues, in my view rightly, that the key question is not about the power of the state *vis-à-vis* particular capitals, but about how a state can support its own capital when it operates abroad.

The essential point is that capital that operates internationally needs the support of a home state to protect its interests. The whole range of needs that are met internally by the state (protection of property, enforcement of contracts, etc.) are met internationally by interstate negotiations and agreements. A large part of the diplomatic apparatus through which nation states deal with each other (in time of peace) has grown up precisely to negotiate the regulation of commercial activities. A stateless corporation, while not perhaps in principle impossible, would be at a crushing disadvantage, since it would have no representation in the system of legalised coercion. [...]

The history of the capitalist world economy has seen periods of acute rivalry between capitalist powers, separated by periods of relative peace. Marx wrote at a time when it seemed reasonable to predict the obsolescence of the nation state, while Lenin and his contemporaries analysed a period when inter-imperialist rivalry was at its most violent. After the Second World War, the United States emerged as very much the strongest capitalist power, and when Marxist discussion of imperialism revived it was generally assumed, almost without debate, that inter-imperialist rivalry had been superseded by US dominance. This seemed particularly obvious to those American writers who took a special interest in Latin America, the area most clearly within the American sphere of influence.

However, the rapid recovery of the European and Japanese economies, the weakness of the US dollar and the American defeat in Vietnam raised doubts about this view of the present stage of imperialism, and opened up the debate again.

The question, then, concerns the kind of relations between the national capitals of the advanced capitalist countries that exist and the future developments that are to be expected. There seem to me to be two issues involved here. Firstly, what are the relative strengths of the different national groups and, in particular, is American capital increasing its lead over other national groups or being overhauled by them? Secondly, are national capitals remaining distinct from each other, or are they tending to merge together with the progress of internationalisation?

If a fusion of national capitals is taking place, one possibility is that it might take place on a relatively equal basis. This is the only case in which the nationality of capital might give way to genuine supranationality, raising questions about the future of the nation state. No one, to my knowledge, has asserted that such a fusion is taking place, or could take place in the foreseeable future, on a global basis; the strength of US capital is such that any fusion would be US dominated. However, a number of writers have anticipated such a fusion on a smaller scale within the EEC, to form a unified European capital. [...]

An alternative possibility is that national capitals are merging together under US dominance by the absorption of enterprises from other capitalist states by American multi-nationals or by their subordination through licensing agreements, subcontracting arrangements and so on. [...]

Prima facie evidence for the dominance of American capital is easy to find. American corporations predominate in any listing of the world's largest firms. American domestic production and overseas investments are much larger than those of any other country, and the American lead is largest in the most advanced branches of production (computers, micro-electronics, automation, aerospace, etc.). The size and growth of American investments in Europe are particularly significant. The breaking up of European colonial empires has enabled American capital to penetrate and, in some cases, dominate areas of the world formerly denied to it (hence American 'anti-colonialism' in the post-war period). American military dominance in the non-communist world is obvious. These facts are not in dispute.

What is in dispute is the *trend* of development. America clearly enjoyed a quite exceptional superiority immediately after the Second World War and one would expect some relative recovery by other powers. Some writers argue that the more rapid recent growth in Europe and Japan as compared to America is no more than a return to the trend, while others argue that it represents a real threat to US dominance, and presages an epoch in which there will be relative equality between the main capitalist powers. Mandel (1967, 1975) and Rowthorn (1971) both predict a narrowing of the gap between America and other imperialist centres and a consequent intensification of rivalry.

Rather oddly, on both sides of the debate attention has focused on the relative strength of American and *European* capital. The relative failure (to date) of movements towards European unity has hampered the competitive strength of European capital, and it has been justly remarked that the largest beneficiary of the formation of the EEC has been American capital in Europe, which has been much quicker to treat Europe as a unified market. However, on present trends it is *Japanese* capital which looks the more formidable rival; it is not divided on national lines, and has maintained a rate of growth quite unprecedented in the history of capitalism for some three decades.

The debate centres on the interpretation of the large flow of capital from America to Europe and the consequent rapid growth of American capital in Europe. Poulantzas (1975) regards this as decisive evidence of American hegemony, on the grounds that the export of capital is the dominant factor in the expansion of capital in the imperialist period; he offers little evidence for this particular assertion other than a reference to Lenin. Rowthorn, drawing on his work with Hymer (Rowthorn and Hymer, 1971), counters this ingeniously. American capital still operates predominantly in America, European capital in Europe; since European economies were expanding more rapidly than the American economy, American capital had to increase its penetration of the European market simply to maintain its relative position. (Expansion in other markets could not offset the loss of ground relative to Europe, since the Japanese market proved difficult to penetrate, and other markets were very small by comparison.) This could be done either by export or by investment in Europe; since lower European wages gave the edge to producers located in Europe, export of capital was chosen. A large net expansion of exports to Europe unaccompanied by capital export would be difficult in any case, since it would upset the European balance of payments and force corrective action (as indeed happened during the post-war dollar shortage). Combining the effects of relative market growth rates and changing market shares, 'big American firms are having and will have increasing difficulty in keeping ahead of their foreign rivals' (Rowthorn, 1971, p. 163).

Rowthorn thus accepts the view that American investment in Europe represents, in itself, a gain by American capital relative to its rivals, but argues that it is offset by the fact that European companies still had the larger share of the more rapidly growing European market. Mandel (1967) similarly argues that American expansion in Europe is a 'defeat' for European capital. However, the relative rate of growth of different markets cannot be taken as given. Not only is the more rapid growth in Europe the result as well as the cause of the greater dynamism of European capital, but the inflow of investment from America may well have contributed to European growth. American investment may thus have helped rather than hindered the expansion of European capital. In more general terms, the expansion of one capital may be complementary to, rather than competitive with, the expansion of others. This is relevant to the question of rivalry.

If we accept that there is a trend towards relative equality between a small number of imperialist centres, as Mandel and Rowthorn argue, we must ask what kind of relation between them is likely. Rowthorn seems to take it for granted that there will be rivalry and antagonism: 'Relations between capitals are always to some extent antagonistic, the degree of antagonism depending both on the area of actual or potential competition and on its intensity' (Rowthorn, 1971). This is undoubtedly true of individual capitals at a micro-economic level; the overall rate of expansion of the market in which they are competing with other firms is beyond their control, and they are struggling over shares of a given market. However, it is not clear that similar antagonism must exist between capitalist *states*. As I have pointed out above, once the overall rate of expansion of the whole economy is treated as a variable, the expansion of one capital may be complementary to that of another. The state is in a position to try to reconcile the two aspects of the relation between capitals, complementarity and antagonism. It may thus be possible to resurrect Kautsky's notion of 'ultra-imperialism', that imperialist powers could agree to cooperate and exploit the world jointly. We do not have to make a simple choice between predicting inter-imperialist rivalry on the one hand or ultra-imperialism on the other; it is more relevant to ask how far the recognition of some common interests can contain the antagonisms generated by other, divergent interests. [...]

Since the date of the main writings discussed here, the world capitalist system has been subjected to a very severe test in the oil crisis and the subsequent world recession. Although co-operation between the major capitalist states has clearly not been perfect, I think that most commentators would have predicted far more severe rivalry than in fact occurred. The measures taken by the oil companies to redirect supplies during the period when some oil-importing states were embargoed by Arab suppliers, and the surprisingly successful expedients taken to preserve the world monetary system from potentially disruptive movements of 'petrodollars', are examples of private sector adaptability based on inter-state co-operation. I would conclude that although the dominance of the United States is coming to an end, it would be unwise for revolutionaries to expect inter-imperialist rivalry to lead to any immediate breakdown of the world capitalist system.

CAPITALIST DEVELOPMENT IN THE 'THIRD WORLD'

The classical Marxists assumed that each country must go through successive stages of development; the capitalist stage performed the historic task of creating a proletariat and laying the material basis for the succeeding stage of socialism. Lenin and Trotsky argued that the bourgeoisie in Russia (then a relatively backward country) was too weak to carry through the political tasks of the bourgeois revolution, so that the proletariat had to take the lead and could then carry straight on to the socialist revolution. The evolution of a relatively backward country differed from that of the more advanced centres. This argument, however, still presupposes the existence of a proletariat adequate to the task, and thus a certain degree of capitalist development.

However, in the first half of the twentieth century, there were few signs of capitalist development in underdeveloped countries, and many Marxists came to argue a position almost diametrically opposed to that of the classics. Where it had been argued that capitalist development had to come first to create the *possibility* of a socialist revolution, it was now argued that the absence of capitalist development made socialist revolution *necessary*. Frank is the leading exponent of this view, summed up in the title of one of his books, *Latin America: Underdevelopment or Revolution*. This shift of perspective entails a shift to a more voluntaristic concept of politics and to treating the peasantry or lumpenproletariat, rather than the industrial proletariat, as the revolutionary class. This trend in political thinking was encouraged by the success of the Chinese and Cuban revolutions.

What are the issues? At the time when Britain, followed by western Europe and North America, industrialised, the world economy was relatively unintegrated. Transport was expensive and risky, so that goods were traded only where production costs were very different in different areas. Most basic subsistence goods and means of production were produced locally, initially by craft techniques. There was therefore scope for local development of capitalist production at the expense of older methods, while competition from more advanced centres was limited. Capital was relatively immobile, and technology was largely embodied in the skills and experience of the labour force. Thus any capitalist development that did take place created an independent local bourgeoisie and a local concentration of skills and technical knowledge. Independent capitalist development in many centres was possible, and its progress was determined largely by local conditions (except where it was suppressed by a colonial state). Frank and Wallerstein would not accept this analysis; they argue that an integrated capitalist world economy has existed from an early stage. I think that the facts are against them. Up to the industrial revolution the bulk of intercontinental trade was in luxuries such as sugar (slaves are an exceptional case), and the impact of European colonial dominance was primarily through its effects on the mode of production in the subordinated areas.

During the later part of the nineteenth century transport costs fell dramatically, organisational forms were found that permitted large scale international capital flows, and the separation of mental from manual labour led to a systematisation of technical knowledge that permitted international transfers of technology. All of this, of course, is the result of capitalist development, and in its turn it led to the progressive creation of a relatively integrated world capitalist economy. The situation facing an underdeveloped country today is therefore quite different from that of earlier periods. One can ask whether industrialisation on the pattern set by, say, Britain is possible today. One can also ask whether industrialisation on that pattern is a relevant standard to set in present day conditions.

On the one hand, underdeveloped countries industrialising now face competition from advanced centres with centuries of capital accumulation and technical progress behind them. As a result, a world pattern of specialisation has been established in which the underdeveloped areas export mainly primary products and import industrial products. Industrialisation means displacing these imports (or breaking into export markets) rather than displacing primitive craft industries. On the other hand, capital and technology can now be imported, and rising wages in the advanced countries offset the advantages they gain from high productivity.

It is generally agreed that there has been a substantial amount of industrial development in the Third World in recent years. Typically this has taken the form, to begin with, of import substitution, starting with the production of relatively 'light' consumer goods using imported capital equipment, often using at least some imported funds and with some sort of involvement of multi-national companies (wholly or partly owned subsidiaries, joint subsidiaries, licensing arrangements, etc.).

The central issue in debate is whether this sort of industrialisation merely reproduces relations of dependence between centre and periphery in new forms (as Amin, Frank, Sutcliffe and others argue) or whether it marks the beginning of a breakdown of the centre–periphery division (as Warren argues).

Sutcliffe (1972) is one of the few writers who have tackled the question of the prospects for development in the present under-developed countries explicitly, and who have recognised clearly how different the present Marxist orthodoxy is from classical Marxism. Sutcliffe recognises the facts of industrial growth in the periphery, but argues that these are not enough to answer the two critical questions: can there be a full independent industrialisation like that of Japan, or failing that, can there be enough development to create 'progressive socio-political forces', i.e. a proletariat like that of Russia in 1917? Apart from some problems of measurement (the figures may over-state the extent of development) he gives two reasons for discounting the observed industrial growth. Firstly, growth has often been by import substitution concentrated in the production of luxury consumer goods for which the demand is limited, and this type of industrialisation reinforces the income distribution and social structure which limit demand. This is the argument of the 'dependency theorists'; to be acceptable it needs to be supported by some explanation of the failure of industrialisation to penetrate into other branches of the economy or into export markets. Secondly, growth of industrial output may not be matched by growth in employment, since high productivity, capital intensive methods are used. With production in the hands of foreign capital, the result is 'the absence of a bourgeoisie and the absence of a proletariat'.

Hence capitalist development may not create the kind of class structure that Marx described, while the great majority of the population are left unaffected or even worse off. This 'marginalisation' of masses of people has been stressed by many writers. It should be remarked that Marx in fact predicted a growing 'relative surplus population', and it could be said that the underdeveloped countries fit Marx's model of capitalist accumulation more closely than do the advanced countries.

Sutcliffe proposed various criteria for 'independent' industrialisation. This, he says, 'does not mean autarky, but carries with it the idea that industrialisation is not merely "derived" from the industrialisation of another economy' (p. 174). I cannot see why the origins of industrialisation matter: the results are surely more important. His criteria for economic independence are that production should be oriented principally to the domestic market, that investment funds should be raised locally or at least should be under local control, that there should be a diversified industrial structure, and that technology should, in some (not very clearly defined) sense, be independent. The basis of these criteria is not clear; they seem to me to show up the rather nebulous character of the concept of dependence.

Economic independence also has its 'social and political counterparts'. Here Sutcliffe's argument seems stronger:

> Economic development only happens when the surplus gets into the hands of those who will use it productively.... This partly implies the need for an industrial bourgeoisie supported by a state that is capable of defending its interests.... The state must be largely independent both of those local social interests opposed to industrialisation and also of foreign interests. (Sutcliffe, 1972, pp. 176–7)

This seems to me to be the nub of the matter: is an independent national bourgeoisie formed? Independence in this sense does require that development be financed locally and under local control, but it requires 'technological independence' only in the sense that use of foreign technology may lead to effective foreign control through conditions attached to licensing agreements, and the like. I see no reason why an independent capitalist class should not be formed on the basis of export-led industrialisation or copying of techniques; in an interdependent world economy a considerable degree of speciali- sation and large scale exchanges of goods, capital and technology are to be expected.

Sutcliffe's concern with technological independence seems to stem mainly from a different concern. He evidently considers that 'foreign' technology (can technology have a nationality?) is unsuitable because it is too capital intensive (p. 176). This is a line that has been widely argued; capital intensive technology means relatively little employ- ment, which has further consequences for the structure of demand. However, it is likely that capitalist firms, whether foreign or national, will adopt the technique that maximises profits. Underdeveloped countries constitute a large enough market for capital goods for it to be profitable to adapt technology to the prices (and in particular, wage rates) that prevail there. It is thus unlikely that national capital using locally devised techniques would make very different choices. There are, in any case, reasons to think that a choice of technique that maximises reinvestible surplus may be the optimum choice from the point of view of long-run growth.

Sutcliffe argues that independent development (in the sense in which he has defined it) is unlikely, unless the links between metro- polis and satellite are disrupted by inter-imperialist war or acute capi- talist crisis. The prospects of development are limited by the relative backwardness of the underdeveloped countries, by monopolistic control based on technological superiority, and by the pumping of surplus out of underdeveloped countries by repatriation of profits and by unequal exchange. These are all familiar arguments.

Warren (1973) makes a frontal assault on the present radical or 'Third Worldist' orthodoxy represented by Sutcliffe. He sums up his conclusions as follows:

> empirical observations suggest that the prospects for successful capitalist development ... of a significant number of major underdeveloped countries are quite good; ... that the period since the Second World War has been marked by a substantial upsurge in capitalist social relations and productive forces (especially industrialisation) in the Third World ... that the imperialist countries' policies and their overall impact on the Third World actually favour its industrialisation; and that the ties of dependence

... have been and are being markedly loosened.... None of this is meant to imply that imperialism has ceased to exist.... What we wish to indicate are elements of change. (Warren, 1973, pp. 3–4)

Warren puts forward a considerable amount of empirical material to substantiate these claims; it would be impossible to summarise it here. It is, in any case, somewhat beside the point, since many writers have conceded (if somewhat grudgingly) the fact of a certain degree of industrialisation; what is really at issue is the interpretation of these facts. Warren shows that industrial production has mainly been for the home market, and that capital is substantially raised within the country concerned, but it has been frequently argued that 'import substitution' (by definition directed to the home market) carried out by multi-nationals using local finance simply reproduces ties of dependence. The empirical facts cited are therefore not decisive.

Warren's essential argument is that development based on foreign (or foreign controlled) capital is complementary to the development of national capital (p. 39), given a state apparatus which exerts pressure on foreign business and promotes national capitalist development. He argues this largely in the context of resource-based international enterprises (fuel and minerals), showing that local governments have successfully extracted greater shares of revenue and greater control. Since the date at which he wrote, of course, the OPEC countries have gone much further in this direction. The same developments, he argues, are taking place in manufacturing. In particular, the position of the 'host' country is strengthened as its nationals acquire greater experience and knowledge in particular industries, which they inevitably do as a result of the simple presence of the industry and even more as a result of government pressures to employ and promote local residents. Partly owned subsidiaries of multi-national companies tend to come more and more under the control of local shareholders, who thus form the basis of a national capitalist class. Multi-nationals serve, in fact, to transfer technology (p. 29), and, more generally, modern capitalism into the Third World.

Warren argues strongly that socialists have implicitly *defined* development in such a way that capitalist development is effectively ruled out. If development is defined by reference to the 'needs of the masses', then Marxists are unlikely to accept that capitalist development can fit the bill, but this leaves us unable to distinguish between continued stagnation, and development that is successful, in capitalist terms, in that it creates conditions for continued reproduction of capital. On this point Warren seems to me to be absolutely right.

What of imperialism as a system for draining surplus value from the periphery to the centre? Warren argues forcefully that even if the outward flow of repatriated profit exceeds the inward flow of investment this does not demonstrate that the economic effect is harmful, since 'what exactly is done with the capital "in between", so to speak, is ignored ... under capitalism exploitation is the reverse side of the advance of productive forces' (p. 39). Capitalism both exploits and promotes development:

> If the extension of capitalism into non-capitalist areas of the world created an international system of inequality and exploitation called imperialism, it simultaneously created the conditions for the destruction of this system by the spread of capitalist social relations and productive forces throughout the non-capitalist world. Such has been our thesis, as it was the thesis of Marx, Lenin, Luxemburg and Bukharin. (Warren, 1973, p. 41)

There is an obvious objection to this view of imperialism. In the time since Lenin wrote, there has hardly been a single example of successful capitalist industrialisation. (Japan was well on the way before the First World War.) Over this whole period, the gap between advanced and underdeveloped countries has been widening, and it was precisely in response to this massively important fact that Marxists turned away from the classical theories. Warren's reply is that the period since the Second World War has seen the breakup of colonial empires and the establishment of independent states in the Third World. We must presumably see the history of imperialism in stages: first the creation of a basis for national (political) independence, and then full capitalist development.

National independence is crucial, according to Warren, both because it provides a political framework for popular pressures for higher living standards, which compel governments to follow policies of industrial development, and also because it breaks the monopoly hold of the colonial power, thus permitting the newly independent state to take advantage of inter-imperialist and East–West rivalries to bargain for favourable treatment. Capitalist development does not require the prior existence of a 'national bourgeoisie'; other ruling classes can and must promote industrialisation. 'These "industrialisers" may themselves become industrial bourgeoisies or may be displaced by the industrial Frankensteins they have created or they may become fused with them' (pp. 42–3). In addition, imperialist states have positively supported development (by right-wing, nationalist regimes) in order to contain socialism. [...]

My main criticism of Warren is that he is too ready to generalise and to argue that industrial development is likely throughout the Third World. His own evidence shows that this development is proceeding very unevenly, and there are good reasons to expect increasing, rather than decreasing, unevenness. If large-scale modern industry establishes itself in a number of centres (and this seems to me to be likely), there will be intense competition between them. The successful 'new centres' will have a tremendous competitive edge, since they will combine the advantages of modern levels of productivity across a wide range of industries with low wages. The advantage of low wages can persist for a long time, since capital-intensive methods of production keep the demand for labour low and the persistence of mass unemployment holds wages down. In these circumstances, both the existing advanced countries (handicapped by high wages and by the costs of safety measures, social expenditures, etc., won by the working class) and the remaining underdeveloped countries (held back by a backward and incomplete industrial structure) would be at a competitive disadvantage and could be faced with severe problems. The prospect thus seems to me to be not of a simple reduction in inequality between nations (as Warren predicts), but rather of a shifting of the relative positions of different areas within a system of inequality that is likely to persist for a very long time (unless it is ended by revolution).

Warren's political conclusions, however, are valid and important. We must recognise that opposition to the dominance of the major imperial powers is not necessarily genuine anti-imperialism, and may represent no more than a desire by a newly formed bourgeoisie to establish itself within a world system that it does not wish to change. Socialists have frequently been deceived by anti-imperialist rhetoric into supporting viciously reactionary regimes. In any Marxist analysis the fundamental division must be that between classes, between capitalists and workers and not between nations.

SUMMARY AND CONCLUSION

Marxist writers since the Second World War have generally predicted continued United States dominance in the capitalist world, and have argued that there is little prospect of underdeveloped countries improving their relative position without a complete break with the world capitalist system. Neither of these propositions has been supported with conclusive arguments, and there are good reasons for expecting that European and, especially, Japanese capital may challenge American dominance, and also that established industries in advanced countries could be seriously threatened by the development of major new industrial centres in low-wage areas. At the present stage of development of Marxist theory it is not possible to make firm predictions.

It will inevitably take some time to sift through the very large volume of work published in the 1970s, but considerable progress has been made and there is a real prospect of creating an integrated Marxist analysis of the world economy.

REFERENCES

Frank, A.G. (1969) *Latin America: Undevelopment and Revolution* (Monthly Review Press, New York).

Mandel, E. (1967) 'International Capital and "Supranationality"', in P. Miliband and J. Savile (eds), *The Socialist Register 1967* (Merlin, London).

Mandel, E. (1975) *Late Capitalism* (New Left Books, London).

Murray, R. (1971) 'The Internationalization of Capital and the Nation State', *New Left Review*, no. 67.

Poulantzas, N. (1975) *Classes in Contemporary Capitalism* (New Left Books, London).

Rowthorn, R.E. (1971) 'Imperialism in the 1970s – Unity or Rivalry', *New Left Review*, no. 69.

Rowthorn, R.E. and Hymer, S. (1971) *International Big Business 1957–1967: A Study of Comparative Growth* (Cambridge University Press).

Sutcliffe, B. (1972) 'Imperialism and Industrialization in the Third World', in R. Owen and B. Sutcliffe (eds), *Studies in the Theory of Imperialism* (Longmans, London).

Warren, B. (1971) 'How International is Capital?', *New Left Review*, no. 68.

Warren, B. (1973) 'Imperialism and Capitalist Industrialization', *New Left Review*, no. 81.

3.10 Marxist theories of the state in world system analysis

Fred Block

Source: Barbara H. Kaplan (ed.), *Social Change in the Capitalist World Economy* (Sage, Beverly Hills, 1978), pp. 27–37.

Block wishes to reformulate Marxist theory which presupposes that the state is controlled by a ruling class. Block argues that it is necessary to identify a division of labour within the ruling class between those who devote themselves to the accumulation of capital and those who manage the state apparatus. He identifies the potential for conflicts of interest between the two groups.

My subject is how we theorize within the world system perspective. The argument has three parts. I begin with the claim that existing Marxist theories of the state place a strong explanatory emphasis on the consciousness of dominant classes in explaining state policy and the use of such theories in world system analysis creates unnecessary analytic problems. In the second part, I argue for an alternative version of the Marxist theory of the state. In brief, the alternative version places more emphasis on structure and relegates class intentionality to a secondary position, which, I argue, is far more consistent with the world system framework. Finally, I try to show how this alternative formulation can be used concretely by reviewing the Marxist debate on 'ultra-imperialism'.

There is a tendency whenever intellectual breakthroughs occur, whenever new concepts are developed, simply to add those new concepts onto an already existing conceptual structure. But the danger in doing that is that the full implications of the new concept are cut short or lost or underdeveloped because it is forced to coexist with the established conceptual apparatus. I am arguing that this has happened with the development and elaboration of the world system perspective. That new perspective has simply been added onto a lot of our existing intellectual baggage, particularly existing theories in Marxism about the relationship between capitalist classes and the state.

This fusion has created some intellectual problems. To start with, Marxist theories of the state, especially those used within world system analyses, place a strong emphasis on the consciousness of the capitalist class, or at least sectors of that class, in determining state policies. Even when writers talk about the relative autonomy of the state, it is still assumed that at some level of analysis, one can talk about the interests or intentions of some sectors of the dominant class being reflected in state policy. In short, even in the more subtle Marxist analyses, it is assumed that some sector of the capitalist class has a fully developed strategic conception of what the state should do both in the international arena and domestically, and that conception is a key input into state policymaking.

This mode of analysis with its emphasis on consciousness and intentionality of class actors clashes with the world system perspective, which, as I read it, is primarily a structural argument. The core of the world system perspective is the idea that standard social science and historiography have been fixated on the level of appearances. When one looks simply at the level of appearances, one sees different nation states and different regions, each with its own unique history, evolving according to its own internal dynamics. In contrast, the world system perspective insists that behind the level of appearances, there is a structured reality, there is a capitalist world system with its divisions among core, periphery, and semi-periphery. That structural reality of the capitalist world system determines a great deal of what goes on in the seemingly independent nation states or regions. The structural thrust of the argument is clearest when Wallerstein (1974a) talks about developments in the Soviet Union and China. In essence, he argues that in spite of what Soviet theoreticians and state managers might have thought, the fundamental reality was that socialist construction was taking place within a capitalist world system and that fundamentally distorted or limited what the Soviets, and the Chinese, are capable of doing. That is a very powerful structural argument because regardless of anyone's intentions, the real forces are the structural relations of a capitalist world system that unfold behind the backs of social actors.

When one combines the world system perspective's structural emphasis with Marxist theories of the state's emphasis on class intentionality, the result is not a dialectical synthesis, but analytic confusion. The two theories just do not fit together properly. The analytic confusion is subtle, but I can give some examples from Wallerstein's (1974b) book that, I think, make the point. There is a strange kind of asymmetry to Wallerstein's argument about the rise and fall of core nations. When the rise of a core nation is discussed, the explanation for the rise often draws heavily on the intentionality of class actors, whereas when a nation's decline is being accounted for, the explanations tend to be structural. For example, nations decline because there is an inflationary process that develops that makes the economy uncompetitive or because there is an overinvestment in the political costs of empire that happens inadvertently. In short, nations rise as a result of class intentionality and decline because of factors that emerge behind the back of social actors. This raises the critical question: 'If they were so smart then, what happened to them later?' Obviously there are ways of answering the question, such as arguing that it is easy to be smart when structural forces are working with you, but as the argument stands, the asymmetry is problematic.

Another problem that Wallerstein slips into results from the fact that within the existing Marxist theories of the state, it is natural to talk about capitalists within a nation state having a developed class consciousness. This class consciousness includes a strategic sense; capitalists, or sectors of the class, know what has to be done to maintain their rule. So when one combines the Marxist theory of the state with the world system perspective, it is only natural to extend that capitalist class consciousness internationally. Hence, Wallerstein suggests at a number of points that capitalist classes within nations have a developed sense of international strategy and this consciousness is reflected in the policies of core states. Now it is already difficult to make a convincing empirical case that capitalist classes have that kind of strategic consciousness in terms of policies within nation states. But when one adds that further level – that capitalists have some kind of international strategic consciousness – I think one runs into real problems of evidence and explanation. Of course, one can always find a few members of a ruling class who possess far-sighted views of what has to be done by the state both domestically and internationally, but to argue that such individuals are some kind of direct representatives of their class seems quite problematic to me.

These criticisms should become clearer as I state the alternative formulations that I think make it possible to avoid some of these analytic confusions. The alternative is a Marxist theory of the state that is primarily structural, relegating capitalist class consciousness to a secondary role. I have developed this argument more fully elsewhere (Block, 1977); what I will try to do here is provide an abbreviated version of the argument. This will obviously be incomplete, raising as many questions as it answers, but my purpose is only to give a sense of the direction in which the alternative line of argument would proceed.

This structural view of the capitalist state does not start with the idea of the relative autonomy of the state because that formulation continues to impute high levels of consciousness to the capitalist class. I want to begin with the idea of a sharp division of labor between those who devote themselves to accumulation and those who devote themselves to managing the state apparatus. I want to argue that the division of labor creates differences of interests – state managers are interested in expanding their own power within the structural situation in which they find themselves – and differences in world views. The ideologies of state managers and capitalists are going to be different because of their different structural locations. The critical point that separates this argument from the liberalism that some people will charge me with is that this division of labor occurs within a structural framework. The structural framework is the reason that, despite the division of interests between capitalists and state managers, the general tendency is for state managers to act in the general interests of capital. Hence, the key to the argument is the analysis of the structural framework.

The two aspects of the structural framework that I want to emphasize are the idea of business confidence and the ways in which demands of subordinate classes are processed. In a capitalist economy, the rate of investment is dependent upon entrepreneurial or managerial decisions and those decisions are made partly in response to simple economic variables. But there is also a more intangible element to investment decisions – the businessperson's perception of how promising is the general political-economic environment. When these perceptions are aggregated across the whole economy, they can be termed the level of business confidence. When business confidence is in decline or threatening to decline (and there was a recent illustration of this in the period between the election and the beginning of the Carter administration when business confidence was threatening to decline, unless Carter made various concessions, such as appointing conservative business types to key posts in the administration), state managers are in trouble. Regardless of their ideology, state managers are dependent upon maintaining adequate levels of business confidence for a series of different reasons. For one thing, the level of business confidence will determine the rate of investment and that will determine the rate of employment. The more unemployment there is, the less political support the regime is likely to have, in general. So in order to protect themselves from political dissatisfaction, state managers want to keep business confidence up. Business confidence is also important because the rate of investment determines the flow of revenues to the state itself. The amount of freedom that state managers have in a competitive nation state system to spend money on armaments is also then a function of the rate of business investment and the level of business confidence. Finally, the level of business confidence has other international ramifications. In a capitalist world economy where trade can move capital across national boundaries in response to market forces, a domestic decline of business confidence will usually generate a decline in international business confidence. International bankers are then reluctant to lend to that nation, and other businesspeople act to disinvest, so the consequence is an international payments crisis. Such a crisis presents state managers with a whole set of difficult problems that they would sooner avoid by acting in the first place to halt the decline in business confidence.

In short, for all these reasons, state managers are generally constrained from doing things that would damage business confidence and they have a strong incentive to use what power they have to improve business confidence, that is, improve the investment climate. The point I want to stress is that business confidence is not like a capitalist class consciousness. On the contrary, business confidence is based on a very short-term, short-sighted perception of the environment. A capitalist class consciousness implies a long-range, strategic point of view. The clearest way of thinking of this difference is the example of FDR during the Great Depression. Roosevelt was continually saying to the business community that he was acting in their general class interest; he was trying to save capitalism. But business confidence remained at low levels; businesspeople were far less impressed by FDR's pleas than they were by such troubling signs as the rise of industrial unionism.

The other key aspect of the structural framework is the way in which demands by subordinate classes (working class, petite bourgeoisie, and peasants) are processed by state managers. It has been demands by such subordinate classes that have played a key role in expanding the state's role in the delivery of services and in the regulation of markets. Faced with demands from below, state managers attempt to avert political turmoil or electoral defeat by pushing outward the boundaries of state action, even against the resistance of business confidence. But even though the pressure to expand the state's role often comes from below, the dynamic is different once the expansion has occurred. Then, state managers have reasons to use their expanded powers to improve the investment climate, that is, in ways that are in the general interests of capital. For example, pressures from below are important in extending educational opportunities in capitalist societies, but once an expanded educational system is created, state managers will orient the educational system toward the creation of the kind of labor force that capital needs. They will do so because they have an interest in improving the investment climate.

Together, these two aspects of the structural framework provide a model in which the rationality of the capitalist state, or its capacity to act in the general interests of capital, cannot be reduced to the consciousness of a sector of capital or the consciousness of state managers themselves. The argument is that the rationality of the capitalist state emerges out of the three-sided relationship between state managers, capital, and subordinate classes. The rationality emerges largely behind the backs of the social actors involved.

The virtue of this model is that it allows one to get away from the standard Marxist methodological tool of assuming that state policies always reflect the intentionality of a social class or sector of a class. It renders obsolete the procedure of looking for a specific social base for any particular state policy. Of course, there are always capitalist special interests attempting to get the state to act in their favor, as, for example, the oil companies lobbying for energy policies that would maximize their profits. But when we are talking about the strategic level, the kind of state policies that rise above specific industrial interests because they are oriented to maintaining the conditions necessary for continued class rule domestically and keeping open possibilities for economic expansion abroad, then such reductionism is unnecessary. The distinction between 'objective' and 'subjective' is useful here. One can say that a policy objectively benefited a particular social class, but that is very different from saying that that social class, or sector of a class, subjectively wanted that policy, or that its intentions were a critical element in policy development.

A historical illustration should clarify what is at stake in this argument. One of the recurring issues in Marxist discussions of the world capitalist system is the consequences of growing economic interpenetration among the core capitalist powers. Writers from Kautsky (1970) to the present have argued that the internationalization of investment is creating a kind of 'ultra-imperialism' in which the interlocking of interests among a small number of giant capitalists in the core nations will create a new international ruling class. The common interests of this international ruling class will then preclude serious conflict among the nations of the core. Not only will inter-imperialist war become unthinkable, but the core nations will present an increasingly united front toward the nations of the periphery and semi-periphery.

The standard critique of this position derives from Lenin (1939, pp. 117–21). It goes as follows: while a system of ultra-imperialism might be stable temporarily, it is bound to happen, because of uneven development, that economic groups in a particular capitalist nation will become dissatisfied with the prevailing arrangements for sharing the global surplus. These groups will push their state to demand a renegotiation of the existing 'rules of the game' on the grounds that their share is no longer commensurate with their increased size and financial power. However, these attempts at revision are likely to be resisted by other nations, and the result would probably be a breakdown of the ultra-imperialist order. Those economic interests that feel they are being cheated will use their respective states to act in an increasingly aggressive way toward the anti-revisionist powers, resulting in trade wars and possibly open interimperialist conflict.

This line of argument, however, seems to become less compelling as the process of economic interpenetration progresses further and further. If some two or three hundred multinational corporations dominate the world economy, and most of these corporations are active in all of the core nations and are closely intertwined with each other in a variety of different arrangements, then it becomes harder to imagine a particular nationally based set of economic interests being aggrieved enough and powerful enough to disrupt the fabric of interimperialist cooperation. On the contrary, one would imagine that such a system would be quite flexible in its capacity to coopt new corporate groups, for example, those that develop in semi-peripheral areas into an elaborate system of interlocking corporate power.

There is, however, another line of criticism of the ultra-imperialism argument, but it requires examining the theory of the state implicit in that position. The ultra-imperialism argument assumes that state policies will generally reflect the intentionality of the dominant capitalists. Once these dominant capitalists recognize that economic interpenetration among core nations has made interimperialist conflict not only unnecessary but positively harmful, they will exert their influence to see that state managers act accordingly. And the results of that influence would be a continuation of interimperialist cooperation.

But what if state policies do not always reflect the intentionality of dominant capitalists? Then it might be the case that even though the dominant capitalists want to preserve interimperialist cooperation, state managers find they have little alternative but to intensify interimperialist conflict. If this were the case, then no matter how far the development of an international ruling class had progressed, ultra-imperialism would still be unstable, and interimperialist conflict might resume.

The argument I have made about the division of labor between state managers and capitalists provides an explanation of how the interests of capitalists and state managers might diverge, but what specific circumstances could lead to such sharp divergences on such a critical issue as the maintenance of interimperialist cooperation? If state managers perceived that the existing rules of the game of the ultra-imperialist system were creating such havoc in their domestic political economy that extremist movements of the left or of the right were threatening their control of state power, then those state managers would very likely begin agitating for a revision of these rules. Their dominant capitalists might well be prospering as a result of global operations, but if high levels of domestic unemployment or inflation or other economic dislocations were creating political turmoil, the state managers might well ignore the pleadings of those capitalists and use their power to disrupt the fabric of interimperialist cooperation. In short, the argument is similar to Lenin's, but it is the state managers who push for a renegotiation of the international arrangements.

As long as one assumes that state policy will reflect the intentionality of the dominant capitalists, the ultra-imperialism argument seems unassailable. But once one adopts a more sophisticated model which recognizes that the intentionality of capitalists is only one part of the structural matrix that shapes the response of state managers operating in a capitalist world system, then the weaknesses of the ultra-imperialism position become apparent. Since a capitalist world economy will always be characterized by combined and uneven development, the process of economic integration among capitals is bound to create severe economic strains in some of the nations of the core. If those economic strains provoke a serious political response, then state managers will be under strong pressure to improve the terms of their nation's integration into the world system. The inevitability of such attempts makes it difficult to conceive of a stable, long-term system of ultra-imperialism.

This argument also makes it possible to resolve a contradiction that has bothered me for a while. Karl Polanyi, whose work was a critical building block in our understanding of the capitalist world system, argued in *The Great Transformation* (1957, pp. 9–19) that *haute finance*, the major banking houses, played a key role in preserving the peace during the second half of the nineteenth century between Waterloo and Sarajevo. According to Polanyi, the great financial families, with their offices in every major European capital, did not want a general European war to break out. Whenever a crisis occurred, the financial interests would use their considerable influence with the heads of state, who were literally indebted to them, to urge them to draw back from the brink of war. But Lenin argued that Finance Capital (which would seem to overlap considerably with haute finance) was responsible for the outbreak of World War I. The two apparently conflicting positions can be reconciled with the distinction between intentionality and structure. Haute finance wanted peace and presumably was an unsuccessful peace interest in the last hours before World War I. It was unsuccessful, however, because the development of the whole structure of finance capitalism had created objective conditions within which state managers felt they had little alternative but to go to war. In sum, one might say that the road to war is paved with peaceful intentions, and the road to analytic confusion in Marxism is paved with an exaggerated concern with class intentionality.

REFERENCES

Block, F. (1977) 'The Ruling Class Does Not Rule', *Socialist Revolution*, 33 (May–June), pp. 6–28.

Kautsky, K. (1970) 'Ultra-imperialism', *New Left Review*, 59 (January–February), pp. 41–6.

Lenin, V.I. (1939) *Imperialism: The Highest Stage of Capitalism* (International, New York).

Polanyi, K. (1957) *The Great Transformation* (Beacon, Boston).

Wallerstein, I. (1974a) 'The Rise and Future Demise of the World Capitalist System', *Comparative Studies in Society and History*, 16 (September), pp. 387–415.

—— (1974b) *The Modern World-System: Capitalist Agriculture and the Origins of the European World Economy in the Sixteenth Century* (Academic, New York).

Part IV
Perspectives and world politics

INTRODUCTION

This Reader has been organized on the basis of competing perspectives on world politics. In this final section, the items have been chosen to throw more light on the nature and significance of these perspectives. As a consequence, the articles raise more overtly philosophical questions about the nature of knowledge and the relationship between theory and practice. It quickly becomes apparent, however, that these are not neutral questions and that the answers to them are influenced by an initial perspective.

Rothstein (4.1) starts from the presumption that theorists and practitioners have been overwhelmingly influenced by the realist perspective – elaborated in the first section of this Reader. The perspective does not prescribe specific policies according to Rothstein but he does insist that it predisposes its adherents to think about international politics in a very circumscribed and ethnocentric fashion. Rothstein goes on to argue that the influence of realism is becoming increasingly dangerous and deceptive because of the revolution taking place in world politics which is invalidating basic realist assumptions. It becomes clear during the course of the argument, therefore, that Rothstein is evaluating realism from the perspective of transnationalism and interdependence. It also becomes apparent that Rothstein is not simply attacking realism because it is presenting an erroneous view of reality but because advocates of realism are endeavouring to maintain a world which Rothstein characterizes as elitist and undemocratic. The article reveals, therefore, that the differences between perspectives can be ethical as well as empirical.

Gilpin (4.2) adopts a much more eclectic approach to perspectives. He identifies three perspectives on the international political economy which to a very large extent overlap with the perspectives identified in this Reader. It is central to his argument, however, that these perspectives are not amenable to empirical verification because they are based on assumptions about individuals and society which are not susceptible to any conclusive empirical test. Adherents of any specific perspective must, therefore, engage in an act of faith. Gilpin, himself, however, believes that he can stand apart from the three perspectives and assess their strengths and weaknesses. On this basis, he is able to draw on all three perspectives in his quest to understand the international political economy. There is, on the face of it, something rather attractive about this eclecticism but in fact it raises a number of difficult philosophical problems which it is not possible to enter into here.

Strange (4.3) who, like Gilpin, believes that it is necessary to adopt a position which transcends the interpretations of competing ideological perspectives argues that academic debates can have profound political significance. She insists that the outcome of the dispute about whether or not we are in the process of observing the demise of the American empire will affect future events. She further asserts, however, that whatever the outcome, the debate has, in the past, been couched in terms of an outmoded perspective which prevents both sides from identifying the nature and amount of power possessed by the United States in the contemporary world.

The position adopted by Cox (4.4) provides an interesting contrast to Strange. The original item is extremely long and only a small portion of it is reproduced here. Nevertheless, the extract is sufficient to make clear that Cox has a very distinctive position on the role of perspectives. He draws a very sharp distinction between a problem-solving and a critical perspective. He argues that the problem-solving perspective takes the world as the theorist finds it. The perspective is designed to reveal how the status quo can be reproduced. By contrast, a critical perspective is designed to transcend the established order and to understand the nature of change. It calls into question institutions associated with the existing order and it makes provision for an ethical position which favours a transformed political and social order. The line of analysis developed by Cox makes it clear that he is unhappy with the established world order and that he wishes to adopt a posture on perspectives which opens up the possibility of radical change. Ironically, the argument has much in common with the one developed by Strange, except that she wishes to develop a critical posture which will ensure that the status quo is maintained.

The final item by Elshtain (4.5) throws fresh light on all the preceding discussion. She is interested in using a feminist perspective as an alternative to the dominant perspectives on world politics and, in particular, realism. But before she can do this, she has to acknowledge the pervasive influence of realism, and she notes how an important strain of feminist thought has been cast in realist terms. She insists, though, that there is an alternative line of feminist ideas which provides the language necessary to engage in a very different form of discourse about international relations. Elshtain does not ascribe an autonomous role for language and discourse but she does insist that the language associated with one particular perspective may preclude consideration of unrealized possibilities which potentially exist in the real world. The language provided by a new perspective may make these possibilities manifest.

The articles in this section are not designed to provide any definitive solutions to questions about the status of perspectives in the study of world politics. The issue is and will probably remain deeply problematic. Nevertheless, we hope that this final section will convince the reader that the identification of perspectives is a necessary feature of any attempt to understand world politics.

4.1 On the costs of realism
Robert L. Rothstein

Source: *Political Science Quarterly*, vol. LXXXVII, no. 3 (1972), pp. 347–62.

After identifying the chief characteristics of the realist view of world politics, Rothstein considers what the effect of this view has been upon politicians and diplomats since World War II and points to the dangers inherent in its continuing to dominate the thinking of foreign policy makers.

[The article begins by pointing to the contrast between the declining satisfaction with realism in academic circles and its continuing attraction for policy makers. It suggests that this contrast can be understood only by recognizing the nature of the realist vision.]

Realism involved commitment to a set of propositions about international politics which were essentially extrapolations from the diplomatic history of nineteenth-century Europe. They were propositions which the generation of statesmen in Europe after 1919 either had lost or misunderstood: re-education in the 'perennials' was clearly necessary. The catechism was simple. All states sought, or would seek, power, given the opportunity. It was an essential prerequisite for the achievement of any other goals. Today's enemy could be tomorrow's ally (n.b., not 'friend', for, as Salisbury put it, 'Great Britain has no permanent friends, only permanent interests'). The use of any means was acceptable (atomic weapons created a dilemma, resolved by silence or metaphysical despair), or at least possible, though only one or two might be appropriate at any single moment. The best operator was the man who possessed 'traditional wisdom'; and the man who possessed 'traditional wisdom' was the best operator.

The scenario and the stage directions are very familiar. The metaphor is deliberate, for many Realists considered international politics a great drama in which wise statesmen made 'hard choices' in a bitter but limited struggle for dominance. They were constrained by their own power and their own fallibility, but at the very least they never fell victim to illusions about the 'true' nature of the world. It was a world in which states were involved in an unending struggle with each other (because that was the nature of states in an anarchic world); power was necessary to survive in it or to continue to fight; all states were potential enemies (Realism requires enemies more than it needs friends), but the worst might be avoided by clever diplomacy and by virtue of the fact that all alike shared a similar conception of rational behavior. It was indeed a dramatic picture, and an especially exciting one, for it was a drama of war in which the wartime mind predominated. This made it particularly attractive to an emerging generation of statesmen whose views had been formed as a response to the failure to stop Hitler before it was too late and who were thus predisposed toward a doctrine which would guarantee that the same errors would not be committed against Stalin.

The Realist model of world politics was simple and elegant. An image of states as billiard balls, interacting within a specific arena and according to established rules, became increasingly prevalent. Once the implication of the metaphor was grasped, that there are only a few immutable patterns of behavior in politics – billiard balls, after all, are not very complex phenomena – the principal preoccupation of statesmen became clear. They were to judge, by experience and intuition, the requisite amount of force necessary to move one or another ball in a preferred direction. Purposes, as in wartime where the need for survival and victory dominated everything, could be taken for granted. Individual idiosyncrasies, which might influence choice of purpose, or domestic politics, which might destroy the elegance of the game, could be safely ignored, for they were hardly significant in comparison to the external imperatives imposed by life in the international arena. All states would respond to the same drummer, irrespective of internal differences, because they had no choice if they wished to survive (at any rate, as a Great Power).

Is there something beyond its elegance and simplicity which has made this doctrine so popular, so to speak so 'natural', to the practitioner? The power of fascination of a doctrine ultimately must rest on its apparent ability to provide answers to practical questions. The answers must be attributable to the doctrine, at least in the sense that some connection may safely be posited between successful practitioners and doctrinal commitment. In the case at hand, the ability to make that connection would imply that a substantive distinction exists between a Realist and a non-Realist.

Is it really that easy to distinguish a Realist from a non-Realist? The difficulty is that commitment to the Realists' image of world politics – a world scarred by a permanent quest for power by potentially wicked men – hardly guarantees realistic decisions about the practical world. Realists and non-Realists may disagree about the permanence of power as the decisive factor in international politics, but they can still reach similar judgments about specific cases. On the other hand, two confessed Realists may reach totally dissimilar conclusions about the same case – in fact, at times, it is difficult to relate an individual Realist's position on policy to his philosophical convictions. Correlating Morgenthau and Kennan on policy with Morgenthau and Kennan on 'Realism' requires a Talmudist's skill and patience, not to say a willingness to suspend disbelief. The difficulty is that reality is so complex and ambiguous that the policies which we choose to call 'realistic' at any particular moment depend to a significant degree on personal predispositions and perspectives.

What this suggests is that Realism involves something more than a temporal perspective on power and the nature of man. It also suggests that lists of characteristics presumably shared by all Realists are irrelevant: statesmen or analysts possessing all the characteristics can act very 'unrealistically' (which we know only after the fact), while others possessing none of the characteristics may act 'realistically' (which we also know only after the fact). The more subtle contention that Realists share an awareness that full security is beyond attainment and that compromise and adjustment of interests are necessary, is more helpful. It implies that Realism involves a state of mind with which to approach problems, rather than the possession of a few characteristics or attachment to the permanent significance of a single operating principle. Nevertheless, some groups have the same sense of the nature of politics and are not considered Realists (for example, some liberals). Moreover, the difficulty of discovering exactly why one policy position is more realistic than another persists.

Various efforts to give Realism an acceptable programmatic content have been inadequate, for the task itself is probably impossible. We can define a Realist arbitrarily as someone who possesses certain characteristics or who believes in certain doctrinal propositions, but there is no way in which we can convincingly relate those characteristics or beliefs to specific choices in the world of action. Realism simply constitutes belief in the wisdom of certain 'eternal verities' about politics, conveniently collected in a few texts and conveniently 'confirmed' by a series of all too recent blunders by non-

Realists. The point surely is not that Realism is unimportant or irrelevant. But its real significance has not been in providing a (non-existent) direct connection between theory and action. Its power and influence over the choice of specific actions has been – and perhaps remains – pervasive, but indirect. It has conditioned the political climate so that some actions seem 'to stand to reason' and others seem naive – by definition. And it has furnished an authentic body of scripture to rationalize 'hard choices', to justify the notion that a democratic foreign policy is inconceivable, and to provide psychic support for the acolyte compelled to lie in defense of his own inter-pretation of the national interest.

The great hero in the Realist canon has always been the successful diplomat – many of the founders and followers of Realism were frustrated Castlereaghs, or better yet, Metternichs – and the great danger the bumbling amateur. Professionals, after all, could always 'work something out'. The very ambiguity and uncertainty of the relationship between the theory and the choice of specific actions guarantee the supremacy of the diplomat's role. What else but experience and intuition allow the necessary connections to be made? And who but the diplomat is trained (rather, one should say, 'experienced') to make the necessary judgments? It is peculiarly true, then, that the lack of an obvious connection between the theory and a practical action, and the ensuing necessity of relying on a corps of skilled intermediaries, has made Realism singularly attractive to professional diplomats. [...]

Realism presumes a world of similar states: it is a doctrine based upon, and beholden to, the behavioral styles of the traditional Great Power. Totalitarian, revolutionary, underdeveloped, and unstable states – as well as Small Powers, international organizations, and nongovernmental organizations, like the multinational corporation or the Ford Foundation – are all unwelcome anomalies. Such states violate and perhaps destroy the notion of a shared, if tacit, sense of a range of permissible behavior for states. It is not altogether in-explicable that many of the events which have surprised us – both theorists and practitioners – in the last twenty-five or so years have been perpetrated by these new kinds of states: the Nazi–Soviet pact in 1939, Pearl Harbor, the German blitz, Soviet acquisition of a nuclear capability, the Berlin blockade, North Korean aggression and Chinese intervention, Nasser's reaction to US Aswan Dam 'diplomacy', the sputniks, the Berlin wall, the installation of missiles in Cuba, and the more recent internal turmoil in both Indonesia and China. It is not that we failed to predict the exact moment or event; it is that we were neither politically nor psychologically prepared for them to happen at all.

It is important to note that many of these failures resulted from the inability of men trained to deal with concrete contingencies as they arise to understand the actions of men or states committed to an ideological interpretation of world affairs – or at least to an interpretation not derived from the history of the European state system. In addition, a congenital bias against planning made it difficult to deal with those who did have a plan. At any rate, both Realists and practitioners shared a bias toward analyzing and evaluating the world according to habits and precepts drawn from European history.

One other aspect of Realism has made it especially attractive to diplomats and practitioners. Concentrating on interaction between states perceived as billiard balls tends to turn attention away from structural alterations in the international system itself. The systemic environment, in the large, is taken as a constant – that is, as a field fluctuating around a metaphorical balance of power. The result has been a static theory concerned only with creating or preserving an equilibrium. As such, only tactical questions – operator's questions about means, not ends – appear truly interesting. The central preoccupation is never why or where the system is going (it is going no place, by definition), but rather how to preserve the existing order of things. It has meant that the Realists have been very poor guides through the thickets of bipolarity, multipolarity, polycentrism, and the like.

Practitioners generally object strenuously to the notion that they all believe in any single doctrine. They point to the indisputable fact that there are sharp disagreements within the government over major issues like Vietnam and the ABM. This mistakes disagreements about specifics for disagreement about general attitudes and approaches. Anyone who reads the memoirs of former practitioners, or who spends any substantial amount of time talking with them, can attest to the existence of widely shared beliefs and very similar perceptions of what can be taken for granted about the conduct of foreign affairs. These shared beliefs and convictions are not held or expounded with anything like the formal elegance or coherence which one finds in a Morgenthau or Kennan text. Nonetheless, they exist and they reinforce – or repeat – the Realist canon. It may be violently unsettling to the political practitioner, but he does indeed 'speak' theory – of a sort. It would be better for all of us if he were aware of it and understood what it implied.

THE PRACTICAL EFFECTS OF REALISM

The extent to which Realism has been elitist and antidemocratic was masked – or ignored – for many years, for the policies which dominated American foreign policy rested on a substantial domestic consensus about the proper way to deal with the Soviet and Chinese threats. Not only the mass public but anyone who disagreed with the conventional wisdom could be disregarded, be they reporters, professors, or 'bleeding hearts' in general. What Realism passed on was a kind of romanticism about both policy – for the 'responsibilities of power' meant that we had a stake as policeman or judge in anything happening anywhere – and the policy-maker – who had to make 'hard choices' in spite of domestic stupidity or indifference. The 'professionals' would give Americans a good and prudent foreign policy even if they had to be tricked into it or misinformed or lied to. In effect, Realism has provided the high tone of necessity for a rather low range of behavior. In this sense, the revelation in the *Pentagon Papers* of a persistent disregard for the democratic process and a persistent fascination with fooling the press and obscuring the truth was entirely predictable.

Realism is also implicitly a conservative doctrine attractive to men concerned with protecting the status quo. It hardly predisposes its followers to look favorably at revolutionary change, for that kind of change threatens all the fences which Realism has erected: it means one might have to deal with some very untraditional states – and 'diplomats' – about some very untraditional issues. It means that disagreement about ends and values might begin to creep into the system, surely an unfortunate development from the point of view of men committed to the notion that only the proper choice of means is ever really at issue.

From one point of view, Realism has always been an eminently sensible doctrine: its emphasis on the virtues of moderation, flexibility, and compromise was an intelligent response to the difficulties and dangers of living in an anarchic world. But from another point of view, Realism has emphasized the necessity for Great Powers to maintain their prestige, status, and credibility. Great Powers, by definition, are compelled to play 'prestige politics', that is to say, a form of politics particularly difficult to compromise or control. Turning the other cheek could be disastrous, or at least imprudent, in a world dominated by the quest for power. In fact, it has always been necessary to use, or to appear to be willing to use, limited amounts of force quickly in order to avoid having to use larger amounts belatedly. This seemingly sensible proposition, so fundamental to a generation who remembered the follies of Chamberlain and Daladier, was very dangerous for men who could remember – or learn – nothing else. Flexibility, moderation, and compromise would have to take a back seat to the necessity of teaching the aggressors a lesson and enhancing the credibility of one's word. An awful lot of 'brinkmanship' and waiting to see if 'the other guy would blink first' could result.

Realism asserts – and it can be neither proved nor disproved – that nothing much can be changed, that the only guide to the future is the past, and that the best interpreter of the way to get there safely is the operator skilled at negotiating limited compromises. It thus gives the 'generalist', the operator armed only with traditional procedural skills, a central role in the conduct of foreign policy. But it is also a conservative and anti-innovative role; as a result, the doctrine has provided a kind of metaphysical justification for the passivity and procedural inertia of the Foreign Service and the State Department, characteristics already built into the policy-making system by incrementalism and the play of bureaucratic politics.

The nature of the role which the practitioner is expected to play also has had a crucial effect on the nature of the training he is expected to undergo. The only unanswered questions are tactical questions about applications. And there is no way to train someone to make correct tactical decisions except 'on the job'. Thus the proper training for the practitioner is never analytical or intellectual; presumably, his proper role is simply to apply known principles to individual cases. That task, which rests on a combination of experience, intuition, and familiarity with the latest details, can be learned only by doing – or, more accurately, by imitating. It is one of the few illustrations of a profession which takes anti-intellectualism as a virtue. In any case, it sharply circumscribes the ability of the practitioner to deal with untraditional events.

The fact that Realism has operated with a strikingly narrow definition of politics also has had a major effect on the behavior of its practitioners. Diplomatic maneuvering to achieve or maintain the gains of 'high politics' became the norm – the analogy with the chessboard, an elegant and intricate arena of play, always seemed appropriate. New developments which undermine the utility of the analogy have to be either ignored or dismissed as irrelevant. Thus the State Department and its denizens have had little influence on a whole range of issues which have dominated foreign policy since World War II: for example, political and economic development in the underdeveloped countries, the relationship between nuclear weapons and political behavior, the control of the arms race, limited and sublimited war, and the erosion of the distinction between foreign and domestic policy. It is misleading to assert, as some critics have done, that these are issues which have been *taken* from the State Department: it is more accurate to say that they have been given away in the apparent hope that they would disappear, or at least not intrude upon the ordered universe of diplomacy.

Realism has the ring of truth to it for men compelled to work in an environment which they can not always understand and can never adequately control. It provides a few simple keys which facilitate understanding (if only, inevitably, by oversimplification) and an intellectual justification for the failure to control (for all is unpredictable – although hardly unexpectable). None of this means that Realism has been responsible for, or 'caused', any particular policy choice: it could just as well have been used, for example, to defend going into Vietnam as staying out. What it has done has been to foster a set of attitudes that predisposed its followers to think about international politics in a particularly narrow and ethno-centric fashion, and to set very clear bounds around the kinds of policies which it seemed reasonable to contemplate. And once decisions have been made, it has provided the necessary psychological and intellectual support to resist criticism, to persevere in the face of doubt, and to use any means to outwit or to dupe domestic dissenters.

THE FUTURE OF REALISM

The appeal of Realism is deceptive and dangerous, for it rests on assumptions about state behavior which have become increasingly irrelevant. It treats one time-bound set of propositions as if they were universally applicable, and thus turns everyone's attention to problems of application – to issues of 'how' not 'why'. It is always a doctrine which takes for granted the primacy of foreign policy and the dominance of the security issue defined in terms of simple notions of power. It is, in sum, not only the classic version of a state-centric doctrine but also an affirmation of the rightful dominance of the Great Powers and the autonomy of their foreign policies.

We could treat this discussion as being of only historical interest but for one fact: despite Realism's increasing irrelevance as an interpretation of the external world, its hold over the mind of the practitioner is still formidable. Why this should be so can only be explained by the dominant – and thus exceedingly attractive – role which Realism assigns to the 'generalist' practitioner (who gets a hunting license on all issues in spite of an absence of substantive expertise); and by the more general consideration that all doctrines persist at the practical level much beyond the point they begin to be assailed at the theoretical level. After all, for the practitioner to abandon or question what he considers to be his own particular expertise is to abandon or question the only thing which separates him from outsiders, and that is very threatening.

The greatest danger in this situation is that Realism is becoming even more irrelevant to the international system in the process of emerging. What we may be witnessing is the first systemic revolution occurring without the intervention of general war or the development of a wholly new kind of military technology. The central point is that the traditional security issue is no longer likely to be the dominant consideration in world politics. I am *very* far from asserting that security will no longer be an issue or that it will somehow disappear from the calculations of states – some analysts of the emerging system seem to take this position, at least implicitly, thus acting as if the realm of security and the realm of inter-dependence were in fact completely autonomous. It is clear, however, that security will be only one of the issues of world politics, albeit a crucial one, for it will have to share prominence with a range of issues heretofore left to technicians or to the play of domestic politics.

The growing interdependence on economic, social, and cultural matters within the state system obviously implies a system in which the autonomy and sovereignty of all the members – great and small – is being eroded. Rational decision-making on such issues requires a degree of international cooperation well beyond anything which has occurred in the field of security. (Even in NATO, for example, the United States always determined strategic questions by itself even though they affected all the allies.) This is particularly true because there is no guarantee that these issues will reduce the degree of conflict in the international system *unless* they are handled in a manner which is minimally satisfactory to all concerned. Interdependence clearly could just as well lead to trade wars and an insane effort to achieve autarchy as it could to increased prosperity and welfare; only a new style of decision-making and a change in basic thought patterns could turn these developments into an opportunity to enhance the degree of cooperation in the system. Finally, it deserves some mention that the security issue itself is becoming (or perhaps one should say, is finally being recognized as) increasingly one involving interdependence, as the recent agreements on the hot line and nuclear accidents attest. It will become even more so if nuclear weapons proliferate and arms technology itself continues to grow in complexity. Even a more mundane, but very critical, security issue like the control of conventional arms cannot be handled by any traditional formula – if it can be handled at all.

The attitudes and predispositions which Realism fosters constitute a classically inappropriate response to these developments. With its overly narrow conception of politics, and with its antiquated notions of sovereignty, Great Power dominance and the autonomy of foreign policy, the Realist response is bound to create conflict and destroy the possibility of working out new forms of cooperation. The potential which these issues have for creating either cooperation or conflict means that they must be deliberately manipulated to encourage cooperation; it may even be necessary to adopt a decision-making style borrowed from domestic politics, or to begin to take functions like planning seriously. We may also be compelled to contemplate other heresies. The Realist mentality would find it virtually impossible to even think about these matters in their proper dimension; worse yet, since Realism presupposes conflict, it is likely to turn the politics of interdependence into another exercise in the politics of security.

4.2 Three ideologies of political economy

Robert Gilpin

Source: *The Political Economy of International Relations* (Princeton University Press, Princeton, 1987), pp. 25–64.

In the book from which this section is drawn, Gilpin uses three ideologies or perspectives – liberalism, economic nationalism and Marxism – to examine a range of specific issues such as trade, investment and development, related to the international political economy. In this section he provides an overview and critique of each ideology and elaborates on what he means by an ideology. Although a liberal by persuasion, Gilpin concludes that Marxism identifies problems which liberalism may not be able to overcome.

Over the past century and a half, the ideologies of liberalism, nationalism, and Marxism have divided humanity. This book uses 'ideology' to refer to 'systems of thought and belief by which [individuals and groups] explain ... how their social system operates and what principles it exemplifies' (Heilbroner, 1985, p. 107). The conflict among these three moral and intellectual positions has revolved around the role and significance of the market in the organization of society and economic affairs.

Through an evaluation of the strengths and weaknesses of these three ideologies it is possible to illuminate the study of the field of international political economy. Although my values are those of liberalism, the world in which we live is one best described by the ideas of economic nationalism and occasionally by those of Marxism as well. Eclecticism may not be the route to theoretical precision, but sometimes it is the only route available.

The three ideologies differ on a broad range of questions such as: What is the significance of the market for economic growth and the distribution of wealth among groups and societies? What ought to be the role of markets in the organization of domestic and international society? What is the effect of the market system on issues of war or peace? These and similar questions are central to discussions of international political economy.

These three ideologies are fundamentally different in their conceptions of the relationships among society, state, and market, and it may not be an exaggeration to say that every controversy in the field of international political economy is ultimately reducible to differing conceptions of these relationships. The intellectual clash is not merely of historical interest. Economic liberalism, Marxism, and economic nationalism are all very much alive at the end of the twentieth century; they define the conflicting perspectives that individuals have with regard to the implications of the market system for domestic and international society. Many of the issues that were controversial in the eighteenth and nineteenth centuries are once again being intensely debated.

It is important to understand the nature and content of these contrasting 'ideologies' of political economy. The term 'ideology' is used rather than 'theory' because each position entails a total belief system concerning the nature of human beings and society and is thus akin to what Thomas Kuhn has called a paradigm (Kuhn, 1962). As Kuhn demonstrates, intellectual commitments are held tenaciously and can seldom be dislodged by logic or by contrary evidence. This is due to the fact that these commitments or ideologies allege to provide scientific descriptions of how the world *does* work while they also constitute normative positions regarding how the world *should* work.

Although scholars have produced a number of 'theories' to explain the relationship of economics and politics, these three stand out and have had a profound influence on scholarship and political affairs. In highly oversimplified terms, economic nationalism (or, as it was originally called, mercantilism), which developed from the practice of statesmen in the early modern period, assumes and advocates the primacy of politics over economics. It is essentially a doctrine of state-building and asserts that the market should be subordinate to the pursuit of state interests. It argues that political factors do, or at least should, determine economic relations. Liberalism, which emerged from the Enlightenment in the writings of Adam Smith and others, was a reaction to mercantilism and has become embodied in orthodox economics. It assumes that politics and economics exist, at least ideally, in separate spheres; it argues that markets – in the interest of efficiency, growth, and consumer choice – should be free from political interference. Marxism, which appeared in the mid-nineteenth century as a reaction against liberalism and classical economics, holds that economics drives politics. Political conflict arises from struggle among classes over the distribution of wealth. Hence, political conflict will cease with the elimination of the market and of a society of classes.

[Gilpin then provides a more detailed discussion of the three ideologies. He concludes that they represent 'intellectual commitments' or 'acts of faith' because they cannot be disproved by logical argument or empirical evidence. He goes on to present several reasons why ideologies are resistant to empirical testing.]

In the first place, they are based on assumptions about people or society that cannot be subjected to empirical tests. For example, the liberal concept of rational individuals cannot be verified or falsified; individuals who appear to be acting in conflict with their own interest may actually be acting on incorrect information or be seeking to maximize a goal unknown to the observer and thus be fulfilling the basic assumption of liberalism. Moreover, liberals would argue that although a particular individual in a particular case might be shown to have behaved irrationally, in the aggregate the assumption of rationality is a valid one.

Second, predictive failure of a perspective can always be argued away through the introduction into the analysis of ad hoc hypotheses. Marxism is replete with attempts to explain the predictive failures of Marxist theory. Lenin, for example, developed the concept of 'false consciousness' to account for the fact that workers became trade unionists rather than members of a revolutionary proletariat. Lenin's theory of capitalist imperialism may also be viewed as an effort to explain the failure of Marx's predictions regarding the collapse of capitalism. More recently, as will be discussed below, Marxists have been compelled to formulate elaborate theories of the state to explain the emergence of the welfare state and its acceptance by capitalists, a development that Lenin said was impossible.

Third, and most important, the three perspectives have different purposes and to some extent exist at different levels of analysis. Both nationalists and Marxists, for example, can accept most of liberal economics as a tool of analysis while rejecting many of its assumptions and normative foundations. Thus Marx used classical economics with great skill, but his purpose was to embody it in a grand theory of the origins, dynamics, and end of capitalism. The fundamental difference, in fact, between liberalism and Marxism involves the questions asked and their sociological assumptions rather than the economic methodology that they employ.

As reformulated by Lenin, Marxism has become nearly indistinguishable from the doctrine of political realism. Political realism, like economic nationalism, stresses the primacy of the state and national security. Although the two are very close, realism is essentially a political position whereas economic nationalism is an economic one. Or, put another way, economic nationalism is based on the realist doctrine of international relations.

Both in Lenin's theory and in political realism, states struggle for wealth and power, and the differential growth of power is the key to international conflict and political change. However, the assumptions of the two theories regarding the basis of human motivation, the theory of the state, and the nature of the international system are fundamentally different. Marxists regard human nature as malleable and as easily corrupted by capitalism and correctable by socialism; realists believe that political conflict results from an unchanging human nature.

Whereas Marxists believe that the state is ultimately the servant of the dominant economic class, realists see the state as a relative autonomous entity pursuing national interests that cannot be reduced to the particularistic interests of any class. For Marxists, the international system and foreign policy are determined by the structure of the domestic economy; for realists, the nature of the international system is the fundamental determinant of foreign policy. In short, Marxists regard war, imperialism, and the state as evil manifestations of a capitalism that will disappear with the communist revolution; realists hold them to be inevitable features of an anarchical international political system.

The difference between the two perspectives, therefore, is considerable. For the Marxist, though the state and the struggles among states are a consequence of the capitalist mode of production, the future will bring a realm of true harmony and peace following the inevitable revolution that the evil capitalist mode of production will spawn. The realist, on the other hand, believes there will be no such nirvana because of the inherently self-centered nature of human beings and the anarchy of the international system itself. The struggle among groups and states is virtually ceaseless, although there is occasionally a temporary respite. It seems unlikely that either prediction will ever receive scientific verification.

Each of the three perspectives has strengths and weaknesses, to be further explored below. Although no perspective provides a complete and satisfactory understanding of the nature and dynamism of the international political economy, together they provide useful insights.

CRITIQUE OF ECONOMIC LIBERALISM

Liberalism embodies a set of analytical tools and policy prescriptions that enable a society to maximize its return from scarce resources; its commitment to efficiency and the maximization of total wealth provides much of its strength. The market constitutes the most effective means for organizing economic relations, and the price mechanism operates to ensure that mutual gain and hence aggregate social benefit tend to result from economic exchange. In effect, liberal economics says to a society, whether domestic or international, 'if you wish to be wealthy, this is what you must do'.

From Adam Smith to the present, liberals have tried to discover the laws governing the wealth of nations. Although most liberals consider the laws of economics to be inviolable laws of nature, these laws may best be viewed as prescriptive guides for decision makers. If the laws are violated, there will be costs; the pursuit of objectives other than efficiency will necessarily involve an opportunity cost in terms of lost efficiency. Liberalism emphasizes the fact that such tradeoffs always exist in national policy. An emphasis on equity and redistribution, for example, is doomed to failure in the long run if it neglects considerations of efficiency. For a society to be efficient, as socialist economies have discovered, it cannot totally disregard the pertinent economic 'laws'.

The foremost defense of liberalism is perhaps a negative one. Although it may be true, as Marxists and some nationalists argue, that the alternative to a liberal system could be one in which all gain equally, it is also possible that the alternative could be one in which all *lose* in absolute terms. Much can be said for the liberal harmony of interest doctrine; yet, as E.H. Carr has pointed out, evidence to support this doctrine has generally been drawn from historical periods in which there was 'unparalleled expansion of production, population and prosperity' (Carr, 1951 [1939], p. 44). When sustaining conditions break down (as happened in the 1930s and threatens to occur again in the closing decades of the century), disharmony displaces harmony and, I shall argue, the consequent breakdown of liberal regimes tends to lead to economic conflict wherein everyone loses.

The major criticism leveled against economic liberalism is that its basic assumptions, such as the existence of rational economic actors, a competitive market, and the like, are unrealistic. In part, this attack is unfair in that liberals knowingly make these simplifying assumptions in order to facilitate scientific research; no science is possible without them. What is more important, as defenders correctly point out, is that they should be judged by their results and ability to predict rather than by their alleged reality. From this perspective and within its own sphere, economics has proven to be a powerful analytical tool. [...]

CRITIQUE OF ECONOMIC NATIONALISM

The foremost strength of economic nationalism is its focus on the state as the predominant actor in international relations and as an instrument of economic development. Although many have argued that modern economic and technological developments have made the nation-state an anachronism, at the end of the twentieth century the system of nation-states is actually expanding; societies throughout the world are seeking to create strong states capable of organizing and managing national economies, and the number of states in the world is increasing. Even in older states, the spirit of nationalist sentiments can easily be inflamed, as happened in the Falklands War of 1982. Although other actors such as transnational and international organizations do exist and do influence international relations, the economic and military efficiency of the state makes it preeminent over all these other actors.

The second strength of nationalism is its stress on the importance of security and political interests in the organization and conduct of international economic relations. One need not accept the nationalist emphasis on the primacy of security considerations to appreciate that the security of the state is a necessary precondition for its economic and political well-being in an anarchic and competitive state system. A state that fails to provide for its own security ceases to be independent. Whatever the objectives of the society, the effects of economic activities upon political independence and domestic welfare always rank high among its concerns.

The third strength of nationalism is its emphasis on the political framework of economic activities, its recognition that markets must function in a world of competitive groups and states. The political relations among these political actors affect the operation of markets just as markets affect the political relations. In fact, the international political system constitutes one of the most important constraints on and determinants of markets. Since states seek to influence markets to their own individual advantage, the role of power is crucial in the creation and sustaining of market relations; even Ricardo's classic example of the exchange of British woolens for Portuguese wine was not free from the exercise of state power. Indeed, as Carr has argued, every economic system must rest on a secure political base (Carr, 1951 [1939]).

One weakness of nationalism is its tendency to believe that international economic relations constitute solely and at all times a zero-sum game, that is, that one state's gain must of necessity be another's loss. Trade, investment, and all other economic relations are viewed by the nationalist primarily in conflictual and distributive terms. Yet, if cooperation occurs, markets *can* bring mutual (albeit not necessarily equal) gain, as the liberal insists. The possibility of benefit for all is the basis of the international market economy. Another weakness of nationalism is due to the fact that the pursuit of power and the pursuit of wealth usually do conflict, at least in the short run. The amassing and exercising of military and other forms of power entail costs to the society, costs that can undercut its economic efficiency. Thus, as Adam Smith argued, the mercantilist policies of eighteenth-century states that identified money with wealth were detrimental to the growth of the real wealth created by productivity increases; he demonstrated that the wealth of nations would have been better served by policies of free trade. Similarly, the tendency today to identify industry with power can weaken the economy of a state. Development of industries without regard to market consider-ations or comparative advantage can weaken a society economically. Although states in a situation of conflict must on occasion pursue mercantilistic goals and policies, over the long term, pursuit of these policies can be self-defeating.

In addition, nationalism lacks a satisfactory theory of domestic society, the state, and foreign policy. It tends to assume that society and state form a unitary entity and that foreign policy is determined by an objective national interest. Yet, as liberals correctly stress, society is pluralistic and consists of individuals and groups (coalitions of individuals) that try to capture the apparatus of the state and make it serve their own political and economic interests. Although states possess varying degrees of social autonomy and independence in the making of policy, foreign policy (including foreign economic policy) is in large measure the outcome of the conflicts among dominant groups within each society. Trade protectionism and most other nationalist policies result from attempts by one factor of production or another (capital, labor, or land) to acquire a monopoly position and thereby to increase its share of the economic rents. Nationalist policies are most frequently designed to redistribute income from consumers and society as a whole to producer interests. [...]

CRITIQUE OF MARXIST THEORY

Marxism correctly places the economic problem – the production and distribution of material wealth – where it belongs, at or near the center of political life. Whereas liberals tend to ignore the issue of distribution and nationalists are concerned primarily with the *international* distribution of wealth, Marxists focus on both the domestic and the international effects of a market economy on the distribution of wealth. They call attention to the ways in which the rules or regimes governing trade, investment, and other international economic relations affect the distribution of wealth among groups and states. However, it is not necessary to subscribe to the materialist interpretation of history or the primacy of class struggle in order to appreciate that the ways in which individuals earn their living and distribute wealth are a critical determinant of social structure and political behavior.

Another contribution of Marxism is its emphasis on the nature and structure of the division of labor at both the domestic and international levels. As Marx and Engels correctly pointed out in *The German Ideology*, every division of labor implies dependence and therefore a political relationship. In a market economy the economic nexus among groups and states becomes of critical importance in determining their welfare and their political relations. The Marxist analysis, however, is too limited, because economic interdependence is not the only or even the most important set of interstate relations. The political and strategic relations among political actors are of equal or greater significance and cannot be reduced to merely economic considerations, at least not as Marxists define economics.

The Marxist theory of international political economy is also valuable in its focus on international political change. Whereas neither liberalism nor nationalism has a comprehensive theory of social change, Marxism emphasizes the role of economic and technological developments in explaining the dynamics of the international system. As embodied in Lenin's law of uneven development, the differential growth of power among states constitutes an underlying cause of international political change. Lenin was at least partially correct in attributing the First World War to the uneven economic growth of power among industrial states and to conflict over the division of territory. There can be little doubt that the uneven growth of the several European powers and the consequent effects on the balance of power contributed to their collective insecurity. Competition for markets and empires did aggravate interstate relations. Furthermore, the average person's growing awareness of the effects on personal welfare and security of the vicissitudes of the world market and the economic behavior of other states also became a significant element in the arousal of nationalistic antagonisms. For nations and citizens alike, the growth of economic interdependence brought with it a new sense of insecurity, vulnerability, and resentment against foreign political and economic rivals.

Marxists are no doubt also correct in attributing to capitalist economies, at least as we have known them historically, a powerful impulse to expand through trade and especially through the export of capital. The classical liberal economists themselves observed that economic growth and the accumulation of capital create a tendency for the rate of return (profit) on capital to decline. These economists, however, also noted that the decline could be arrested through international trade, foreign investment, and other means. Whereas trade absorbs surplus capital in the manufacture of exports, foreign investment siphons off capital. Thus, classical liberals join Marxists in asserting that capitalist economies have an inherent tendency to export goods and surplus capital.

This tendency has led to the conclusion that the nature of capitalism is international and that its internal dynamics encourage outward expansionism. In a closed capitalist economy and in the absence of technological advance, underconsumption, surplus capital, and the resulting decline in the rate of profit would eventually lead to what John Stuart Mill called 'the stationary state'. Yet, in an open world economy characterized by expanding capitalism, population growth, and continuing improvement in productivity through technological advance, there is no inherent economic reason for economic stagnation to take place. [...]

The principal weakness of Marxism as a theory of international political economy results from its failure to appreciate the role of political and strategic factors in international relations. Although one can appreciate the insights of Marxism, it is not necessary to accept the Marxist theory that the dynamic of modern international relations is caused by the needs of capitalist economies to export goods and surplus capital. For example, to the extent that the uneven growth of national economies leads to war, this is due to national rivalries, which can occur regardless of the nature of domestic economies – witness the conflict between China and the Soviet Union. Although competition for markets and for capital outlets can certainly be a cause of tension and one factor causing imperialism and war, this does not provide an adequate explanation for the foreign policy behavior of capitalist states.

The historical evidence, for example, does not support Lenin's attribution of the First World War to the logic of capitalism and the market system. The most important territorial disputes among the European powers, which precipitated the war, were not those about overseas colonies, as Lenin argued, but lay within Europe itself. The principal conflict leading to the war involved redistribution of the Balkan territories of the decaying Ottoman Empire. And insofar as the source of this conflict was economic, it lay in the desire of the Russian state for access to the Mediterranean. Marxism cannot explain the fact that the three major imperial rivals – Great Britain, France, and Russia – were in fact on the same side in the ensuing conflict and that they fought against a Germany that had few foreign policy interests outside Europe itself.

In addition, Lenin was wrong in tracing the basic motive force of imperialism to the internal workings of the capitalist system. As Benjamin J. Cohen has pointed out in his analysis of the Marxist theory of imperialism, the political and strategic conflicts of the European powers were more important; it was at least in part the stalemate on the Continent among the Great Powers that forced their interstate competition into the colonial world. Every one of these colonial conflicts (if one excludes the Boer War) was in fact settled through diplomatic means. And, finally, the overseas colonies of the European powers were simply of little economic consequence. As Lenin's own data show, almost all European overseas investment was directed to the 'lands of recent settlement' (the United States, Canada, Australia, South Africa, Argentina, etc.) rather than to the dependent colonies in what today we call the Third World. In fact, contrary to Lenin's view that politics follows investment, international finance during this period was largely a servant of foreign policy, as was also the case with French loans to Czarist Russia. Thus, despite its proper focus on political change, Marxism is seriously flawed as a theory of political economy.

[Despite its serious limitations as a theory of the capitalist world economy, Gilpin insists that Marxists have drawn attention to three important issues in the contemporary world: (1) the economic and political implications of uneven economic growth; (2) the impact of the market economy on foreign policy; and (3) the capacity of a market economy to reform its less desirable features. Gilpin disagrees with the Marxist analyses of these issues and argues that the development of the welfare state has alleviated some of the problems identified by the Marxists. But he acknowledges that the future of capitalism remains problematic. He concludes by looking at the capacity of capitalism to survive.]

WELFARE CAPITALISM IN A NON-WELFARE INTERNATIONALIST CAPITALIST WORLD

[...] It is possible that, with the advent of the welfare state, the inherent contradictions of capitalism have simply been transferred from the domestic level of the nation-state to the international level. At this level there is no welfare state; there is no world government to apply Keynesian policies of demand management, to coordinate conflicting national policies, or to counter tendencies toward economic disequilibrium. In contrast to domestic society, there is no state to compensate the losers, as is exemplified in the dismissal by wealthy countries of the demands of the less developed countries for a New International Economic Order (NIEO); nor is there an effective international government response to cheating and market failures.

In the anarchy of international relations, the law of uneven development and the possibility of intracapitalist clashes still applies. One could even argue that the advent of national welfare states has accentuated the economic conflicts among capitalist societies. The new commitment of the capitalist welfare state to full employment and domestic economic well-being causes it to substitute interventionist policies for the free play of market forces and thereby brings it into conflict with the policies of other states pursuing a similar set of economic goals.

Welfare states are potentially highly nationalistic because governments have become accountable to their citizenry for the elimination of economic suffering; sometimes the best way to achieve this goal is to pass on economic difficulties to other societies. In times of economic crisis public pressures encourage national governments to shift the burdens of unemployment and economic adjustment to other societies; thus, economic and interstate competition through the market mechanism subtly shifts to interstate conflict for economic and political advantage. This nationalistic struggle to gain economic advantage and to shift the costs of economic distress to others again threatens the future of international capitalism.

The issue of the future of capitalist society in the era of the welfare state is central to the question of the applicability of the core of Marx's general theory of historical development to the world of the late twentieth century. One proposition of Marx's theory was that 'no social order ever perishes before all the productive forces for which there is room in it have developed; and new, higher relations of production never appear before the material conditions of their existence have matured in the womb of the old society itself' (Marx, 1977 [1859], p. 390), that is, one mode of production is not transcended by the next until it has exhausted its inherent productive potential. Each phase of human experience, according to Marxism, has its own historical mission to fulfill in elevating human productive capacities and thereby setting the stage for the phase to follow. Each mode advances until further progress is no longer possible; then historical necessity dictates that the fetters holding back society are removed by the class chosen to carry it to the next level of material achievement and human liberation.

The implications of this formulation are intriguing for the future of capitalism envisioned by Marxist theory. According to Marx, the historical function of capitalism was to develop the world and its productive potential and then to bequeath to its heir, socialism, a fully developed and industrialized world economy. Although Marx provided no timetable for this cataclysmic event to take place, he lived out his life in the expectation that the revolution was imminent.

As Albert Hirschman has shown, Marx failed to recognize (or more likely suppressed) the significance of these ideas for his analysis of the eventual demise of capitalism, that is, if no mode of production comes to an end until it plays out its historical role and if the assigned task of capitalism is to develop the world, then the capitalist mode of production has many decades, perhaps centuries or even millennia, yet to run (Hirschman, 1981, ch. 7). If one further discounts, as Marxists do, the 'limits to growth' argument, capitalism's assigned task of the economic development of the planet, including its oceans and nearby space, will require a very long time indeed.

Hirschman suggests that this must have been an uncomfortable thought for Marx, who until his dying day was so frequently disappointed in his longing to see the coming of the revolution. In Hirschman's view, this explains why Marx focused on European capitalism as a closed rather than an open economy and why he failed to develop a theory of imperialism even though one would have expected this of him as an assiduous student of Hegel. As Hirschman points out, Hegel anticipated all subsequent theories of capitalist imperialism.

Hirschman concludes that Marx, in his own writings, suppressed Hegel's theory of capitalist imperialism because of its disturbing implications for Marx's predictions concerning the survivability of capitalism. If no social system is displaced by another until it exhausts the productive potential inherent in it, then an imperialistic capitalism as it expands beyond Europe into Asia, Africa, and elsewhere will add new life to the capitalist mode of production. Through the mechanisms of overseas trade and foreign investment, the inevitable collapse of capitalism may thus be postponed for centuries. Indeed, if such a collapse must await the elevation of the developing world to the economic and technological levels of the most advanced economy, then in a world of continuing technological advance, the requisite full development of the productive capacities of capitalism may never be reached.

Rosa Luxemburg appears to have been the first major Marxist theorist to appreciate the historic significance of this reasoning; she argued that as long as capitalism remains an open system and there are underdeveloped lands into which the capitalist mode of production can expand, Marx's prediction of economic stagnation and political revolution will remain unfulfilled. In response to this troubling (at least for Marxists) prospect, Lenin's *Imperialism*, as noted earlier, transformed the Marxist critique of international capitalism. He argued that although capitalism does develop the world and is an economic success, the closing-in of political space through capitalist imperialism and the territorial division of the globe among rising and declining capitalist powers leads to international conflict. Thus, Lenin argued that the masses would revolt against capitalism as a war-prone political system rather than as a failed economic system.

Whether or not one accepts these several formulations and reformulations of Marxist thought, they do raise a fundamental issue. As Marx himself pointed out, the logic of the dynamics of a market or capitalist economy is expansive and international. The forces of the market reach out and bring the whole world within their confines, and they are destructive of traditional ways. The basic anarchy of the market mechanism produces instabilities in the lives of individuals and whole societies.

The modern welfare state and protectionism have developed to cushion these deleterious effects, and herein lies the most serious problem for the capitalist system and its survival. As Keynes appreciated, the logic of the welfare state is to close the economy, because the government must be able to isolate the economy from external restraints and disturbances in order to control and manage it. The international flow of trade, money, and finance undermines the Keynesian management of an economy by decreasing domestic policy autonomy. Goods, Keynes wrote at the height of the Great Depression, should be 'homespun', and capital should stay at home where it can benefit the nation and the nation's working class.

Thus, the logic of the market economy as an inherently expanding global system collides with the logic of the modern welfare state. While solving the problem of a closed economy, the welfare state has only transferred the fundamental problem of the market economy and its survivability to the international level. The problem of reconciling welfare capitalism at the domestic level with the nature of the international capitalist system has become of increasing importance.

The resolution of this basic dilemma between domestic autonomy and international norms is essential to the future viability of the market or capitalist economy. How can one reconcile these two opposed means of organizing economic affairs? Which will prevail – national economic interventionism or the rules of the international market economy? What are the conditions that promote peace and cooperation among market economies? Is a dominant or hegemonic power required to resolve the conflict? A look at the past successes and failures of international capitalism reveals that temporary resolutions of this dilemma or failures to resolve it have been crucial in recent history. In the 1980s the future of the world market economy and the continuing survival of the capitalist mode of production are dependent upon solutions developed or not developed by the United States and its major economic partners.

In another guise this was the problem posed by Richard Cooper in his influential book, *The Economics of Interdependence* (1968). An increasingly interdependent world economy requires either an international agreement to formulate and enforce the rules of an open world market economy and to facilitate the adjustment of differences or a high degree of policy coordination among capitalist states. Without one or the other, a market economy will tend to disintegrate into intense nationalist conflicts over trade, monetary arrangements, and domestic policies. With the relative decline of American power and its ability or willingness to manage the world economy, this issue has become preeminent in the world economy. If there is no increase in policy coordination or decrease in economic interdependence among the leading capitalist economies, the system could indeed break into warring states, just as Lenin predicted.

The long-term survivability of a capitalist or international market system, at least as we have known it since the end of the Second World War, continues to be problematic. Although the welfare state 'solved' the problem of domestic capitalism identified by Marx, continuing conflicts among capitalist societies over trade, foreign investment, and international monetary affairs in the contemporary world remind us that the debate between Lenin and Kautsky over the international nature of capitalism is still relevant. As American power and leadership decline due to the operation of the 'law of uneven development', will confrontation mount and the system collapse as one nation after another pursues 'beggar-my-neighbor' policies, as Lenin would expect? Or, will Kautsky prove to be correct that capitalists are too rational to permit this type of internecine economic slaughter to take place?

REFERENCES

Carr, E.H. (1951/1939) *The Twenty Years' Crisis, 1919–1939*, 2nd edn (Macmillan, London).

Cooper, R. (1968) *The Economics of Interdependence: Economic Policy in the Atlantic Community* (McGraw-Hill, New York).

Heilbroner, R.L. (1985) *The Nature and Logic of Capitalism* (W.W. Norton, New York).

Hirschman, A.O. (1981) *Essays in Trespassing: Economics to Politics and Beyond* (Cambridge University Press, New York).

Kuhn, T.S. (1962) *The Structure of Scientific Revolutions* (University of Chicago Press, Chicago).

Marx, K. (1977/1950) *Karl Marx: Selected Writings*, edited by David McClellan (Oxford University Press, Oxford).

4.3 The future of the American empire

Susan Strange

Source: *Journal of International Affairs*, vol. 42, no. 1 (1988), pp. 1–17.

Strange insists that arguments about the hegemonic decline of the United States have failed to take account of what she calls the structural power of the modern state. To do this, however, it is necessary to break away from the territorially based conception of power which has acted as a perspectival strait-jacket on attempts to understand the contemporary international system.

[Strange begins by arguing that the outcome of the debate about whether or not the US has lost its hegemonic status in the international system has practical consequences which will affect future policy choices by people in business, banking and government. The 'school of decline' is seen to make three claims: (1) the power of the US has declined; (2) Great Powers inevitably decline; (3) a likely consequence of the US decline will be political instability and economic disorder in the international system. Strange goes on to challenge each of these claims while accepting that we are approaching a fork in the road and that governments are facing 'momentous choices' ahead which may dwarf the outcome of the debate about US decline.]

AMERICAN POWER

Paul Kennedy, in common with the rest of the decline school, starts from the age-old premise that 'to be a great power demands a flourishing economic base'.[1] Following Adam Smith the liberal, and Friedrich List the mercantilist, this is then interpreted to mean an economic base of manufacturing industry located within the territorial boundaries of the state. It is this interpretation of 'a flourishing economic base' that is obsolete and therefore open to doubt. Smith and List are both long dead. More recent changes, noted by Peter

Drucker[2] among others, in the character of the world economy throw doubt on whether it is manufacturing that is now most important in developing the sinews of war; and, whether it is location within the boundaries of the territory that matters most.

My contention (which should surely be sustained by the champions of American service industries) is that it is the information-rich occupations, whether associated with manufacturing or not, that confer power, much more now than the physical capacity to roll goods off an assembly line. Secondly, I contend that the location of productive capacity is far less important than the location of the people who make the key decisions on what is to be produced, where and how, and who design, direct and manage to sell successfully on a world market. Is it more desirable that Americans should wear blue collars and mind the machines or that they should wear white collars and design, direct and finance the whole operation?

That is why all the figures so commonly trotted out about the US share of world manufacturing capacity, or the declining US share of world exports of manufactures are so misleading – *because they are territorially based.* Worse, they are irrelevant. What matters is the share of world output – of primary products, minerals and food and manufactured goods and services – that is under the direction of the executives of US companies. That share can be US-directed even if the enterprise directly responsible is only half owned by an American parent, and even, in some cases of technological dependence, where it is not owned at all but where the license to produce is granted or refused by people in the United States. The largest stock of foreign direct investments is still held by US corporations – even though the figures are neither precise, complete nor comprehensive. The fact that the current outflow from Japan is greater than that from the United States merely means that the gap is narrowing. But the Japanese still have a long way to go to rival the extent of US corporate operations in Europe, Latin America, Australasia, the Middle East and Africa, the assets of which are often valued at their historical prices not at their current values. [...]

At this point some people will object that when production moves away from the territory of the United States, the authority of the US government is diminished. At the same time, the same people sometimes complain against the 'invasion' of the United States by Japanese companies, as if 'selling off the farm' is diminishing the authority of the United States government. Clearly, both cannot be right. Rather, both perceptions seem to me to be wrong. What is happening is that the American Empire is spilling out beyond the frontier and that the very insubstantial nature of frontiers where production is concerned just shows the consolidation of an entirely new kind of nonterritorial empire.

It is that nonterritorial empire that is really the 'flourishing economic base' of US power, not the goods and services produced within the United States. One obvious indication of this fact is that foreign central banks last year spent roughly $140 billion supporting the exchange value of the dollar. Another is that Japanese and other foreign investors financed the lion's share of the US government's budget deficit by buying US government securities and investing in the United States. An empire that can command such resources hardly seems to be losing power. The fact that the United States is still the largest and richest (and mostly open) market for goods and services under one political authority means that all successful foreign companies will want to produce and sell there and will deem it prudent also to produce there, not simply to avoid protectionist barriers but in order to be close to the customers. And the worldwide reach of US-controlled enterprises also means that the capacity of the United States to exercise extraterritorial influence and authority is also greater than that of any other government. If only for security reasons, the ability of Washington to tell US companies in Japan what to do or not to do is immeasurably greater than the ability of Tokyo to tell Japanese companies in the United States what to do.

This points to another major fallacy in the decline school's logic – its inattention to matters of security. The US lead in the ability to make and deliver the means of nuclear destruction is the complement to its lead in influencing, through past investments overseas, the nature, modes and purposes of modern industrial production. Here, too, the gap may be narrowing as South Africa, Israel, India and others claim nuclear capability. Yet there is still no comparison between the military power of the United States to confer, deny or threaten the security of others with that of minor non-Communist states. That military power is now based far less on the capacity to manufacture nuclear weapons than on the capacity to recruit scientists, American or foreign, to keep ahead in design and invention, both offensive and defensive.

HISTORICAL PARALLELS

The decline school so far has succeeded in promoting the idea that history teaches that it is 'normal' for great states and empires to decline, especially when they become militarily overextended, or else when they become socially and politically sclerotic, risk-averse and resistant to change or when they overindulge in foreign investment, and for any or all of these reasons when they lose preeminence in agricultural and industrial production, or in trade and military capability. In almost all this American literature on the rise and fall of empires, great attention and weight is characteristically (and for reasons of language and culture, perhaps understandably) given to the British experience. But the trouble with history, as the first great realist writer on international relations, E.H. Carr, rightly observed, is that it is necessarily selective – and that the historian selects facts as a fish shop selects fish, choosing some and discarding or overlooking others. In this debate, the historical analogy between Britain and America is particularly weak; and the other examples selected for consideration show a strong tendency to concentrate on the empires whose decline after the peaking of their power was more or less steady and never reversed.

First, it is not too difficult to show that what Britain and America have had in common – such as a tendency to invest heavily overseas – is much less important than all the differences that mark their experience. Britain's economic decline, beginning around the 1880s, was the result of a neglect of the then advanced technologies – notably in chemicals and engineering. This neglect reflected the weakness and low status of manufacturing industry in British politics and society – a social disdain such as American industry has never had to contend with. Even more important was the effect of two long debilitating wars on the British economy, by comparison with which the American experience of Vietnam was a flea bite. It is arguable that the British economy, dependent as it was on financial power, would not have suffered so great a setback if the whole international financial system on which it lived and prospered had not been twice destroyed – first in the Great War and then in the Second World War. The interwar period was too short – and policies were also ill-chosen – to allow a reversal of this British decline.

Finally, there is the great difference between a small offshore island running a large territorial empire and a great continental power managing (or sometimes mismanaging) a large nonterritorial empire. The island state made the fatal mistake after the Second World War of relying on sheltered colonial and sterling area markets – with disastrous effects on the competitiveness of its export industries and even some of its old, established multinationals. The continental power's confidence in its ability to dominate an open world economy, plus the strong commitment to antitrust policies at home, has created no such weakening crutches for its major transnational corporations.

Secondly, any historical study of empires of the past fails to reveal any standard or uniform pattern of rise and fall. They are like trees. Some grow fast and fall suddenly without warning. Others grow slowly and decay very gradually, even making astonishing recoveries from shock or injury. One author, Michael Doyle, who has shared less in the media attention perhaps because his work lent itself less readily to deterministic interpretations, drew an important conclusion from an analytical survey of empires that included those of the ancient world as well as the later European ones. It is worth quoting:

> The historical alternatives had divided between persistence, which necessitated imperial development in both the metropole and the periphery, and decline and fall. Persistence in an extensive empire required that the metropole cross the Augustan threshold to imperial bureaucracy, and perhaps became in effect an equal political partner with the metropole.[3]

In plainer language, what I interpret this to mean is that the empires that lasted longest were those that managed to build a political system suited to the administration of the empire out of one suited to managing the core. In addition, those empires that survived managed to blur the distinction between the ruling groups of the core and the participating allies and associates of the periphery. This is a notion closely related to Gramscian concepts of hegemony and explanations of the persistent strength of capitalist political economies.

Michael Doyle's attention to the Roman Empire, which was much longer-lived than any of the nineteenth-century European empires, is important for the debate. This is so partly because there have been so many conflicting interpretations of its decline, from Edward Gibbon and Thomas Macaulay to Joseph Schumpeter and Max Weber, and partly because most historians seem to agree that it passed through periods of regeneration and reform before it finally broke up in disorder. Michael Mann, for instance, recently identified one such period of reform and regeneration in the twenty years after the accession of Septimus Severus in AD 193:

> Severus began withdrawing crack legions from the frontiers to mobile reserve positions, replacing them at the frontier with a settler militia. This was a more defensive, less confident posture. It also cost more, and so he attempted financial reform, abolishing tax farming and the tax exemption of Rome and Italy.[4]

This comment by a sociologist is interesting because it focuses on two important elements of power in imperial states: relations with key groups in the periphery, and the fiscal system by which unavoidable imperial expenditures are financed. When we consider the future of the American Empire, we find that these two issues are once again crucial to the outcome between Doyle's two alternatives – persistence or decline. Mann describes the Roman Empire as a 'legionary empire', indicating that the role and character of the legions were important in explaining Roman power.

I would argue that America's 'legions', in the integrated financial and production economy of today's world, are not military but economic. They are the corporate enterprises on which the military depends – as President Dwight Eisenhower foresaw in talking about the military–industrial complex. The American Empire in sociological terms therefore could be described as a 'corporation empire' in which the culture and interests of the corporations are sustained by an imperial bureaucracy. But this bureaucracy, largely set up after the Second World War, was not simply a national American one based in Washington, DC. A large and important part of it was and is multinational and works through the major international economic organizations such as the International Monetary Fund (IMF), the World Bank, the Organization for Economic Cooperation and Development (OECD) in Paris and the General Agreement on Tariffs and Trade (GATT) in Geneva.

The other feature of the Roman Empire that I believe is relevant to the current debate is that citizenship was not a matter of domicile, and that there were gradations of civil and political rights and responsibilities, ranging from slaves to senators, which did not depend on what we, today, understand by 'nationality', indicated by possession or nonpossession of a passport. If we can once escape the corset-like intellectual constraints of the conventional study of international relations and liberate our minds to ask new questions we begin to see new things about America's nonterritorial empire. Here, too, citizenship is becoming much more complex and graded than it used to be. The managers of US corporations, in Brazil, for example, may hold Brazilian and not US passports. But they are free to come and go with indefinite visas into the United States and they often exercise considerable delegated power in the running of US-directed enterprises vital to the Brazilian economy. Participation in the cultural empire depends not on passports but on competence in the American language and in many cases participation in US-based professional organizations – like the International Studies Association, for example. Similarly, participation in America's financial empire depends on the possession and use of US dollars and dollar-denominated assets and the ability to compete with US banks and in US financial markets.

Rather like a chrysalis in the metamorphosis from caterpillar to butterfly, the American Empire today combines features of a national-exclusive past with features of a transnational-extensive future. In military matters, it is still narrowly exclusive – though where advanced technology is concerned, even that is changing. Certainly, in financial and cultural matters, the distinction between first-class, passport-holding citizens and second-class, non-passport-holding participants is increasingly blurred. The peripheral allies have been unconsciously recruited into the American Empire. [...]

POWER AND SYSTEMIC DISORDER

The third proposition of the decline school has been the one under longest discussion among scholars in international relations. Over most of the past decade, the lead in these discussions has been taken by specialists in the study of international organizations (for example, Joseph Nye, Robert Keohane, John Ruggie and Ernst Haas). It seems to me that they share a wishful reluctance to admit that international organizations, when they are not simply adaptive mechanisms through which states respond to technical change, are either the strategic instruments of national policies and interests, or else merely symbolic gestures toward a desired but unattainable world government. This reluctance to admit the inherent limitations of international organizations leads them subconsciously to the conclusion that it must be hegemonic decline that is the cause of economic instability and disorder and the coincident erosion of earlier international regimes.

This is a proposition that does not stand up well either to the record of recent international economic history or to structural analysis of power in the international political economy. I do not want to repeat myself, but *Casino Capitalism* was an attempt to show two things (among others): there were more ways than one of interpreting recent developments in the international monetary and financial system; and, these developments of the last fifteen years or so could be traced to a series of crucial (and mostly permissive) decisions by governments. Hence, the precarious and unstable state of the global financial structure – which has already been dramatically demonstrated once and probably will be so again – was no fortuitous accident of fate or history.[5]

Since that book was written, I find confirmation that it was not a decline of American power but rather a series of American managerial decisions of dubious wisdom that accounts quite adequately for financial and monetary disorder, without any need to adduce the decline of American hegemonic power. Not only is this the theme of David Calleo's *The Imperious Economy*,[6] it is also to be found buried in the text of Robert Gilpin's chapters on international money and finance:

> Beginning with the Vietnam war and continuing into the Reagan Administration, the United States had become more of a 'predatory hegemon' to use John Conybeare's terms (1985), less willing to subordinate its own interests to those of its allies; instead it tended more and more to exploit its hegemonic status for its own narrowly defined purposes.[7]

Gilpin repeats the point twenty pages later, adding: 'Most of the troubles of the world economy in the 1980s have been caused by this shift in American policy.'

It will not escape careful students of this important text that Gilpin's historical analysis, and the use of the word 'mismanagement' with reference to American domestic and foreign financial policy, fundamentally contradicts his concluding thesis that a stable and prosperous world economy in the future calls for an American–Japanese condominium because of lost American hegemony.

Similarly, *States and Markets* extends the definition of international political economy beyond the conventional politics of international economic relations to ask more basic who-gets-what questions.[8] In that volume I find that a structural analysis of the basic issues in any political economy, when applied to the world system, strongly suggests that on balance American structural power may actually have increased in recent decades. It has done so through four interlocking structures. These structures concern the power conferred by the ability to offer, withhold or threaten security (the security structure); the ability to offer, withhold or demand credit (the financial structure); the ability to determine the locus, mode and content of wealth-creating activity (the production structure); and, not least, the ability to influence ideas and beliefs and therefore the kind of knowledge socially prized and sought after, and to control (and, through language, to influence) access to and communication of that knowledge (the knowledge structure).

Such a structural analysis suggests the existence under predominant American power and influence of an empire the likes of which the world has never seen before, a nonterritorial empire, whose only borders are the frontiers of the socialist great powers and their allies. It is not, in fact, such an eccentric idea. Two former US secretaries of state recently wrote:

> Far into the future, the United States will have the world's largest and most innovative economy, and will remain a nuclear super-power, a cultural and intellectual leader, a model democracy and a society that provides exceptionally well for its citizens.[9]

WHAT, THEN, MUST BE DONE?

[Strange concludes by warning that because the world is at a 'critical juncture' the US must use it enormous structural power and take the lead in future developments. This will involve forging a symbiotic relationship with Japan on the basis of an international 'new deal'. Other new deals will need to be struck with other areas of the world.]

New Deals, however, do not drop like manna from heaven. They do not come about without political vision and inspiration, or without hard intellectual effort to find the sustaining optimal bargain. Optimal bargains are those that last because they go some way to satisfy the needs and aspirations of the governed as well as those of the governors. Only then can the power of those in charge of empires (as of states, local party machines or labor unions) be sustained over the long run. The next four years will show not only Americans but the rest of us who live and work in the American Empire whether the defeatist gloom of the school of decline can be dissipated. They will show whether the necessary vision can still be found in the White House for a series of global New Deals and whether the necessary intellectual effort to design and negotiate them will be generated not only in the bureaucracies, national and international, but in the universities and research institutes of all our countries.

NOTES

1   Paul Kennedy, *The Rise and Fall of the Great Powers: Economic Change and Military Conflict from 1500 to 2000* (New York, Random House, 1987).
2   Peter F. Drucker, 'The Changed World Economy', *Foreign Affairs*, 64: 4 (Spring 1986), pp. 768–91.
3   Michael Doyle, *Empires* (Cornell University Press, Ithaca, 1986), p. 353.

4   Michael Mann, *The Sources of Social Power*, vol. 1 (Cambridge University Press, New York, 1986).
5   Susan Strange, *Casino Capitalism* (Basil Blackwell, New York, 1986).
6   David P. Calleo, *The Imperious Economy* (Harvard University Press, Cambridge, Mass., 1962).
7   Robert Gilpin, *The Political Economy of International Relations* (Princeton University Press, Princeton, New Jersey, 1987), p. 345.
8   Susan Strange, *States and Markets* (Frances Pinter, London, 1988).
9   Henry Kissinger and Cyrus Vance, 'Bipartisan Objectives for American Foreign Policy', *Foreign Affairs*, 66: 5 (Summer 1988), pp. 899–921.

4.4 Social forces, states and world orders: beyond international relations theory

Robert W. Cox

Source: *Journal of International Studies: Millennium*, vol. 10, no. 2 (1981), pp. 126–55.

Cox is interested in the way that the structure of world order can change and he argues that to understand this process it is necessary to develop a methodology which can transcend the outlook of any specific perspective. The problem with the dominant perspective of realism is that it claims to have identified ahistorical truths. The claim, according to Cox, is ideological. He identifies realism as a problem-solving form of theory which works within and helps to sustain a state-dominated world order. Cox argues in favour of a critical form of theory which focuses not only on how a particular form of world order is maintained but also on how it can be transformed.

[Cox begins by arguing that theory must always be based upon changing practice and empirical historical study.]

ON PERSPECTIVES AND PURPOSES

Theory is always *for* someone and *for* some purpose. All theories have a perspective. Perspectives derive from a position in time and space, specifically social and political time and space. The world is seen from a standpoint definable in terms of nation or social class, of dominance or subordination, of rising or declining power, of a sense of immobility or of present crisis, of past experience, and of hopes and expectations for the future. Of course, sophisticated theory is never just the expression of a perspective. The more sophisticated a theory is, the more it reflects upon and transcends its own perspective; but the initial perspective is always contained within a theory and is relevant to its explication. There is, accordingly, no such thing as theory in itself, divorced from a standpoint in time and space. When any theory so represents itself, it is the more important to examine it as ideology, and to lay bare its concealed perspective.

To each such perspective the enveloping world raises a number of issues; the pressures of social reality present themselves to consciousness as problems. A primary task of theory is to become clearly aware of these problems, to enable the mind to come to grips with the reality it confronts. Thus, as reality changes, old concepts have to be adjusted or rejected and new concepts forged in an initial dialogue between the theorist and the particular world he tries to comprehend. This initial dialogue concerns the *problematic* proper to a particular perspective. Social and political theory is history-bound at its origin, since it is always traceable to a historically conditioned awareness of certain problems and issues, a problematic, while at the same time it attempts to transcend the particularity of its historical origins in order to place them within the framework of some general propositions or laws.

Beginning with its problematic, theory can serve two distinct purposes. One is a simple, direct response: to be a guide to help solve the problems posed within the terms of the particular perspective which was the point of departure. The other is more reflective upon the process of theorizing itself: to become clearly aware of the perspective which gives rise to theorizing, and its relation to other perspectives (to achieve a perspective on perspectives); and to open up the possibility of choosing a different valid perspective from which the problematic becomes one of creating an alternative world. Each of these purposes gives rise to a different kind of theory.

The first purpose gives rise to *problem-solving* theory. It takes the world as it finds it, with the prevailing social and power relationships and the institutions into which they are organized, as the given framework for action. The general aim of problem-solving is to make these relationships and institutions work smoothly by dealing effectively with particular sources of trouble. Since the general pattern of institutions and relationships is not called into question, particular problems can be considered in relation to the specialized areas of activity in which they arise. Problem-solving theories are thus fragmented among a multiplicity of spheres or aspects of action, each of which assumes a certain stability in the other spheres (which enables them in practice to be ignored) when confronting a problem arising within its own. The strength of the problem-solving approach lies in its ability to fix limits or parameters to a problem area and to reduce the statement of a particular problem to a limited number of variables which are amenable to relatively close and precise examination. The *ceteris paribus* assumption, upon which such theorizing is based, makes it possible to arrive at statements of laws or regularities which appear to have general validity but which imply, of course, the institutional and relational parameters assumed in the problem-solving approach.

The second purpose leads to *critical theory*. It is critical in the sense that it stands apart from the prevailing order of the world and asks how that order came about. Critical theory, unlike problem-solving theory, does not take institutions and social and power relations for granted but calls them into question by concerning itself with their origins and how and whether they might be in the process of changing. It is directed toward an appraisal of the very framework for action, or problematic, which problem-solving theory accepts as its parameters. Critical theory is directed to the social and political complex as a whole rather than to the separate parts. As a matter of practice, critical theory, like problem-solving theory, takes as its starting point some aspect or particular sphere of human activity. But whereas the problem-solving approach leads to further analytical subdivision and limitation of the issue to be dealt with, the critical approach leads toward the construction of a larger picture of the whole of which the initially contemplated part is just one component, and seeks to understand the processes of change in which both parts and whole are involved.

Critical theory is theory of history in the sense of being concerned not just with the past but with a continuing process of historical change. Problem-solving theory is nonhistorical or ahistorical, since it, in effect, posits a continuing present (the permanence of the institutions and power relations which constitute its parameters). The strength of the one is the weakness of the other. Because it deals with a changing reality, critical theory must continually adjust its concepts to the changing object it seeks to understand and explain. These concepts and the accompanying methods of inquiry seem to lack the precision that can be achieved by problem-solving theory, which posits a fixed order as its point of reference. This relative strength of problem-solving theory, however, rests upon a false premise, since the social and political order is not fixed but (at least in a long-range perspective) is changing. Moreover, the assumption of fixity is not merely a convenience of method, but also an ideological bias. Problem-solving theories can be represented, in the broader perspective of critical theory, as serving particular national, sectional, or class interests, which are comfortable within the given order. Indeed, the purpose served by problem-solving theory is conservative, since it aims to solve the problems arising in various parts of a complex whole in order to smooth the functioning of the whole. This aim rather belies the frequent claim of problem-solving theory to be value-free. It is methodologically value-free insofar as it treats the variables it considers as objects (as the chemist treats molecules or the physicist forces and motion); but it is value-bound by virtue of the fact that it implicitly accepts the prevailing order as its own framework. Critical theory contains problem-solving theories within itself, but contains them in the form of identifiable ideologies, thereby pointing to their conservative consequences, not to their usefulness as guides to action. Problem-solving theory stakes its claims on its greater precision and, to the extent that it recognizes critical theory at all, challenges the possibility of achieving any scientific knowledge of historical processes.

Critical theory is, of course, not unconcerned with the problems of the real world. Its aims are just as practical as those of problem-solving theory, but it approaches practice from a perspective which transcends that of the existing order, which problem-solving theory takes as its starting point. Critical theory allows for a normative choice in favor of a social and political order different from the prevailing order, but it limits the range of choice to alternative orders which are feasible transformations of the existing world. A principal objective of critical theory, therefore, is to clarify this range of possible alternatives. Critical theory thus contains an element of utopianism in the sense that it can represent a coherent picture of an alternative order, but its utopianism is constrained by its comprehension of historical processes. It must reject improbable alternatives just as it rejects the permanency of the existing order. In this way critical theory can be a guide to strategic action for bringing about an alternative order, whereas problem-solving theory is a guide to tactical actions which, intended or unintended, sustain the existing order.

The perspectives of different historical periods favor one or the other kind of theory. Periods of apparent stability or fixity in power relations favor the problem-solving approach. The Cold War was one such period. In international relations, it fostered a concentration upon the problems of how to manage an apparently enduring relationship between two superpowers. However, a condition of uncertainty in power relations beckons to critical theory as people seek to understand the opportunities and risks of change. Thus the events of the 1970s generated a sense of greater fluidity in power relationships, of a many-faceted crisis, crossing the threshold of uncertainty and opening the opportunity for a new development of critical theory directed to the problems of world order. To reason about possible future world orders now, however, requires a broadening of our inquiry beyond conventional international relations, so as to encompass basic processes at work in the development of social forces and forms of state, and in the structure of global political economy. Such, at least, is the central argument of this essay.

[Cox goes on to argue that there are two currents of thought – realism and Marxism – which have something important to say about international relations and world order. He suggests that while both draw on problem-solving and critical theory, realism is primarily informed by problem-solving theory whereas Marxism is informed by critical theory. He then restates the basic premises which underlie critical theory.]

(1) An awareness that action is never absolutely free but takes place within a framework for action which constitutes its problematic. Critical theory would start with this framework, which means starting with historical inquiry or an appreciation of the human experience that gives rise to the need for theory.

(2) A realization that not only action but also theory is shaped by the problematic. Critical theory is conscious of its own relativity but through this consciousness can achieve a broader time-perspective and become less relative than problem-solving theory. It knows that the task of theorizing can never be finished in an enclosed system but must continually be begun anew.

(3) The framework for action changes over time and a principal goal of critical theory is to understand these changes.

(4) This framework has the form of a historical structure, a particular combination of thought patterns, material conditions and human institutions which has a certain coherence among its elements. These structures do not determine people's actions in any mechanical sense but constitute the context of habits, pressures, expectations and constraints within which action takes place.

(5) The framework or structure within which action takes place is to be viewed, not from the top in terms of the requisites for its equilibrium or reproduction (which would quickly lead back to problem-solving), but rather from the bottom or from outside in terms of the conflicts which arise within it and open the possibility of its transformation.

FRAMEWORKS FOR ACTION: HISTORICAL STRUCTURES

At its most abstract, the notion of a framework for action or historical structure is a picture of a particular configuration of forces. This configuration does not determine actions in any direct, mechanical way but imposes pressures and constraints. Individuals and groups may move with the pressures or resist and oppose them, but they cannot ignore them. To the extent that they do successfully resist a prevailing historical structure, they buttress their actions with an alternative, emerging configuration of forces, a rival structure.

Three categories of forces (expressed as potentials) interact in a structure: material capabilities, ideas and institutions (see Figure 1). No one-way determinism need be assumed among these three; the relationships can be assumed to be reciprocal. The question of which way the lines of force run is always a historical question to be answered by a study of the particular case.

Figure 1

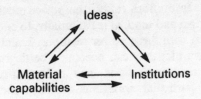

Material capabilities are productive and destructive potentials. In their dynamic form these exist as technological and organizational capabilities, and in their accumulated forms as natural resources which technology can transform, stocks of equipment (for example, industries and armaments), and the wealth which can command these.

Ideas are broadly of two kinds. One kind consists of intersubjective meanings, or those shared notions of the nature of social relations which tend to perpetuate habits and expectations of behavior. Examples of intersubjective meanings in contemporary world politics are the notions that people are organized and commanded by states which have authority over defined territories; that states relate to one another through diplomatic agents; that certain rules apply for the protection of diplomatic agents as being in the common interest of all states; and that certain kinds of behavior are to be expected when conflict arises between states, such as negotiation, confrontation, or war. These notions, though durable over long periods of time, are historically conditioned. The realities of world politics have not always been represented in precisely this way and may not be in the future. It is possible to trace the origins of such ideas and also to detect signs of a weakening of some of them.

The other kind of ideas relevant to a historical structure are collective images of social order held by different groups of people. These are differing views as to both the nature and the legitimacy of prevailing power relations, the meanings of justice and public good, and so forth. Whereas intersubjective meanings are broadly common throughout a particular historical structure and constitute the common ground of social discourse (including conflict), collective images may be several and opposed. The clash of rival collective images provides evidence of the potential for alternative paths of development and raises questions as to the possible material and institutional basis for the emergence of an alternative structure.

Institutionalization is a means of stabilizing and perpetuating a particular order. Institutions reflect the power relations prevailing at their point of origin and tend, at least initially, to encourage collective images consistent with these power relations. Eventually, institutions take on their own life; they can become a battleground of opposing tendencies, or rival institutions may reflect different tendencies. Institutions are particular amalgams of ideas and material power which in turn influence the development of ideas and material capabilities.

There is a close connection between institutionalization and what Gramsci called hegemony. Institutions provide ways of dealing with conflicts so as to minimize the use of force. There is an enforcement potential in the material power relations underlying any structure, in that the strong can clobber the weak if they think it necessary. But force will not have to be used in order to ensure the dominance of the strong to the extent that the weak accept the prevailing power relations as legitimate. This the weak may do if the strong see their mission as hegemonic and not merely dominant or dictatorial, that is, if they are willing to make concessions that will secure the weak's acquiescence in their leadership and if they can express this leadership in terms of universal or general interests, rather than just as serving their own particular interests. Institutions may become the anchor for such a hegemonic strategy since they lend themselves both to the representations of diverse interests and to the universalization of policy.

It is convenient to be able to distinguish between hegemonic and nonhegemonic structures, that is to say between those in which the power basis of the structure tends to recede into the background of consciousness, and those in which the management of power relations is always in the forefront. Hegemony cannot, however, be reduced to an institutional dimension. One must beware of allowing a focus upon institutions to obscure either changes in the relationship of material forces, or the emergence of ideological challenge to an erstwhile prevailing order. Institutions may be out of phase with these other aspects of reality and their efficacy as a means of regulating conflict (and thus their hegemonic function) thereby undermined. They may be an expression of hegemony but cannot be taken as identical to hegemony.

The method of historical structures is one of representing what can be called limited totalities. The historical structure does not represent the whole world but rather a particular sphere of human activity in its historically located totality. The *ceteris paribus* problem, which falsifies problem-solving theory by leading to an assumption of total stasis, is avoided by juxtaposing the connecting historical structures in related spheres of action. Dialectic is introduced, first, by deriving the definition of a particular structure, not from some abstract model of a social system or mode of production, but from a study of the historical situation to which it relates, and second, by looking for the emergence of rival structures expressing alternative possibilities of development. The three sets of forces indicated in Figure 1 are a heuristic device, not categories with a predetermined hierarchy of relationships. Historical structures are contrast models: like ideal types they provide, in a logically coherent form, a simplified representation of a complex reality and an expression of tendencies, limited in their applicability in time and space, rather than fully realized developments.

For the purpose of the present discussion, the method of historical structures is applied to the three levels, or spheres of activity: (1) organization of production, more particularly with regard to the *social forces* engendered by the production process; (2) *forms of state* as derived from a study of state/society complexes; and (3) *world orders*, that is, the particular configurations of forces which successively define the problematic of war or peace for the ensemble of states. Each of these levels can be studied as a succession of dominant and emergent rival structures.

The three levels are interrelated. Changes in the organization of production generate new social forces which, in turn, bring about changes in the structure of states; and the generalization of changes in the structure of states alters the problematic of world order. For instance, as E.H. Carr (1945) argued, the incorporation of the industrial workers (a new social force) as participants within western states from the late nineteenth century, accentuated the movement of these states toward economic nationalism and imperialism (a new form of state), which brought about a fragmentation of the world economy and a more conflictual phase of international relations (the new structure of world order).

The relationship among the three levels is not, however, simply unilinear. Transnational social forces have influenced states through the world structure, as evidenced by the effect of expansive nine-teenth-century capitalism, *les bourgeois conquérants*, upon the de-velopment of state structures in both core and periphery. Particular structures of world order exert influence over the forms which states take: Stalinism was, at least in part, a response to a sense of threat to the existence of the Soviet state from a hostile world order; the military–industrial complex in core countries justifies its influence today by pointing to the conflictual condition of world order; and the prevalence of repressive militarism in periphery countries can be explained by the external support of imperialism as well as by a particular conjunction of internal forces. Forms of state also affect the development of social forces through the kinds of domination they exert, for example, by advancing one class interest and thwarting others.

Considered separately, social forces, forms of state, and world orders can be represented in a preliminary approximation as par-ticular configurations of material capabilities, ideas and institutions (as indicated in Figure 1). Considered in relation to each other, and thus moving toward a fuller representation of historical process, each will be seen as containing, as well as bearing the impact of, the others (as in Figure 2).

Figure 2

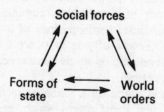

HEGEMONY AND WORLD ORDERS

How are these reciprocal relationships to be read in the present historical conjuncture? Which of the several relationships will tell us the most? A sense of the historicity of concepts suggests that the critical relationships may not be the same in successive historical periods, even within the post-Westphalian era for which the term 'state system' has particular meaning. The approach to a critical theory of world order, adumbrated here, takes the form of an interconnected series of historical hypotheses.

Neo-realism puts the accent on states reduced to their dimension of material force and similarly reduces the structure of world order to the balance of power as a configuration of material forces. Neo-realism, which generally dismisses social forces as irrelevant, is not much concerned with differentiating forms of state (except insofar as 'strong societies' in liberal democratic polities may hamper the use of force by the state or advance particular interests over the national interest), and tends to place a low value on the normative and institutional aspects of world order.

One effort to broaden the realist perspective to include variations in the authority of international norms and institutions is the theory of 'hegemonic stability' which, as stated by Robert Keohane (1980), 'holds that hegemonic structures of power, dominated by a single country, are most conducive to the development of strong international regimes, whose rules are relatively precise and well-obeyed'. The classic illustrations of the theory discussed by Keohane are the *pax britannica* of the mid-nineteenth century and the *pax americana* of the years following the Second World War. The theory appears to be confirmed by the decline in observance of the norms of the nineteenth-century order which accompanied Britain's relative decline in state power from the late-nineteenth century. Exponents of the theory see a similar decline, since the early 1970s, in the observance of norms of the postwar order, relating it to a relative decline in US power. Robert Keohane has tested the theory in particular issue areas (energy, money and trade) on the grounds that power is not a fungible asset, but has to be differentiated according to the contexts in which a state tried to be influential. He finds that, particularly in the areas of trade and money, changes in US power are insufficient to explain the changes that have occurred and need to be supplemented by the introduction of domestic political, economic and cultural factors.

An alternative approach might start by redefining what it is that is to be explained, namely, the relative stability of successive world orders. This can be done by equating stability with a concept of hegemony that is based on a coherent conjunction or fit between a configuration of material power, the prevalent collective image of world order (including certain norms) and a set of institutions which administer the order with a certain semblance of universality (that is, not just as the overt instruments of a particular state's dominance). In this formulation, state power ceases to be the sole explanatory factor and becomes part of what is to be explained. This rephrasing of the question addresses a major difficulty in the neo-realist version signalled by Keohane and others, namely, how to explain the failure of the United States to establish a stable world order in the interwar period despite its preponderance of power. If the dominance of a single state coincides with a stable order on some occasions but not on others, then there may be some merit in looking more closely at what is meant by stability and more broadly at what may be its sufficient conditions. Dominance by a powerful state may be a necessary but not a sufficient condition of hegemony.

The two periods of the *pax britannica* and the *pax americana* also satisfy the reformulated definition of hegemony. In the mid-nineteenth century, Britain's world supremacy was founded on its sea power, which remained free from challenge by a continental state as a result of Britain's ability to play the role of balancer in a relatively fluid balance of power in Europe. The norms of liberal economics (free trade, the gold standard, free movement of capital and persons) gained widespread acceptance with the spread of British prestige, providing a universalistic ideology which represented these norms as the basis of a harmony of interests. While there were no formal international institutions, the ideological separation of economics from politics meant that the City could appear as administrator and regulator according to these universal rules, with British sea power remaining in the background as potential enforcer.

The historical structure was transformed in its three dimensions during the period running from the last quarter of the nineteenth century through the Second World War. During this period British power declined relatively, losing its undisputed supremacy at sea, first with the German challenge and then with the rise of US power; economic liberalism foundered with the rise of protectionism, the new imperialisms and ultimately the end of the gold standard; and the belated and abortive attempt at international institutionalization through the League of Nations, unsustained either by a dominant power or a widely accepted ideology, collapsed in a world increasingly organized into rival power blocs.

The power configuration of the *pax americana* was more rigid than that of the earlier hegemony, taking the form of alliances (all hinging on US power) created in order to contain the Soviet Union. The stabilization of this power configuration created the conditions for the unfolding of a global economy in which the United States played a role similar to that of Britain in the mid-nineteenth century. The United States rarely needed to intervene directly in support of specific national economic interests; by maintaining the rules of an international economic order according to the revised liberalism of Bretton Woods, the strength of US corporations engaged in the pursuit of profits was sufficient to ensure continuing national power. The *pax americana* produced a greater number of formal international institutions than the earlier hegemony. The nineteenth-century separation of politics and economics had been blurred by the experience of the Great Depression and the rise of Keynesian doctrines. Since states now had a legitimate and necessary overt role in national economic management, it became necessary both to multilateralize the administrative management of the international economy and to give it an intergovernmental quality.

The notion of hegemony as a fit between power, ideas and institutions makes it possible to deal with some of the problems in the theory of state dominance as the necessary condition for a stable international order; it allows for lags and leads in hegemony. For example, so appealing was the nostalgia for the nineteenth-century hegemony that the ideological dimension of the *pax britannica* flourished long after the power configuration that supported it had vanished. Sustained, and ultimately futile, efforts were made to revive a liberal world economy along with the gold standard in the interwar period. Even in the postwar period, British policy continued to give precedence to balance of payments problems over national industrial development and employment considerations. A 'lead' case is that of the United States, where the growth indicators of material power during the interwar period were insufficient predictors of a new hegemony. It was necessary that US leaders should come to see themselves in ideological terms as the necessary guarantors of a new world order. The Roosevelt era made this transition, including both the conscious rejection of the old hegemony (e.g. by torpedoing the world economic conference in 1933 and abandoning the gold standard) and the gradual incorporation of New-Deal principles into the ideological basis of the new world order. There followed US initiative to create the institutions to administer this order. Neo-mercantilists in the United States now warn against a danger of repeating the British error, urging US policymakers not to continue to operate according to doctrines appropriate to the *pax americana* when the United States can no longer afford to act as guarantor for a universalist world order. Their persuasive efforts underline the point that in these matters ideology is a determining sphere of action which has to be understood in its connections with material power relations.

[In the final section (not reproduced here) Cox goes on to argue that social forces now flow across state boundaries. As a consequence, states have started to play an intermediate, albeit autonomous, role between local and global structures. Using this insight, it becomes possible to understand how the nature of states and the configuration of power between them has changed over the last century.]

4.5 Reflections on war and political discourse: realism, just war, and feminism in a nuclear age

Jean Bethke Elshtain

Source: *Political Theory*, vol. 13, no. 1 (1985), pp. 39–57.

Elshtain accepts that the study of international relations and war has been dominated by a realist tradition, despite the existence of the long-standing rival just war tradition. She asserts, however, referring to the work of Hannah Arendt, that a feminist perspective not only makes it possible to deconstruct realist rhetoric and reveal its inconsistencies, but also can be used to open up a new and more hopeful line of discourse about war and international relations.

WHAT MAKES REALISM RUN?

[...] Historic realism involves a way of thinking – a set of presumptions about the human condition that secretes images of men and women and the parts they play in the human drama; and, as well, a potent rhetoric. Whether in its uncompromising Hobbesian version or the less remorseless Machiavellian narrative, realism exaggerates certain features of the human condition and downgrades or ignores others. Interpreting foundational realist texts from a vantage point informed by feminist concerns, one is struck by the suppression and denial of female images and female-linked imperatives, hence alert to the restricted and oversimplifying terms through which realism constitutes symbolism and narrative roles more generally.

For example, Hobbes describes a world of hostile monads whose relations are dominated by fear, force, and instrumental calculation. Yet (and almost simple-mindedly) we know this to be anthropologically false. From the simplest tribal beginnings to the most complex social forms, women have had to tend to infants – no matter what the men were up to – if life was to go on in any sustained manner. That important features of the human condition are expunged from Hobbes's universe suggests that his realism is a dramatic distortion rather than a scientific depiction of the human condition at rock bottom. To acknowledge this by insisting that the state of nature is an

457

analytic fiction fails to address the concerns I raise here. Fictions are also truths and what gets left out is often as important as what is put in and assumed.

To be sure, the contemporary realist is unlikely to endorse a full constellation of Hobbesian presumptions. He might reject Hobbes's vision of the state of nature, and his depiction of social relations, as dire and excessive. It is likely, however, that he would continue to affirm the wider conclusions Hobbes drew by analogy from the miserable condition of human beings in the state of nature to the unrelenting fears and suspicions of states in their relations to one another. Yet it seems plausible that if Hobbes omitted central features of human existence internal to civil societies and families, perhaps he is guilty of similar one-sidedness in his characterization of the world of states. To take up this latter possibility is to treat Hobbes's realism as problematic, not paradigmatic.

Machiavelli goes down more smoothly in large part because we have internalized so much of his legacy already. We all know the story. Human beings are inconstant and trustworthy only in their untrustworthiness. Political action cannot be judged by the standards of Christian morality. Civic virtue requires troops 'well disciplined and trained' in times of peace in order to prepare for war: this is a 'necessity', a law of history. *Si vis pacem, para bellum*, a lesson successive generations (or so the story goes) must learn, though some tragically learn it too late, others in the nick of time.

Machiavelli's narrative revolves around a public–private split in and through which women are constituted, variously, as mirrors to male war-making (a kind of civic cheerleader) or as a collective 'other', embodying the softer values and virtues out of place within, and subversive of, *realpolitik*. Immunized from political action, the realist female may honor the Penates but she cannot embark on a project to bring her values to bear on the civic life of her society. J.G.A. Pocock calls Machiavelli's 'militarization of citizenship' a potent legacy that subverts (even for some feminists, as I argue below) consideration of alternatives that do not bind civic and martial virtue together. Military preparedness, in this narrative, becomes the sine qua non of a viable polity. Although women cannot embody armed civic virtue, a task for the man, they are sometimes drawn into the realist picture more sharply as occasions for war (we must fight to protect her), as goads to action, as designated weepers over the tragedies war trails in its wake, or, in our own time, as male prototypes mobilized to meet dwindling 'manpower' needs for the armed forces.

Rethinking realism using feminist questions defamiliarizes its central categories: the male *homme de guerre* retains his preeminent role, to be sure, but we recognize explicitly the ways in which his soldierly virilization is linked to the realist woman's privatization, and so on. But matters are never quite so simple. There are variants of modern feminist argumentation indebted to realist discourse in its Hobbesian and Machiavellian modes respectively.

Hard-line feminist realists, for example, endorse a Hobbesian social ontology and construe politics as a battleground, the continuation of war by war-like means. They advise women to learn to 'fight dirty'. Making generous use of military metaphors (Who is the enemy? Where is he located?), Hobbesian feminists declare politics and political theory inevitably a 'paradigm case of the Oppressor and the Oppressed'.[1] There is tough talk about sex-war, shock troops, and the need for women to be integrated into the extant power structure construed as the aggregate of all those who defend law and order, wear uniforms, or carry guns for a living – 'the national guard ... state troopers ... sheriffs'. Women are enjoined to prepare for combat as the only way to end their 'colonization'.[2]

Such feminist realists share with their Hobbesian forefather a self-reproducing discourse of fear, suspicion, anticipated violence, and force to check-mate force. Their discussions are peppered with worst-case scenarios and proclamations of supreme emergency that reaffirm the bleakest images of 'the enemy' and pump up the will to power of combatants. Possibilities for reciprocity between men and women, or for a politics not reducible to who controls or coerces whom, are denied in much the same way Hobbes eliminates space for any noninstrumental human relations.

This hard-line position is less important, however, than the modified realism, more Machiavellian in its claims and categories, expressed in a 1981 legal brief filed by the National Organization for Women as part of a challenge to all-male military registration. Beginning with the claim that compulsory, universal military service is central to the concept of citizenship in a democracy, NOW buttresses an ideal of armed civic virtue. If women are to gain 'first-class citizenship' they, too, must have the right to fight. Laws excluding women from draft registration and combat duty perpetuate 'archaic notions' of women's capabilities; moreover, 'devastating long-term psychological and political repercussions' are visited upon women given their exclusion from the military of their country.

NOW's brand of equal opportunity or integrationist feminism here loses a critical edge, functioning instead to reinforce 'the military as an institution and militarism as an ideology' by perpetuating 'the notion that the military is so central to the entire social order that it is only when women gain access to its core that they can hope to fulfill their hopes and aspirations'.[3] In its deep structure, NOW's legal narrative is a leap out of the female/private side of the public/private divide basic to Machiavellian realism and straight into the arms of the hegemonic male whose sex-linked activities are valorized thereby. Paradoxically, NOW's repudiation of 'archaic notions of women's role' becomes a tribute to 'archaic notions of men's role'. Because of the indebtedness of their discourse to presumptions geared histori- cally against women and the values to which they are symbolically if problematically linked, feminist realism, whether in its Hobbesian or less extreme 'armed civic virtue' forms, fails to provide a sustained challenge to the Western narrative of war and politics. Ironically, female-linked symbolism is once again suppressed or depreciated this time under a feminist imprimatur as a male-dominant ideal – the 'dirty fighter' or the 'citizen-warrior' is urged on everyone.

JUST WARS AS MODIFIED REALISM

In a world organized along the lines of the realist narrative, there are no easy ways out. There is, however, an alternative tradition to which we in the West have sometimes repaired either to challenge or to chasten the imperatives realism claims merely to describe and denies having in any sense wrought.

Just war theory grows out of a complex genealogy, beginning with the pacifism and withdrawal from the world of early Christian communities through later compromises with the world as Chris- tianity took institutional form. The Christian saviour was a 'prince of peace' and the New Testament Jesus deconstructs the powerful metaphor of the warrior central to Old Testament narrative. He enjoins Peter to sheath his sword; he devirilizes the image of manhood; he tells his followers to go as sheep among wolves and to offer their lives, if need be, but never to take the life of another in violence. From the beginning, Christian narrative presents a pacific ontology, finding in the 'paths of peace' the most natural as well as the most desirable way of being. Violence must justify itself before the court of nonviolence.

Classic just war doctrine, however, is by no means a pacifist discourse. St Augustine's *The City of God*, for example, distinguishes between legitimate and illegitimate use of collective violence. Augus- tine denounces the *Pax Romana* as a false peace kept in place by evil means and indicts Roman imperialist wars as paradigmatic instances of unjust war. But he defends, with regret, the possibility that a war may be just if it is waged in defense of a common good and to protect the innocent for certain destruction. As elaborated over the centuries, noncombatant immunity gained a secure niche as the most important of *jus in bello* rules, responding to unjust aggression is the central *jus ad bellum*. Just war thinking requires that moral considerations enter into all determinations of collective violence, not as a post hoc gloss but as a serious ground for making political judgments.

In common with realism, just war argument secretes a broader world-view, including a vision of domestic politics. Augustine, for example sees human beings as innately social. It follows that all ways of life are laced through with moral rules and restrictions that provide a web of social order not wholly dependent on external force to keep itself intact. Augustine's household, unlike Machiavelli's private sphere, is 'the beginning or element of the city' and domestic peace bears a relation to 'civic peace'.[4] The sexes are viewed as playing complementary roles rather than as segregated into two separate normative systems governed by wholly different standards of judgment depending upon whether one is a public man or a private woman. [...]

My criticisms of just war are directed to two central concerns: one flows directly from just war teaching; the other involves less explicit filiations. I begin with the latter, with cultural images of males and females rooted, at least in part, in just war discourse. Over time, Augustine's moral householders (with husbands cast as just, meaning neither absolute nor arbitrary heads) gave way to a discourse that more sharply divided males and females, their honored activities, and their symbolic force. Men were constituted as just Christian warriors, fighters, and defenders of righteous causes. Women, unevenly and variously depending upon social location, got solidified into a culturally sanctioned vision of virtuous, nonviolent womanhood that I call the 'beautiful soul', drawing upon Hegel's *Phenomenology*.

The tale is by no means simple but, by the late eighteenth century, 'absolute distinctions between men and women in regard to violence' had come to prevail.[5] The female beautiful soul is pictured as frugal, self-sacrificing, and, at times, delicate. Although many women empowered themselves to think and to act on the basis of this ideal of female virtue, the symbol easily slides into sentimentalism. To 'preserve the purity of its heart', writes Hegel, the beautiful soul must flee 'from contact with the actual world'.[6] In matters of war and peace, the female beautiful soul cannot put a stop to suffering, cannot effectively fight the mortal wounding of sons, brothers, husbands, fathers. She continues the long tradition of women as weepers, occasions for war, and keepers of the flame of nonwarlike values.

The just warrior is a complex construction, an amalgam of Old Testament, chivalric, and civic republican traditions. He is a character we recognize in all the statues on all those commons and greens of small New England towns: the citizen-warrior who died to preserve the union and to free the slaves. Natalie Zemon Davis shows that the image of warlike manliness in the later Middle Ages and through the seventeenth century, was but one male ideal among many, having to compete, for example, with the priest and other religious who foreswore use of their 'sexual instrument' and were forbidden to shed blood. However, 'male physical force could sometimes be moralized' and 'thus could provide the foundation for an ideal of warlike manliness'.[7] This moralization of collective male violence held sway and continues to exert a powerful fascination and to inspire respect.

But the times have outstripped beautiful souls and just warriors alike; the beautiful soul can no longer be protected in her virtuous privacy. Her world, and her children, are vulnerable in the face of nuclear realities. Similarly, the just warrior, fighting fair and square by the rules of the game, is a vision enveloped in the heady mist of an earlier time. War is more and more a matter of remote control. The contemporary face of battle is anomic and impersonal, a techno-logical nightmare, as weapons technology obliterates any distinction between night and day, between the 'front' and the 'rear'. [...]

Few feminist writers on war and peace take up just war discourse explicitly. There is, however, feminist theorizing that may aptly be situated inside the broader frames of beautiful souls and just warriors as features of inherited discourse. The strongest contemporary feminist statement of a beautiful soul position involves celebrations of a 'female principle' as ontologically given and superior to its dark opposite, masculinism. (The male 'other' in this vision is not a just warrior but a dangerous beast.) The evils of the social world are traced in a free-flowing conduit from masculinism to environmental destruction, nuclear energy, wars, militarism, and states. In utopian evocations of 'cultural feminism', women are enjoined to create separate communities to free themselves from the male surround and to create a 'space' based on the values they embrace. An essentially Manichean vision, the discourse of feminism's beautiful souls contrasts images of 'caring' and 'connected' females in opposition to 'callous' and 'disconnected' males. Deepening sex segregation, the separatist branch of cultural feminism draws upon, yet much exaggerates received understandings of the beautiful soul.

A second feminist vision indebted implicitly to the wider discursive universe of which just war thinking is a part features a down-to-earth female subject, a soul less beautiful than virtuous in ways that locate her as a social actor. She shares just war's insistence that politics must come under moral scrutiny. Rejecting the hard-line gendered epistemology and metaphysic of an absolute beautiful soul, she nonetheless insists that ways of knowing flow from ways of being in the world and that hers have vitality and validity in ways private and public. The professed ends of feminists in this loosely fitting frame locate the woman as a moral educator and a political actor. She is concerned with 'mothering', whether or not she is a biological mother, in the sense of protecting society's most vulnerable members without patronizing them. She thinks in terms of human dignity as well as social justice and fairness. She also forges links between 'maternal thinking' and pacifist or nonviolent theories of conflict without presuming that it is possible to translate easily particular maternal imperatives into a public good.

The pitfalls of this feminism are linked to its intrinsic strengths. By insisting that women are in and of the social world, its framers draw explicit attention to the context within which their constituted subjects act. But this wider surround not only derogates maternal women, it bombards them with simplistic formulae that equate 'being nice' with 'doing good'. Even as stereotypic maternalisms exert pressure to sentimentalize, competing feminisms are often sharply repudiating, finding in any evocation of 'maternal thinking' a trap and a delusion. A more robust concept of the just (female) as citizen is needed to shore up this disclosure, a matter I take up below.

RESCUING POLITICS FROM WAR: HANNAH ARENDT'S HOPE

[Elshtain then raises a number of concerns about a dominant form of discourse, encouraged by living in a world which is characterized by 'armed' peace which draws on the belief that politics is an extension of war.]

Hannah Arendt's *On Violence* responds to these concerns by exposing our acceptance of politics as war by other means. Arendt asks what historic transformations and discursive practices made possible a consensus 'among political theorists from Left to Right ... that violence is nothing more than the most flagrant manifestation of power?"[8] (The violence Arendt has in mind is that of groups or collectives, not individual outrage culminating in a single violent act; Melville's *Billy Budd* is her example.) Her answer is multiple: teleological constructions of historic inevitability (known to us as Progress); theories of absolute power tied to the emergence of the nation-state; the Old Testament tradition of God's Commandments that fed command-obedience conceptions of law in Judaeo-Christian discourse; the infusion of biologism into political discourse, particularly the notion that destruction is a law of nature and violence a 'life promoting force' through which men purge the old and rotten. All these 'time-honored opinions have become dangerous'. Locked into dangerously self-confirming ways of thinking, embracing 'progress' as a standard of evaluation, we manage to convince ourselves that good will come out of horrendous things; that somehow, in history, the end does justify the means. Both classical liberals and their Marxist adversaries share this discursive terrain, Arendt argues, though she is especially critical of 'great trust in the dialectical "power of negation"' that soothes its adherents into believing that evil 'is but a temporary manifestation of a still-hidden good'.

By conflating the crude instrumentalism of violence with power, defined by Arendt as the human ability to act in concert and to begin anew, we guarantee further loss of space within which authentic empowerment is possible. In this way violence nullifies power and stymies political being. One important step away from the instrumentalism of violence and toward the possibility of politics is to resist the reduction of politics to domination. Arendt evokes no image of isolated heroism here; rather, she underscores the ways in which centralized orders dry up power and political possibility. If we recognize the terms through and means by which this happens, we are less susceptible to unreflective mobilization and more open to finding and creating public space in the current order. As citizens through their actions break repetitive cycles of behavior, power as the 'true opposite' of violence reveals itself.

Arendt's discourse constitutes its subjects as citizens: neither victims nor warriors. She paints no rosy picture of her rescue effort. Just as Grey argues that the will to war is deepened by the emptiness of a false peace, Arendt believes that the greater a society's bureaucratization, the greater will be secret fantasies of destruction. She repudiates grandiose aims and claims, refusing to dictate what politics should do or accomplish instrumentally, for that would undermine her exposé of the future oriented teleologies on which violence and progress feed. To the extent that we see what she is doing and let it work on us, her symbolic alternative for political being offers a plenary jolt to our reigning political metaphors and categories – state of nature, sovereignty, statism, bureaucratization, contractualism, nationalist triumphalism, and so on. If we remain entrapped in this cluster of potent typifications, each of them suffused with violent evocations or built on fears of violence, we will face only more, and deadlier, of what we've already got. Contrastingly, Arendt locates as central a powerful but pacific image that engenders hope, the human capacity that sustains political being.

Evidence of hopelessness is all around us. The majority of young people say they do not believe there will be a future of any sort. We shake our heads in dismay, failing to see that our social arrangements produce hopelessness and require it to hold themselves intact. But the ontological possibility for hope is always present, rooted, ultimately, in 'the fact of natality'. Arendt's metaphor, most fully elaborated in the following passage from *The Human Condition*, is worth quoting in full:

> The miracle that saves the world, the realm of human affairs, from its normal, 'natural' ruin is ultimately the fact of natality, in which the faculty of action is ontologically rooted. It is, in other words, the birth of new human beings and the new beginning, the action they are capable of by being born. *Only the full experience of this capacity can bestow upon human affairs faith and hope, those two essential characteristics of human existence* ... that found perhaps their most glorious and most succinct expression in the new words with which the Gospels accounted their 'glad tiding': 'A Child has been born unto us.'[9]

The infant, like all beginnings is vulnerable. We must nurture that beginning, not knowing and not being able to control the 'end' of the story.

Arendt's evocation of natal imagery through its most dramatic ur-narrative is not offered as an abstraction to be endorsed abstractly. Rather, she invites us to restore long atrophied dispositions of commemoration and awe; birth, she declares, is a 'miracle', a beginning that renews and irreversibly alters the world. Hers is a fragile yet haunting figuration that stirs recognition of our own vulnerable beginnings and our necessary dependency on others. Placed alongside the reality of human beginnings, many accounts of political beginnings construed as the actions of male hordes or contractualists seem parodic in part because of the massive denial (of 'the female') on which they depend. A 'full experience' of the 'capacity' rooted in birth helps us to keep before our mind's eye the living reality of singularities, differences, and individualities rather than a human mass as objects of possible control or manipulation.[10]

By offering an alternative genealogy that problematizes collective violence and visions of triumph, Arendt devirilizes discourse, not in favor of feminization (for the feminized and masculinized emerged in tandem and both embody dangerous distortions), but politicalization, constituting her male and female objects as citizens who share alike the 'faculty of action'. At this juncture, Arendt's discourse makes contact with that feminism I characterized as a modified vision of the beautiful soul. Her bracing ideal of the citizen adds political robustness to a feminist picture of women drawn to action from their sense of being and their epistemic and social location. Arendt's citizen, for example, may act from her maternal thinking but not as a mother – an important distinction that could help to chasten sentimentalism or claims of moral superiority.

But war is the central concern of this essay. Does Arendt's discourse offer a specifiable orientation toward international relations? Her discourse shifts the ground on which we stand when we think about states and their relations. We become skeptical about the forms and the claims of the sovereign state; we deflate fantasies of control inspired by the reigning teleology of progress; we recognize the (phony) parity painted by a picture of equally 'sovereign states' and are thereby alert to the many forms hegemony can take. Additionally, Arendt grants 'forgiveness' a central political role as the only way human beings have to break remorseless cycles of vengeance. She embraces an 'ascesis', a refraining or withholding that allows refusal to bring one's force to bear to surface as a strength not a weakness.

Take the dilemma of the nuclear arms race that seems to have a life and dynamic of its own. From an Arendtian perspective, we see current arms control efforts for what they are – the arms race under another name negotiated by a bevy of experts with a vested interest in keeping the race alive so they can 'control' it. On the other hand, her recognition of the limiting conditions internal to the international political order precludes a leap into utopian fantasies of world order or total disarmament. For neither the arms control option (as currently defined) nor calls for immediate disarmament are bold – the first because it is a way of doing business as usual; the second because it covertly sustains business as usual by proclaiming 'solutions' that lie outside the reach of possibility.

Instead, Arendt's perspective invites us – as a strong and dominant nation of awesome potential force – to take unilateral initiatives in order to break symbolically the cycle of vengeance and fear signified by our nuclear arsenals. Just as action from an individual or group may disrupt the automisms of everyday life, action from a single state may send shock waves that reverberate throughout the system. Arendt cannot be pegged as either a 'systems dominance' nor 'sub-systems dominance' thinker – a form of argumentation with which she has no patience in any case. She recognizes systemic imperatives yet sees space for potentially effective change from 'individual (state) action'. The war system is so deeply rooted that to begin to dismantle it in its current and highly dangerous form requires bold strokes.

At this juncture, intimations of an alternative genealogy emerge. Freeman Dyson suggests the *Odyssey* or the theme of homecoming rather than the *Iliad* or the theme of remorseless force as a dominant ur-political myth if we break the deadlock of victims versus warriors. Socrates, Jesus of Nazareth, and Nietzsche, in some of his teachings, emerge as articulators of the prototypical virtues of restraint and refusal to bring all one's power to bear.[11] For it was Nietzsche, from his disillusionment, who proclaimed the only way out of 'armed peace' to be a people, distinguished by their wars and victories who, from strength, not weakness, 'break the sword' thereby giving peace a chance. 'Rather perish than hate and fear', he wrote, 'and twice rather perish than make oneself hated and feared.'[12] Historic feminist thinkers and movements who rejected politics as force take center stage rather than being relegated to the periphery in this alternative story.

To take up war-as-discourse compels us to recognize the powerful sway of received narratives and reminds us that the concepts through which we think about war, peace, and politics get repeated endlessly, shaping debates, constraining consideration of alternatives, often reassuring us that things cannot really be much different than they are. As we nod an automatic yes when we hear the truism (though we may despair of the truth it tells) that 'there have always been wars', we acknowledge tacitly that 'there have always been war stories', for wars are deeded to us as texts. We cannot identify 'war itself' as an entity apart from a powerful literary tradition that includes poems, epics, myths, official histories, first-person accounts, as well as the articulated theories I have discussed. War and the discourse of war are imbricated, part and parcel of political reality. Contesting the discursive terrain that identifies and gives meaning to what we take these realities to be does not mean one grants a self-subsisting, unwarranted autonomy to discourse; rather, it implies a recognition of the ways in which received doctrines, 'war stories', may lull our critical faculties to sleep, blinding us to possibilities that lie within our reach.

NOTES

1 Ti-Grace Atkinson, 'Theories of Radical Feminism', Notes from the Second Year: *Women's Liberation*, edited by Shulamith Firestone (n.p., 1970), p. 37.
2 Susan Brownmiller, *Against Our Will: Men, Women and Rape* (Simon and Schuster, New York, 1975), p. 388.
3 Cynthia Enloe, *Does Khaki Become YOU? The Militarization of Women's Lives* (Pluto Press, London, 1983), pp. 16–17.
4 Henry Paolucci (ed.), *The Political Writings of St. Augustine* (Henry Regnery, Chicago, 1967), p. 151.
5 Natalie Zemon Davis, 'Men, Women and Violence: Some Reflections on Equality', *Smith Alumnae Quarterly* (April 1972), p. 15.
6 G.W.F. Hegel, *The Phenomenology of Spirit*, trans. A.V. Miller (Clarendon Press, Oxford, 1977), pp. 399–400.
7 Davis, 'Men, Women and Violence', p. 13.
8 Hannah Arendt, *On Violence* (Harcourt Brace, New York, 1969), p. 35.
9 Hannah Arendt, *The Human Condition* (University of Chicago Press, Chicago, 1958), p. 247.
10 Arendt, *On Violence*, p. 81.
11 Freeman Dyson, *Weapons and Hope* (Basic Books, New York, 1984).
12 Cited in J. Glenn Gray, *The Warriors: Reflections on Men in Battle* (Harper Colophon, New York, 1970), pp. 225–6.

Index